PRAISE

"These essays are political theory, cultural critique, movement memoir, and ethnographic study. Together, they are a crucial analysis of the decade of tumult that brought us here. Shanahan writes with brilliance, humor, and—above all—love, love for those who dream of better horizons and take to the streets to build them. *Every Fire Needs a Little Bit of Help* is a chance to reflect, to dream, and to plot—a true gift to the left."
—Eman Abdelhadi, coauthor of *Everything for Everyone: An Oral History of the New York Commune, 2052–2072*

"Rather than pondering politics from a distance, Shanahan writes from within the political moment itself. We find in these pages not simply an appraisal of America's slow decline into social anomie or even an activist account of recent political movements but instead a picture of history in all its murky motion, where the antipolice riot gives way to the Trump rally, while apocalyptic myths play out on TV. This book therefore offers both a treasure trove of careful observations tracking the trends of our chaotic moment and an example to be followed by others seeking real social change."
—Phil A. Neel, author of *Hinterland: America's New Landscape of Class and Conflict*

"A banger! Tracing the morbid symptoms of late capitalism and collective responses from Occupy Wall Street to the rise of the far right and everything in between, Shanahan's activism and writing remain deeply committed to building movements that demand 'everything for everyone.' Coming at a time of great despair and disillusionment with liberal politics, this collection offers today's revolutionaries a sober analysis of past and present political experimentations, all the while remaining hopeful and engaged with our fiery future."
—Zhandarka Kurti, coauthor, *States of Incarceration: Rebellion, Reform, and America's Punishment System*

T0387628

"*Every Fire Needs a Little Bit of Help*, and so do we. Jarrod Shanahan delivers on the promise. He is a fine writer, perhaps the best of his generation among far-left activists—a participant-journalist and a revolutionary who thinks while he acts. These essays are grounded in his experiences in mass mobilizations against police terror, some days and nights in jail, watching some good and not so good movies, and personal underground investigations into the alt-right. Because of his writing, we go where he goes. And we're all better prepared for what comes next."
—John Garvey, editor of *Race Traitor*, *Insurgent Notes*, and *Hard Crackers*

"Searching, and hilarious—Shanahan writes from, about, and for the people. These essays document more than a decade of struggle and reflection from an expansive thinker and committed writer; Shanahan is a relentless and astute interpreter of the present American landscape."
—Jack Norton, coeditor, *The Jail Is Everywhere: Fighting the New Geography of Mass Incarceration*

"Protests against police and the carceral logic of racial apartheid in the United States have swept the nation, from organized militant movements such as Stop Cop City in Atlanta, to protracted street battles in Ferguson, to widespread popular resistance during the George Floyd Rebellion. *Every Fire Needs a Little Help* offers an urgently needed collection of essays written from the heart of this conjuncture, with crucial insights that will be necessary for navigating out of the liberal cooptation of struggle."
—Danielle Carr, author of *The Brains of the Living: The Rise, Fall, and Second Coming of Neural Engineering*

"Alternately funny and furious, this collection is a radical guide to the history of the present—something we all need."
—Malcolm Harris, author of *What's Left: Three Paths Through the Planetary Crisis*

Every Fire Needs a Little Bit of Help

A Decade of Rebellion, Reaction, and Morbid Symptoms

Jarrod Shanahan

Every Fire Needs a Little Bit of Help: A Decade of Rebellion, Reaction, and Morbid Symptoms
This edition © 2025 PM Press

ISBN: 979-8-88744-126-9 (paperback)
ISBN: 979-8-88744-127-6 (ebook)
Library of Congress Control Number: 2025931206

All rights reserved. No part of this publication may in any form be reproduced, transformed, duplicated or distributed without prior authorization from the publishers.

Cover by prole.info
Interior design by briandesign

10 9 8 7 6 5 4 3 2 1

PM Press
PO Box 23912
Oakland, CA 94623
www.pmpress.org

Printed in the USA.

To my affinity family, Fiorella and May.

Contents

INTRODUCTION Get Back Up Again *by A.M. Gittlitz*   ix

PART 1 RUPTURE

The Old Mole Breaks Concrete: The Ongoing Rupture in New York City   2

Some Bullshit   20

Noel Ignatiev, 1940–2019   28

PART 2 THE ROCK

Checking Out   38

Days Spent Doing Too Much of Fucking Nothing   47

The Secret Lives of Rikers Island Jail Guards   55

The Surreality of Rikers Island   72

PART 3 MORBID SYMPTOMS

Death to the Walking Dead   80

Friday the 1312   96

Zoomers Go to Hell   102

Hybrid Moments   117

The Future Belongs to the Mad   134

PART 4 LOOKING RIGHT

Three Months Inside Alt-Right New York   162

Thankful for President Trump: Thanksgiving with Stop the Steal   178

The Big Takeover   188

Iowa Bluffs   196

PART 5 EVERY FIRE NEEDS A LITTLE BIT OF HELP

Every Fire Needs a Little Bit of Help   218

AFTERWORD Toward Something Else   261

NOTES   272

ABOUT THE AUTHORS   291

INTRODUCTION

Get Back Up Again

by A.M. Gittlitz

The title of this book references the song "Give the Anarchist a Cigarette" by the Yorkshire "anarchist pop group" Chumbawamba. The track, from their 1994 album *Anarchy*, comments on a bit of dialogue from D.A. Pennebaker's documentary of Bob Dylan's controversial 1965 UK tour, *Don't Look Back*. Like Chumbawamba, Dylan was a radical musician midway through his climb up the music industry ladder. In the previous two years, he had performed at the Great March on Washington and Silas McGhee's SNCC-headquarters farm in Greenwood, Missouri, and wrote protest songs for the ex-Communists of Pete Seeger's "topical-song movement." But once he picked up an electric guitar to combine West Village folk revival with the then lowbrow art of rock 'n' roll, pledging in beatnik lyrics to toil on "Maggie's farm" no longer, the UK Communist Party mobilized pickets. "They've started calling you an anarchist," his manager, Albert Grossman tells him in his limo after a concert, "just 'cause you don't offer any solutions." Leather-clad Dylan laughs and cooly removes his Ray-Bans, pouting "Give me a cigarette. Give the anarchist a cigarette."

Perhaps recognizing their similar trajectory to Dylan, Chumbawamba firmly came down on the side of those decrying him as a Judas to the movement:

Give the anarchist a cigarette
A candy cig for the spoilt brat
Give the anarchist a cigarette
We'll get Albert to write you a cheque ...
Give the anarchist a cigarette / You know I hate every pop star that I ever met

In the chorus, Chumbawamba reveal their own theory of pop as an incendiary device to inspire and support future rebellions: *"Nothing ever burns down by itself, every fire needs a little bit of help."*

Three years later, the band released their smash hit "Tubthumping." Before its infamous Trump and Biden-quoted refrain of "I get knocked down, but I get up again," it opens with a muffled sound clip from the 1996 film *Brassed Off*, in which the conductor of a Yorkshire coal miners' brass band refuses a music award to protest the wave of privatizations that will cost his band their livelihoods. "Truth is . . . I thought that music mattered. But does it? Bollocks! Not compared to how people matter."

The *Tubthumper* album sold many millions worldwide, with unknown thousands more stolen from record stores with the band's encouragement. Most listeners, however, bought it in earnest, taking its title track as a mindless anthem of substance abuse. Predictably, some of their old fans now believe the band had become Dylanesque *Judases* themselves.

Like Chumbawamba, Jarrod Shanahan is drawn to the radical poptimism without the same conflicted contempt for the political ambiguity that is an inevitable trade-off for mass-market appeal. His method draws inspiration from the Trinidadian marxist theorist and organizer C.L.R. James, who argued in *American Civilization* that the entertainment industry was creating "new conditions of the relation between art and society" that "will give us deep insight into modern political psychology and help us to knit together various currents in what is a world movement towards the creation of man as an integral human being." Jarrod's essays in this volume thus analyze the arsonous riots of Ferguson and the George Floyd Rebellion, the American carceral system, and the Trump movement with near equal consideration to the low-culture phantasmagoria of punk bands like the Misfits and horror franchises like *Hellraiser*. Shanahan writes on these subjects as an active participant and enthusiastic consumer, seeing in the confused violence of proletarian riots and zombie-apocalypse fantasies the expressed neuroses of a society materially driven towards confrontation with the class order.

Other contemporary leftist cultural critics, like the black-pilled meme theorists of *Do Not Research*, or *Jacobin* magazine's film critic Eileen Jones, often sound like the anti-Dylan Leninists when they cover this territory, seeing pop culture as valid only when it conveys a message adequate to the platform of a not-yet-existing vanguard party. As a result, their work ironically comes off like a Dylanesque sneer that the

INTRODUCTION

entirety of American politics, from the alt-right to the seemingly spontaneous bursts of Black liberation, is uniformly absurd noise, signaling little more than a hopeless future.

Shanahan, on the other hand, echoes the conclusions of the intro to "Tubthumping"—while there may be little hope in the catchiest conventional narratives of class society, extreme and grotesque art and cultural moments represent the violence of everyday desires to burn down the cruel excesses of the old world and build communism from what remains.

I first encountered the indefatigably optimistic milieu that connected James to Jarrod at the *Hard Crackers* journal release parties at Freddy's Bar in Brooklyn. During the aughts, this working-class watering hole became notorious as the final holdout against the massive developmental project that razed blocks of Brooklyn's downtown for luxury high-rises and the Barclays Center. Freddy's fought eminent domain to the bitter end, opening its backroom to grassroots meetings of neighbors, like writer and longtime anti-apartheid activist Mike Morgan, long after the project's main opponents, the Democrat-machine NGO ACORN, sold out to the developers for a role in administering a percentage of "market-value" apartments. Freddy's was eventually demolished and moved to South Slope in Brooklyn, where Morgan held regular release parties for a new journal founded by himself, Shanahan, and former *Race Traitor* editors John Garvey and Noel Ignatiev in 2016.

Race Traitor was a ubiquitous novelty among the anarchist zine tables at the punk shows and infoshops of my youth. Its central thesis, which remains surprisingly controversial among US marxists, was that the American class order was structured around the keystone of white supremacy. Every revolutionary movement in modern American history, from John Brown's attempted slave insurrection to the general strikes of runaway slaves that won the Civil War, to the civil rights movement of the sixties, to the Movement for Black Lives of our previous decade, has shown the country's white majority the path towards liberation. They were only defeated by the reaction of white workers who came to believe the ongoing immiseration and hyperexploitation of their Black counterparts was integral to the modest privileges that Du Bois called the *wages of whiteness.* In this narrative, the greatest barrier to American revolution is clearly the perpetuation of *whiteness* itself as a cross collaboration that promises to exploit white and nonwhite workers to different degrees. *Race Traitor,* and later, *Hard Crackers,* argued for a mass refusal of this ever-fluctuating alliance far more profound than mere privilege checking; nothing less than the *abolition of whiteness* could establish a truly autonomous, international, and interracial working-class force that could fight seriously for the demands of the Black proletariat, and to eventually overcome the divisions of wage labor, nations, and race altogether.

At Freddy's I was honored to meet the septuagenarian Ignatiev in the flesh. Gigantic, slight, kind, and stunningly ambitious, he truly believed the zine would spread the politics and methods of their milieu like wildfire, just as *Race Traitor* had in the nineties. It was a similar affect to the other '68ers Jarrod and I have encountered, like Loren Goldner, Silvia Federici, George Caffentzis, and Phil Wohlstetter—undying commitment to the long march lost to nearly all our millennial comrades. These clear-eyed partisans of the *real movement that abolishes the present state of things* (Marx and Engels's concise definition of communism) had witnessed the certainty of revolution in the late sixties, the Movement's pitiful liquidation into cults and sects, and the reputed *end of history* in the nineties. Even as they watched their friends become apolitical careerists or political prisoners, they were impervious to the cycles of pessimism and optimism that immobilized me and other comrades in the lulls between struggles.

This political depression is especially epidemic in our *current year,* as progressives and social-democrats alike abandon their civil rights movement and BLM-era commitments to social and racial justice in the face of fascism's reemergence. The most likely source of stability in the chaotic era of capitalist decline, social disorder, and climate chaos, this new bleak bipartisanship asserts, is border walls, law-and-order policing, and ever-expanding prisons to discipline the working-class and exterminate all resistance. The race traitors, of course, have seen this nadir of struggle before, and always quieted overwhelming doubts in the viability of proletarian revolution with the pounding certainty that capitalism cannot last forever.

Shanahan's contributions to *Hard Crackers* bridged the gap between the New Left elders of *Race Traitor* and the more subjective literary styles of anarchopunk zinesters like Aaron Cometbus, Cindy Crabb, and Ericka Lyle. His writing situates the subversive joy of what proto-punk Raoul Vaneigem called *the revolution of everyday life* within the post-Leninist strategy of *Race Traitor*'s sixties mentors. Believing the activity of

INTRODUCTION   xiii

ordinary, nonparty workers had surpassed the orthodox marxist focus on union bureaucracies or political parties, C.L.R. James, James Boggs, and Grace Lee Boggs, and the *Facing Reality* group called on communists to "recognize and record" developments of the class struggle at its quotidian origin on the factory floor. In the half century since the *Facing Reality* group developed this method, capitalism dramatically restructured and radically altered American class composition. The New Left likewise expanded its understanding of the primal source of revolt from the workplace to everywhere capitalist social relations are produced—homes, universities, neighborhoods, the streets, and even countercultural enclaves, online and off.

Beyond zinester personalism and New Left marxism, Shanahan adopts the experimental honesty in encountering these recreative realties typical of the beatnik prose of Henry Miller and Samuel Delany, the passionate rock criticism of Greil Marcus, Lester Bangs, Ellen Willis, and Chuck Klosterman, and the "gonzo" journalism of Hunter S. Thompson and Normal Mailer. His contributions to recognizing and recording American cultural history especially stand out in his direct reports from within the eye of society's most ferocious storms. The second section of this book, for instance, describes his experience with America's carceral system not as a social worker or undercover prison guard, à la Shane Bauer, but as an inmate.

His thirty-day sentence was the result of a climactic march over the Brooklyn Bridge, after Eric Garner's killer was cleared of charges in December 2014, during which he broke an officer's nose during a melee. In the days afterwards, a citywide search for the perpetrators ensued, complete with a wanted poster featuring Jarrod's blurry face on the cover of the *New York Post*. A year and a half later, as Trump ascended through the Republican primaries, I visited Jarrod at the Rikers gymnasium. When I solemnly asked how he was, I was shocked that he excitedly answered "Great!" He was filling notebooks with every detail of bastille life and his fellow inmates' stories, he told me. When I asked if he was able follow the news of the world, he grinned and said there was no need. "I'm in the center of it."[1]

A year later, Trump was president and Jarrod and I watched in horror as the alt-right smashed the Overton window wide open in a Gramscian attempt to transform the GOP into the Nazi Party. Seeking insight into the scheme, Jarrod began posting on the forums of the *Daily Stormer* in the persona of a skinhead named "Irish Jay." Within no time, he was invited to their "Book Club" and "Hate Hikes," working his way up to their most secretive midtown conference. As the rally wound down, he texted me the location of its beer-hall afterparty, where I was to listen in on conversations outside his earshot and assist in the event that he slipped up in some way that exposed him as an infiltrator. Around two in the morning, when Jarrod was confident he had accumulated enough material and could finally be free of this sad little world, I overheard him lightheartedly admit to one of the subjects that he was an antifascist, and their whole cabal would soon be exposed. The Nazi looked at him in stony silence for a tense moment before the two burst out laughing.

On the morning of August 17, 2017, the day the entirety of the alt-right movement arrived for the "Unite the Right" rally in Charlottesville, Virginia, some details of Jarrod's investigation were leaked to the public. With the double lives of these small-business owners, tech-workers, neo-volk pagans, and wealthy intellectuals now exposed to their "normy" friends, family, and coworkers, they undoubtedly received a barrage of furious texts as they marched toward battle. But even after they were defeated in the streets by thousands of brave antifascists and Charlottesville locals, and Jarrod had published his *Commune* magazine tell-all on the operation, the race warriors could not believe they had been bested by ordinary people who hated their politics enough to risk life and limb to fight them. Victims of their own narrative that the MAGA movement emerged from the economic anxiety of downwardly mobile whites, many still argued that Irish Jay had been a Nazi all along, and had only betrayed the movement in an act of cowardice.

After the alt-right's fracture following Charlottesville, Shanahan continued to probe this narrative within the broader MAGA movement by enduring several Trump rallies. Where some edgy social democrats, like Angela Nagel, saw a blue-collar revolt against neoliberalism, Jarrod found instead "an interconnected web of small-time hucksters, politicized police and Border Patrol, Christian chauvinists, ideological white supremacists and xenophobes, and local petty bourgeois prone to representing themselves as "the white working class."

After Trump lost his reelection, tens of thousands of this coalition mobilized to support his attempted coup by storming the Capitol to prevent the electoral vote tally on January 6, 2021. Some antifascists were so horrified to see Carhartt cosplayers battling their way through police lines that they regretted not mobilizing in defense of Biden, and began participating in a campaign to identify the rioters and turn them over to the FBI. Jarrod, on the other hand, judged the moment to be a parodic, but potent petit bourgeois recreation of the May 28 precinct burning that initiated the George Floyd Rebellion. Fearing the significance of J6 and M28 alike would be lost, he wrote: "Collective actions like the siege of the Capitol register in the minds of millions of people the idea that drastic measures can be taken by ordinary people. What is our alternative?"

Jarrod and I are, of course, not "ordinary people." We are partisans of a centuries-long class war, students of its great theorizers like Hegel, Marx, Du Bois, James, and Ignatiev, and writers that connect isolated moments of proletarian rage through long cycles of burst and bust. We treat these great episodes the same way record collectors and film nerds do often-obscure genre waves—important marginalia striving towards some culmination still past the horizon of marxist prognostication.

This archive of their failures and triumphs has been compiled in hopes that future generations of rebels will enjoy them as something more than subversive songs satisfying the riot-porn itch of depressed radicals contemplating defection. Instead, think of these texts as a carton of smokes that can provide both yard-time relief, or kindling for tomorrow's fires; an invitation to *do* what the anarchist sang: *strike another match and start anew.*

PART 1
RUPTURE

The Old Mole Breaks Concrete: The Ongoing Rupture in New York City

This text was first circulated in a pamphlet in December 2014, under a pseudonym. It was written in a hurry, to be distributed amid the street movement that would come to be called Black Lives Matter. For the ease of the reader I have made basic copyedits, added citations, and removed stray passages that are either irrelevant to a broader audience or are today mysterious even to their author.

■

> "When history is written as it ought to be written, it is the moderation and long patience of the masses at which people will wonder, not their ferocity."
>
> –C.L.R. James, *The Black Jacobins*

Toward a Practical Grasp of the Present

The US working class is on the move. The militants of Ferguson, Missouri, are the vanguard of a rebellion threatening to generalize across the United States. Individual cases of police murder are escaping the confines of their particular context and blurring into the total condition of life under white supremacist capitalism. The ruling class is breaking ranks on the question of police violence. The movement politicians are running behind the movement. The police are scared. There is no talk of the 99%.

As unarmed Black men murdered in the street by pigs the state calls innocent, Michael Brown and Eric Garner have many things in common. But most important to understanding the last four months in the United

States is that they both stood up and said *no more*. Ordered rudely out of the street in Ferguson, Michael Brown refused. Harassed constantly by the NYPD, Eric Garner took a stand: "This stops today!" We can cite a million subtle causal factors for the ensuing mass movement, but we should not lose sight of its grounding in brave acts of defiance that cost two Black people their lives.

If we are to understand this as something besides a movement against "police brutality"—a liberal myth purporting that police existence can be any other way—how do we view these acts of refusal, and the movement they have catalyzed? It is surely a Black struggle against white supremacy. But is this movement simply playing out within the institutions of official society? One could hardly argue that to be the example set by Ferguson's sustained militancy. Is it verging on a more generalized rebellion? The events of the past two weeks make this hard to dispute. In any case, central is the figure of the refusal—the refusal of a racialized position in the capitalist division of labor, the refusal of policing as the central figure of social reproduction, and the refusal of an ever downward standard of living for the US working class, disproportionately weighing on working-class Black and brown people. This refusal has not been voiced in the halls of justice into which liberals now seek to push it, but as with Michael Brown, Eric Garner, and the militants of Ferguson who kicked off this rupture, the refusal has been in the streets, articulated with one's body on the line.

As we work toward an understanding of this refusal, what it means in terms of racialized class stratification, and what it portends for the coming class struggle, we'd like to also take a slightly more empirical look at the struggles in the wake of the Ferguson rebellion as they have played out in New York City. On a practical level, what do we make of the movement in the US since the Ferguson rebellion, and now Darren Wilson's and (Eric Garner's murderer) Daniel Pantaleo's nonindictments? What is this movement, where is it headed, and what is the role of revolutionaries?

If what follows seems amateurish, improvised, frantic, eclectic, and riven with contradictions, it will have perfectly grasped the flavor of the present rupture. The term "far left," used throughout, refers loosely to a local agglomeration of anarchists, autonomists, left communists, communizers, and other antistate communists: a rowdy bunch indeed. This piece has benefited tremendously from their insights, actions, courage, genius, and love. Special thanks are due to the Trayvon Martin Organizing Committee, and of course the countless anonymous proletarians who are always the real heroes of every class struggle and whose reward is almost always anonymity, at best.

Blurred Snapshot of a Rupture in Progress

In New York City there have been four major mobilizations since the Wilson nonindictment, two of which corresponded with the nonindictment in the case of Eric Garner's choking death by the NYPD. Each mobilization originated from multiple points (or at least times) of convergence, and almost constantly featured multiple marches disabling major infrastructure simultaneously. While these larger marches have mostly been called by traditional organizers, like various front groups for the old Stalinist parties, the leadership quickly becomes irrelevant, especially as marches split. (Notably the Trayvon Martin Organizing Committee, comprised solely of anarchists and antistate communists, has managed to call and lead two massive mobilizations, complete with militant chants and literature.) Marches of thousands converged at strategic (or miraculous) moments to outflank police, and diverged just as fluidly as police struggled to keep a handle on the situation. Diverse as the city itself and equally unwieldy, on New York's streets the class has become once more a "many headed hydra," popping up in three places when repressed in one.

More importantly, there have been an almost daily diffusion of small activities by small or unaffiliated crews, spontaneous breakaway marches, unaffiliated folks new to organizing calling for marches that receive tens of thousands of responses. Everyday New Yorkers have been joining spontaneously, blocking traffic, at times confronting the police, and demonstrating a tactical militancy that would have put them in league with the far left only six months ago. While much has been made in the media of the prevalence of white faces at the New York demonstrations (so much so that a French comrade reached out to us for an explanation of this), this is largely bullshit, as the demographics at these marches, while skewing toward youth, have been a wonderful representation of the diversity of New York, and heavily Black to boot. One protester on the West Side Highway remarked during an intense skirmish with the NYPD in which the police were embarrassingly outflanked and at times assaulted: "It's Black on blue tonight!"

THE OLD MOLE BREAKS CONCRETE

While of course this is a large umbrella of organizations, we can broadly define the base as working class, and potentially militant, but organized under the banner of reformist politics (sometimes in radical garb). This tension in itself, between enthusiastic young people trying to change the world, and the cold reality of the bureaucratic statist nonprofits that trade in their enthusiasm and energy, is worth keeping an eye on, though we are not aware of any prominent splits at present. (A more satisfactory topography of this tension, and technical definition of the admittedly overgeneral signifier "nonprofit" used throughout this piece, is forthcoming in future analysis.) There has also been an upsurge of unaffiliated proletarians of color taking part in these protests, rolling in small groups of friends or even alone, joining the marches from the streets and canceling whatever plans they had. Once in the streets, these young proletarians are quick to block traffic, lead militant chants, spontaneously hatch, advocate for, and execute direction changes to outmaneuver the police, and in many places surround and sometimes shove officers arresting marchers. This is at odds with (at least the leadership and guiding principles of) the more established nonprofit sector, which is much more conservative in chants and tactics, to say nothing of a hard line against the police.

The major tactical figures we have witnessed are the unpermitted street march, the intersection blockade, the highway blockade, the bridge crossing, the bridge blockade, "die-ins," and various actions inside major retail stores to impede or shut down consumption. While none of these are totally new, what is remarkable is how general, diffuse, deprofessionalized, and almost instinctive they have become, in addition to how frequently and coextensively they have been executed. Many far-left comrades here predicted some months ago that a highway blockade the night following the Wilson nonindictment would be an unprecedented act of escalation, only to watch in surprise as three different bridges were blocked the night before the announcement was even made. It is impossible to imagine these tactics being so popular before Ferguson. Ironically, they would have no doubt been met with charges of "putting Black and brown bodies at risk." Perhaps it was only when the proletarians of Ferguson elevated this risk to an accepted premise of the class struggle in the US that the class could move en masse elsewhere.

This level of mass militancy is something we haven't seen since Occupy, or arguably before that. What we have seen is the better parts of Occupy (emphasis on cohesive street tactics, socializing the response to police violence, media savvy mobilizations, ostensibly horizontal organizing structure) breaking free from the ghetto of the middle-class professional organizer and taking hold within the consciousness of large numbers of New Yorkers. Chants of "Slow down stay together!" have emanated from all corners of snake marches, and an often excessive insistence on form (e.g., locking arms when not necessary) by very young marchers would be irritating if not so beautiful to behold. On the flip side, much of Occupy's liberal illusions, such as "the cops are the 99%," have a harder time taking root in an issue that attacks the crisis of social reproduction, not from the perspective of Occupy's demand for a return to/of the middle class (which, tellingly, was nonetheless still greeted by police violence), but aimed at the central figure of contemporary social reproduction, which has replaced the welfare office: the violent police.

The degree of decenteredness is something definitely not seen even during Occupy. Since the marches do not emanate from a central position, it is harder to bureaucratize them under a common leadership. Further, the plethora of existent organizations, community groups, student groups, and generally pissed off people around the issue of the police is almost endlessly multiplicitous, and for many of these groupings this is not their first rodeo. At the present the imposition of a centralized authority has proven impossible, with so much spontaneous activity emanating from seemingly nowhere. This is a momentary tactical advantage for antiauthoritarians, but it is also fleeting. Soon enough, and this is already underway, the media-savvy and well-funded organizations around "Black Lives Matter" and the various statist nonprofits accustomed to swallowing up disorganized networks will attempt to gobble up all diffuse activity into one cohesive strategic umbrella, relying heavily on the "good protester / bad protester" dichotomy and a healthy dosage of liberal identity politics to purge the official movement of confrontational tactics and the larger revolutionary element. This will be compounded by the moment of street tactics meeting their limit, with a militant minority earning the ire of the mass movement, which has yet to noticeably occur but could be right around the corner.

Despite the best intentions of academic identity politics, there is no clear political line along the lines of race. What has emerged instead are the class ruptures within racial designations, as well as long-standing political lines between sects and organizations. At a march in East New

York called after the murder of *another* unarmed Black man (Akai Gurley) just before the Ferguson decision was announced, a group of older Black militants berated the multiracial crowd for chanting "Hands up, don't shoot!" advocating instead "Arms down, shoot back!" This chant naturally caught on with the multiracial far left. However, it has met much resistance along the supposed lines of race by the nonprofit crowd. We've witnessed non-Black chanters being told to "check your privilege," and the Blackness of the Black people chanting it questioned.

Similarly, militant street tactics have been pursued by a diverse swath of New Yorkers, perhaps most predominantly young Black and brown people with no discernible group ties, while the right wing of the nonprofits and more conservative voices advocate respectable behavior and nonprovocation of the police (which extends right down to using unkind words). The class and political tensions within such abstract entities as "communities of color" are coming to the fore in the streets. With all due respect to the immense differences between people in different racialized strata of the working class, the foremost division in the streets, as usual, remains between those who want things to stay under control and those who want to push the envelope toward more militant tactics, both camps being thoroughly multiracial.

Interestingly, this movement does not appear to be an extension of the so-called movement of the squares.[1] This concept as described by *Endnotes* includes occupations across several city centers that involved alliances between multiple fractions of the working class and middle class. Outside of Ferguson, there has been no attempt to seize a piece of land and hold it while surrounded by police. Perhaps it is a shortcoming of these marches that the organic mass instincts seem to be wanting to outmaneuver, outsmart, and otherwise get away from the police. Nonetheless the success of the mobilizations and their momentum call into question the wisdom of a "square" for a movement comprised of locals in contemporary New York. If we can have daily activities carried out by well-rested folks not constantly braving the winter elements, if we are freed from focusing on the practical questions of holding a small piece of property, are we not the better? Can we bypass the square? Do we need the square? Do we need an occupation? Did we ever? Or have we simply surpassed that moment?

It can of course be objected that the social relations being produced in the square or the occupation, especially taking on the reproduction of the class outside of the state as a concrete problem, created a qualitative shift in the relationships in the movement of the squares, and qualitatively shifted the content of the politics toward, in some cases, a revolutionary paradigm. However we should not discount that these relations are being forged in the streets, and that these shifts are occurring on the run. This question, which is in no way answerable by mere analysis, should be of paramount practical importance to all revolutionaries.

If not the square, what? What is the highway blockade? What is the bridge crossing? What is the Macy's disruption? What is the seemingly endless (up to *ten hours* in some cases) snake march, diverging from one march, converging with another, flowing amorphously from one major infrastructure blockade to another? In our view this is the class groping toward a form of militant action in a period when direct confrontation with the state seems to be off the table. Ferguson has set the tone for the class struggle in the US, but Ferguson, where rioting has flared and at times live ammunition has been fired at the police, is difficult to emulate outside of its context. In New York City, state violence is advanced far beyond the rest of the US. Not only are the formal police the most developed in perhaps the world, but the informal police—from a gamut of nonprofits to trade unions, to local politicians like Charles Barron, Jumaane Williams, Letitia James, and even the mayor himself—serve the state well, demobilizing militant struggle and channeling it into legal channels. Unlike the pigs in Ferguson, the NYPD didn't need tanks in the street when the Black youth of East Flatbush rose up after Kimani Gray was murdered last year, because they had Charles Barron and Jumaane Williams to give the counterinsurgency a softer touch.[2] This is also what the New York ruling class has in mind when they decry the out of touch white ruling class in St. Louis. Up here, they congratulate themselves; class domination, like everything else New York's ruling class loves, is so much more *authentic, organic,* and *locally grown!*

But beyond the "shock absorber" politicians, there seems to be something stubbornly intransigent about a general aversion to property destruction, skirmishes with the police, and the like in this present upsurge in NYC. The difficulty may be an ideological barrier, a practical fear, or perhaps overall a bedrock reality of the moment. One tactic that seems to be used to bridge the gap between demonstrators who are unwilling to face the police but simultaneously are interested in outmaneuvering and otherwise escaping police is the "de-arrest" (the forcible removal of a seized person from police hands), which should be put in the forefront by practice and propaganda (including shaming those who interfere). More generally there is a need to recognize the widespread class activity capable of bridging the current gulf between the most advanced actors of the class struggle (directly confronting the state with property destruction and violence) and the broader mobilized masses, and to push forward these activities wherever they are found.

It is of course possible that the emphasis on entering retail stores in particular is a sign of the kind of "consumerist" fixation that many bring to contemporary politics, in a period where many on the left externalize political projects from their participation, and literally review them on the internet as if they are rating a restaurant on Yelp ("I wasn't welcomed with a smile, the rhetoric was a bit alienating, I didn't feel comfortable," etc.). However, may we not infer that this is a groping toward what it means to stop production in a largely postindustrial setting like Midtown Manhattan? Is there not an instinctive wisdom to blocking the site of commodity purchase—understood as a moment in the expanded repro-duction of capital—that is just as disruptive as grinding the factory to a halt? Surely the emphasis on spectacle (e.g., the selection of glitzy shop-ping districts instead of more proletarian shopping areas like Brooklyn's Atlantic Terminal Mall, across from the Barclays Center, a popular spot for "die-in" actions) raises some skepticism on this note.

Regardless, tactics have ranged from active disruption through chanting and literally running around, to the more docile and media-oriented "die-in," which is nonetheless disruptive in its own right in the right place. And is it not so tantalizing to have so many taking direct action in such close proximity to so many wonderful commodities? In any case, the fact remains that the class is getting more comfortable entering "private property," disrupting the flow of the city, and generally breaking the law, and in a period that's conservative as hell, that's saying a lot and we should be attentive to its minutiae.

On a very basic level, the tactical ensemble of the moment boils down to a slogan that has been oft chanted from everywhere and nowhere in particular: "Shut it down!" The instinct to stop business as usual, no matter the panoply of political possibilities this implies, should be taken very seriously (and is perhaps here understated). Everyday people want to "shut it down," echoing Eric Garner's words "This stops today!" and Michael Brown's refusal to get out of the street. The instinct to "shut it down," to be diffuse, mobile, amorphous, and all the while belligerent, is a defining characteristic of this period. At the risk of being excessively literary, it is tempting to imagine this as a broader call to cease the suicidal momentum of capitalism toward untold debasement of human life and the planet itself. Given the vast diversity of protesters' perspectives and agendas, even within the liberal camp, it is perhaps more pragmatic to imagine this impulse to "shut it down" as devoid of overarching positive political content beyond this refusal. Perhaps this places the "shut down" space on par with the square of the "movement of the squares," in which an opening is created through the cessation of daily life, in which a politics must be created (not inserted). Shutting it down could be a constitutive act, towards a praxis which does not yet exist. The question becomes: From what will this concrete political content arise? How much of its form will be determined by the conscious activity of political actors, and how much will arise from the conditions themselves?

The Thorny and Overdetermined Question of Consciousness

Much of how we situate these tactics, their underlying impetus, and the broader questions they imply hinges on our understanding of consciousness, a subject which we find to be overrepresented in revolutionary theory and underrepresented in revolutionary praxis. Beyond all the grand theories addressing this issue in toto with proper names neatly affixed to them like a hermetic seal, the questions surrounding consciousness are more likely to be slogged out on an individual basis with the folks we meet in ones and twos. What's important to keep in mind is that these experiments, groping toward a new form of expression and pushing the limits of the present form of political activity, remain open ended and their horizon is by no means clear.

Predictably, the foremost observable contradiction has been that between what people say and what they do. This much is reminiscent of Occupy: liberal rhetoric of justice and democracy accompanying the (sometimes felonious) breaking of the law. Some of us have found ourselves in the paradoxical situation of militant chants meeting resistance amid such unprecedented acts of mass illegality as thousands blocking Manhattan's West Side Highway in defiance of explicit police orders, and then police violence. This is not simply a matter of "dual consciousness," in which militant actions outpace ingrained ideology.

Instead, this marks a contradiction central to the movement itself, between civil disobedience as a tactic of achieving civil rights, and direct confrontation with the state as that which has lost all legitimacy. It is of course impossible to extricate where one ends and the other begins, as the two are often coextensive. And it is equally important to emphasize the qualitative role mass action plays in advancing class consciousness.

In mass action, the radical ambiguity between "sending a message to the masses/lawmakers," taking on capitalism as an object of attack, and building social cohesion—which are so hopelessly intertwined it almost doesn't make sense to parse it all out on paper—prevents us from making any definitive analysis of these tactics. However, we can only point to the fact that none of these explanations are a given on their own, and it is possible for this tactic (and other blockade tactics) to definitively break in one or another direction. In many ways this contradiction is contained within the blockade tactic itself. The act of blocking a highway, obstructing a store, and so forth, can be (1) civil disobedience meant to call public attention to a wrong to be righted by the state and civil society (the liberal perspective); (2) the weakening of the circulation of capital, in itself a victory against our foe the state (the "block the flows" perspective, however vulgarized); or (3) an exercise in building social relationships toward increasingly militant confrontations and breaks from legality (the communist perspective—according to which the bridge itself is meaningless, and if the social relations could be better forged elsewhere doing something else, even with less media attention, that would be desirable). To be fair, as much was characteristic of the "civil rights movement," to which today's movement is being hastily compared.

Let's keep this discussion brief and take our questions to the streets. In advancing forward we advocate an agnostic position on grand theories of consciousness, which nonetheless takes them seriously. The emphasis however should fall on an experimental approach to engaging revolutionary openings, with an emphasis on the particularity of the situation encountered, mirroring the experimental nature of this entire period.

The Bedrock of the Present Moment

To return to the civil rights comparison, there is a key difference today from the civil rights era: the intransigent impossibility of reform. As the communizers have argued compellingly, the contemporary police force is the twin of the nonreproduction of the class by capital.[3] As labor power is purchased below the rate necessary to procure means of subsistence, and supplementary programs traditionally provided by the state (welfare, public housing, public sector work, school lunches, childcare, etc.) are continually withdrawn, a vast and disproportionately racialized fraction of the class is left with its social reproduction ensured by the threat of violence and with no other incentive to keep working. This is not due simply to the greed of bankers or the so-called 1%, but to the worldwide reconfiguration of capitalism away from productive labor in the advanced industrial countries, where its value had risen thanks to workers' struggles, an increasingly falling rate of profit due to mechanization, and the transformation of capital accumulation based on exploiting variable capital to the trade of fictitious capital (which generates no value of its own but only circulates speculative capital that often doesn't exist).[4] Even the utopian liberal economist and anti-Marxist Thomas Piketty had to settle for a plan for remedying worldwide income inequality that would be slightly more difficult to implement than world revolution itself.

Contrary to the quixotic police reformers, we know that in order to even begin to end wholesale police murder the state would have to somehow manage to reproduce the class by traditional social-democratic means. And even then, with perhaps the most egregious murders out of the headlines, the racist imperative of devaluing and disciplining Black labor power, to say nothing of the racist imperative central to the foundation of the police and the state itself, would of course remain. While politicians like Bill de Blasio and the army of nonprofits and unions who channel grassroots energy into electoral campaigns have made much of the desire to return to a mythic golden age of American capitalism, it has proven to be quite impossible. This does not mean there is no desire on the behalf of a fraction of the ruling class to escape this situation, quite the contrary. The current tension between the mayor and the NYPD—the latter denouncing the former through the mouthpiece of their company union, the Police Benevolent Association, and the former distancing himself from the latter as they double down on their paranoid mantra: "It's better to be judged by twelve men than carried by six"—is emblematic of the growing rift in the ruling class among its ideological figures (the *New York Times*, Obama, Holder, De Blasio, Hollywood, etc.) and the executors of its practical functions (the police).

It is possible that the police have fewer illusions in this case; namely, they know it is impossible to reproduce the racialized lowest rungs of

THE OLD MOLE BREAKS CONCRETE

the class in any other way, while the ideological mouthpieces of capital still proclaim a twentieth-century line on upward mobility and the rule of law, which was never true to begin with and is now incommensurable with even the pretense of reality. This tension is particularly important to pay attention to. If the mayoralty and the NYPD continue to break ranks, an opening unprecedented in recent NYC history may present itself. Have you heard any news out of Oakland lately?[5]

Further, in the chasm created by the nonreproduction of the class, the nonprofit complex and its growingly indistinguishable partners the business unions have emerged as a powerful force in political organizing, as well as a powerful economic and political presence in the reproduction of the class. Able to provide resources the state refuses to provide, including employment, to communities of color, while simultaneously espousing far-left rhetoric and channeling all political energy into the mechanisms of state reform, the nonprofits are a daunting challenge to revolutionary activity in this period and will no doubt comprise the bulk of the coming reaction to this spontaneous mass activity. This reaction will surely draw heavily on identity politics, taking the multiracial composition of the protests as a threat to the hegemony of established movement leaders and the liberal ideology in radical garb which they push on the movement. When the multiracial nature of the protests is attacked using identity politics, especially by legitimately enraged Black and brown people, much of it comes from a genuine place of defending the autonomy of Black political subjects, and not wishing to deracialize the movement, place it under white leadership, or otherwise abstract from the historical context and lived experience of white supremacy. But from many liberal, academic, and definitely nonprofit circles, especially those that traditionally funnel revolutionary enthusiasm into reformist channels, what is also being attacked is the threat of continued breaks with legality and the specter of a multiracial revolutionary movement escaping the framework of liberal institutions.

At the risk of being alarmist, this pushback is actually already underway. A march planned for this coming Saturday titled the Millions March, originally called by a small group of friends, has earned the attention of the entire city, including many professional activist groups. Suddenly a permit has been acquired (the first of the entire upsurge, and perhaps its death certificate), a stage planned and speakers announced, a list of social-democratic demands quickly affixed to the website, and the organizers are now scrambling to poetically qualify the event's original "Day of Anger" subtitle. "Millions" proclaims itself to be in the spirit of the previous marches, only more organized and centralized, which of course defies the spontaneous tactical genius of the previous marches, and the empowerment of countless New Yorkers this enabled. "Millions" threatens to discipline and demobilize the momentum of the class by returning to the rigid parade-style marches, led by politicians and penned in by police barricades, so beloved by the moribund NYC institutional "left." This little band of amateurs could prove to be the accidental Thermidor of the entire present rupture. Of course whether this disciplining of autonomous class action will be possible remains to be seen. And our experience of the last two weeks tells us that they will need a lot of "marshals" (paid movement police, likely union or nonprofit staffers who they plan to have on hand) to push the class back into the pens it has been pushing out of for two weeks.

What Is It that We Should Consider Perhaps Suggesting to Be Done?

For the revolutionary (the term meaning here the self-identified far leftist, though this is surely not the horizon of revolutionary actors) not simply content with writing on the sidelines, organizing mass marches, or giving canned speeches to captive audiences—and especially for those of us who see independent class activity as a goal far more important than bolstering our particular sect—this is a dizzying moment. While it may be possible to rest content with the class in action, and seek only to push things along tactically in the streets, or to call for the next big march (or occupation), we are presented in part with the fundamental problem of mass activity outpacing mass consciousness. Refusing antipolice chants while defying police orders to cease blocking a major artery of the city, or even while actively fighting back against police, is a puzzling subject position indeed. We must grapple to understand it in theory while experimenting constantly in practice.

It is always a given that the working class taking decisive action does not need our leadership or sanction; and that's a good thing, because events never seem to pan out that way. But if we as revolutionaries are to avoid abstracting ourselves from the class (of which we are surely a part) altogether, and consigning ourselves to inactivity and idle speculation, it doesn't hurt to reflect on our position and its relation to the struggle.

First and foremost, what is needed is for us to find the most advanced layers of the class in action, document and publicize their activities, assist when strategic, and help by any means necessary to generalize this activity more broadly across the class. And in each situation, like all combatants in the proletarian class struggle, we must weigh heavily whether our activity helps or hinders the class in motion.

It is in the spirit of this humility, and the foreknowledge that such prescriptions as follow always lend themselves to easy parody, that we offer up discussion points for what we can and should do amid the present rupture. It is of course a common mistake we constantly risk as revolutionaries to assume we are the most advanced elements of the class, one that typically finds us comically chasing after the very masses we kid ourselves into imagining tail behind us. It is from some controversial premises—that not everything self-identified revolutionaries do is a meaningless waste of time that leaves the struggle worse off than it would be without us, and that we may have a thing or two to show for our years of study, debate, and experimentation—that we move to the following points of discussion meant to inform taking action amid the present rupture.

Revolutionaries should operate on the wager that consciousness is surely helped along substantially by mass action, and qualitative shifts of sociality are no doubt affected by common experiences, but ultimately there exists a basic necessity for intellectually articulated political alternatives to liberalism. It is difficult in 2014 to imagine spontaneously arising consciousness rising to this task, though it is surely not without historical precedent. In any case the class is hungry for news, analysis, and debate. If people don't get it from us they will likely get it from the "police reform" liberals, or worse.

One of the strengths of the nonprofits is that they take people seriously as capable of learning and debating complex political positions. The city is awash in liberal identity politics, individualized privilege theory (think Tim Wise, not Noel Ignatiev), talk of reforming the police, or simply removing Police Commissioner Bratton (to be replaced with another functionary with the same social role), and so forth. This is not spontaneous mass consciousness. This is the product of a hard-working segment of the New York City political establishment—the nonprofits, the community-based organizations, the alternative parties (Working Families, etc.), shadowy political action committees like New York Communities for Change (NYCC), the "alt-labor" movement (like Fast

Food Forward), and a slew of academic institutions, anti-oppression workshops, etc.—taking working-class people seriously as capable of engaging political questions. These reformists provide the liberal ideological framework, which has been challenged by the street activity but remains standing and will likely carry the day.

So where is our framework? Are we relying on mass action to solve the problem of mass consciousness? Do we seriously think that a highway blockade (and most certainly the more toothless "die-in") can't easily be recast as an act of "civil disobedience" intended to influence legislation? Most importantly, in our engagements with the people that we meet on the streets, how do we understand and represent the questions of race, and more broadly, difference itself, in this period? Coherent and actionable theories of white supremacy, patriarchy, homophobia, transphobia, and the like, should be the hallmark of any political groupings deserving of the class's attention right now. Otherwise these burning questions will happily be answered by the liberals, or the nationalists among the revolutionaries, or the outright white supremacists. For those who take their groupings seriously, this should be a time of self-clarification, advancing positions, and engaging in rigorous principled debate.

When in the streets, we must continue to push the situation while laying the foundation for groupings and political projects that will sustain and entrench a baseline of the present level of militancy should this movement prove to have hit its crest. To be clear, we should be among the last to accept that this movement has hit its crest. But we should be prepared for it at all times. This is not a defeatist position (that the struggle certainly has hit its limitations, and that the Millions March is evidence of this, etc.) but a responsible consideration that we should be ready for the lull period, and should be asking ourselves how we can best position ourselves for that time right now. This could be distributing literature and critiques at the coming marches, meeting as many new folks as possible, and most importantly, populating or helping to build sustainable radical projects (social centers, solidarity networks, community speak-outs, reading groups, writing projects, Cop Watches, public debates, social events, and so forth).

Further, we must push against the centralization of this movement by recuperators wherever they arise, including being open to the possibility that they are in fact us. In power struggles against centralization and co-option we must find the dissidents already struggling and bloc with them. We must find those practicing the most promising escalatory street tactics and support them. We must keep an eye out for the fissures of promising leftward splits in ruling-class organs, especially the nonprofits, and position ourselves to facilitate these splits, and give them political context if necessary. We must fight the deployment of identity politics as a tactic of "de-escalation" back to the framework of civil society and legality, even when we're told we don't have a right to intervene. And we must call out and shame the "de-escalating" peace police in the streets, online, and wherever their despicable collaborationism with the state can be publicly denounced.

The flip side of this last item is popularizing militant street tactics, not only by our example, but also by popularizing the reasons for them. Why do we throw trash barrels in the streets during marches? To many liberals this is simply a symbol of lifestyle anarchism. Will peace police still interfere with this practice, and put the barrels back in place, when they know that this is a measure meant to prevent NYPD scooters from charging them and potentially running them over? Likewise with de-arresting, will people still get in the way of de-arrests when they are confronted with the facts that not only does this maneuver successfully keep people from the brutal hands of the state, but that interfering with it makes one an agent of the state itself, no matter how well-meaning they may be? This all remains to be seen, but in moments of mass upsurge we should try to err on the side of the masses of people wanting to do the right thing for the movement, without falling into pure naivety.

So just what should we be striving to build? For the first time since Occupy and perhaps for longer, the possibility is on the table for a serious antistate, anticapitalist (as opposed to "anticorporate") political and cultural milieu in the city capable of attracting, educating, building with, and most importantly, learning from people outside of the traditional academic or subcultural pipelines to revolutionary politics. We should take seriously the panoply of social and political institutions this entails, and a practical critique and analysis of the success of the nonprofits and community-based organizations in engaging the class (albeit in a disempowering way) is a project to consider. For those of us in the left, with active projects and perhaps a little baggage, now is the time to talk to each other, see if we can network our projects, set aside old differences, and figure out what really matters, even if it means we hate each other all over again (maybe this time for better reasons).

Likewise there is now the capability to coordinate meaningfully on a national scale, to socialize resources and experiences, and coordinate actions together. The risk of course, as always, is falling in love with our own organizations, and putting them ahead of the imperatives of class struggle. But this ever-present risk is no excuse for inactivity on the national level when the struggle seems so likely to generalize. What we need is no less than a radical alternative to the nonprofits on the local and national scale, not a project in building a better nonprofit, "boring from within" to change them, or forming blocs with the "radical ones." Right now we on the far left have our own shit, with its own momentum, and if we can't meet people outside an institutional framework, that says more about us as organizers than it does about the importance of working within reformist institutions.

This also means engaging as much as possible with the new groupings, the hastily constructed infrastructures, and all other forms of social relations that have arisen out of necessity over the past two weeks, and more broadly since the Ferguson uprising began. Many informal networks, small organizing crews, social media groupings, and so forth have sprung up out of necessity. In many cases attempting to formalize such entities beyond their role as mere tools of advancing struggle kills them. But it is important to begin asking what they are, how they relate to already existing groupings (if at all), and most importantly, how they relate to each other. Most political groupings never overcome the accidents of their birth, and while this may help sustain small crews, it is not necessarily a good thing. We should be encouraging and facilitating the generalization of as many projects as possible, or at least the facilitation of a common ecosystem for them to inhabit in relation to each other without forfeiting their autonomy. This will be messy; it will entail nasty splits, bitter polemics, lots of hurt feelings and maybe some tears, but this work is as risky and uncomfortable as it is necessary. In other words, it is in keeping with the order of the day.

It is now tempting, in the fashion of the day, to conclude with some grand theory that casts all these goings-on in a neat framework. But that would sell the presently polymorphous phenomena short, and not do us any favors by reducing their complexity. Instead we must outline a tentative and actionable map of the movement's contradictions, be careful not to downplay them, and be ready to take decisive action on its fault lines. The real resolution to the questions this piece raises, and

THE OLD MOLE BREAKS CONCRETE   19

thousands more unspoken above, can't be obtained by forcing these
events into a theoretical schema, but by engaging with these questions
in the streets on a micro level, by meeting individual people, pushing
along individual acts of defiance toward their generalization, forming
blocs with the right voices in meetings, boldly making mistakes, and
occasionally getting it right. And the theory we write should serve this
purpose, or will otherwise be met with detached curiosity.

It is impossible to say almost anything definitive about any rupture
from the midst of it. Nor is it possible to periodize with finality the recent
present (or distant past, really). For all the critiques leveled at Occupy,
many of which remain justified and relevant today, it is possible that on
a long enough time frame we will come to see the Occupy moment as
part and parcel of the rupture now underway. It is not important right
now to make such judgments; we can leave it to posterity, or more likely,
the US's fail-safe memory hole. What we do know for sure is that most
of what happens in the course of human social relations is outside of
the control of the small pockets of self-identified revolutionaries like
ourselves the world over. The question, paramount at moments like
this, is not: What is outside of our collective power? Instead, let's ask:
What isn't? And this is a question that only tireless experimental praxis
can resolve.

Some Bullshit

This text first appeared in issue 1 of *Hard Crackers: Chronicles of Everyday Life,* Summer 2016.

∎

In late December 2014, the New York Police Benevolent Association coordinated a work slowdown that effectively brought street-level policing to a halt in New York City. For the previous month, diffuse direct actions that would come to be called "Black Lives Matter" had proliferated like the mythical "many-headed hydra": no sooner had the police pushed an unpermitted march off the street, or cleared protesters out of a shopping center, than did one or two or three seemingly unrelated actions spring up elsewhere in all reaches of Manhattan, often by the spontaneous initiative of New Yorkers far removed from the professional activist set. In the face of a political machine that treats human lives as disposable or otherwise subject to arbitrary violence and systematic humiliation, this movement celebrated an unknown recent high school grad from Ferguson, Missouri, named Michael Brown, and a Staten Islander who sold loose cigarettes on the corner to make ends meet named Eric Garner, along with many other obscure names which rang out loudly in a city normally obsessed with the wealthy and glamorous.

As the protest movement grew, the newly elected liberal mayor Bill de Blasio enraged the police by expressing sympathy with the protesters and spurning the hardline tactics of his predecessors in favor of a hands-off approach to policing the movement. A police force, which for over twenty years had grown accustomed to exercising petty tyranny over working-class New Yorkers of color through "stop and frisk," brutalizing the homeless, and generally answering to nobody did not take lightly to being undermined by a massive multiracial, multigenerational movement against these privileges, and their anger was only exacerbated by the ostensibly divided allegiance of the city's mayor. Perhaps eyeing their upcoming contract negotiations, the PBA used the shooting deaths of two officers by a seemingly deranged man as the occasion for a rare workplace action. Though the slowdown was officially denied, President Pat Lynch slyly called for all officers to not make arrests "unless absolutely necessary." Arrests and tickets for most street-level offenses dropped to almost nothing. But contrary to the portended return to a Hobbesian state of nature, daily life basically went on as usual. Except, of course, life went on without the police harassing low-income people of color or issuing frivolous tickets and fines to fill the city's coffers. This doesn't mean the lives of everyday New Yorkers were any less fodder for the machinations of the city's power elite during this time. But at least for a welcome change of pace, human life was cynically instrumentalized by the powerful in a way that kept people out of jail. Most of them, anyway.

During this strange period, while most New Yorkers enjoyed a tantalizing glimpse of life without policing as we know it, I was one of the lucky few to find myself behind bars in Manhattan's Central Booking. I had been apprehended belatedly in connection with my participation in the street demonstrations, which by this point had calmed down substantially. Street politics had given way to capital P politics in the city's halls of power, and for a hot moment, quite against my intentions, I felt very intimately the weight of the conflict over just who ruled New York's streets. But more importantly, I got to see up close an unwitting experiment in, to rephrase a popular antiwar slogan, imagining if they built a jail and practically nobody showed up.

The 1%
Four years earlier, I had been held in this exact facility during the wildest days of Occupy Wall Street, when I was arbitrarily arrested in a routine police exercise in reclaiming the streets from the throngs of the so-called 99% who had taken a stand of their own against the impossibility of a dignified existence. On that warm November evening in 2011 Central Booking was sweaty, stinking, and swarming with recent arrestees, packed thirty or more to a cell, farting, snoring, and bragging of their

various prowesses all the way down the long subbasement corridor illuminated by oppressive fluorescent lights beaming twenty-four hours a day. I was mercifully split off from the other Occupards, in a seemingly arbitrary decision for which I was made grateful as their ceaseless sloganeering wafted down the hallway to my cell where the discussion was limited to the various charges we faced, comparing criminal histories, and the heaps of marijuana which would be collectively consigned to the air upon our release. Each newcomer to my cell, after being sized up from all corners of the room, was asked the same question: "What are you in for?" And each, without fail, offered the same answer: "Some bullshit."

The charges for which these men had been abducted, kept locked away from their families in piss-soaked squalor, forced to miss work without even the chance to call, kept awake for days, and fed inedible sandwiches useful only as pillows while cockroaches inched toward their feet, were, in fact, some bullshit. Possession of small amounts of marijuana. "Loitering" in a housing project hallway after leaving a friend's apartment. Smoking a blunt in a project stairwell because where else are you going to do it. Low-level drug dealing. Property disputes with friends. Fistfights with cousins. Smoking a cigarette for a few drags too many on the way down the subway steps. In a processing center for all arrestees in Manhattan, located in the southernmost tip of the island, there were scarcely any detainees picked up south of 120th Street, never mind white faces, excepting of course the Occupy protesters. You would have thought quite wrongly that the island of Manhattan isn't packed to the gills with white people who love to get drunk and fucked up on drugs and act like morons. But the fact of this racial double standard was so obvious, so uncontroversial, so ubiquitous, that it was simply unmentioned. The moralistic indignation with which activists rightfully rail against this racist double standard was completely absent, save only for the Occupards who were hard at work sloganeering about exploitation and oppression to some of New York's most exploited and oppressed people. This was some bullshit, all right, but to huff and puff against it would be like railing against the force of gravity. It just was.

What Evidence?

While there were no clocks, the guards who occasionally passed by felt no need to respond to questions, and the "one phone call" of the popular imagination was only good for those with quarters or numbers

SOME BULLSHIT   23

memorized to call collect; the time nonetheless passed in my cell.
Detainees practiced innocence narratives for the judge, seeming to
convince even themselves. A middle-aged father on his way to Rikers
recognized his son across the hallway and enjoyed some catching up. This
reunion led to brokering an exchange of a plastic glove stolen from the
police during processing (which it turns out is a hot commodity, useful
for keistering illicit objects on the island) for a small amount of marijuana
similarly stashed up someone's ass. The glove was promptly delivered
across the hall, under the cell bars in a single-serving cereal box, but
the deal hit a snag when the marijuana failed to materialize. "Don't rush
me!" yelled a squat Mexican man flushed red in the face as he sat on the
toilet grunting and everyone jeered. Thankfully for the integrity of this
informal economy, everything came out just fine in the end.

Meanwhile a young Black kid not a day over twenty painted an
unforgettable portrait of his arrest for street dealing. Thinking fast, he
had managed to get his stash of crack vials into his mouth, and battled
to swallow them while one cops held either arm and a third strangled
him to prevent the bag from going down his throat. When he choked
it down nonetheless, the arresting officers furiously charged him with
destruction of evidence. He paused, and wondered "What evidence?"
with a sly laugh that brought the cell to its feet. Soon after, a severely
stoned heavyset man arrived complaining morosely of being arrested for
petty drug possession in a restaurant at the exact moment his food was
coming out. That plate of food was clearly haunting him, and the moldy
cheese sandwich and crumpling apple he received for his stay were scant
compensation for the meal that got away. All the while an older, seasoned
convict's ceaseless sleeping farts in the direction of an already aggra-
vated young man slowly built to a heated altercation, or, more precisely,
the performance of one. The two men made exaggerated gestures and
issued grave threats of bodily harm, though it was obvious that neither
wanted to fight. The younger man got in close and demonstrated quite
delicately how he would choke the elder, to which the elder said not so
fast, and took the phone off the hook to demonstrate how he would use
it to break the choke. The pantomime became increasingly convivial
until they discovered that they hailed from the same block in Harlem,
and after that they just compared mutual friends.

I was released after thirty-five hours, and while I hadn't necessarily learned anything I didn't already know about the racist brutality of

Broken Windows policing, I had glimpsed the banal subjective dimension that can be all-too-often lost in a sea of data or saccharine political rhetoric. These were human beings, whose lives are the playthings of the shifting winds of city politics, academic theories of policing, targeted arrests to make way for condominiums, political campaigns desperate for the mantle of "tough on crime," nonprofit organizations claiming to champion the down-trodden, and so forth.

Absolutely Necessary

Upon my return in early January 2015, amid the PBA's police slowdown, the place was almost unrecognizable, though unmistakably unchanged. The architecture was the same, the food was the same, the stale air reeking of bleach and body odor remained eternal, but gone were the people. The endless corridor between intake and the door to see the judge seemed so much shorter, and silence reigned, belying the everydayness and shabbiness of the space, made from quite ordinary materials after all. The subtle threat of violence, which had previously undergirded an otherwise oddly fraternal atmosphere, gave way to the dullest of boredom. The soft time of short-term incarceration stretched out even further as the hours failed to tick by. In twenty hours I met about ten people, and reminiscent of an episode of *The Twilight Zone*, we soon figured out that ours was the only cell, and began to worry the guards had forgotten about us. In the parlance of the police slowdown, these must have been the baddest of the bad, those whose arrests, never minding "some bullshit," were absolutely necessary. Who were they?

One Black man in his mid-forties had been in and out of the system his whole life, and had a story for each cell in the hallway. Ten years prior the cell diagonally across the hall had held him for a day before he was extradited all the way to Texas for a sentence he had already served. This clerical error was corrected a year after he was taken from Manhattan Central Booking in a van that stopped off at various jails to sleep and to feed him Burger King along the way, always Burger King. He proudly hailed from Harlem, and had written a novel based in part on his hardscrabble upbringing. When I later searched for the title, I found a review by an amateur critic who disputed my cellmate's claims to have mastered ten languages ("when he barely speaks English!"), and to have sold tens of thousands of copies of his self-published book, and concluded the review by complaining that a previous bad review had earned him a personal

SOME BULLSHIT

message from the author threatening his safety. As a writer, I can relate. But it wasn't threats against his reading public that earned my friend a two-day stay in Central Booking, this time at least. My new friend had argued with his schizophrenic mother, and when she called the police on him, they arrested him for property destruction—his own property, in the form of a small hole he had punched in his own wall. The police were reluctant to take him in, not least because they recognized him from YouTube. He was also a well-known local rapper, though not as famous as his cousin in the Wu-Tang Clan.

A similar story (local fame notwithstanding) came from another Black man around the same age but with no prior experience in the system. He had wrestled with his pubescent son as I had with my own father at that age, but in this case his son, bested, had come away with a wildly reckless case of sour grapes and called the police. Even in cases so seemingly innocuous, cops responding to a domestic call have two options: leave the scene and risk being held accountable should some-one commit assault or murder once they leave, or make a bullshit arrest that will likely result in the charges getting dropped later. But that's not always clear to the arrestee. A longtime employee of the NYC Parks Department, this poor man was frantic that he would lose his job over his first-ever brush with the law. Worst of all, he had thoughtlessly commented to the arresting officers that he was in such despair he wanted to kill himself, which earned him a twelve-hour observation at Bellevue before our paths crossed downtown. Having experienced both holding areas, I can say he was in a much better place now, by a mile, and he bore every symptom of having been held in a truly barbarous place.

I tried to reassure him and others followed my lead—his son would drop the charges, he would not lose his job, and all would be well. We finally got him to calm down sufficiently to confirm a long-standing observation I couldn't resist running past him: weren't the toilets in Central Booking the same as those in the Parks and Recreation pools and weight rooms? He had to concur. Perhaps more out of boredom than altruism, I took this admission as my chance to put in a good word for the mostly Black young kids who populate the Parks and Rec system's after-school hours. In my facility, they are treated very badly by the city workers who patrol these facilities, harassed for ID (which most people lock up before working out) and generally given no respite from the school-to-prison pipeline even when following the mayor's admonitions to keep fit. Why else did stray pieces of exercise equipment, useless outside the gym, always go missing? He hadn't thought about it that way. More generally, he couldn't get over how poorly he'd been treated. Maybe some of those kids would have an easier time from now on.

Another man, a little younger, was a Puerto Rican from Springfield, Massachusetts, who was arrested visiting his cousin in New York. His crime was possession of a knife in violation of New York's draconian knife law, which as many carpenters, art-handlers, or movers will tell you, is a very common experience, compounded by the fact that like many street-level offences, no two police officers seem to agree on what constitutes illegality. We couldn't quite figure out why this poor bastard had been taken in, except that he looked the part of a seasoned hood, with the criminal record to match, and hailed from out of state and therefore would likely just ignore a ticket. Unsure what to make of the rest of us, he cautiously alternated, as most men in lockup seem to do, between the ridiculous performance of exaggerated masculinity necessary among low-income men, and the more approximate reality of a vulnerable, playful, and generally affable man scared out of his wits by his own perceived inadequacies. He was gracious enough when I recommended he make a pillow out of the otherwise useless sandwiches they provide, but was prevented from sleeping by his nagging (and well-founded) dread of ending up stuck at Rikers.

De Blasio Sucks

When the guards brought in another white guy, he generated the same buzz that had greeted me—what the hell did you do to get in here, on any day, but today of all days? Sharply dressed and noticeably groggy, this twenty-something just wanted sleep and didn't want to talk. His addition to the pack occupied everyone's imagination, to which wordless sidelong glances from every direction were testament. Finally, as the unofficial ambassador to white world, I loosened him up sufficiently for him to tell us with some hesitation "I helped myself to something that wasn't mine." After further prying, that something became a taxicab. And soon we learned the taxicab was running. And the driver was chasing after it on foot. And it perhaps went without saying that the perpetrator of this brazen theft had no motive besides being very, very drunk. Perhaps thankfully, he didn't make it very far. For every block of his adventure he had incurred another charge: grand larceny, reckless endangerment, operating under the influence of alcohol, and everyone's favorite, failure to pay a fare. During my two-day stay I would meet one other white guy, the next day in the Tombs. He was a knucklehead from Framingham, Massachusetts, who, also drunk out of his mind, had knocked a police officer out cold, and despite claiming no memory of the incident, had it on good authority that the cop was a head taller than him. I told him that he should probably consider getting help for his drinking, and half delirious with lack of sleep, shared my own experiences getting sober. "Some good it did you!" he replied.

I waited to make bail in the Tombs, where I could have been kept for weeks if the money didn't come through. This place was meaner than Central. The lead guard figured the case I was caught up in, and tried to threaten me while his subordinates half-heartedly played along. He taunted me with an unexpected salvo: "De Blasio sucks." Well, we agree on one thing, I told him. I was preparing myself to hunker down for indefinite sustained hostilities, when the strangest thing happened. There was a shift change, from afternoon to night. The white commanders were replaced with Black commanders, who began to tell me how much they supported the protest movement. One guard gave me extra food "for a brother." The officer-in-charge told me she proudly owned an "I Can't Breathe" T-shirt, and she would be sure that I got out ASAP if she had anything to do with it.

My cellmates were a young Black man and a young Latino man who knew the place well and explained the hierarchy of the various guards and various bureaucratic points of process to me while we waited. They were in on some credit card fraud charge I couldn't quite understand, and they passed the time comparing the comparative disadvantages of Rikers and upstate prisons, with the former praised for its better comfort and later lights-out time. If he could get his charges knocked down to a misdemeanor, the Black man told me, he was going to become a corrections officer. Then the Black corrections officer with the "I Can't Breathe" shirt, who told me her sister begged her not to wear it to work, called my name and I was set free, for a while at least.

Redux
A few days later, the slowdown that supposedly wasn't happening was called off, and some bullshit kicked back into high gear.

Noel Ignatiev, 1940–2019

This text first appeared on the *Commune* magazine website in November 2019.

■

Noel Ignatiev, who died on November 9 at the age of seventy-eight, believed that emancipation from the misery and stupidity of capitalist society was not only possible but present in germinal form within the daily struggles of everyday working people. These beliefs guided his life's work, and led him to place a particular emphasis on combating headfirst the disaster that white supremacy has visited upon all working people, including the white ones. "Labor in the white skin cannot be free," he often quoted from Marx's *Capital*, "where in the black it is branded." In death as in life, Noel will be remembered as an autodidact steelworker, an eccentric genius, a groundbreaking theoretician, a firebrand historian, a lapidary cultural critic, an unlikely Harvard PhD, and a bitter enemy to white chauvinists everywhere, in whose scorn he basked with delight. Friends and family might remember Noel as a wisecracking Romeo, a loving father, a generous mentor, a gourmet cook, and a fierce adversary. Noel was all these things, but above all a revolutionary.

Noel became a steelworker to help instigate a revolution. He became a prominent theoretician of "whiteness" as part of a revolutionary project to abolish white supremacy and capitalism together. He studied history obsessively in order to draw from it lessons for revolutionaries. He paid scrupulous attention to the daily lives of the so-called "ordinary people" around him because he believed therein lay the key to instigating a revolution. While Noel was a dear friend of mine, I doubt I'd have heard from him quite so much if he didn't imagine our relationship as somehow instrumentally connected to these goals. Noel died a stone-cold revolutionary. Until the very end he strove for nothing short of the abolition of capitalism through revolutionary struggle, by any means necessary. He got old, but unlike others of his generation didn't discover with age the hidden wisdom of the progressive wing of the ruling class.

Noel was born in Philadelphia in 1940, into a working-class Communist Party family of Russian-Jewish émigrés struggling to make ends meet. He began his political life an avowed "antirevisionist," still believing in the revolutionary potential of the USSR and dedicated to upholding a distinctly Leninist conception of revolutionary Marxism against Nikita Khrushchev's 1956 disavowal of Stalin. Noel joined the Communist Party USA in 1958 and gravitated toward its "ultraleft" faction, the Provisional Organizing Committee to Reconstitute the Marxist-Leninist Communist Party (POC). The POC offered for Noel the most viable option for advancing immediate revolution, grounded in the daily struggles of working people around him. Accordingly, Noel dropped out of college in 1961 to organize full-time in factories, as he would continue to do for nearly twenty-five years. Cutting his teeth in hard-bitten Leninist microsects and arduous industrial labor organizing helped mold what already must have been a sharp and ferocious mind into a weapon dangerous to foe and friend alike. It also marked the beginning of a lifetime of movement experience and practical wisdom, which he was always willing to share with younger comrades, even if we didn't always want to listen.

I once confided in Noel, following my arrest at a demonstration, that I was having a hard time stomaching the wildly exaggerated sense of self-importance my comrades ascribed to our tiny group and the legal case we had stumbled into. With a smile, Noel recalled his own arrest while flyering for the POC fifty years earlier. Since joining POC, Noel had heard movement elders raving endlessly about the sophisticated police conspiracy against their tiny organization, summoning an image of impending dual power before which the state trembled. When he finally got cuffed for "disturbing the peace"—a law Noel would consistently flout for the remainder of his years—he learned the harsh truth: "They had no idea who we were," he recalled, chuckling, "and they didn't care." Noel loved to recount the story of a Trotskyist he saw selling newspapers outside his factory, with the bold headline "The Working Class *Demands* Our Party." Barely getting to the punchline without laughing, Noel would chortle: "And nobody was buying it!" I laughed every time, even though I'd heard the joke and lived it many times. Noel could grin, with a twinkle in his eye, at the tragicomic vainglory of revolutionary leftism, but in the next breath return to plotting our grand entry onto the stage of world history. How else can you spend a life in the movement without burning out or selling out?

Once a group of us younger comrades teased Noel about sticking with Stalinism for so long. He had been giving us shit all night, gleefully destroying some post-Marxist nonsense about "immaterial labor" by citing the first page of *Capital* off the top of his head, and we thought we had him at last. "Oh," he replied, waving us off, "if you were all alive then, you would have been in the CP too, complaining about it just like we did." When our little collective fell apart shortly thereafter, for reasons of ego and personality rather than coherent political disagreement, Noel called to cheer me up. "Say what you want about the Party," he remarked, "but people didn't just pack up and go home at the first disagreement like they do today."

Noel didn't voluntarily pack up and go home from the POC. He was expelled in 1966 during one of the frenzies of self-examination such groups pass through when their relevance wanes. He soon came to count it as a blessing. "I think that the first fish that managed to crawl up onto dry land from the ocean slime," he later wrote, "and discover a world of light and fresh breezes could not have been more shocked than I on being propelled from that cultish environment." But Noel's definitive break with Stalinism came not then, but when Don Hamerquist, another CP veteran, advanced a simple proposition. "Khrushchev's policies were not an abandonment of Stalin's," Hamerquist told him, "but a continuation of them." In short, Stalin was not a Leninist revolutionary, but an architect of state capitalism. In telling me this, Noel was quick to clarify that Hamerquist did not in fact change Noel's mind. His mind had already been made up, he assured me, he just hadn't realized it. If this was ego—and I've surely never encountered a bigger one—it was equally rooted in Noel's theory of how consciousness develops. "I've won every argument I've ever had," he would often say, "but I never changed anyone's mind." For the revolutionary, this Wildean quip has enormous implications. Winning people over, Noel believed, is not a matter of sloganeering and evangelizing rote clichés, but of finding within people's daily lives revolutionary premises they already agree with, but have not yet recognized as such.

The thorny and contradictory nature of working-class consciousness was a consistent preoccupation of Noel's work, as he demonstrated an all-too-rare ability to face with sober senses the enormous evil the working class was capable of while simultaneously holding in mind its ability to save the world. In 1967, Noel and his mentor Theodore Allen coauthored the germinal essay "The White Blindspot." At the time, major left organizations advanced a line characterized by the slogan, "Black and white, unite and fight," meaning that differences should be set aside in the name of some abstract common struggle. Pointing to the structural white supremacy baked into the workplace by hundreds of years of US history, Noel and Allen argued that any struggle that did not address white supremacy head-on, lining up behind the demands of the workers on the lowest racialized tier, was bound to reinforce the racial division of labor, to the ruin of any strategic program for actual unity. Drawing from W.E.B. Du Bois's classic *Black Reconstruction in America*—a book Noel told me "every American radical ought to have their face rubbed in"—the duo formulated the concept of "white-skin privilege" to indicate the perks offered to white workers by the US ruling class, in exchange for which the former forswears all meaningful solidarity with their nonwhite coworkers and bind themselves instead in a self-defeating alliance with the white ruling class. The task of the revolutionary, they argued, is to break this alliance.

Older and more experienced than the average student activist of the late 1960s, Noel became an important member of the New Left, serving as a national officer in Students for a Democratic Society (SDS) in 1969. He subsequently emerged as a powerful voice amid its dissolution, first within the Revolutionary Youth Movement (RYM), and then as one of the leaders of the Revolutionary Youth Movement II (RYM II), a split from the faction of RYM that became the Weathermen. Noel penned a legendary polemic against the nascent Weathermen, entitled "Without a Science of Navigation We Cannot Sail in Stormy Seas," which addresses with remarkable lucidity questions that continue to plague the left and in places reads as if it were written last week.

Beyond the polemic at which he excelled, Noel's adult life was defined by practical work at the point of production. In late 1969,

Noel, Hamerquist, and a small group of former RYM II cadre and other Chicago-area radicals formed the Sojourner Truth Organization (STO), a group dedicated in its early years to revolutionary factory organizing. STO drew upon and developed the theses offered in "The White Blindspot," alongside the organizational theory of Antonio Gramsci, the praxis of C.L.R. James's Johnson-Forest Tendency (JFT), and the radical organizational experiments of Detroit's League of Revolutionary Black Workers (LRBW). Following these influences, STO developed novel forms of independent shop-floor organizing while actively contesting the white supremacy intrinsic to factories, trade unions, and the broader capitalist society.

Honoring the true spirit of Lenin, STO based their practice not on inherited scripture and rehashed platitudes from different times and places, but concrete engagement with the particular circumstances in which they lived. And like the League, STO thus dispensed with any lingering romantic notions about labor unions as revolutionary instruments: "Unions are a necessary development out of workers' spontaneous struggles against their oppression. While many of those who fought and died to build unions were moved by far loftier aspirations ... unions have emerged as institutions which channel workers' discontent into paths which are compatible with bourgeois rule. Most important of these is the widely recognized complicity of US unions in maintaining and promoting national and sexual divisions in the working class."[1]

Just as the League had to work outside union officialdom to contest white supremacy and advance a revolutionary strategy, so too did STO push for independent and experimental worker-led initiatives outside the structures of union officialdom, as part of a coherent revolutionary strategy. My favorite offering from STO's numerous workplace publications, which to be clear were largely serious affairs, was the candidacy of "Filthy Billy," a trashcan, for shop steward. He was, his campaign literature declared, "the can-do can-didate." Similarly, Noel told me he was always opposed to automatic dues checkoffs, a sacred cow of reformist unionism to this day. "I just liked to see my union rep every now and then," he told me, chuckling at the fact that union officials had to come to seek him out to collect.

This spirit of playful subversion accented a serious commitment to workplace militancy that declined prefigurative "movement-building" in favor of a militant minoritarian praxis, inspired by the nineteenth-century abolitionist movement against slavery. Noel tirelessly argued that the abolitionists presented a better model for revolution in the United States than the revolutions in Russia or anywhere else. In a recent and indispensable reflection on revolutionary strategy, Noel called their approach "creative provocation." According to this strategy, the biggest problem facing a small group is not how to attract the masses into its ranks, but how to best make its modest forces reverberate throughout society with maximum impact. "Politics," Noel would often say, "is not arguing with people you disagree with, but finding people you agree with, getting together, and doing things." Political action is therefore not a matter of convincing people of your point of view, but orchestrating the circumstances under which they can take action together. It's no coincidence that Noel lived his life in emulation of John Brown, who he claimed was perhaps the only white person to ever completely transcend whiteness.

Noel hung on to the industrial strategy until 1984, shouting the words of James and Marx over the clanging and whirring of the machines on the slowly depopulating shop floor. Thankfully, by his own telling, at least one factory where Noel worked for some years, US Steel, never got an honest day's work out of him. Instead he roamed from station to station, toolkit in hand, agitating and listening, with careful attention, to the revolutionary potential of even the most banal workaday gripe. By the time he was receiving vile threats on the internet, he told me, he'd become used to it from decades of reading cowardly invectives anonymously scrawled on the men's room walls of the factories where he daily defied the color line. I also knew he got a kick out of it. Noel believed that a white person can judge their antiracist praxis not by how many nonwhite friends they have but by how many enemies they'd made of white racists.

In the mid-eighties, when factory employment became untenable and STO was on the wane, Noel charmed his way into a Harvard graduate program, despite never having completed his bachelor's degree. When a nasty back injury ended my own (thankfully shorter) blue-collar career and I entered a doctoral program, I asked Noel if he had any trouble making this transition himself. "It was the easiest thing I ever did in my life!" he boomed, offended by the question. "The professors were afraid of me!" I didn't doubt it. He recalled sitting in a smooth leather chair in a cozy student lounge, listening to jazz performed live by his classmates, and thinking to himself there was absolutely no way he'd ever go back. "If the guys back in Gary, Indiana, knew how good I have it here," he recalled musing, "the entire steel industry would come to a halt!"

Though the early days of STO were the period Noel considered his most effective political work, he is best known, loved, and reviled for his writing and editing of the journal *Race Traitor*. Below a banner proclaiming "treason to whiteness is loyalty to humanity," Noel and STO fellow traveler John Garvey produced sixteen volumes of provocative theory and analysis geared toward the practical abolition of "whiteness," therein theorized as a social pact foreclosing solidarity based on common humanity. Noel contemporaneously released the classic historical study, *How the Irish Became White*, popularizing for a wide audience the history and theory that he and Allen had espoused for decades. Noel's work from this era, and its significant cultural reverberations, influenced an entire generation of activists and thinkers, popularizing the then-fringe notion that race was a "social construct" determined by a confluence of political and economic forces. It also led to an unfortunate trend within so-called white studies, of clinging to whiteness and white identity rather than taking it apart in practice. The point of studying whiteness, Noel never tired of pointing out, was to abolish it. Needless to say, an entire academic field reifying "whiteness" drove Noel as nuts as the "privilege checking" industrial complex, which owed some of its origins to "The White Blindspot." Noel fought both opportunistic trends tooth and nail in the pages of *Race Traitor*.

Throughout his years working on the magazine, Noel remained very active in revolutionary organizing, offering sage advice to younger organizers, and making himself available for whatever the struggle demanded of him. His final project was *Hard Crackers: Chronicles of Everyday Life*, a journal we conceived and edited together along with a motley, multigenerational crew of revolutionaries Noel had assembled over fifty years of class struggle. By focusing on stories that capture contradictions at the core of American life, *Hard Crackers* demonstrated the commitment to the revolutionary potential of everyday working-class life that had oriented Noel since the beginning. "American society is a ticking time bomb," an editorial statement declared with Noel's characteristic flair, "and attentiveness to daily lives is absolutely essential for those who would like to imagine how to act purposefully to change the world."

In his political and personal lives, which often overlapped, Noel possessed an irresistible charisma. Like a lunar body that alternatively pulls or repels others into its orbit with a great force but with ultimate indifference to the collisions and chaos it catalyzes, Noel's strengths were also his weaknesses. The indefatigable adherence to clarity of principles which propelled his projects for decades simultaneously became the source of a kind of petulance, or badgering, or sometimes, bullying. Noel's thirst for conflict could not be slaked; if he finally won you over or just wore you down, he'd change his position just to keep the fight going. For a long time I told myself that this was probably what it was like to hang out with Lenin, and just tried to just roll with it. Recently, however, I had to tell Noel, to his great disappointment, that unlike him I actually did not enjoy arguing. He complied with a grumble, but not before trying to pick a fight about it!

While this foible surely helped him through decades of hardscrabble sectarian dogfighting, dangerous political work in factories, and the death threats at which he laughed until his final days, it was of less help when running our blog. And it became more serious when it coupled with his isolation from the movement activity that nourished his best work, and led to a contrarian spirit which sometimes verged on outright trolling. While I will forever cherish the honor of working with Noel on *Hard Crackers*, and seeing my name alongside his on the masthead of a publication, I must confess that every time a new post went up on the blog, my stomach sank. While Noel likely had more faith in "ordinary people" than I did, believing as he did that they have no need whatsoever for seemingly any of the left organizations existing in our moment, I nonetheless retain practical and personal affinity with much of the actually existing left, to whom Noel delighted in offering one big, flaming middle finger after another. This tendency was particularly noxious on Facebook, where rhetoric becomes inflated in inverse proportion to substance and political stakes. The several times I broached the issue with him, suggesting that his time could be better spent writing about the US Civil War, or attending to his memoirs, or doing *fucking anything* besides taking on all comers all day long online, I felt a bit like Engels must have trying to convince Marx to set aside his own outraged essays about this or that benighted contemporary and finish his goddamned books already.

A mutual friend put it best: "Noel was an institution, and what institution aren't we critical of?" The older I get the more I appreciate how these big personalities and monumental egos that every leftist loves to hate and hates to love are an essential part of political organizing, no matter how much we wish they weren't. Through charisma, coercion, or the amazing power of sheer bullshit, they hold combustible compounds together for as long as possible before the whole thing blows sky high. All the while they provide consistency, clarity, and focus. They anchor projects for years as countless others come and go with the passing wind. They challenge us to be stronger, and wiser, and better, and if we fail, they are strong and better and wiser for us. And when the going gets tough, they are the first ones to get punched in the face, figuratively and sometimes literally, and it helps that many, like Noel, seem to enjoy it. Usually we have to kill them in the end, and something tells me Noel would have been fine with that too, if the ravages of time hadn't done the job first.

Noel's legacy is impossible to capture in one place, and I'm grateful that both his friends and enemies are weighing in to provide a robust picture of the enduring impact he has made on the world. I only wish to add that at a moment when both the far right and many on the left are hard at work fortifying and defending the walls between the so-called races, whether under the guise of "culture," "experience," or "biology," the approach Noel advanced in word and deed throughout his entire life furnishes us the tools to take race seriously while also taking it apart. While Noel's death leaves a terrible void in my life and the lives of countless others, perhaps there is a silver lining: Noel is now being talked about more than he has been in decades, at the moment when a *Race Traitor* revival stands long overdue, striking as it does an arduous path between the Scylla of race blindness and the Charybdis of race fetishism.

A few years back, on a long drive from western Massachusetts to Brooklyn, I asked Noel a question that sometimes keeps me up at night, as civil society across the globe unravels at a pace matched only by the degeneration of the very ecosystem upon which human life depends, and as the messiah of working-class revolution patiently idles in the wings of the world stage.

"What if there's nothing underneath it?" I asked.

"What do you mean," he replied.

"What if there's no future society underneath ours?"

He paused, as if he'd never given the question any thought.

"Well," he said at last, with a twinkle in his eye, "I guess we'd be in real trouble!"

We laughed heartily.

PART 2
THE ROCK

Checking Out

This text first appeared in *Insurgent Notes* issue 13, October 2016.

In mid-June 2016, tension between workers and their boss in a small New York City retail shop reached the boiling point. Even during a normal week these workers would have toiled under the insults of their overseer for a subminimum wage, sweltering in the summer heat, and abused by customers and managers alike as they hustled merchandise at a rapid pace. But in the preceding days they had been subjected to an especially breakneck speedup, open wage theft, taunts that they were "privileged" and "should be happy to have their job," and threats of replacement by "a bunch of Mexicans." They pleaded their case to the boss, demanding to be treated as human beings worthy of respect, but these entreaties met deaf ears. As labor conditions worsened and employer retaliation escalated, the workers met behind the boss's back and planned to stop work in a dramatic fashion, by all quitting at once. The action was designed to paralyze the shop at a moment calculated to cause maximum havoc for the boss, to send a clear message that they were more powerful than he had judged, and to walk away with a little bit of dignity intact. True to their word, about two-thirds of the staff quit at once, right before the busiest day of the week. The result was chaos for a hated overseer, and the sweet aftertaste of an assertion of people power all too rare in their line of work.

For the workplace organizer, a mass quitting is usually an option of last resort. If your aim is to build collective power in your shop, the last

CHECKING OUT

thing you want is for the most militant, or even belligerent, workers to leave without a fight, which they usually do anyway, one by one, without anyone organizing it. But this is no ordinary shop. It is a commissary in the Eric M. Taylor Center (EMTC, formerly known as C-76) at New York City's notorious Rikers Island correctional facility, where inmates shop for basic necessities not provided by the jail. These workers are themselves inmates, and their boss was a corrections officer with nearly unbridled power over their lives. At work or back at home in their dormitories, inmates at EMTC are carefully monitored for being "influential," for their alleged gang affiliations, and for being a bit too quick to stand up for themselves. They are routinely moved around the facility both deliberately and randomly, with no appeal possible. They are kept silent in the hallways and deliberately segregated from other prisoners as a means of limiting communication. No matter what kinship defies these strictures, the average stay for a prisoner is just under two months, so the turnover in Rikers dorms is even higher than the most unbearable retail or fast-food job on the outside.

Taken together, these factors drastically undermine any possibility that inmates will join together and build any kind of collective resistance against the well-documented daily indignities of life at Rikers. And the fear of retaliation that plagues the typical precarious worker is multiplied in the face of seemingly boundless power by a notoriously abusive prison staff. The dour sentiment that no organized resistance is possible, which we encounter in daily life outside of prison, is amplified considerably by these repressive conditions. By all accounts, this work stoppage was rare. And limited though it was in scope and efficacy, it certainly contradicted the general sentiment among inmates at Rikers that collective resistance is impossible, and pointed toward the possibility for coordinated resistance within what is perhaps New York City's most dense concentration of exploitation, oppression, and proletarian misery.

As an inmate myself during this time, I spoke to one of the militant commissary workers on the day of their action, and dozens of inmates working numerous occupations over the course of my own month-long incarceration on the island. Thankfully, like most of the inmates I met, I was not held long enough to be considered for most jobs, and thanks to some great friends on the outside, I had enough cash in my account to use the phone and shop in the commissary. Nonetheless, though duly limited to a small sample of discussions and observations at EMTC, I received an illustrative glimpse into the daily lives and attitudes of inmate workers in this facility.

My observations must be situated in the particular context that there is little compulsion to work at Rikers in the sense that many imagine prison workers as forced to work. The state of New York retains the right to impose labor on all "able-bodied" men at EMTC, but this compulsion is rarely if ever exercised. Jobs can be switched, or simply quit, with a quitting inmate having little trouble finding employment elsewhere. I met only one inmate who had been assigned a job that he did not want, and who was weighing whether to refuse. To refuse would be to possibly risk losing "good time," potentially prolonging his stay, and to risk being moved from a relatively calm and peaceful "working dorm" into what could be a more hectic and violent living situation. These are certainly serious threats for inmates trying to get out in one piece as quickly as possible. But by all accounts, these penalties are rarely if ever imposed. Besides this one man, every other assigned worker I spoke with either wanted his job, wanted a second job, or wanted a better job. This is a place where inmates *want to work*. And the reason is scarcely reducible to their pitiful wages.

Inmate workers are notoriously underpaid and more often than not labor under conditions hidden from public sight by mortar and razor wire. At Rikers, full-time workers can expect anywhere between $80 and $112 per week for working well beyond forty hours. Besides the commissary, inmates work in the cafeteria, laundry, clinic, law library, carwash for corrections buses (and unofficially, I was told, the guards' cars), and perform general building maintenance including painting, construction, and janitorial services, and perhaps the oddest job I learned of, burying the city's unclaimed bodies in New York's potter's field. The most basic janitorial upkeep of EMTC's minimum security dorms, where upwards of sixty inmates live in one open room, is maintained by "house detail" inmates, who then become responsible for, often quite aggressively, enforcing the rules of hygiene and cleanliness on those around them. Sometimes house detail work is even done for free as a means of buttering up the guards to get on the rolls officially. It is not uncommon for inmates in the hallway or dining hall to make a quick break away from the guard escorting them to give their name and number to an official they believe can get them a coveted job. Inmates allowed to work outside the facility walls are dressed in bright orange stripes, kept starched and impeccably

CHECKING OUT

clean compared to the grubby greens of the homebody inmate worker. This clear marking of the relatively privileged inmate workers cuts to the core of the incentive for inmate workers: mobility across the facility and outside of it, escape from the boredom and brutality of life in the dorms, and most generally, an increased control over daily life.

Wages are of course important to Rikers inmates, especially low-income inmates with no commissary funds and dependents on the outside. But one need not understate the value of the wages in order to appreciate the extramonetary incentives for inmate labor. First of all, it is not as if the most enthusiastic inmate workers don't realize they are being egregiously exploited by wages far below even the pitiful minimum wage. I spoke to one inmate who worked well over forty hours per week, as a painter, for $112. He didn't even bother keeping track of his hours. He would half-heartedly brag about the money, but he didn't seem to believe his own bluster, and everyone knew that deep down he knew that the money was nothing to brag about. His compensation was of a different sort. As a worker with outside clearance, he was able to leave the often-chaotic dorms for a good part of the day and night. He sometimes traveled across the seemingly endless bridge leading off the island into a vanishing point of flashing sirens—an occasion about which most inmates must be content to fantasize for the tenure of their incarceration. He was able to eat food from the outside, the topic of endless hours of wan reminiscences over sparse plates of bland prison fare. He could relate to his coworkers not as fellow victims of a debased situation, but as part of a cooperative project. And the impatient, aggravated way he related to his free time on days off from work suggested what is perhaps the principal motivation for him and many inmate workers: escaping boredom, making time go by faster, and getting out of the dormitories for as long as possible.

An inmate, with outside clearance, worked all day and well into the night in the kitchen at another jail. He rolled his eyes at the money, and anyway had enough support on the outside to do without it. So why did he look forward to his job? He wasn't in jail, he told me, when he was there. A chef by training, he worked at his own pace in the kitchen, under his own direction, and could get lost in his work. The guards at his worksite treated him as more of a colleague than a prisoner, even helping him correct a clerical error that had extended his sentence beyond his release date. He had freedom to prepare his own food, and even eat food from outside. And for a few hours each day he had some down time to watch TV or otherwise enjoy the indescribably rare privilege of solitude, far from the imposed stupidity of dormitory life. Back at Rikers he winced at the constant shrieking of the house guards, the hostilities of the inmates, and the countless indignities built into even the smoothest day at EMTC. He was happy to rise before the sun and get away from all this.

A fellow new arrival I spent my first week with in the intake dormitory had been to Rikers dozens of times and couldn't wait to get a job. But he wasn't really thinking about the pitiful salary, and he seemed to somehow have everything he needed already. What he was after was the excuse to move around freely. One day he left with a pass for the clinic and came back having shopped at the commissary by himself, which to the average inmate would be completely impossible, and the mere attempt would probably lead to disciplinary action. This man knew the island inside out, and only needed the privilege of circulation throughout the institution to run in different social circles, to nourish mutually beneficial quid pro quo relationships with powerful guards, and most of all, to circulate items. Beyond the items everyone would guess, like tobacco, it is just as common for a tightly rationed commodity as banal as jelly or matzo bread to be wildly popular, giving whoever has access to these items an upper hand in informal economies, social hierarchies, or simply being a mensch. Some items seemed to only circulate through this sort of gray market, such as "two-piece" inmate uniforms. Inmates are given ill-fitting, uncomfortable jumpsuits upon arrival, but there are shirts and pants of the same color that circulate through back channels, and mark the wearer as someone who knows their way around the place. In my month-long incarceration I saw no legitimate channels through which to secure these garments, and their informal circulation occurred unhampered by any authorities. Needless to say this also applies to less innocuous contraband, but I'll leave the snitching to someone else.

The oddest character I met actually cleaned the grimy bathroom for free, when he wasn't on the schedule, just for something to do. A Russian friend who had served time back home assured me that doing this there would place you at the bottom rung of the prison hierarchy, with the untouchables. But to the Americans, it lacked any kind of stigma or even appearance of abnormality. Better than sitting around, doing nothing. With food and shelter guaranteed, there is almost nothing to do all day besides watch garbage TV, listen to the same increasingly boring

CHECKING OUT

war stories from those around you, play repetitive games, or steal some reading over the incessant shouting of inmates and guards. There is scarcely any access to education, exercise, quiet reflection, any kind of creative outlet, or source of personal fulfillment, to say nothing of escape from physical confinement within a small and overcrowded space. The basic necessities of life like eating, showering, shaving, even clipping your nails, though guaranteed, are regulated by the whims of capricious guards, and subject to draconian restrictions with no appeal. Necessary items are paltry and scarce, for no good reason. Meaningful activity is even rarer to come by than the kosher meal matzo crackers everyone seems to desperately want. ("We don't even really eat those," a puzzled Jewish friend told me.) In sum, prisoner work cannot be understood without reference to this totalizing environment. It is possible the actual labor is the least important element of the complex relationship between inmate workers and the most basic activities of their daily lives. Cast in this light, the struggle over conditions of labor becomes the struggle over the nature of free time.

This brings us back to mid-June, when a critical mass of commissary workers joined together and lit their boss's hair on fire, figuratively speaking of course. The commissary in question is akin to when a bodega stays open after midnight but conducts all business through a plexiglass window, making communication a bit difficult, and the line slow-moving and impatient. Shopping, as it is called, is done on a designated day and hour, with upwards of fifty shoppers lined up to be served, called one by one by name to rattle off a shopping list as quickly as possible through muted slots in dingy plexiglass. The workers behind the plexiglass fill buckets on a kind of assembly line amid shouts, accusations of theft, gossip conducted loudly between men who don't see each other often, names ringing out mispronounced over and over, and in this general environment of confusion, violence lurking just below the surface, and sometimes above it. When not attending to shoppers, these workers are also responsible for unloading trucks and stocking the storerooms, which requires climbing a ladder with boxes of goods in tow. The guards decline this work, and stick to running the final tally at checkout and delegating responsibility.

Work in the commissary is unique in this facility in that it comes with the bonus of "tips," items which the commissary worker rather firmly suggests each shopper donate in exchange for their hard work.

And it really is the least we can do. Tips usually consist of tiny bags of chips, cookies, or sweets ranging in price from fifty cents to two dollars. Such items, unremarkably common on the outside, assume an inflated importance in the prison environment of enforced scarcity, and serve as the cornerstone of the informal economy that brings licit and illicit items into one market with a generally agreed rate of exchange. This is to say that what is immensely valuable to commissary workers is almost worthless to the guards, who have no shortage of access to miniature bags of Doritos or little strudel cookies in their daily lives. However, this does not stop the guards who run the commissary from extorting their share of the tips from the workers (when not outright campaigning to end the practice of tips, which the more righteous among them consider to be itself a form of extortion). Theft of petty commissary by staff, a commonly reported indignity suffered by inmates, seems mostly to be a raw display of power, though looking at these guards gives one the sense that the cookies and Doritos are not going to waste. "Render unto Caesar what is Caesar's," one guard told a comrade, charitable enough at least to quote Jesus Christ while ripping him off. Meanwhile the same guard reserved the right to leave pay slips unsigned, as a punitive measure, a show of power, or simply an expression of apathy, which could result in a worker not getting paid on time. This had become common practice by the time these workers took action.

The always simmering labor relations of this particular shop came to a head after a day-long, building-wide lockdown backed up the commissary even further than usual. The commonly accepted story ran that one inmate was cut by another in the dorm upstairs from mine, and what followed was a small-scale rebellion. When the riot squad showed up in response to the stabbing, the men of the dorm came alive. They defied orders to disperse by the riot gear clad "turtles," and were sprayed with the powerful chemical weapon MK-9. A noxious breeze wafted through our windows below as we rushed to screw them shut, amid defiant chanting and singing ringing out throughout the courtyard, spreading to other dorms. A disembodied voice upstairs excitedly shouted play by play out his window to a man in our dorm who was broadcasting the news live to the rest of us. Soon the hubbub died down, and the reaction of the island's veterans told me this was not an uncommon occurrence.

Predictably enough, inmates throughout the building were placed on lockdown the following day, subjected to an invasive and humiliating

CHECKING OUT

search (during which a different class of workers, those who clean up during shakedowns, were roundly accused of theft, for which they are rightly or wrongly well known—my own experience suggesting the former), denied basic services, and above all, denied our trip to commissary. A lockdown responds to a particular act of violence, limited to a specific time and place, by creating a general atmosphere of violence throughout the entire facility. While logically justified to prevent repercussions from the original act, they far more resemble what one friend of mine called "some revenge shit." Inmates are kept home from work, packed in close quarters, disallowed to shower or use the dayroom, invasively searched, bullied in the hallway by guards, denied access to the phone, denied hot water to make food while meals operate on an unpredictable schedule, and sometimes kept on their beds. In this environment, heated arguments break out between inmates or with guards, and individual loudmouth inmates (and guards) deliver angry soliloquies which ramp up the tension. The guards who try to be "cool" with the inmates by flirting or talking about basketball or allowing special privileges have no choice but to enforce these rules, participate in shakedowns, and defend the most overzealous of their peers, the foremost of whom boast of a military background and act accordingly. In short, the reality of daily life, sometimes buried beneath pleasantries and fringe benefits, is brought into the sharpest relief at these moments.

Already agitated by the lockdown and quickly approaching point zero, these commissary workers returned to work the following day to be met with a breakneck speedup and a dramatic extension of their work hours meant to quickly fill the gap left by a missed day of service. In short, they were forced to bear the brunt of the very lockdown that had debased them the day prior. Slowly they began to openly rebel, egging each other on, picking fights with the guard in charge and antagonizing him whenever possible. "Your soul is required in Hell!" one worker bellowed over and over to the laughter and approval of others. At the end of a long, stressful day playing catch-up after the lockdown, the guard in question confiscated half of the tips for the day, totaling a hundred or more dollars per worker in Rikers currency. To make matters worse, he had caught wind that the inmate workers were planning to quit, so he refused to sign all their pay slips for the day, meaning they would have no choice but to come back. He knew that the following workday, a Monday, was to be "bag day," when items are delivered to the houses instead of the inmates coming to shop. This is quite labor intensive compared with regular shopping, and yields no tips. A shortfall on a Monday would hit the boss hardest. If the wage theft was provocation, this was a clear challenge: if they wanted their back wages, they'd have to come back to work. But he overestimated the dependence of his workers on this wage. He thought he had them beaten by the threat of withdrawing their checks. But in the end, they said pay slips be damned, lockdowns be damned, daily life at Rikers Island be god-fucking-damned, we're quitting anyway. And they did.

Days Spent Doing Too Much of Fucking Nothing

This text first appeared in the "Abolish" issue of *The New Inquiry*, volume 59, March 2017.

■

> "*The Price Is Right* was on in the dayroom. I tried to play along, but just kept thinking about how this place is wrong."

Lil Wayne's *Gone 'Til November* (Plume Books, 2016) is, in all likelihood, a faithful, if slightly amended, reproduction of Weezy's actual diary from the eight months in 2010 that he spent at the Eric M. Taylor Center (EMTC) at Rikers Island, home to sentenced inmates serving one year or less. It is designed to resemble a composition notebook, inside and out, right down to its faux-handwritten font. Inside, Weezy's writing is stream of consciousness, unvarnished, and primarily focused on the banalities of daily life at EMTC, widely regarded as the calmest facility at Rikers. Despite his celebrity and the recent attention being paid to the island prison, Lil Wayne's account of his incarceration has drawn remarkably little notice, and it's not his fault: He has simply captured daily life at EMTC in a way that doesn't fit with the splashy headlines of Rikers's corruption and violence. Still, his account represents the facility just as damningly and faithfully.

"I got back up early enough to get a shave," Weezy writes, "Yeah!" In fits of manic enthusiasm punctuated by melancholy (Yeah! is a common rejoinder, as well as its opposite, "Damn!"), he documents the major events of each day: the triumphs of waking up early, often before dawn, for the coveted packets of sugar that come with breakfast, and a bit later for access to a tightly controlled razor for shaving; "being able to escape the harshness of jail" through visits but dreading the accompanying strip searches where the COs tell you to squat and "lift up ya nutsack!"; scoring a two-piece uniform, a cherished Rikers commodity to replace his one-piece jumpsuit; chatting with the male COs about sports and flirting with the women; and being exasperated with how everyone in jail would "yell regular conversations at the top of their lungs and say everything twice: 'Eh yo, them niggas down there be buggin' ... them niggas be buggin'! That's my word, that's my word, son!'" He wonders, "I don't know if it's a jailhouse thing, New York thing, or a New York jailhouse thing, but it's for damn sure an annoying-as-fuck thing!"

Weezy's entries end with nightly rituals of communal commissary meals and some combination of push-ups, prayers, slow jams, sports radio, and then sleep. He relates to the outside world through twenty-one-minute phone calls, biweekly visits, and the more unique experience of hearing himself and his friends on the radio. He befriends the other inmates on his block, including Al, the white ex-cop who one day jokingly dons a do-rag saying, "if Eminem can do it"; Coach, the gay man ("you know it had to be one of those") who braids Weezy's hair; and Jamaica, who makes tasty jailhouse fare for the other guys and begs Wayne for assistance with his deportation case until one day he is packed up and deported. "I guess he really did need a better lawyer," Wayne writes. "Damn!"

Otherwise, Weezy lounges in the dayroom watching *American Idol*, *Undercover Boss*, and on "DVD day" (a cherished privilege), a *Martin* marathon. He plays his hand in the informal economy: "I traded a coffee pack for a pack of noodles. Damn ... I'm really in jail!" He briefly tries his hand at a job, suicide prevention aid, Rikers's highest paid position—over $100 each week, an additional $50 if you stop someone from hanging themselves, or $25 if you find them dead—before tiring of the night shift, where he can only really chat with whoever is awake. Weezy writes letters, argues and reconciles with his various lady friends, and surprises a few lucky fans with phone calls. Unlike most of his fellow inmates, he gets regular visits, a torrent of mail, and even some unsolicited business offers: "Received a movie script ... Damn and Yeah! First the 'yeah' ... It was a script for *New Jack City 2*, and I was to play the son of mothafuckin' Nino Brown! Now the 'damn' ... They only sent it to me in hopes I'd fund the project."

DAYS SPENT DOING TOO MUCH OF FUCKING NOTHING

There's a little bit of action here and there. Wayne and the boys play a trick on their friend Dominicano by setting up an elaborate wedding with Coach as the willing bride, and later, Wayne is punished for having an MP3 player in his cell, and after a confrontation with a high-ranking officer, flanked by twenty goons, in the shower, Wayne is sentenced to thirty days in solitary confinement—an increasingly common practice at Rikers since the early 1990s for minor disciplinary infractions such as possession of harmless contraband. In fact, this practice—widely considered a form of torture and recently eliminated for detainees and inmates under twenty-one following a concerted activism campaign—is deployed so frequently that Wayne is put on a waiting list.[1]

For the most part, this book could take its title from one of Wayne's entries, "Days spent doing too much of fucking nothing," when Wayne and his friends are locked in their cellblock for almost the entire day and with nothing to do. This is not just because they're in protective custody—boredom is the policy at EMTC. EMTC has no library, except for a "Law Library" staffed by inmate-workers who don't know anything about the law, and where an equally ignorant CO monitors inmates' work to ensure it pertains to a legal appeal, ejecting them after an hour. Inmates are offered an hour to stand around in the yard each day, often when many are out getting medicine or methadone, in which case their hour is up until tomorrow. The same goes for medical care of any kind. Inmates sign up on a list for the following day and may or may not be called. Inmates requesting emergency services are accused of faking and told to wait.

Deprived of anything to do except work menial jobs—which are in limited supply, especially for the short-term inmates who make up the bulk of the EMTC population—days come to revolve around procuring basic necessities and, of course, stupid conflicts. Violence between inmates erupts on a nearly daily basis, often around issues like inmate control of payphones (indicated by socks of different colors on different receivers). CO-on-inmate violence is also rampant, as documented recently in a scathing report from the Department of Justice, especially at EMTC's juvenile facility, where assault rates are among the highest on the island.[2] But equally, if not more prominent is a sense of crushing boredom and futility. In Wayne's words: "I had to get my blood pressure and shit checked out. Of course everything checked out OK. It would have been a different story if they had scanned my brain for being bored out of my fucking mind."

Weezy, of course, enjoys privileges and pitfalls in accordance with his status as Rikers's most famous inmate: He learns a nurse only began wearing makeup when he showed up, other inmates kiss his ass, and he's apologetically told he's being sent to the box so the Department of Corrections can save face when the story of his MP3 player leaks. But to dismiss his experience as an outlier would be a mistake because his account of it illuminates many common elements of life at EMTC. While it was certainly not built for the rich and famous, reading Weezy's jailhouse experiences as exemplary of how and why the institution functions can shed some light on why, despite the author's best intentions and skill at capturing the poetry of the banal, his book is so unbelievably goddamned boring.

The EMTC, the Rikers Island facility also known as building C-76, opened in 1964 as the New York City Corrections Reception and Classification Center. The center was conceived as a humane alternative to the decrepit and purely punitive conditions of incarceration at nearby Hart Island. The latter, in its rich history, has hosted a Foucauldian smorgasbord of institutionalized subjects—juvenile delinquents, psychiatric patients, inveterate alcoholics, disobedient sailors, incapacitated senior citizens, the homeless, and convicted prisoners serving short sentences—all in a gloomy and decrepit penal colony revolving around New York City's burial ground for unclaimed bodies and amputated limbs, still operating to this day. With Hart Island as a foil, the Classification Center was based on a model for prisoner rehabilitation championed by corrections commissioner Anna Moscowitz Kross, a former judge and distinguished criminal justice reformer, suffragist, and one-time labor lawyer. In Kross's design, the center would provide intensive evaluation of all inmates coming into the New York Department of Correction system by using clinicians and social workers to craft plans for rehabilitation tailored to each inmate in days jam-packed with activities and programs meant to put the inmates on the right track to reenter society.

In 1965, Kross wrote: "Although the present Reception & Classification Center building was originally planned to replace the old traditional workhouse, our growing understanding of the mechanics of true correction and of the need for something far beyond the haphazard work assignments of time-worn practices led us to our present short-term pioneering effort. A new phase of our Rehabilitation Program is being undertaken there."[3]

When Mayor John Lindsay dedicated the bridge connecting Rikers Island to mainland Queens, the mile-long span was effusively dubbed the Bridge of Hope. Today the crumbling stretch is known as the Bridge of Pain.

While there is evidence that Kross may have in fact pioneered a method of intensive rehabilitation at C-76, it can only be speculated whether her experiment would have succeeded in the long term. What we do know is that in the face of nascent neoliberalism, deindustrialization, and the rise of "law and order" policing—the ingredients of what would become mass incarceration—Kross's dream didn't stand a chance.

Already in 1968, as a bellwether of changes to come, C-76 had been renamed the New York City Corrections Center for Men. While retaining the practice of intake classification—which continues at an extremely reduced capacity to this day—it also began to function as a more traditional holding facility for inmates serving "city time" of one year or less, including housing juvenile offenders. Inmates are housed in dormitory-style units with upwards of eighty beds, and confined to these quarters for almost the entire day. Numerous lawsuits filed since the 1970s, journalistic exposés, and a stream of first-hand testimonials from formerly incarcerated people paint a picture of this facility as it has operated for the vast majority of its existence: as a place where just about anything can happen except, it seems, "rehabilitation."

In 2000, C-76 was renamed again—this time after a former corrections chief, who got his start when he was laid off from the NYPD during the 1970s economic crisis and found that the New York City Department of Corrections was hiring. Alongside Norman Seabrook and Bernard Kerik, Eric M. Taylor introduced a program called the Total Efficiency Accountability Management System (TEAMS), a statistically driven corporate-management program in the style of NYPD's CompStat. Taylor's reforms are touted as dramatically reducing violence in the corrections system in the mid-1990s. However, these reforms also entailed the explosion in the punitive use of solitary confinement, like Wayne experienced, and increased restriction on inmate movement within the facility, which Wayne's case typifies to the extreme.

This was all enforced by the growth of a "culture of violence" denounced in the previously mentioned Department of Justice report, which it claims is largely kept off the radar of official statistics by the widespread institutional practice of inmates being instructed to "hold it down," or not report violence from COs or other inmates. To date, the only "progressive" program that can be found in most EMTC blocks is the Key Extended Entry Program (KEEP), which keeps inmates zonked out on high dosages of methadone all day, as an alternative to intensive drug treatment.

But even more pervasive than the violence, which rightfully grabs headlines and dominates the lion's share of prison reform rhetoric, is the enforced immobility, combined with the withdrawal of programs and services, that produce endless days in which there is quite literally nothing for most inmates to do but sit around. There is no effort at rehabilitation of any kind. The COs refer to inmates as "bodies" and "packages," and treat them as inanimate objects to be transported, with minor requirements for upkeep such as regular meals. On its face, this may seem like a grave mistake, as many prison reformers are wont to argue, pointing to humane programs in the Netherlands as alternatives. It is commonly said that people are locked up out of hatred or other strong emotions. But this misunderstands the dispassionate banality of mass incarceration.

Most people who find themselves in a place like EMTC are not locked up in order to make them better citizens capable of reintegration into gainful employment. On the contrary, they are locked up because there is nowhere else to put them. Addiction, mental illness, homelessness, and chronic unemployment account for a vast majority of the inmate population. For the lowest (and highly racialized) rungs of the labor market, there is little work, little housing, and put bluntly, little space for them in the current economy. The US ruling class has no interest in income redistribution through social welfare policies; these were rejected the 1970s in in favor of what's known as the carceral state.

Accordingly, the only public sector unions with substantive political power are prison guards and police officers, and these forces receive the lion's share of funding to deal with issues such as unemployment, mental health, drug abuse, and homelessness, which are directly related to the neoliberal disinvestment from social services that were inadequate in the first place. Thus, in the case of EMTC, a facility that was envisioned as a humane alternative to the brutish workhouse of Hart's Island has itself become a brutish place where daily life is so degraded that work is coveted above all other activities. The inmate is bored because there is no need for the inmate to be anything but bored.

The beauty of *Gone 'Til November* is that it captures not only the crushing debasement of human life but also the perverse flowering of the human spirit in such an intellectually, materially, and spiritually impoverished setting. Friendships bloom, laughter echoes throughout the blocks, and flashes of joy, triumph, and sentimentality momentarily remove the inmate from the reality of a debasing institution. A multi-millionaire, Weezy quickly finds himself rejoicing over iced Gatorade, makeshift meals seasoned with crushed up Doritos, adding extra sugar to the cereal he eats out of a recycled peanut butter jar, and listening to slow jams on a low-quality radio.

But more striking than the material comforts are the social ties Wayne forges: the goofy jokes, the transmission of local knowledges like recipes, tricks of the trade, and general survival skills in pithy adages. In the conditions at EMTC, camaraderie blooms alongside conflict, and intense bonds are formed, though they are rooted more in proximity than in anything more enduring. "I pray for everybody in here," Wayne admits, "but I don't really see myself keeping in touch with anybody but a couple of COs who never acted like dicks toward me."

As the campaign to close Rikers Island gains momentum as more people realize that this rotting avatar of mass incarceration cannot be reformed, it is necessary to argue that even the boredom at Rikers is indefensible. Lil Wayne's most boring days are tied to the most violent days at Rikers: They are interrelated symptoms of a larger social ill that must be eradicated in all its parts. Far from a minor side effect of incarceration, boredom and the sheer futility of life behind bars is a key element of the prison experience that often takes backseat to sensationalist stories. In terms of explanatory power, the acute boredom communicates the impersonality and dispassionateness of mass incarceration far more accurately than the tales of impassioned violence. In short: You are not locked up because society cares so much about you that they want to hurt you, stem your advancement, or assert supremacy over you. You are locked up because nobody with any social power cares about you enough to make it stop or to give you a better life.

This is where boredom in prison becomes political. It is often argued that it would be futile to close a place like Rikers while changing nothing else about our society, which has little to offer the people who would suddenly be free. But this is not a cause for defeatism; instead, it is a reminder that the struggle for prison abolition must be done with a

broader eye to the social conditions that make boredom at Rikers necessary: namely, the concentration of private property in an ever-shrinking
set of hands. To end incarceration as it is practiced at Rikers and to begin
to end incarceration as we know it requires a corresponding movement to
redistribute wealth and social power throughout our society. It demands
the end of the existence of a class of people who just sit around all day
and rot.

The Secret Lives of Rikers Island Jail Guards

This text first appeared on the *Hard Crackers: Chronicles of Everyday Life* website in January 2018.

"Corrections should rehabilitate the inmates," writes C. René West in *Caught in the Struggle*, "but who has the time. The officers are so busy trying to sift through all the confusion in the parking lots, locker rooms and in the corridors with all the animosity and foolishness that there is no time or consideration to assist the inmates with their issues." West worked in the New York City Department of Correction (DOC) from 1991 to 2004, when she published *Caught in the Struggle* as an exposé of "the Real Rikers Island." Robin K. Miller worked from 1983 until 2005, self-publishing *Inside the Dark Underbelly of Rikers Island* in 2016. Gary Heyward worked from 1997 until his arrest for drug smuggling in 2006, self-publishing *Corruption Officer* in 2011, which caught the eye of a major publisher and became a mass market paperback (Atria Books, 2015). These books form a trio of self-published memoirs by former New York City jail guards offering gritty, tell-all accounts of the sex, violence, and corruption that define the lives of guards at the city's secluded Rikers Island jail complex. Rooted in the tradition of self-published "street lit," these books are written in a straightforward, conversational tone meant to convey not only the dialect of the Rikers guards' social universe, but also the values that animate it. "Though some of the language may not be considered proper English," West writes, "it is my intention to keep it ... true to the actual conversations and experiences that only those who have lived these experiences may truly understand or can actually relate."

West, Miller, and Heyward paint Rikers as a place of widespread predation between inmates, routine guard brutality, and systematic cover-ups erasing these phenomena from the DOC's statistical tables. The authors describe drugs, weapons, and other contraband circulating freely throughout the jail system, often brought in by the guards themselves. They depict the management of the inmate population as either accomplished by brutal guard violence or simply left to powerful inmates who extort and victimize the powerless, ruling by intimidation and violence with often explicit guard approval. Rikers emerges from these accounts as a place of danger and indignity for inmates, patrolled by "glorified babysitters," in Heyward's words, who are preoccupied with their own social universe and otherwise counting their days to retirement without even pretending to be *correcting* anything or anyone. In the process, a detailed picture emerges of day-to-day life for Rikers Island jail guards, providing a rare glimpse into a secretive and repressive world, which nonetheless offers social mobility and considerable power and prestige for the working-class New Yorkers who seek employment in the Department of Correction.

What follows is an attempt to reconstruct the social universe of Rikers Island jail guards as it emerges from these three books, relying heavily on direct, unedited, and sometimes lengthy quotations. While it is not my intention to fact-check particular details of the guards' accounts, the skeptical reader should note that these books not only corroborate each other on most major themes, but are also largely corroborated by decades of investigative journalism and special investigations of the DOC and Rikers Island, especially a recent report from the Department of Justice (DOJ) detailing the island's brutal "culture of violence," defined by systematic intimidation and elaborate cover-ups, and two reports from the New York City Department of Investigation detailing the ease of staff smuggling and the widespread social proximity of guards to inmates conducive to smuggling and sexual relationships.[1]

The Blue-Collar Jackpot

City employment in New York has historically been a source of upward mobility for low-income people of color, and all three authors emphasize the prestige of a city job and the social mobility it afforded them. West claims that many of those who become guards escape lives defined by welfare, drug addiction, and sex work. West herself was hired at age twenty-two, and found the salary and benefits impossible to pass up, no matter what Rikers threw at her: "Our pension slogan was 'hired in my 20's retired in my 40's, can't touch this.'" Miller agrees, and surmises that most guards do the job for a salary that places them in the "upper middle-class range." Today guards start out making a $43k/year base salary, and within five and a half years are making nearly $100k, not including overtime, which is a major source of additional income that can more than double a guard's total earnings. The immense change of fortune this job represents is especially salient given that, like many guards, the authors all hail from low-income communities of color. "In the ghetto," writes Heyward, who grew up in the Polo Grounds projects in Harlem, "everybody knows that if you land a city or state job you hold onto that job, you do your twenty years and retire young." Heyward is the most explicit about his change of fortune upon becoming a guard, attaining what he dubs "made man status":

> The made status goes as follows: 1) consistent money, never worrying when or where your next check is coming from; 2) consistent coochie, the chicks that would not give the "one step up from a summer job" brother a look, are now constantly dropping the draws because of BEN-O-FITS; and 3) the perks, everybody in the hood will now know that nigga got a gun and a motherfuckin badge. Traffic stops—whip out the badge—BAM. Bouncer at the club—stop—BAM! Subway and bus—BAM! Chicks putting up a coochie stop sign—BAM! BAM! BAM! HA! I felt like Master P in the projects because the badge sometimes had NO LIMITS.

West is a bit more subdued but echoes Heyward in sentiment. "With excellent health benefits and a pension after twenty years of service, working as an officer is like hitting the blue collar jackpot."

However, this newfound status comes at a high cost, inside and outside the island jail complex. Heyward describes his initial chagrin at a workplace that smells like "a combination of funky sweat, funky asses, and three-day-old cabbage that's been sitting out." West emphasizes the high rate of guard mortality due to stress, including heart attacks and suicide. Guards' lives are quickly defined by bad diet, smoking, substance abuse, and the collapse of outside relationships including marriages, all of which seem to go hand in hand with the job. Drinking on the job is tolerated and sometimes encouraged by supervisors, some of whom send their subordinates on liquor runs. Heyward's depicts himself and his colleagues as drunk on the job for the better part of his nine-year tenure. Often reeking of booze, they sip liquor in plain sight of inmates using water bottles, but "Poland Springs ain't never made water that tastes like this." The physical isolation of Rikers, the long hours, and the insularity of guard culture—reinforced by a commonality of experience that is surely unique, but also an "us against the world" siege mentality—combine to isolate the guards from their loved ones, destroy outside relationships, and relegate their social lives to a sort of compulsory community rooted in self-destructive behavior, rampant and incestuous promiscuity, and shared complicity in covering up misdeeds that extend from slacking off on the job to horrendous acts of violence against inmates. When a new female guard says she's spoken for, West writes, the male guards ask how her partner feels about her job. "If you say that he doesn't like you working on Rikers … it will only be a matter of time before you're on the available list."

Dodging Bullets

Guards' complicity with the island's repressive culture is reinforced by the constant threat of retaliatory transfer, suspension, or firing, which keeps them from challenging the status quo or bruising the egos of super-visors who wear "their fear of being proven incompetent on their sleeves." West notes the toll that this complicity takes on the guards. "I couldn't understand why, when others were being degraded, humiliated and totally disrespected by supervisors, they would act as if it was ok and it did not bother them. But soon I found out that those same officers were affected in a variety of ways either by an increase in cigarette smoking, drinking coffee, gaining weight, being abusive to inmates or using alcohol or drugs." Whether or not guards speak up against the island's status quo, they pay the price with their health, safety, and sanity.

As a most basic punishment, transfer can be effected arbitrarily, and robs the guard of their set schedule, as well as the seniority, comfort, and society of their established work station, which can also be the site of a sexual relationship, or a lucrative market for smuggling contraband. Outside the workplace, the loss of a steady schedule can be devastating to the health and family life of a guard, especially if it means a move from steady hours to the alternation of day and night shifts, which wreaks havoc on relationships but also health and sanity. Suspension and firing can result from gross misconduct, as ultimately befell Heyward when he was fired and arrested for smuggling contraband into Rikers in an episode that grabbed headlines. But workplace penalties can also result from simply being unpopular enough to be singled out when someone must be held accountable for anything that embarrasses the correction administration, especially the death of an inmate, as befell two of Heyward's friends. Most commonly, however, transfer and other retaliation seem to result from pettiness, sexual jealousy, or outright sexual harassment.

Female guards are forced to either accept the sexual attention of male superiors, or face retaliation. Played off one another by male guards who dole out perks, women fight over preferential treatment on the schedule, vying for assignments where they can leave early, avoid inmate contact, or get outside food delivered. They also just fight over lovers. West warns that ranking female guards who are the jailhouse "girlfriends" of male guards will pick fights with new hires they find threatening, knowing that due to the probationary period they'll get fired. This practice is called "get[ting] the bitch fired." "I can literally count on one hand the female officers who never gave me a problem," Miller recounts. West scratches her head at female colleagues who fistfight over married men, or otherwise harm each other as much as possible, socially, professionally, and physically, just to gratify the egos and appetites of the men who rule what Miller dubs "the land of testosterone." West seems a bit more understanding of a female colleague who cut a male guard on his face for manipulating her in a love triangle to serve his ego: "When you live foul, expect the same thing you dish out to return to you."

West writes that complaints of racism or sexual harassment are met with retaliation. In this climate of violence and intimidation, most guards "just walk with the 'herd' and pray they are not the next victim" in West's words. "This behavior is commonly referred to as 'dodging bullets.'" And these "bullets" are not simply professional retaliation. Miller was assaulted by a senior guard for rejecting his advances, including sniffing her seat on the cross-island staff bus after she stood up. Like his harassment, the assault occurred publicly, this time in front of inmates, but was covered up by their superiors despite documented injuries. West was attacked in the parking lot of a retirement party by a woman guard jealous of her dancing with a captain, who anyway happened to be married, and being in her probationary period, she was lucky not to lose her job. Miller recalls a colleague who reported sexual harassment to administration: "Once she made a complaint, she stated the officers retaliated. I find that hard to believe, not my colleagues, they stick together. Just bullshitting, of course they retaliated." Conversely, sexual relationships and sex appeal can be leveraged to gain preferred assignments, like the Control Room, which by West's account is a cushy gig, air conditioned "unlike the smelly hot dorms," doesn't require much inmate contact, and serves as a hub for gossip. This assignment is often given to women either dating or pursued by male superiors, because "some of the male supervisors wanted a harem of women around them."

The Playboy Mansion

"Many spouses worry about what their mates do after work," West writes, "but they need to concern themselves with what happens at work, and with whom they are doing it." The lion's share of these books focuses on courtship and dating rituals between guards, and the attendant drama. The reader is halfway through *Caught in the Struggle* before much is said about inmates at all, and West is clear that "the struggle" is almost completely within the social world of the guards. "Working at Rikers was similar to being in the projects or back in high school," she writes. "There was no age limit to foolishness or the viciousness that was to be dealt with; and this came from all staff and your supervisors. All this drama and nonsense was before you even stepped foot in the housing area to face the inmates. Oh yeah, the inmates; that's the reason we are there but that's last on the list after dealing with all of the above." Heyward refers to dormitory searches, the most disruptive possible occurrence in the daily life of inmates, as "when officers from one jail get to visit another jail and catch up with officers that they have not seen in a long time. Oh, and they come to wreak havoc and search the jail, too." Miller agrees with West that almost all of her trouble came from her fellow guards, not the inmates: "Working in an all-male prison was a walk in the park; literally. I grew up in the Brownsville housing projects, so for me, it was like walking down Stone Avenue." West and Miller found their major problems to stem from the fraught sexual underground of the island's institutional life, which seems to completely dominate its day-to-day functioning. The thousands of human lives under the DOC's "care, custody, and control" are an afterthought.

"All you have is time" writes West, "and the one thing about being in jail is that there are many locked doors and secluded areas to handle whatever business you desire with whom you desire to handle it with." Miller complains: "We are a quasi-military establishment and should be conducting ourselves in a professional manner. Instead some are gallivanting around wearing their sexuality on their sleeves participating in oral sex, sexual intercourse, orgies, ménage à trois and anal sex, at work, as though we are at the playboy mansion." West describes used condoms littering the guards' parking lot, or as Heyward calls it, the "cocking lot," where West claims guards get "paid in full" for sex work. No sooner did new guards set foot on the island, West writes, "whether you did or did not want to participate, the race was on between the men and the women to be the first to fuck the new meat." When not simply the product of aggressive sexual harassment by male superiors, courtship begins at lunch time, with the gifts of outside food—a coveted item due to the commonly held belief that inmates contaminate guards' food with bodily fluids. In West's experience, the gift of a turkey and cheese sandwich in the guards' dining room is the most popular courtship ritual. Heyward calls the gift of a sandwich from a female to a male guard "the first telltale sign they're fucking."

Miller dedicates a chapter of *The Dark Underbelly* to "the elephant in the room": her affair with a high-ranking and married DOC official named Eric M. Taylor, a famous chief of operations whose name today adorns the island's C-76 facility, where, incidentally, they met when he was her superior. Miller complains bitterly of Taylor's childish behavior after she broke off their short-lived romance, including him bragging about their sexual relationship in the locker room and calling her "my woman" for years thereafter. Their three-month relationship, she writes, "would haunt me for the rest of my career." "Most officers are proud to say their wife isn't on the job, or they wouldn't let their woman work a job like correction's," writes West, "but these are the same men who are quick to have affairs with the first female officer who gives them the chance." This behavior is typical of West's and Miller's accounts of the conduct among male guards, complete with what West calls a "wall of shame" in men's locker rooms, containing embarrassing information about female guards, which inmate cleaners can read and repeat back in the cell block. Heyward certainly offers no contestation of this in his graphic accounts of workplace sexual conquest and "running through the jails swinging my dick from left to right."

Miller and West take pride in their own abilities to navigate this terrain with dignity and street smarts, and disdain the women who fail to do so. Miller implores her female colleagues to "Stop! being a door knob and letting your male colleagues take turns on you." West is pragmatic in her approach to jailhouse dating: "My advice to women in corrections is to limit yourself, and control your lustful desires. The maximum number of guys women should date at work, if any at all, should be no more than two guys per jail. Any more than two who are in the same jail at the same time would be playing yourself." Heyward's claims to be the target of female coworkers who want to have his children just for the child support money may seem like braggadocio, but West completely agrees that the male guards are an easy mark for "the 17% trap," her name for child support. She claims "one female officer is known to have four children by officers from various ranks within the department and is now living a life of luxury, not to mention her own $60,000 annual salary." Miller decries this "jailhouse prostitution," "the scam of sleeping with ranking officers just so you can take them to court for child support and double your salary."

Miller and West never suggest that women are simply helpless prey in the sexual free-for-all of the Rikers Island guard culture, but the vastly unequal gender dynamic is palpable. "Women have to be extremely careful about whom they associate with at all times" writes West, "because their failed relationships tend to linger more often than the men's and when they move up in rank, they look silly unlike the men whose sex life increases with each promotion." Miller addresses an entire chapter to the men working in correction, who "assume the roles of predator and sexual abuser." She writes: "You decide you want to have sex with us and make us comply, if we do not, you isolate and treat us as if we are yesterday's trash and [you] will intentionally place our lives in danger … not every female officer is your property for the choosing. Our body parts do not belong to you. If we decline to become part of your harem, you go after our jobs and try to make our lives a living hell. Instead of focusing on care, custody and control, your primary focus is ego, vagina and who has the most testosterone."

Between the unwanted sexual attention of superiors, and supremely childish behavior of male guards in consensual sexual relationships, these passages leave the reader wondering if the widespread reckoning surrounding the "#MeToo" moment may be headed for the New York City Department of Correction.

THE SECRET LIVES OF RIKERS ISLAND JAIL GUARDS

The sexual free-for-all between the guards also extends to relations between guards and inmates, who are legally unable to give consent. West claims that sex with inmates is pervasive, "male officers with female inmates; female officers with male inmates; female officers with female inmates; male officers with male inmates. In other words, any combination it can come in, it happens and it gets done." Heyward brags not simply of having sex on the job—and don't worry, he'll tell you exactly how it went down—but of serving as a pimp, negotiating sex between female guards and male inmates. West claims that some female guards target the sex-starved male inmates for amorous attention. Miller implores her female colleagues to "Stop! sleeping with inmates and stop being their illegal narcotics and weapons mules. These inmates do not give a damn about you. These inmates are not cute or you bae, or boo. If you are that insecure, go seek counseling to figure out why you falling for the oldest inmate trick in the book." This conduct is unambiguously against the law, and it seems to be only the tip of the iceberg in the culture of illegality that defines the staff life of Rikers Island.

The Inmates Are Not the Problem

"I'm often asked what it is like to work on Rikers surrounded by murderers, rapists, burglars, and the mentally ill," West reflects. "People are often surprised when I tell them that the inmates are not the problem on Rikers ... it wasn't an inmate who stole fur coats, money, and uniform equipment out of the locker rooms. Nor did an inmate scratch the paint off of brand-new cars, break windows, steal radios, or flatten tires in the staff parking lot. When I was physically assaulted, robbed of my jewelry, and my life threatened, it was not at the hands of an inmate, but at the hands of my fellow officers."

West recounts how guards who have made an enemy might return to the locker room at the end of their shift to find their lockers glued shut and the items inside soaked in bleach. In the guards' parking lot, where the general public is not allowed, cars are keyed and spray-painted with race and gender slurs, windows are smashed, and valuables are stripped for resale. Thefts by guards range from basic supplies like jackets, flashlights, command insignias, and ties, stolen when left around the workplace, to jewelry, jackets, phones, credit cards, and cash stolen out of lockers by breaking the locks. Guards who die on the job have their lockers immediately sealed as a memorial, but Heyward recounts that even those are burglarized. "Security doesn't even conduct an investigation" when these break-ins occur, West complains. "All people say is 'that's fucked up.'" Miller got her sister a job as a guard, only for her to be turned onto smoking crack by a coworker, who used it and sold it to the other guards.

West describes a spate of tax evasion schemes and other frauds promoted by her colleagues and marketed as a package service across the jails. One service offered to trick out cars with luxury parts somehow available at bargain prices. Some guards claimed to be pastors for the tax breaks, or encouraged their coworkers to simply claim ninety-nine dependents to receive their entire paycheck tax-free. Others operated a variety of pyramid schemes, which Heyward confirms were a lucrative source of revenue for guards. West documents a particularly bizarre episode in which a group of guards marketed a tax evasion service that changes the claimant's address to "a country I couldn't find on the map" and changes their last name to a variant of "Bey," thereby somehow evading US taxation. West recalls a time when both the ninety-nine dependents scam and the Bey scam became popular simultaneously, especially after they actually worked on a number of consecutive paychecks—until quarterly salary figures were tallied. "The new cars started rolling in; the diamonds and furs started appearing everywhere. Everyone was living large until the bottom fell out and the jig was up." Worse yet, the Bey scam threatened the unforeseen side effect of forfeiting one's status as a civil servant along with US citizenship. West watched the demise of many of her colleagues with disdain. She never got involved with the scams because she knew their day of reckoning was coming. "Uncle Sam will seize your accounts to get his money and will set your shit out in the street," she warns. "I don't play with him because I know he's not trying to play with me."

All three books were published before the most famous instance of Rikers guard corruption to date, the 2016 arrest of Correction Officers Benevolent Association president Norman Seabrook for bribery and fraud surrounding his handling of COBA retirement funds. But with impressive prescience, Miller directly addresses not just corruption in COBA, but Seabrook himself: "Remember this Mr. Seabrook; all good things come to an end. What goes up must come down and judging on the history of COBA, I can almost guarantee a front-page scandal of you Norman Seabrook.... For your sake, I hope you are squeaky clean, but who is, with that much power."

Red Meat and Venom

Heyward, on the other hand, was too busy with smuggling drugs and cigarettes into the jails to concern himself with cheating on his taxes. Between his smuggling contraband, acting as a pimp for fellow guards, and even conducting armed robbery using his DOC issued weapon, the stories in *Corruption Officer* place Heyward in a league of his own, even by the standards of Rikers Island. But interspersed with his gritty noir tales of action and adventure are offhand references to belittling and beating inmates and denying them basic dignity. In one episode Heyward is drunk on the job and an inmate asks him for toilet paper. "I bark at him and say, 'You ain't getting shit! Go wipe yo ass with your hand!'" The inmate is incensed and launches into a tirade "ranting and raving about how we as officers use our power to take advantage of them and treat them like slaves but don't realize that we are the real Uncle Toms doing the white man's dirty work for him by oppressing our own people." The conflict escalates and Heyward winds up viciously beating a man who had simply requested toilet paper. The story ends when a powerful inmate pressures the man Heyward had beaten, who Heyward derisively calls "Mandela," and "our civil rights leader," to not report the assault. The casual and largely anecdotal way Heyward narrates this and other stories of violence and indignity demonstrates what Rikers inmates already know, namely, that inmates are at the bottom of the guards' list of priorities—if they're lucky.

Miller recalls that guards are fed "red meat and venom from the door" of the academy, setting the table for brutality and callousness against the inmate population. Any guards who speak against the assault and debasement of inmates are labeled "inmate lovers" and open to the consequences of breaking the island's social contract. In the academy, Heyward recalls, the "instructors told us point-blank that these individuals (the inmates) don't care about you or your family. They don't have anything to do all day but scheme on you. They focus on what they can get from you or what they can get you to do for them." Heyward's narrative of his own smuggling career relies heavily on this popular theory, in which inmates contaminate staff with contagious criminality disguised as basic requests for necessities or dignified human interaction. When inmates are not perceived as the enemy, they are simply understood in relation to the guards' ability to either make their job easier, shirk their responsibilities, or avoid getting into trouble. West emphasizes the common guard fear that when an inmate dies overnight, the temperature of the body upon discovery could reveal that a guard was not making their regular rounds and was probably sleeping. "God forbid an inmate dies as you doze," writes West, "with time of death down to science, that inmate's body had better not be cold, or you will be left holding the bag." She recalls one negligent guard who tried to warm up a dead inmate to modify the time of death, but just burned the dead flesh on the heater and was caught.

Heyward recalls that when he first began patrolling the dorms he followed procedure and tapped sleeping inmates to wake them up for a count. An inmate woke up and almost punched Heyward before realizing what was going on. The inmates yelled to the ranking guard to "call off your man Dudley Do-right. He walking around waking motherfuckas up." The guard told Heyward to forget everything he's learned in training, and soon enough, he was drunk on the job, "sleeping most of my second tour, letting whatever inmate had the most power run the housing area." Heyward discovers another key to the staff management of inmate life when he is stationed in the mental observation area, "aka the Nut House": "Right now these fools are jumping off the wall until they hear their favorite call, which is MEDICATION! Ah, right on time. They all line up at the front entrance of the housing area to receive their prescribed meds for the day and then, bam! It's like the house has done a 360-degree turn. No more yelling at the television or nothing, just the walking dead." Similarly West learns how complaint reports against inmates actually function, after she writes up an inmate for verbally abusing her, and is told by a senior guard to make reports more "juicy" so they will stick: "A small curse like 'fuck you bitch' turned into a threat to kill my mother, rape me or to visit me once he was released." West describes being subsequently confronted by the inmate whose words she'd falsified, who asks her why she lied. Feeling ashamed, she vowed not to do it again. "I felt if his actual words couldn't get him penalized for what he did or said, then that was the way it would be."

The Right to Kick Ass

Nowhere is the antagonism between inmate and staff interests more palpable than in incidents of so-called use of force, a euphemism for the violence staff use to maintain discipline. Heyward calls the "use of force" regulation "the right-to-kick-ass rule," noting that in the academy,

THE SECRET LIVES OF RIKERS ISLAND JAIL GUARDS

"many of the Caucasian recruits paid close attention to this lesson, foaming at the mouth and shit." But soon enough Heyward learns how to hide cavalier cruelty behind "use of force" protocol, relying on the systematic fabrication of official reports to cover his actions. In one instance Heyward viciously beats a helpless inmate wearing "black leather gloves with metal plates sewn in them." At the end of the beating Heyward threatens the inmate: "'When you go to the clinic you know what to say.' He nods and says, 'the shower.'" The inmate will say he has fallen in the shower, and not only will Heyward avoid disciplinary action, but the "use of force" will stay off the official statistics.

Miller recalls the violence she witnessed as a rookie and the cover-ups that ensued: "I personally witnessed some of the most horrific beatings any human being should have to endure.... I can still visualize and replay some of those beatings ... and what surprises me is the inmates did not die." "I would watch the beatings," she continues, "and the cover-up machine instituted immediately. A pen and a piece of paper goes a long way. The sad part is many of the superior officers assist in these cover-ups to avoid demotion and lawsuits." While Miller is writing about the early 1980s, the recent DOJ report on violence at Rikers echoes much of her claims. Miller also casts doubt on the reforms that took place under a mayor she declines to name but who is almost certainly Rudolph Giuliani. "Under this Mayor's leadership he equipped his appointees with enormous power to institute his Arnold Schwarzenegger crush kill destroy approach. His cohorts condoned and encouraged correction officers to use force and whatever means necessary to maintain order in the jails." Under this mayor, Rikers "became worse, even though on paper, it appeared he was doing a terrific job."

As a case study of sorts, Heyward describes in detail his education in the art of the cover-up. As an overzealous newjack, he led a group of guards in a vicious gang beating of an inmate accused of giving a female guard a bloody nose—which she claimed in the heat of the moment—but who turned out to have simply caused her stress that triggered the nosebleed. After the beating, word got around that "Big Heyward had put the work in," earning commendation from his superiors, nods from the men, and lustful stares from some of the women. Big Heyward was riding high.

But a more experienced guard quickly burst his bubble, explaining to him that once he'd earned the reputation as an enforcer, he would be called upon as backup to settle guards' scores against inmates whenever there's a beating to be doled out. While this practice is part of the de facto institutional protocol, she warned him, an enforcer can only beat up so many inmates and write it up like he "slipped in the shower" before the hospital staff begins to wonder "how his jaw, ribs, and arm all got broken from one fall." And "don't let the inmate be smart enough to remember one of y'all's badge numbers and name" she scolded. "You know some of y'all ain't smart enough to take your shield off or at least cover it up before y'all get into some shit." Once an investigation got rolling, she concluded, the enforcer can only hope "the inmate's family may not have money for a lawyer," but if they do, and a lawsuit follows, it becomes every man for himself, fighting alone to save their jobs and stay out of jail.

Heyward began to panic, but she consoled him:

> Listen, if you get into some shit and you got a real muthafuckin' supervisor, I mean one that came up through the ranks, that didn't get put into position by way of a family member that has pull, that is an officer's supervisor, your ass is good. That kind of supervisor will know what to tell you to write in your report. That kind will know who to get to sign off on anything that we say happened in an incident, use of force or whatever. We have the power to manipulate the system and can get away with just about anything up in here.

Heyward is also cautioned by many of his coworkers "not to start shit outside their jails, because when it comes down to writing reports and coming up with lies to cover your ass; you'd rather they come from officers from your jail that you have a bond with, that you trust."

A chance detail of Heyward's story adds an additional layer of complexity to the relationship between inmates and guards, who often hail from the same low-income communities of color, and often know each other from the streets. Eager to prove himself to his new colleagues, Heyward had rushed headlong into a skirmish and beaten a man with a hoodie pulled over his head. When the man's face was revealed, Heyward recognized his victim as someone he knew from the projects. Heyward worried what would happen if word got back to his neighborhood that he had joined the other side, meaning that not only was he doing the job, but he was taking it seriously. In a striking passage, West reflects on the extensive overlap between the housing project and the jail:

It wasn't until I worked in a jail setting that I realized the same paint colors on the walls were the same colors used in the hallways and stairwells in the projects: A color I would call institutional gray, drab yellow or drab yellow and orange.... The floor areas in jails are very similar to the lobby areas in many of the projects apartment buildings; and the inmate's housing areas have the same tiles on the floor, which is an almost beige and a not quite white color.... When you look out of the jail windows, the view is basically the same as in the projects, with a slight view of grass or trees. You will see gates and bars; often you face a brick wall both in jail and in the projects.... When you look in the institutional mirrors, you see a blurred vision of who you actually are since the mirrors are made of a scratched metal that is screwed into the walls just to give you an image but not a clear view. Could this be a coincidence or a way of subtly being told, "Welcome home."

What It Boils Down To

West finally quits after a guard drops dead in the staff dining hall. "Officer Wight was dead," she recalls "and nothing stopped. The inmates wanted their soap and toilet paper as usual and they received their services on time as usual. One officer came to my post and just stared off into space mumbling that he didn't want to die at work. I agreed with him. He said he didn't want to die around people he worked with for over 17 years and were still complete strangers to him." This story and countless others contained in these books could be set in just about any workplace. Across lines of work, people compelled to earn a wage struggle against immense inertia to attain basic control over the activity they have to spend most of their time doing. Hemmed in on all sides by coercive social relations they never asked to be born into, and faced with no clear prospects of advancing a common agenda of liberation with the people around them, the degrading effects of wage labor take their toll. Alcohol and drugs fill the longing for oneness denied by the objective constraints of a society defined by atomization and compulsory competition, predatory sex or vapid social rivalries provide meaning to the daily performance of activity for which no salvageable purpose exists. Men draw on their disproportionate social power to pursue sexual gratification, women do the best they can to empower themselves or else simply survive under these circumstances while getting some kicks of their own in the process.

Amid imposed competition and the debasement of human creative faculties, the most puerile pettiness one can drudge from the depths of the human spirt is allowed to reign supreme. Above all, most workers are left with a supreme contempt for any obstacles to an easy work day, demands for doing things "by the book," or any other impediments to doing as little as possible and doing everything possible to make the time stolen from the worker by their employer into the worker's own time—no matter the moral or ethical implications.

Like most workers, guards rebel against constraints placed on their labor and the general wasting of their time that the job represents. But this places them fundamentally at odds with the safety and dignity of inmates whose basic human rights interfere with the guards' ability to stay out of trouble for doing whatever they please. And this says nothing of the predatory and violent relationships between workers that are found in many workplaces but seem to especially thrive in the uniquely hierarchical, paramilitary setting of a place like Rikers Island. While it is tempting to depict the participants in many of these stories as monsters—just as many would like to portray the people they guard— by all appearances the people on both sides of the bars at Rikers Island are pretty much just the people we ride the train with. These books describe ordinary human beings, a few of whom are utterly despicable, but most of whom are just struggling to keep their head above water, to make the best of their short lives amid severe structural constraints, to support themselves and their families, and to gratify whatever desires they can along the way. It just so happens they are doing so in one the most notorious and repressive jail complexes in the world, and they, often carelessly, wield immense power over the lives of some of the city's most powerless people. Ultimately these works suggest that while nobody in DOC employ seems to be a candidate for outstanding ethical citizenship, the real problem at Rikers Island is not the failing of the individual people guarding it, or even the "culture" of their workplace, but the fact that ordinary people are forced to do a job that simply shouldn't exist.

Miller puts it a bit more bluntly:

> Think about everyone in your immediate workplace ... Some of your coworkers are cool and some are idiots, some are book smart but lack common sense, lazy, gossipers, ass kisser, mean, hateful,

always arriving to work late, complainers, stink, loose, whorish, and backstabbers.... Picture them with badges and guns and ask yourself would you be okay if they worked in law enforcement, and if you or your family member were arrested and under their custody and supervision. Well that is ... what it boils down to being a "Correction Officer."

The Surreality of Rikers Island

This text first appeared on the *Hard Crackers: Chronicles of Everyday Life* website in October 2019 under the title "The Crucifixion of Rikers Ysland."

■

In February 1965, Salvador Dalí was invited to visit a Rikers Island prisoner art program by longtime correction commissioner Anna M. Kross. The wily reform commissioner appealed to the artist's thirst for publicity by promising a high-profile visit under the banner "Salvador Dalí Goes to Prison." When the appointed day arrived, however, Dalí had fallen ill. Unable to fare on the frigid ferry ride that transit to Rikers required in the days before the Buono Memorial Bridge, and with the press impatiently awaiting his descent in the hotel lobby below, Dalí seized a pencil and some india ink and got to work.

Within two hours he had produced *The Crucifixion of Christ*, an abstract though recognizable likeness of Christ on the cross, spattered in red blood, his head bowed, awaiting deliverance from torturous punishment. It's tempting to imagine the image as a poignant reflection on the injustice of incarceration, told through the allegory of the tortured Christ panting the wan prayer: "Father, forgive them, they know not what they do." Alternatively, however, as one Dalí biographer later remarked, the surrealist master "was certainly somebody who could dash off a crucifixion when the need arose."

In any case, satisfied with his work, Dalí dedicated the drawing to "the dinning [*sic*] room of the prisoners, Rikers Ysland [*sic*]" and

THE SURREALITY OF RIKERS ISLAND

deputized a friend to deliver it to the prisoners in his place. The drawing, though rudimentary, clearly bears the mark of the master's touch. "It is a bird's nest of dark lines," a critic later wrote of the three-by-five-foot piece, "indecipherable at first glance. Then the cross comes clear, strong and clean and square. Then a man's bloodshot eye, glaring through a tangle of hair, possibly thorns. Then blood or maybe just a stain [from its subsequent tenure in the prisoners' dining hall] dripping down the long, ravaged body."

Like all matters big and small on Rikers Island, the origins of the Dalí drawing were soon forgotten amid the banal and terrifying humdrum of life in a twenty-four-hour penal colony. *The Crucifixion of Christ* hung anonymously in a prisoners' dining hall at the Correctional Institution for Men (known today as the Eric M. Taylor Center, or EMTC) for sixteen years, until an incarcerated art critic pummeled it with a coffee cup, smashing its glass casing and permanently staining the paper beneath. Removed from the dining hall, the work subsequently spent some time in mothballs, briefly featured in a gallery exhibit on prison art, and eventually found its way to a staff corridor of EMTC because, as one warden later rationalized, "prisoners couldn't understand it, they couldn't appreciate it, and they thought some crazy person put it there."

Hanging in an obscure corridor, unseen by practically anyone, least of all prisoners, the artwork once more slipped quietly into the island's memory hole. And there it would remain, save for the faint murmuring, among the few guards who beheld it on a daily basis, of its mythical price tag.

"Wouldn't it be funny to take it?" assistant deputy warden Benny Nuzzo polled a group of colleagues and subordinates gathered in the EMTC commissary in October 2002. Like most jokes, this was simply tentatively proffered truth-telling. Nuzzo planned to steal the drawing, and was recruiting accomplices. Thanks to his "joke" Nuzzo enlisted fellow assistant deputy warden Mitchell Hochhauser, and by February the duo had recruited Timothy Pina and his carpool buddy Gregory Sokol, two captains who could be stationed in the hallway the artwork called home.

The plan Nuzzo masterminded was an ornate cloak-and-dagger escapade. The high-ranking quartet orchestrated a late-night fire drill, to be announced by Hochhauser, in order to distract the guards working within sight of the Dalí. If any guards failed to vacate the corridor, as ended up occurring, the captains could simply order them off by citing their superior rank, as they ended up doing. The captains were then free to use Nuzzo's key to open the locked case, remove the drawing, and replace *The Crucifixion of Christ* with a forgery Nuzzo had composed based on several months of reconnaissance and some surreptitious Polaroid photos. Nuzzo, who would direct the whole operation, could then spirit the artwork off the island in the trunk of his SUV. Once off the island, Nuzzo anticipated selling the artwork for $500,000, $400,000 of which he would split with fellow assistant deputy warden Hochhauser, and the remaining $100,000 he would divide between their subordinates Sokol and Pina.

The heist itself went off more or less without a hitch. In spite of this—or more accurately, because of it—the theft of *The Crucifixion of Christ* soon earned a place in the colorful annals of art theft history not simply for its peerless status of occurring within a prison, but more broadly for its sheer ineptitude.

It turned out Nuzzo had laid the perfect plan, save for one detail: the forgery failed to fool anyone. From its immediate discovery by a pious guard who prayed daily to *The Crucifixion of Christ* and therefore knew the original quite well, a consensus quickly spread across EMTC that the artwork hanging on the wall that morning was not the same one that had hung there the day before. "It looks like the painting has been replaced by a copy," a DOC spokesman reported. "That appears to be the case based on a consensus of nonexpert opinion, people who work near the painting and see it day in and day out."

This opinion needed not be "expert." Nuzzo's forgery was, for starters, comprised of different coloration and different proportions than the original, striking the observer immediately as brighter and otherwise just different. It had moreover been composed with different materials; instead of india ink on paper, it was oil paint on canvas—and canvas of a different size than the original drawing. In terms of quality, witnesses described the forgery as appearing to have been crafted by a child, and one lacking artistic talent, even for a child. Worst of all, Nuzzo's forgery was affixed to the wall with staples instead of its gilded frame, which had simply vanished. In its place, a new "frame" had been lazily painted directly onto the canvas. It wasn't even gold.

"There's no question," an investigator concluded, "that the real one is in the wind." A DOC spokesman put a finer point on it: "What's there

THE SURREALITY OF RIKERS ISLAND

ain't the real thing." This unanimous sentiment likely did not come as a complete shock to all conspirators. "Anybody who comes up here is definitely going to see that this is a duplicate," Sokol later recalled telling Nuzzo, who was nonetheless satisfied with the forgery and gave it his stamp of approval. Nuzzo's fellow assistant deputy warden, Hochhauser, agreed with Nuzzo that the forgery would suffice, quieting all dissent. The skeptical Sokol, for his part, complied with his superiors.

As the embarrassing story spread, investigators turned up the heat on the tiny circle of Rikers staff who could have carried out the heist. Pina flipped immediately, implicating Sokol, who himself began to cooperate with the state, implicating the others. As the final insult, the irreplaceable artwork, dedicated to the prisoners of Rikers Island by Salvador Dalí, was by all accounts destroyed by Nuzzo in a blind panic. In the aftermath, three of the four conspirators were convicted, and all four were fired. Despite the testimony of his coconspirators and considerable circumstantial evidence, Nuzzo rejected a plea bargain, and opted instead for a jury trial, in which he was miraculously found not guilty. He was nonetheless fired, after a search of his mother's Bushwick home for the missing artwork discovered a trove of office supplies stolen from Rikers Island.

The resulting media coverage made light of the thieves as a quartet of hopelessly inept bunglers, ill-suited for a life of crime—in contrast, of course, to those they guard. The admittedly droll affair became a citywide punchline. "Rikers Island just got a little less surreal," quipped the New York Daily News in an article subtitled "It's Goodbye, Dalí." The ordinarily staid New York Times took to its own headlines to dub the plot "Far from a Masterpiece." The city had a good chuckle and then, like the drawing itself, the story vanished.[1]

In recent years, however, with the proliferation of online content farms and the increased notoriety of Rikers Island, the case of the Dalí heist has resurfaced episodically in clickbait article after rehashed clickbait article, recounted over and over in nearly identical detail. (In all fairness, as I can attest, it's a fun one to write.) Even when told well, as James Fanelli of Esquire accomplished in a 2018 return to the caper that featured interviews with principal characters and oodles of juicy new details, the story remains a mere object of curiosity, devoid of context, and offered up as an entertaining chaos yarn somewhere between the Coen Brothers and the Marx Brothers. But beyond the shopworn trope of "stupid crooks," with which writers are all too willing—though with no shortage of evidence—to frame the story, a simple question has never been satisfactorily addressed: How on earth did they expect to get away with it?

I find this neglected question to be illuminated by an unlikely source: an extensive 2014 report by the DOJ on the systematic and long-term guard violence against adolescent prisoners, including at the facility from which the Dalí was stolen, and the considerable manipulation of official records that accompanies this violence.[2] This report is most famous for chronicling the island's long-standing "culture of violence," and played an important part in what became the zeitgeist favoring the closure of Rikers Island for good. It also helps explain why Nuzzo and company were comfortable enough to risk their lucrative careers switching the work of a master painter with an apparent finger painting.

As part of this "culture of violence," the report found adolescent prisoners to be not only regularly assaulted by brutal guards, but subsequently told to "hold it down," meaning to not report the assault or to seek medical attention that would create documentation. When their injuries are so serious as to require medical attention, assaulted prisoners are instructed to report "slip and fall" accidents in official paperwork, which the DOJ found to be widespread. This obfuscation, which the DOJ found ran up and down the chain of command, functions not just to protect individual guards from charges of assault, but to generally keep the island's quantified instances of violence down, which is of keen interest to its bureaucrats at the top covetous of favorable statistics.

The DOJ also found that the formally prohibited practice of punching prisoners, including in the face, is nonetheless widespread among Rikers guards. In their subsequent paperwork, punches are rhetorically recast as sanctioned "control holds," or described as "guiding" detainees to the floor. Such "use of force" reports (itself a bureaucratic euphemism) regularly state that the responding guard was assaulted "out of nowhere" by prisoners. This narrative is almost always upheld, even in the absence of any injury on the part of the guard, and sometimes against considerable evidence that the guard violence was unprovoked—including testimony by prisoners. Moreover, guards cynically utter the phrase "stop resisting" as they assault prisoners, in order to justify assault as a response to prisoners allegedly "resisting" more peaceful forms of coercion. The DOJ found the phrase "stop resisting" features prominently in "use of force" reports.

THE SURREALITY OF RIKERS ISLAND   77

The DOJ also found that the creative writing process underlying these reports is not done in secret by individual rogue guards, but is instead a common and communal act, the product of concerted efforts conducted out in the open. Reports made by multiple guards who witness and partake in violent incidents are often written in identical language. This indicates not only a widespread practice of conspiring to get a story straight before putting it down on paper, but also a lack of concern that this process will be detected by superiors. Even the existence of contradictory video evidence—when not "lost" or compromised by a camera conveniently pointed away from a violent act at a strategic moment, as often happens—is sometimes not enough to discredit the guards' stories as these accounts move up the chain of command. In the rare case that a red flag is raised and superiors cannot turn a blind eye to the patent falsehoods on paper, the guards usually don't have too much to worry about. Instances of censure for violence typically amount to a "re-training," consisting of some seminars and video screenings.

Throughout this process, captains and assistant deputy wardens like Nuzzo, Hochhauser, Pina, and Sokol play a key role in sanctioning, and sometimes crafting, the alternative reality that becomes the official story of guard violence against prisoners. The DOJ report details how "use of force" reports make their way up the chain of command uncontested, no matter how questionable, and are essentially rubber-stamped by the highest authorities on the island. Almost no investigation is ever mustered, absent considerable external pressure. The word of a guard who has used violence against a prisoner, no matter how absurd, is almost as good as truth at the moment its scrawled down on paper. By the time it gets to the top, it becomes ordained as nothing short of God-given truth, even when significant conflicting evidence is available. The result is the systematic institutional acceptance, at face value, of improbable and sometimes outright ridiculous stories, which are at times contradicted by empirical evidence.

In light of the DOJ reports and other accounts of how the books are cooked on Rikers Island, the case of the Dalí art heist seems less like the sort of tragicomic tale of "stupid crooks" so amusing to tabloid news consumers, and becomes instead a vivid portrait of how reality and truth are constructed by state power to cover up traumatic violence meted out against powerless people. After all, if a captain says a punch in the face is a "control hold," and a deputy warden can dismiss video evidence in favor of an incoherent account offered by an assaultive guard, then surely four such high-ranking Rikers officials, working together, can claim that a poorly conceived forgery of a Dalí is in fact an original Dalí, and have that be the final word. And if the frame is missing, so what. It never existed.

It's telling that when the forgery failed to deceive, the four thieves went into a panic and had no idea what to do. They were in the throes of a new experience; it had likely never occurred to them that what they decided would constitute reality would be questioned, especially by their underlings. Even Sokol, who saw the forgery for the failure that it was, took comfort that his superiors could cloak it in the usual mantle of bullshit behind which they were all accustomed to hiding. The subsequent unraveling of their plot tells us almost nothing about their aptitude for crime, for which countless Rikers officials have distinguished themselves over the years. Instead, it tells us much about the dangerous malleability of reality itself in the violent maw of Rikers Island and all institutions of human caging, rotten beyond all reform.

PART 3
MORBID SYMPTOMS

Death to the Walking Dead

This text first appeared on the *Hard Crackers: Chronicles of Everyday Life* website in February 2022.

■

After twelve years of blood and guts, AMC's postapocalyptic zombie epic *The Walking Dead* (TWD) is finally being laid to rest. With almost all of the original cast long torn to shreds since its 2010 debut, and much of the show's dramatic events a distant memory, TWD can be likened to a postapocalyptic *General Hospital*, melodrama and all. But even following the departure of main character Sheriff Rick Grimes (Andrew Lincoln) in the show's ninth season, TWD still draws millions of American viewers per week, and more on streaming platforms and a massive international market, sufficient to spawn two spinoff shows, with more in the works, and a series of video games. Fans pack the halls of comic conventions to hear cast members and creators speak. Even as its ratings have fallen in the later seasons, TWD remains the most-watched show on cable TV now, or ever. What accounts for this massive interest in such a grim topic, leading millions to spend their precious few hours outside work watching other people tormented, brutalized, and mauled to death?

"The mass is not merely passive," writes C.L.R. James. "It decides what it will see." Popular culture is a great feedback loop through which the dreams, desires, and darkest fears of billions of people are served up by ruling-class institutions like Hollywood. While entertainment corporations serve to reinforce predominant values friendly to the ruling class, there is no grand conspiracy; they are above all in the business of making money, and must therefore give people what they want, or else their competitor will. Mass cultural goods, then, depict "if only negatively ... some of the deepest feelings of the masses, but represent them within the common agreement—no serious political or social questions which would cause explosions."[1] The most popular entertainment of our moment, then, teaches us a great deal about the people who consume it, as it simultaneously educates us in the means by which ruling-class organs decipher dissatisfaction with our world and our striving for a better one, while attempting to neutralize it.

If James is correct, we can surmise that millions of people, including some in our families, neighborhoods, and workplaces, identify on some level with the travails of small bands of survivors navigating the nihilistic hell of a zombie apocalypse, a world where it is not the zombies, but those condemned to live, who constitute the titular *walking dead*.

So just what is this television show that has held the notorious attention spans of American viewers for over a decade? TWD is derived from the comic series of the same name created by writer Robert Kirkman and artist Tony Moore, which debuted in 2003, and which the show has followed with varying degrees of fidelity across its staggering 193 issues. Kirkman and Moore originally pitched a science fiction epic set in the twenty-seventh century, when minerals from another planet destroy what had become a utopian society on Earth.[2] It was rejected by the Image Comics publishing house. The duo then proposed a period piece set in the aftermath of George Romero's original *Night of the Living Dead* film, but were encouraged to develop their own unique zombie universe set in the present, largely to have sole proprietary rights over the content. They did, but were told their story was too ordinary. So Kirkman got creative.

"Look, you're right," he told *Image*, "it does need a hook and that's why after a few issues I'm gonna reveal that this is actually an alien invasion story. That these zombies are actually put on Earth by aliens and it'll eventually be revealed that it's this really cool sci-fi epic involving alien invasion. You know, the seeds will be planted very early on, but it will be a while before it's actually revealed."[3] Kirkman, who had no intention of writing such a plot twist into TWD, was bluffing. It paid off; the comic series quickly became a critical and commercial success, and the alien invasion was soon forgotten. Kirkman and Moore had tapped into a profound cultural appetite for stories exploring the dissolution of society, daily life as a Herculean struggle, and above all, meditations on how people are transformed by the hardships they must endure and the choices they are forced to make to survive. Despite their publisher's concerns, they had in fact created a novel story unique to their time and place. But the figure of the walking dead is nothing new.

From *Zonbis* to *Night of the Living Dead*

As many scholars have pointed out, unlike the classical figures of European gothic horror—ghosts, werewolves, vampires, Frankenstein's monster, and all the rest—the zombie mythology is a distinct product of the New World, tracing its origins to the slave society of the French colony Saint-Domingue, known today as Haiti. In his masterpiece *The Black Jacobins*, James describes life in Saint-Domingue as remarkable, even among slave societies, for its brutality, squalor, and high rate of mortality from violence, disease, and malnourishment. Under the draconian 1685 Negro Code, the "slave received the whip more certainly than they received their food," alongside far more ghastly tortures that codified grisly sadism into the cold execution of nascent managerial science.[4] Though Black Haitians were able to abolish slavery and shake off direct European rule through the slave revolution that lasted from 1791 to 1804, the horrors of slavery left an indelible mark on Haitian culture, seen in the original story of the *zonbi*.

The original walking dead of Haitian lore derived from the Afro-Caribbean belief in an afterlife, symbolizing the transcendence of slavery to deliverance back to Africa. But this possibility of a felicitous hereafter also came with the threat of the dead being once more taken captive, whether as a punishment for suicide (a belief encouraged, in part, by slave drivers), or as innocent victims of the same avarice that drove enslavement. The creation of zombies is a complex Voodoo ritual overseen by the *bokor*, or Voodoo priest. In this belief system, one's hapless soul could be enslaved in a bottle, and forced into spiritual labor for the bottle's owner, or else one's body itself could be seized upon and forced to perform arduous labor as the soul looks on helplessly, conscious but unable to intervene. A body that can be made to do anything the *bokor* wants is, of course analogous to the capitalist seizing control of bodies and putting them in motion for much of their waking time, which reached its most barbaric excesses under chattel slavery. The brutality of the slave trade in particular, and its central ethical issues surrounding the meaning of freedom and bondage, left sufficient impact on Haitian society that *zonbi* rituals are still performed in the present day, including the transmission of bottles purported to contain souls, and festivals where the trade in undead bodies is reenacted.

The practice of *zonbi* rituals, argues anthropologist Elizabeth McAlister, "diagnoses, theorizes, and responds mimetically to the long history of violent consumptive and dehumanizing capitalism in the Americas from the colonial period until the present."[5] The original incarnation of the *zonbi* represented a consuming fear of, and opposition to, compulsory service in the most brutal labor process known to human history, the West Indian slave trade, which stood as a cornerstone of the development of contemporary capitalism. In the present, the persistence of the *zonbi* in Haitian culture also demonstrates a pervasive identification with perpetually unfree souls among a critical mass of people subjected to sustained underdevelopment and imperialism.

It is among history's many ironies that this cultural trope would be taken up with great gusto in the slave-built seat of imperialist power, the United States of America. Fittingly, the story of the zombie, as the undead came to be called, seems to have found its way into US culture during the American occupation of Haiti, between 1915 and 1935. During this time Victor Halperin's 1932 film, *White Zombie*, marked the creature's Hollywood debut. Its villain is the Haitian sugar baron and Voodoo master Murder Legendre (Bella Lugosi), who commands a multiracial army of the undead. Jacques Tourneur's 1943 film, *I Walked with a Zombie*, also attempts loyalty to the Haitian roots of zombie lore, setting the story at a formerly slaveholding sugar cane plantation on a fictitious Caribbean island, thematically evoking slavery through both symbolism and overt references to the island's slave past. These films represent a bridge between the original Haitian iteration of the zombie and the distinct form it would assume when fully subsumed into American pop culture, thanks largely to George Romero.

Beginning with his 1968 *Night of the Living Dead*, the films of George Romero served as the template for the zombie film genre that took root in the United States and subsequently spread around the world. Spawned in the turbulence of the late 1960s, Romero's zombie narratives enlist hordes of the undead as a roving metonymy for the decay and brutality lurking beneath the shiny veneer of postwar American society. Romero cast Black men and white women in leading roles, among the films only likeable characters, as the collapse of society is exacerbated, if not outright caused by, the toxic paternalism of the nuclear family (*Night of the Living Dead*), the crass materialism of consumer culture (*Dawn of the Dead, 1978*), and the suicidal drive of militarism (*Day of the Dead, 1985*).[6] The death of the Black protagonist Ben (Duane Jones) in *Night of the Living Dead*, at the hands of a white posse who may or may not think he's a zombie, has been widely likened to the contemporaneous assassination of Martin Luther King Jr. The degree of scandal generated by this film in particular would be incomprehensible to most devotees of TWD, given that nothing in it remotely approaches the hyperrealistic gore that AMC gleefully splashes across the screen on an average Sunday night. Roger Ebert described viewing the film in a theater full of traumatized children, as calls for censorship dogged the film's initial run.[7] For better or worse, today's kids would be excused for falling asleep.

Befitting both the international division of labor and the deindustrialization plaguing much of the US by the late 1960s, whereas Haitian zombies are productive laborers, American zombies are consumers. Not only do the living dead crave the flesh of the living, or, as specified by Dan O'Bannon's 1985 punk rock masterpiece *The Return of the Living Dead*: "Braaains!" Romero's zombies also return to "an important place in their lives," which, in the case of his 1978 *Dawn of the Dead*, is the deliberately disorienting consumerist phantasmagoria of the American shopping mall. *Dawn*'s stupefied zombies bear an uncanny resemblance to dazed shoppers basking in the waning bounty of America's postwar boom—though Romero is often given a bit too much credit for the profundity of this fairly common elitist aspersion on the supposedly philistine culture of middle-class America. Regardless, whether as workers rendered docile for their exploiters, or consumers stupefied by the goods they have traded their lives for, zombie mythology cuts to the heart of modernity, which is to say, of capitalism. "The only modern myth is the myth of the zombies," write the dependably opaque Gilles Deleuze and Félix Guattari, "motrified schizos, good for work, brought back to reason."[8] Born of the most violent expression of the capitalist mode of production, the zombie genre inherently evokes the specter of class politics, social dissolution amid the chaos of capitalism, and the ethical quandaries of life under a mode of production where human life is cheap and the lives of great masses of the Earth are simply a means to enrich a few.

The dynamism of Romero's influence on the zombie genre lasted roughly two decades, with notable entries by directors like Lucio Fulci,

DEATH TO THE WALKING DEAD

who launched his own take on the genre with *Zombi 2*. The real horrors of the 1980s and 1990s, however, belonged to the living; the slasher film, catapulted to prominence by the success of John Carpenter's 1978 *Halloween*, spawned numerous imitators and innovators. Whereas the zombie film depicts hordes of ghouls working in concert to menace organized bands of survivors, the slasher film evinces a cultural turn toward radical individualism; the killer almost always works alone, picking off isolated victims in secluded cabins or else that bastion of monadic despair, the American suburb. The triumph of the slasher over the zombie horde also reveals the shift in cultural apprehension of crime, from the act of dangerous classes of people produced by structural economic factors outside their control, which was a mainstream position amid the rebellions of the 1960s, toward a conception of the lawbreaker as an individual, pathological case with no economic cause, and no redress save for hard punishment. By the early 1990s, an increasingly campy and absurd take on the walking dead offered by Jim Booth's 1992 *Braindead* and Sam Raimi's *Evil Dead* series was the only real innovation to be found in a sea of rip-offs and rehashing. The end of the Cold War and attendant inward turn of American society spawned a postmodern turn in horror, seen in self-referential exercises in deconstruction like Wes Craven's 1996 *Scream*. This did not bode well for the class politics of the zombie horde. Instead, the undead had become a punchline.

We're All Carriers

The turn of the century saw a reinvention of zombie film, thanks in large part to Danny Boyle's *28 Days Later* (2003), itself spurred by the success of the Japanese *Resident Evil* video game series. Boyle in particular succeeded by shedding the goofy camp and shopworn clichés of an aging genre, to reimagine through gritty realism just how terrifying roving bands of the undead would actually be. Boyle also cultivated an atmosphere of sustained dread apart from the usual jump scares and gore, depicted the undead running full speed, which is widely cited as the scariest part of the film, and above all, rediscovered Romero's insight that the worst thing about a zombie apocalypse could very well be the behavior of the living. Clearly indebted to *28 Days Later*, *The Walking Dead* even begins the same way, with the protagonist waking up alone in the hospital, having missed the apocalypse altogether. Kirkman claims this was a coincidence, and it is not difficult to believe him; harking back to Romero at his best, this new genre of zombie films derived less of its substance from imagining society's grisly collapse, and more from the fact it was already underway.[9] This was part of a growing cultural sensibility that the end of the world is not a speculative event in the future that we must imagine, but a process through which we are presently living.

AMC's *The Walking Dead* (TWD) premiered on October 31, 2010, part of a weeklong rollout in 120 countries. The show became an overnight commercial and critical success. (Spoilers ahead.) Millions of viewers were drawn each week to the serialized story of Sheriff Rick Grimes, a cop who was shot in the line of duty and subsequently hospitalized, only to wake up in the aftermath of the fall, as it is called on TWD, with no idea what had hit him or the world. An unlikely hero, Grimes begins his odyssey weakened, disoriented, and scantily clad. He has no greater objective save for finding his wife and son, and bumbles through the series premier learning the realities of the new world the hard way at almost every juncture. Doomed by his ineptitude in this new world, Grimes is saved only by a chance encounter with a motley crew of survivors who have formed an unsteady alliance. They have set up a camp outside Atlanta in an impossibly indefensible position that characterizes the amateurism of the survivors in the show's early days. After proving his mettle, Grimes is welcomed back to the camp, only to discover his wife Lori (Sarah Wayne Callies) and son Carl (Chandler Riggs) are living there, along with his former cop partner and best friend Shane Walsh (Jon Bernthal), who told Lori that Rick had died as an overture to beginning a relationship with her.

The stage is thus set for *Peyton Place* plus zombies. But one detail sets the show apart and lends it a nastiness so suitable for our moment. Under Grimes's leadership (contested by Walsh, in a predictable clash of wills that the latter will not survive), the survivors make their way to the Center for Disease Control office in Atlanta, searching for answers and leadership. Instead, they find a lone scientist on the brink of suicide, who lets Grimes in on a chilling secret: "We're all carriers." Everyone is infected. Following the ordinary playbook, of course, TWD's zombie bites turn living people into the walking dead, but only because they cause death. Turning, as the process is known, is also the necessary outcome of any death that does not destroy the human brain. In short,

DEATH TO THE WALKING DEAD

everyone will turn. There is no escape, no illusions that a better future can be built free from the scourge of zombification. The resurgence of the zombie, that undead avatar of capitalism's deadly contradictions, has come to define a moment when no future is possible save for the end of the world, already in progress. All the living can do is ward off contamination by those who have already succumbed to the end, for as long as they can, until they too succumb to the inevitable.

Fear the Living

Kirkman later claimed to regret the scientist's big reveal; TWD is, after all, not concerned with the how or why of social collapse, but the obtrusive reality of the end of the world, and how people navigate it.[10] Even the dead are generally just an excuse to talk about the living. The characters who aren't killed off early in the narrative generally become adept at handling all but the largest groups of the zombies single-handedly. By the later seasons, death at the hands of a walker, as the zombies are called, is a hazard akin to getting hit by a car in our world. TWD's protagonists, however, find much worthier adversaries among other survivors. "Fight the dead," ran the show's tagline, beginning in the second season, "fear the living." The show's narrative arc pits Grimes's gang against one microsociety after another of humans reduced to sociopathic survival machines. Despite episodic flashes of idealism, to defeat these external threats the show's protagonists must also embrace wanton brutality, duplicity, and the winner-take-all survival of the fittest. Like all the others, Grimes's tribe organizes itself into a small insular unit, viewing all outsiders as a mortal threat, or in the very least, not their problem. Midway through the show, they are indecipherable from their worst foes. Thus, after spelling out the futurelessness of humanity in scientific argot, Kirkman only regrets overstating his case; the scientist's secret simply puts too fine a point on the mean-spirited nihilism that characterizes TWD's entire outlook.

In *The Walking Dead,* the sentimentalism of humanity's more prosperous days is not simply anachronistic, it is a death sentence. Any threat, living or dead, who a TWD character hesitates to kill is likely the gravedigger of someone they love. Characters unwilling to face the harshness of the new world, such as Andrea (Laurie Holden), who refuses to destroy the brain of her dead sister, or Hershel Greene (Scott Wilson), who keeps zombies penned up in his barn awaiting a cure that is never coming, are dangerous liabilities to the rest of the survivors. Hardness in the face of unspeakable trauma is the show's chief virtue, weakness a perennial lament. The young Carl becomes something of TWD's patron saint after killing his own mother to prevent her from turning, and then taking his own life when he is later bitten. The young people who come of age after the fall are depicted as having a much easier time adapting to its exigencies, much like the people who are spared the worst atrocities appear ill-prepared to face up to what they must do, and who they must become, in order to survive.

This contrast is dramatized in season five when Grimes and his battle-scarred band of survivors take up residence in the Alexandria Safe-Zone, a walled-in community that has weathered much of the hardships unfolding outside. At first, Alexandrians are scandalized by the violent and totalitarian tendencies Grimes and his cohort have brought with them, but soon enough, these traits are revealed to be the keys to survival. TWD's ethical questions therefore do not concern the best possible course of action, since there is only one. The show instead explores whether or not characters are strong enough to follow it, and how the decisions they make change them over time. And it is not just the living who adapt; as time goes on, the zombies begin to roam in herds, exponentially increasing their destructive potential. The tribalism of Sheriff Rick Grimes and his tight band of loyalists, mimicking the vision of sheriff-led autonomous counties offered by the far-right Posse Comitatus movement, thus meets its worst foe in the form of the zombie herd, a roving band of social junk, whose collective action makes them the existential threat to civilization itself. In other words, it is a social outlook we could only call *petty bourgeois*. The return of class politics to mass culture in the US and beyond, spurred by protracted economic crisis that has swelled the ranks of the lower classes, becomes negatively reflected by cultural goods like TWD, recast as a terrible threat to the prosperity of the self-determining, property-owning patriarchal family central to middle-class American ideology.

And while Grimes retaining his role as cop betrays an impoverished imagination that can imagine the end of human society but not the end of cops, the gradual reveal of what each character did before the fall constitutes one of TWD's most interesting subplots, as it explores the great transformations that the imperative to survive forces people to adopt. The great tactician Glenn Rhee (Steven Yeun) spent his days before the apocalypse delivering pizzas. The governor (Brian Blake), the authoritarian leader of the town of Woodbury and central antagonist of seasons three and four, worked as a low-level office clerk before coming into his own after the fall. Similarly, TWD's arch antagonist Negan (Jeffrey Dean Morgan) was an unemployed gym teacher living off of his wife as he played video games in their basement, prior to changing with the times and reinventing himself as the charismatic leader of a powerful extortion racket calling themselves the Saviors. Carol Peletier (Melissa McBride) was a housewife and the survivor of ongoing domestic abuse before the death of her husband and the trials of life after the fall transformed her into a powerful warrior and leader. By contrast, Father Gabriel Stokes (Seth Gilliam) attempts to remain a priest after the fall; beset by doubts and haunted by his failures to live up to his calling amid the new reality, he experiences severe emotional distress that places his comrades in danger time and again.

Though it is mostly only teased at and disclosed in throwaway dialogue, the question of what TWD characters did for work before the fall cuts to the central appeal of the show to its record-breaking audience. When the sword-wielding warrior Michonne Hawthorne (Danai Gurira) was revealed to have been a lawyer before the fall, living in a bougie apartment and loving every minute of it, I recall speaking with a group of leftist TWD fans who were shocked that the show's central Black woman character, a fierce fighter who could handle any situation, was not of working-class origin. To me this missed the point altogether; TWD is not a show about people in our society who already possess the versatility they need to face a cruel world. With the exception of the lumpenproletarian misfit Daryl Dixon (Norman Reedus), whose life perhaps improved after the zombie apocalypse, TWD characters already suited for the hardships of the new world are, for better or worse, the show's villains. Instead, characters like Michonne refer to real people who are today challenged by a world they are *not* prepared for. The real Michonne, out there somewhere today, buried herself in debt to earn a law degree, but cannot find well-paying work in a field that is at once racist, sexist, and saturated with degrees. She is instead forced to take on precarious legal work in an inhuman system, interacting with indigent clients in desperate need of assistance, but who she lacks the power to help, while she struggles to stay afloat and anxiously eyes a downward slide ever further down the class ladder. This point is made clearly enough by the first several seasons, characterized by one tragic blunder after another, befitting survivors attempting to navigate a new world with the mindset of the old.

We Are the Walking Dead

TWD's ultimate appeal, then, is rooted in a decades-long race to the bottom in working and living conditions for most working people. In recent decades, the primary fixation for working-class life has increasingly been reduced to simply surviving, defined as avoiding consignment to a growing class excreted from the world of living wages altogether and doomed to a realm between life and death. The show's enduring motif of *before* and *after* the fall typifies the collapsing expectations for increasing numbers of people who must put their hopes and dreams aside and be content to simply avoid the growing underclass. As an emotional Rick proclaims in the heat of season five: "We are the walking dead!" And isn't the Romero-era zombie, clad in tattered clothing and reduced to its most animal functions, the ultimate symbol for both downward social mobility and the crippling fear of its contagion among those closest to the bottom? The true revulsion of the zombie is not its dissimilarity, but its profound proximity to the living; the latter know that they are one chance event away from joining the ranks of the ragged hordes. Thus TWD viewers recognize their lives in the tragic but often heroic struggles of characters who represent everyday humans navigating the collapse of society, facing unprecedented decisions that pit their capacity for compassion and humanity against the will to survive at all costs in increasingly hostile terrain.

In keeping with James's observation that popular culture must only recognize mass feelings negatively, and steer sentiments away from collective solutions, TWD is scrupulous in presenting a generalized condition of working-class life that clearly resonates with great numbers of viewers, but simultaneously reduces this general social condition to the struggles between insular pockets of individuals locked in zero sum combat. Central to this feat is the show's ethos of cruelty and sadism, which drips from nearly every inch of film. Much like the process of turning disfigures and dehumanizes a person succumbing to the zombie virus, TWD attempts to make the very face of humanity despicable beyond recognition. Acts effacing life itself are not simply depicted on screen in ample doses, but are also practiced by the show's makers themselves through their very mode of exposition. Just about any inkling of love or tenderness among characters, especially the highly disposable minor characters, only serves as the prelude to the violent demise of one or more of the sentimental parties in gut-wrenching spectacles the camerawork greedily leans into, lingering and sharpening its focus on grotesque images of brutality and mutilation, and cutting away only to show the face of the survivors watching on in crippling anguish. Characters who believe in anything greater than the survival of themselves and a handful of those closest to them are quickly educated, by means of the most brutal tools at the show's disposal, in the folly of anything approaching human solidarity. Surely this is not lost on the viewer, who has come to TWD with a set of ethical problems, and finds therein a deranged moral compass for navigating them.

Of particular note is the figure of Negan, a fast-talking sociopath loosely modeled after Henry Rollins, who gleefully murders those who resist his extortion racket in front of their loved ones as a calculated warning that *all* must comply. Like Grimes and the gang, Negan considers himself the good guy, forced to do whatever he can to protect his narrowly defined community, a view that TWD's showrunners may or may not share. And as Negan glibly wisecracks his way through grisly and highly aestheticized executions carried out with a barbed wire-coated baseball bat, it is hard to shake the suspicion that Negan and the showrunners actually have a lot in common. They both go to great lengths to rub their viewer's nose in brutality visited upon innocent people they have grown attached to, just to turn around and make the point that society has regressed to the point where you must either pay Negan tribute or fight like hell to take his place. TWD's use of extreme violence, far surpassing anything to ever appear on cable, to make this shopworn point, or no point at all, even earned the scorn of Romero himself. As the late genre pioneer later recounted, he refused offers to direct episodes of the show, clarifying the difference between their zombies: "I use them to sort of make fun of what's going on in a number of societal events ... I don't use them to just create gore. Even though I use gore, that's not what my films are about, they're much more political."[11]

If only the *Walking Dead* franchise stayed out of politics. While the flagship show has largely refrained from documenting the fall, the 2015 spinoff *Fear the Walking Dead*, cocreated by Kirkman, fills in the gaps and gives viewers a telling glimpse into how it all went down. *Fear* follows

Travis Manawa, who is, like Grimes, a father simply trying to protect his family, this time amid the chaos of the fall. Set against the heavy-handed backdrop of Los Angeles, however, the fall itself becomes a reactionary fever dream. It starts when LAPD cops kill a zombie. They are immediately confronted by angry mobs of the living, who hysterically impede their ability to rescue humanity at this crucial juncture. The confrontation quickly spirals into an orgy of looting and arson, as the hapless protesters are picked off by the very zombies they would not allow the cops to protect them from. Looking on with wan disgust, the Manawa clan holes up in a small business owned by the Salzar family, hard-working Latino immigrants. That is, until arsonists force them to flee into the danger of life amid the fall, and we're off to the races. Produced in the immediate aftermath of the 2014 rebellion in Ferguson and the national anti-cop movement that came to be known as Black Lives Matter, *Fear the Walking Dead* drew from these events, alongside a variety of conservative tropes central to petty bourgeois American neurosis, to craft a portrait of societal collapse suitable for the pages of *Breitbart*. It is an outlook identical to the ideology that drove Kyle Rittenhouse and his comrades across the United States to take up arms against a mass movement they deemed a nihilistic threat to civilization itself.

This leads to the TWD's most ambiguous terrain: its politics of race. Early in the story, the show and comic alike constituted an unapologetic celebration of localized patriarchal white power and settler colonialism. The main dramatic tension boiled down to which of the white police officers would rule the new world, secure leadership of the same white family, and tame the wild all over again, with a smattering of nonwhite characters thrown in. This was not lost on critics, especially of the show, who largely failed to recognize its overt rightist politics and instead decried its lack of diversity among the murderous bands of survivors.[12] Befitting "diversity and inclusion" under capitalism, TWD responded by increasing the heterogeneity of its cast, while retaining the same political core. TWD thus remains a tale of white "revanchism," as scholar Neil Smith once put it, meaning the imperative to take back terrain from the mindless destruction of a feral underclass.[13] This a common political outlook dating back to the urban rebellions of the 1960s and Nixon's "Silent Majority" and the rise of "law and order," running through the aggressive gentrification of American cities in the 1990s and 2000s, and underlying the Trump movement and Blue Lives Matter in the present.[14]

DEATH TO THE WALKING DEAD

It's likely not a coincidence that the silver long-barrel revolver toted by Grimes as a symbol of his authority bears a striking resemblance to Charles Bronson's 475 Wildey Magnum from the *Death Wish* series, the ultimate Hollywood avatar of vigilante white backlash against the urban crisis of the 1960s and the political movements of Black and brown power.[15]

But as TWD rehashes familiar racial themes, it simultaneously practices the "colorblindness," as Michelle Alexander put it, of the era that spawned it. After its first few episodes, TWD hardly mentions race at all.[16] Earl Dixon (Michael Rooker), Daryl's older brother and the show's only committed white supremacist, is killed off early on, freeing Daryl to quickly overcome his ill-defined racial prejudices and join the multiracial group. It is even revealed that Daryl's motorcycle, bearing the Nazi SS insignia, actually belonged to Earl, further exonerating him. The Maori Travis Manawa, the Korean Glenn Rhee, and even the Black Michonne Hawthorne all effectively marry into whiteness, adopting a Silent Majority orientation to the menacing hordes outside their walls as they join white families and enact the same narrative driving Sheriff Grimes to fight for law and order in the face of social collapse. The show's color blindness is especially pernicious, as TWD represents so viscerally how the deepening tribalism of our present society plays out against increasing disorder, scarcity, and a generalized state of fear. In the real world, these lines are drawn, more often than not, along the lines of race and ethnicity, which lend inescapable substance to the *us versus them* distinctions that serve as TWD's bread and butter. *The Walking Dead* therefore offers a thoroughly racialized narrative which, through refusing to take the subject seriously, tacitly endorses the present paradigm of white power by allowing it to go unnamed.

Fight the Dead

As *The Walking Dead* prepares to conclude its eleventh and final season, it really doesn't matter how the story ends. With thousands of grisly deaths stretched across hundreds of hours of television, TWD has chiseled into the popular culture a barbaric vision of the present, which celebrates the worst human responses to social crisis, and alternatingly ridicules and vilifies anyone who believes in a way out. Beyond the political intricacies of the show's worldview, which fans can debate in endless detail as fans do, this is evident enough simply in the show's gleeful celebration of human disposability, at a historical juncture when life is cheap and getting cheaper. The regular TWD viewer might need to be reminded, as the show's most foolish and naive characters are wont to say, that the zombies slaughtered and dismembered by the hundreds each season with great gusto were once humans, and might be considered as such still. If the pornographic revelry of unceasing violent death can be brushed off as mere entertainment, it is clear that TWD, which offers a portal into the darkest reflection of our present world, is anything but escapism. As critics Travis Linnemann, Tyler Wall, and Edward Green write: "If you can kill a zombie, you can kill anyone."[17]

Does all of what has been said amount to killing the messenger? As a longtime fan of the show, I'd like to believe it. But for that to be true, TWD would have to offer a harsh reality, which is nonetheless inescapably true, rendering its creators blameless heralds of a new world coming into being. This is, however, not so clear. For a fictional world where time is commonly designated either "before" or "after," TWD, by the metric of our own time, increasingly feels like it belongs in the time *before*. The comic and show debuted before Occupy Wall Street, the rebellion in Ferguson and Black Lives Matter, the struggle at Standing Rock, and the George Floyd Rebellion, in addition to popular struggles across the globe ranging from the Arab Spring and the movement of the squares to popular revolt throughout much of Latin America, Africa, Asia, Europe, and the Middle East. While these movements are sufficiently diverse that speaking of them in a single sentence might seem unjust, they are part of a worldwide rebuke to the proposition that surviving the present can only be undertaken by small bands of self-interested individuals, to the exclusion of all else. Such mass action, vilified in the universe of TWD as the stuff of zombie herds and their clueless enablers, serve instead as the only serious alternative to the show's darkest reflection of our present reality becoming the only one.

The world of *The Walking Dead*, writes media scholar Sherryl Vint, is "one that simultaneously dehumanizes and makes monstrous these survivors. This is true both of the zombies in the series, reduced to endless walking and consuming, and those able to adjust themselves to the new order, who draw a narrow circle of community and demonize all those outside of it."[18] It makes sense why so many people are drawn to this show; the apocalypse has already arrived, and we are struggling to survive it. But reality is not a comic book. Living under the very real threat of human extinction, facing biological contagions in our world sufficient to expose millions of our most helpless people to miserable deaths, and facing down the possibility of barbarism on a global scale overwhelming any hopes of redress, it is time to put *The Walking Dead,* and the reactionary pessimism it lends such visceral support, out of its misery.

Friday the 1312

This text first appeared on the *Hard Crackers: Chronicles of Everyday Life* website in May 2021.

■

It's a dark and stormy night in Swinton, Louisiana. Officer Kevin Ganning shakes off the rain as he enters a dingy diner ensconced in the ambience of gritty cop noir. He is not welcomed. The Black server, Pops, keeps his back turned to Ganning while a Black woman behind the counter shoots him dirty looks. They are both glued to a television piping in images of riot cops clashing with Black protesters. "A now familiar scene," the reporter intones, "an officer accused of shooting an unarmed African American man ... has been found not guilty." Ganning orders a coffee, to which Pops growls back "not working," his eyes fixed on flickering images of Black revolt and police repression.

"All across the city, and nation, including Swinton," the broadcast continues, "spontaneous protests have erupted to decry the verdict as well as to oppose police violence." Pops watches as protesters push back against police lines, kick away tear gas canisters, and brandish a stolen cop vest as a trophy. The reporter recounts how allegations of a police conspiracy to frame the victim and plant a gun did not sway the jury. Ganning orders a medium Coke, met with silence, and a long hard stare. "Various peaceful protests escalated as objects were thrown at City Hall as well as police vehicles," the reporter continues, as Ganning nervously notes dirty looks from the diner patrons, white and Black, while donning a mask of anguish in the face of the injustice he must suffer.

"You're not welcome here today, Kevin," Pops at last tells Ganning, sliding him a sad looking soda in a paper cup. "Not today man." It doesn't matter that Ganning, portrayed by Latino actor Ian Casselbury, is not the kind of good old boy, Derek Chauvin–looking white cop traditionally associated with police violence against Black men. His tormented visage tells us as much; Ganning is not indignant in the face of Pop's discrimination against him as a cop, but just endlessly sad at the tragedy of it all. Don't they know he's only doing his job? Those bad cops don't represent him. Why should he be lumped in with them? Back in his patrol car, cutting forlornly through the darkness of the storm, Ganning consoles his daughter over the phone. "I know, I wish I could be there too," he tells her. "I'm doing this for us ... I won't miss anything else."

The call ends abruptly when a van with no license plate cuts across Ganning's path. He pulls it over. The driver is obscured behind a black-tinted window, and initially refuses to come out. Ganning becomes agitated, drawing his gun and shouting orders. It's a familiar scene to the American viewer, made doubly canny by multiple cuts that show the scene through Ganning's body cam and the cop car's dash cam, which usually ends in the death of the motorist at the hands of the cops. At last the door opens and a petite Black woman steps out, hands up, shaking and afraid. But Ganning keeps on shouting. "Don't make me hurt you, please!" he barks, ordering her onto the ground. At that, he is abruptly snatched off the ground by an unseen supernatural force. Shrieking in pain, Ganning hurtles through the air as the ground below vanishes through the view of his body cam.

The first four minutes of the 2020 film *Body Cam* deftly outline the film's moral economy, part and parcel of the political moment that produced it. Make no mistake: though undeniably atmospheric and not without a few technical tricks, including the clever use of dash and body cams, *Body Cam* is a thoroughly mediocre work of horror, hardly capable of mustering an effective jump scare. It was also completed at least a year before the George Floyd Rebellion kicked off in Minneapolis, ushering in a qualitatively new era in the struggle against racialized police violence in the United States, and the sympathy it attempts to evoke for the injustice against the poor defenseless cops may (hopefully) come off as tone deaf and dated. Nonetheless, the film has proven to be remarkably prescient and profound, if only by accident. Directed by *Imperial Dreams* director Malik Vitthal and starring R&B legend Mary J. Blige, *Body Cam* offers an honest view of the social crisis around American policing as it appears through the eyes of the progressive wing of the US ruling class.

Around the time of Ganning's ill-fated traffic stop, Officer Renee Lomito-Smith (Mary J. Blige), fresh off a suspension for assaulting a civilian who called her a racial slur, patrols nearby streets with her white rookie partner, Officer Danny Holledge. The duo comes across a young Black boy playing unattended in the middle of the street. When they attempt to help the child find his parents, an angry mob gathers, pushing them back to their car amid verbal abuse, including from the child's careless mother, who we gather ought to be thankful. The pain on Lomito's face is the same worn by Ganning in the diner; one can picture the actors practicing it together. Back in the car, they're summoned to the scene of Ganning's last traffic stop. Lomito views replays of Ganning's dash cam, and watches his death in shock. Then the whole apparatus shorts out, deleting the video. Following a grisly trail of blood and broken teeth, the duo finds Ganning's mutilated body hung up on a nearby fence. Did I mention this is not a subtle film?

When the higher-ups arrive on the scene, nobody believes what Lomito has seen. She has a unique standpoint throughout the film that allows her to identify with the cops, sympathize with their victims, and above all understand the danger of the consent of the governed falling apart. Holledge, who cannot see the world through Lomito's eyes, must decide whether he trusts her enough to take her word for it. The rest of the film unfolds around Lomito dealing with the consequences of her startling vision: the violence and injustice of American policing has opened the vortex, summoning an inchoate force of pure destruction. The killer is nameless, ill-defined, does not speak, and makes no demands. Its form is a shadow, at best, seen only when it appears in order to mete out ruthless violence. There is no chance of dialogue, coming together, reconciliation, or healing, only vengeance and destruction. And Ganning is of course not the only casualty. As the bodies pile up and Lomito's superiors stonewall her queries, she must undertake her own investigation to put the genie back in its bottle and restore social order.

What does it take to close the vortex? Spoiler alert: Lomito knows. She has tracked down its origins in a conspiracy among her fellow officers to cover up the murder of a young Black boy. The child's mother, who has helped summon the monster into existence, initially considers Lomito the enemy. But through Lomito's persistent hard work, she comes to believe that there is at least one cop who is on her side. Lomito also succeeds in winning over Holledge, who at last reveals a secret that has been eating him: he witnessed the murder and captured it on his body cam. He leaves this evidence behind and shoots himself in the head. Armed with this evidence, Lomito stands up to the cops behind the cover-up, and with a little help from the supernatural, reveals the truth. Since most of the cops involved in the murder have already been eviscerated by this point, a lone superior complicit in the coverup is made to stand trial. Following "a stunning trial that riveted the public," a news anchor tells us, he is found guilty. The monster is satisfied, and stops killing cops. Hailed as a hero, Lomito remarks that she is just doing her duty.

The motif of the body cam, a small camera worn on cops' vests to film their interactions with the public, is a seemingly odd choice for a film that throws its weight behind the imperative to reform the police. A popular demand in the early days of Black Lives Matter (BLM), championed by Barack Obama's Justice Department, body cams have been adopted across the United States—and have proven to do very little to prevent police violence. They have a nasty habit of accidentally turning themselves off in moments of police violence, or else police departments fight tooth and nail to avoid releasing the footage they capture, or else viewers have been forced to watch body cam videos of killer cops who often face no repercussions for their acts. All of the cops involved in George Floyd's death were wearing body cams, but this did not prevent Floyd's murder, or stop the Minneapolis police from issuing a fraudulent account of Floyd's lethal ordeal, which glosses over Chauvin's acts entirely, claiming only that Floyd suffered "medical distress." The statement is sure to add: "Body worn cameras were on and activated during this incident." It was only a bystander's video that told the real story.

This choice of motif is however easily understood in light of Lomito's central role in the resolution of the violent conflict that animates *Body Cam*. Lomito represents in one character the figure of "community policing," the demand for more diverse cops, the axiom that cops and the communities they terrorize need to simply open up a "dialogue," and the persistent liberal cant that "not all cops are bad"—as if the functionaries tasked with overseeing racialized class domination could somehow escape this role by being nice. There might be individual cops who are racist, ill-tempered, mean, and in need of "sensitivity training," a common panacea in police reform circles for at least half a century, but

US policing is, of course, only as violent and nasty as the capitalist order it props up. The violence at the heart of US society—its enduring racial hierarchy, staggering inequality of wealth and power, and abandonment of much of its population to destitution and death—is simply expressed through the violence of the cops who hold this combustible compound together. The horizon for change offered by *Body Cam* is therefore a kind of pantomime of change draped in the language of "social justice" that modifies nothing about how society is organized. This perspective speaks of reconciliation but only means the cessation of hostilities between irreconcilable social forces in the name of the status quo. What better metonym for this outlook than that useless decoration, the body cam?

Surely this is not your average white boy cop drama. *Body Cam* is part of an innovation in copaganda that incorporates some of the main themes of movements like BLM, along with diverse faces representing the cops, to argue that "distrust" between police and working-class communities of color must be repaired so that the former can effectively do its necessary work keeping the latter in line. *Body Cam* therefore acknowledges that there is some justification to the payback that the cops have coming to them, but concerns itself far more with putting disorder to an end than with ending the circumstances that produce it. It also plays a good amount of violin for American cops in the process—you know, the good ones who are only doing their jobs—deploying a comparison of antipolice prejudice with racism that is of course a common argument of the Blue Lives Matter movement. The real tragedy, the film tells us, is that people no longer trust the cops. In other words, like many dominant social institutions in the US, the film's major problem is not that killer cops exist but that finally someone is fighting back. It is among *Body Cam*'s virtues that it fails as a horror movie, lest the viewer be distracted by cheap scares from beholding the poverty of this worldview allowed to plead its case for ninety-six painful minutes.

While this largely forgettable film was unceremoniously dumped onto streaming services just days before the murder of George Floyd, it remains remarkably attuned to the zeitgeist that produced it. In its heavy-handed plucking of the raw nerves of the post-BLM years, *Body Cam* captures at once the great anti-cop fury that would soon be released, culminating in the attack on the Third Precinct, alongside the urgent need among movement managers and their allies in the police to deescalate the rebellion, define it within the terms of liberal democracy, and channel its energy into dialogue with the powerful and the theatrics of procedural justice, instead of a direct attack on the carceral state.

It might be a stretch to say that *Body Cam* predicts not only the rebellion, produced by the ongoing and racialized structural violence of American life, but also the conviction of Derek Chauvin, undertaken by systematic cooperation throughout the Minneapolis city government to placate the George Floyd Rebellion and quell it once and for all. The film does, however, depict the near inevitability of the rebellion, and the mechanisms by which it was diluted and sidelined in the name of business as usual, including Chauvin's conviction. *Body Cam* transports to the realm of supernatural horror the concrete material fact that the capitalist order of the United States and the police that violently uphold it up can conjure a ruthless force dedicated to the destruction of both.

After rearing its head in the summer of 2020, it seems that this monster has been subdued. But what good horror creature stays dead for long?

Zoomers Go to Hell

This text first appeared on the *Hard Crackers: Chronicles of Everyday Life* website on Halloween 2022.

This October marked the release of *Hellraiser* (2022), a putative reboot of the 1987 horror classic and the eleventh entry into the *Hellraiser* franchise. It is especially significant for the involvement of creator Clive Barker, who has been absent from *Hellraiser* films for decades, as their intellectual property owner, Dimension Films, cranked out one direct-to-video mediocrity after another. The original *Hellraiser*, by contrast, based on Barker's 1986 literary novella *The Hellbound Heart*, remains nothing short of a masterpiece. Barker's direction brought arthouse sensibility and queer eroticism to bear on gross-out splatterpunk imagery at the glorious apex of practical special effects, driven by a story so memorable that it has been retold and reimagined dozens of times. Made with just a million dollars, *Hellraiser* became an instant classic in the genre, with its iconic Pinhead joining the pantheon including Michael Myers, Jason Vorhees, and Freddy Krueger. The film even earned accolades from many normie critics, who are ordinarily loath to say anything positive about a horror film.

A substantive reboot has been in the works since at least 2006, when Barker announced his intentions to write the film and oversee its production.[1] This fell apart, time and again, due to producer Bob Weinstein's insistence that the queer splatter fest be sanitized and straightened up for a mainstream teenage audience.[2] But the downfall of the Weinstein brothers, and Barker's 2020 recapture of cinematic rights, has opened the door for more serious entries into the *Hellraiser* canon.[3] The new film represents *Hellraiser*'s introduction to Generation Z, the so-called zoomers born around the turn of the century. Thirty-five years after Barker's startling vision first debuted, his mythology once more offers itself up for a new generation to decide whether they recognize their fears and anxieties in the curious figure of the demon with pins protruding from his head, promising the tantalizing curse of fulfilling one's ultimate desires.

Fertile Ground for the Seeds of Torment

The original *Hellraiser* draws influence from gothic literary figures like Mary Shelley and Edgar Allan Poe, horror auteurs like Dario Argento and David Cronenberg, the crimson theatricality of the Grand Guignol theater, and Barker's own stage exploits in the transgressive Dog Company. As scholar Giorgio Paolo Campi observes, the 1987 film bears the deliberate marks of the underground counterculture percolating in the London of Barker's formative years, specifically punk rock, queer nightlife, BDSM, and the body modification scene.[4] Critic Mark Derry calls it "an S&M rewrite of the Faust legend," while scholar Lúcio Reis Filho dubs the film "a sadomasochistic take on the myth of Pandora's box."[5] But above all else, *Hellraiser* is a love story, albeit one suitable for its age.

The Hellbound Heart begins with an epigram from seventeenth-century metaphysical poet John Donne: "I long to talk with some old lover's ghost / Who died before the god of love was born."[6] The story follows Julia and Larry Cotton (named Rory in the novella) taking possession of the latter's gloomy family home, hoping to salvage a marriage "stale, like this house," as the screenplay puts it, and establish a nuclear family firmly anchored by the four walls of 55 Lodovico Street.[7] Larry is childish and naive, sexually inept, and largely clueless to the simmering dissatisfaction consuming Julia as he presses toward his staid middle-class dreams. In the screenplay, Barker describes Julia as "beautiful, but her face betrays a barely buried unhappiness. Life has disappointed her … and Larry has been a major part of [her] disappointment." (Spoilers ahead.)

In the parlance of today, Larry is a cuck. Beyond her ordinary middle-class disaffection, Julia is haunted by an adulterous encounter years old with Larry's brother, Frank, consummated in the days before their wedding—in their marital bed, atop the bridal gown, no less. Brother Frank is an archetypal hedonist, scouring the Earth obsessively striving to transcend "the dull round of desire, seduction, and disappointment that had dogged him from late adolescence."[8] Julia had pursued the opposite course, a monogamous heterosexual relationship, but later came to rue her wedding day for "the promise it had failed to fulfill," leaving her similarly forlorn, but fixed within four walls.[9] In the film, their tryst has scarcely concluded when Frank bemoans: "It's never enough!" Julia, by contrast, is hooked on their impossible romance, yet similarly doomed to remain unsated. The *Hellraiser* story, then, revolves around the unlikely symmetry between globe-trotting sybarite and sedate housewife as they pursue, in their own ways, the fool's errand of reaching desire's definitive end.

Following her wedding to Larry, Julia settles down for a life of quiet yearning, and Frank resumes his relentless roaming, obsessed with rumors of a metaphysical puzzle box called the LeMarchand Configuration. To solve it is to summon an order of otherworldly deities who demolish all limits to pure satisfaction, opening a doorway "to pleasures no more than a handful of humans had ever known existed, much less *tasted*—pleasures which would redefine the parameters of sensation."[10] These beings are the supernatural Cenobites, devotees of the Order of the Gash, inhabiting a realm where pleasure and pain are indistinguishable. Frank obtains the box, and takes up residence in the master bedroom of 55 Lodovico Street in the months before Julia and Larry's arrival, working frantically to summon them. Soon enough, he receives the ultimate punishment: his deepest desires come to pass.

Explorers in the Further Regions of Experience

The appearance of the Cenobites staggers Frank. Their rotting flesh, disfigured bodies, and ghastly torture instruments defy his earthly conception of extreme pleasure. For all his self-conceit as a transgressor beyond all boundaries, the novella reveals that Frank mainly expected the Cenobites to show up with a legion of naked women looking to party. The beings he encounters instead are "explorers in the further regions of experience" who have progressed far beyond intercourse as humans understand it. Pleasure to them is the most extreme of sensation, attainable by tortures no mortal could survive. They are, as the film's working title famously put it: "Sadomasochists from Beyond the Grave."[11]

The novella introduces the as-yet-unnamed franchise star Pinhead in familiar terms: "Every inch of its head had been tattooed with an intricate grid," writes Barker, "and at every intersection of horizontal and vertical axes a jeweled pin driven through to the bone." But while the film's Pinhead presents as a man and speaks with a stentorian boom, in the novella, the Cenobites are "sexless *things*." Encountering Pinhead, Frank "had difficulty guessing the speaker's gender with any certainty," Barker writes. "Its voice ... was light and breathy—the voice of an excited girl." While the novella says little about the Cenobites' manner of dress, except that their clothing is interwoven with their mutilated flesh, the film's costume designer equipped the quartet in their now iconic BDSM-inspired gear.[12]

In short order, this gruesome quartet whisks Frank away to the land of their god, the Leviathan, where he is ruthlessly tortured until nothing remains of him but stray scraps of flesh and bone. "The Cenobites gave me an experience beyond limits," he recalls in the film. "Pain and pleasure, indivisible." But his spirit lingers on in the walls of the room where he exited Earth, so that when Julia arrives at 55 Lodovico, she is assaulted with memories of their tryst, and becomes convinced of his presence within the house. Their inevitable reunion is enabled when Larry, struggling to move their bed in through the front door, cuts himself and sheds blood on the floor, bringing his wayward brother back to life.

The being that stalks the second act of *Hellraiser* is not the hunky Frank depicted in the photograph Julia clasps in secret; this Frank is a ghastly skinless monster, craving blood to make himself whole. Julia's obsession with Frank, however, proves stronger than her initial shock and revulsion at his wretched condition. In the film, a flashback reveals Julia pleading with Frank not to leave her, insisting: "I'll do anything you want. Anything." When Frank returns as the horrid creature dubbed "Frank the Monster" in the film's credits, Julia keeps this vow. To procure the blood he demands, Julia picks up strange men at nearby bars to bring home, murder, and feed to Frank, all while Larry is at work. This arrangement places Larry in grave danger, and before long he has joined the pair's victims. In a grisly denouement, Frank removes his brother's skin to wear as his own, allowing him to walk the Earth freely, and evade recapture by the Cenobites. That is, save for the intrusion of one meddling kid.

Some Things Have to Be Endured

The heroine of the original *Hellraiser* story is a young woman named Kirsty. In the novella she is a nebbishy and adoring friend of Larry. In the film, Kirsty is crucially reimagined as Larry's adoring daughter from another marriage, whose mother is long dead, and who Larry wishes to move in with him and Julia to reform their family in a new home. Both Kirstys are distrustful of Julia, and are the first to discover her and Frank's infernal pact. After confronting Julia and Frank the Monster, Kirsty narrowly escapes with her life—and the LeMarchand Configuration. Kirsty solves the puzzle by accident, and when the Cenobites arrive to claim their new captives, she strikes one of the story's many bargains: in exchange for her freedom, she will lead them to the escaped Frank. They accept, and the pieces are in place for a final showdown at 55 Lodovico Street. Frank greets Kirsty in Larry's skin, but fails to fool her for long. She reveals his trick, and the Cenobites are close behind. Frank then kills Julia before the Cenobites whisk him back to his eternity of torment. In the novella, Kirsty is left as the keeper of the box. In the film, it is seized by a winged demon and returned to the merchant who first sold it to Frank, setting up *Hellraiser* for the first of many sequels.

Kirsty's survival makes her *Hellraiser*'s contribution to the pantheon of '80s horror's "final girls" first described by scholar Carol J. Clover.[13] In the dramaturgy of 1980s horror, final girls must reject the absent, abusive, or inadequate authority structure imposed on them by the adult world, especially that of father figures. Final girls once believed themselves safe within an orderly world, sheltered by family and state. The arrival of the monster only serves to dramatize their discovery that this was all a fantasy. As their less adept friends drop dead left and right—usually as a result of indulging in drugs, alcohol, or sexual gratification—final girls are forced to figure out what this new world demands of them, incorporate it into their previously naive conception of reality, and confront the threat head-on. In the process, they not only survive, but attain agency as adults, facing a hostile universe on their own two feet, able to navigate the absence of competent authority in their lives. The weight of this common horror narrative, then, comes not from the fantastical intrusion of supernatural killers, but from the banal, everyday dilemmas attendant to coming of age, with which the audience is meant to relate, however unconsciously.

Kirsty, who in scholar Sarah Trencansky's words, "ably rises to the challenge of accepting the unbelievable events around her," is nonetheless not the typical final girl.[14] "Barely twenty," as the screenplay describes her, instead of a teenager, Kirsty drinks alcohol and engages in sexual activity, behaviors that consigned many of her teenage forebears to death. She also lives on her own, outside of the family home. In Kirsty, we see the family's oppressive grip, which characterizes much of '80s horror, clearly devolving: Kirsty has already escaped, and, as scholar Matthew Sautman points out, must return to the family home for the story's monsters to harm her.[15] This detail is key; while the *Hellraiser* franchise is virtually unrivaled in the scope and complexity of the netherworld from which the Cenobites hail, it is close to home, at 55 Lodovico Street, where the real horror resides.

Demons to Some, Angels to Others

While the Cenobites are now synonymous with the *Hellraiser* franchise, their ghoulish forms cut a slender figure in the original story, receiving roughly seven minutes of screen time in the 1987 film. This should come as no surprise. As scholar Levi Ghyselinck wisely concludes: "Frank and Julia are the real monsters."[16] Julia's is certainly the titular "hellbound heart," and she is likely the principal hell-raiser as well. This means the real source of *Hellraiser's* horror is not the monstrous world the Cenobites inhabit. Central to the film's dramatic tension is the dissolution of the nuclear family, landlocked in its lodestone, the family home. The Cotton family's demise is a fact more stubborn than the Cenobites' pursuit of them; the harder Larry tries to force his traditional conceptions of family into existence, the more the very foundation of his home rebels. Accordingly, critic Paul Kane notes the film's direct lineage from English postwar "kitchen sink" realist dramas like Tony Richardson's *Look Back in Anger* and *A Taste of Honey*, which examine the social forces undercutting family life, and their impact on the people forced nonetheless to live together.[17]

Fusing this tradition with the macabre and supernatural, *Hellraiser* thereby makes a unique contribution to the genre of "domestic horror." "Hitchcock urges us to 'put horror back where it belongs, in the family,'" writes critic Gina Wisker.[18] Heeding this call, domestic horror focuses on "the oppressive, the threatening, the perverse, and the sickening flip side of 'domestic bliss.'" Traditional horror, as Kane argues, pitted the "moral supremacy of the nuclear family and all it stood for" against external threats.[19] Films like *Hellraiser*, by contrast, locate the danger precisely within the family itself, and the ground changing underneath its feet, in the "terrible house." "The image of the 'terrible house,'" writes critic Robin Wood, "signifies the dead weight of the past crushing the life of the younger generation, the future."[20] As *Hellraiser* unfolds, Kirsty must therefore contend quite literally with the weight of dead generations, concentrated in the terrible house at 55 Lodovico Street, the film's sole site of danger.

Barker has wryly described the original Hellraiser as "Ibsen with monsters."[21] The Cotton family was so much the centerpiece of the original *Hellraiser* that, according to franchise writer Peter Atkins, Barker intended Julia to be his Freddy Krueger, before Pinhead surprised his creator by becoming the fan favorite.[22] And it's hardly a coincidence that so much of the film's early action revolves around the Cottons' marital bed, that hallowed cornerstone of the proper family unit, where Larry strives to realize his vision of domestic bliss, oblivious that Julia and Frank have already consummated a union of their own. In a tragically unused line from Barker's original screenplay, one of the movers struggling to get the mattress up the stairs tells Larry: "Who are you calling a fucking asshole? It's this bastard bed that's your fucking problem."

As critic Scott Jeffrey argues, the original *Hellraiser* uniquely fuses such domestic horror, rooted in the claustrophobic world of the nuclear family, with cosmic horror, which conversely confronts humans with a vast universe of ghastly alterity and cosmic apathy toward human concerns.[23] While surely a monument to the imagination of Clive Barker, this juxtaposition is above all a reflection of the historical moment that produced the film.

The Worst Nightmare of All: Reality

So what was really rumbling beneath the foundation of 55 Lodovico Street? The original film's setting was deliberately vague, given the aspiration of English filmmakers to reach an American audience. The house therefore fell in what franchise writer Peter Atkins dubbed "a country of the imagination" somewhere between England and the United States.[24] In the 1980s, however, this terrain was nonetheless quite common, unified by the dual governing regimes of Thatcherism and Reaganism, constituting what we today call neoliberalism. This governing technique responded to deindustrialization, international capital flight, and declining profit rates by slashing public services, allowing wages to stagnate, and insulating ruling-class financiers from the ravages of the free market.[25] This burden was borne instead by working people caught in a downward spiral of wealth, job security, and purchasing power. Most cruelly of all, this brutal retrenchment came packaged as a celebration of home ownership by the heterosexual nuclear family, at the precise time when this was becoming an impossibility for a growing number of people, in trends that continue to the present day.[26]

It is not far-fetched, then, that scholar Patricia Allmer reads *Hellraiser* as a critique of the tragic ruse of 1980s neoliberalism. In *Hellraiser*, she writes, "far from the Thatcherite promises of 'freedom' and 'liberty,' ownership leads to death, destruction, and fragmentation, not least of the very individuality that ownership tries to establish and protect."[27] Further, while Thatcherism and Reaganism pushed moral panics against feminists and LGBTQ people as supposed threats to the family, scholar Matthew Sautman argues: "Barker shows *Hellraiser*'s viewers that the hegemonic family formation exalted during the 1980s American backlash against feminism is seemingly incapable of ensuring familial prosperity, and that patriarchs have the capacity to transform any given domestic space into a private hell for anyone else who values their bodily autonomy."[28]

In the original *Hellraiser*, then, the destabilization of the family home stands as an avatar for broader transformations in social relations that had been long pulling people away from traditional, heteropatriarchal living arrangements and making the existing ones unstable and prone to fall apart. As the journal *Endnotes* argues, deindustrialization and attendant transformations of social reproduction have long undercut the gendered division of labor in these countries, sending large numbers of men into traditionally feminized occupations like clerical and service work. Subjectivities based on this division, especially genders traditionally organized around men's work and women's work, could not but be destabilized as well. This transformation has been further accelerated by the demise of the single-paycheck families in the upper tiers of the working class, and the entry of large numbers of women into the middle tiers of the workforce, where they work as much, if not more, than the men in their households, and even supervise men at work. These factors combine to make the traditional nuclear family, and the identities it imposes, make increasingly less sense.[29]

Simultaneously, as scholar John D'Emilio has argued, the tendencies of capitalism to break up traditional social forms and free laborers for the market, compounded with the rise of urbanization and self-selected communities, has enabled the consolidation and proliferation of queer identities and so-called alternative lifestyles, the likes of which Barker, himself a gay practitioner of BDSM, took part in with great enthusiasm.[30] Meanwhile, developments in elective surgery and pharmacology dramatically opened the possibility for human bodies to be reconfigured, and further destabilized the notion of embodiment as a fixed destiny. Barker was not alone in finding this fertile ground for creative imagining; films like David Cronenberg's 1983 *Videodrome* and Stuart Gordon's 1986 *From Beyond* prefigured *Hellraiser* by juxtaposing so-called body horror with BDSM and queerness, demonstrating a keen intuition of profound and intractable social transformations underway—if not always portraying these themes in a favorable or respectful light.

You Opened It, We Came

Just as Marx's *Capital* begins with the commodity, so too does Barker's *Hellraiser*. Central to the story is the puzzle box, a gilded fetish if there ever was one, obtainable through a market transaction and promising the fulfillment of its owners' ultimate desires. As scholar Patricia Allmer notes: "*Hellraiser* opens with commercial exchange," the purchase of the LeMarchand (French for merchant) Configuration, bringing with it the same contractual relations that define the free market so lauded in the time of Thatcher and Reagan.[31] In the Cenobites' world, as in theirs, there are no innocent victims; everyone is considered free to choose, and must therefore be held accountable for whatever happens to them as a result. The central illusions that structure capitalist ideology are therefore also key aspects of the Cenobites' moral economy. And the disproportionate power they wield is disguised by the illusion of free assent. In the original film, those who desire to open the box, and do so, are automatically treated as consenting parties. In the novella, even after Frank opens the box, he must provide nothing short of enthusiastic consent to enter the realm of the Leviathan; the Cenobites ask him multiple times if he is sure he wishes to enjoy their pleasures, even cautioning him: "There's no going back."

When the fruits of this transaction prove too much for Frank to bear, he does not fault the Cenobites. Having internalized their guiding ideology and its celebration of free choice, the novella's Frank reasons that "his real error had been the naive belief that *his* definition of pleasure significantly overlapped with that of the Cenobites." Like a loyal capitalist subject insistent on blaming themselves for taking out a predatory loan or signing an exploitative labor contract, Frank would rather cling to his illusion of freedom than question the validity of the system in which it unfolds. In an unused exchange from the screenplay, Julia insists that Frank was cheated by the Cenobites. "Oh no," he replies, defending his tormentors. "They kept to their bargain. They gave me experiences I'd never forget." Far from disputing the validity of his captivity, Frank plots his escape via a "loophole" in their contract, as the novella phrases it.

The Cenobites' scrupulous attention to consent is, however, offered in bad faith; they know that Frank is a desperate man, and has no other options left but to turn himself over to them. "We understand to its breadth and depth the nature of your frenzy," one tells him in the novella. "It is utterly familiar to us." Driven by compulsions beyond his control, Frank elects to enter the realm of the Leviathan no more freely than a laborer chooses to work for wages, the consumer chooses to purchase food, or the working-class college student goes into debt to get an education. The Cenobites are aware that their agreement with Frank is under duress and he will come to regret it, but his interests do not concern them. All that matters is that he signs on the dotted line. Frank, for his part, is possessed by a frenzy that points his desire toward the mystical character of the puzzle box. When the flesh and blood reality of the commodity's secret is revealed at last, it is too late; he has already been chewed up and spit out.

A Waste of Good Suffering

To make the original film, Barker made a Faustian pact of his own, forfeiting the cinematic rights to his most memorable characters. On the heels of *Hellraiser*, Barker wrote and produced a 1988 sequel *Hellbound*, which largely followed the mythology of the original, while expanding its vistas to include Kirsty's sojourn through the Escheresque land of the Leviathan. Barker acted as a nominal producer, albeit with rapidly diminishing interest, on two subsequent installments, *Hell on Earth* and *Bloodline*, pushing the original story as far as it would go in space and time. The latter in particular shoehorned *Hellraiser*'s mythology into a three-century timeline spanning LeMarchand's creation of the box in postrevolutionary France to his descendant's victorious final battle with Pinhead on a space shuttle in the year 2127. The ambitious *Bloodline* was, however, brutally recut by the studio, leading to director Kevin Yagher crediting himself as "Alan Smithee," the Director's Guild's official designation of a disavowed final cut. This would set the tone for the rest of the series, which continued largely without the involvement of Barker, and represented cheap attempts to cash in on his loyal fans, while paying no respect to the complexities of the original mythology.

Lúcio Reis Filho argues that the first four films, overseen by Barker, generally follow the philosophical underpinnings of H.P. Lovecraft's "Cthulhu Mythos," characterized by "deadly encounters between gods and hapless human beings who stumble across them and discover, to their horror, a universe far darker and more hostile than they had ever imagined."[32] Importantly, this mythos has no place for the good/evil binary of Judeo-Christianity, which projects human value systems onto the order of the cosmos. Instead, it is the indifference of the universe to such human concerns that constitutes the core of the horror. The rest of the series, by contrast, quickly devolved into shopworn moralism, featuring Pinhead punishing evildoers, his Sadean sermons traded for such vapid Christian platitudes as: "Your flesh is killing your spirit." In short Barker's brilliant exploration of a realm beyond human values became yet another unimaginative rehashing of the Christian concept of hell.

Critic Katie Rife once observed: "Watching all nine *Hellraiser* movies is an exercise in masochism."[33] There are now eleven, including *Inferno* (2000), *Hellseeker* (2002), *Deader* (2005), *Hellworld* (2005), *Revelations* (2011), and *Judgment* (2018). At least three of these films feature mere cameo appearances from Pinhead, clearly retrofitted into preexisting, unrelated scripts. But the unquestioned nadir of a series full of lows comes in *Revelations*. The sole purpose of this dismal seventy-five-minute slog was for the Weinstein Company to legally retain rights to the *Hellraiser* characters, which would otherwise default back to Barker for lack of use. The company generated a script virtually overnight, and allocated a $300,000 budget for two weeks of shooting. These conditions were so dismal that even Doug Bradley, whose Pinhead had weathered one forgettable sequel after another, refused to participate.[34] Similarly, Clive Barker announced: "I have NOTHING to do with the fuckin' thing. If they claim it's from the mind of Clive Barker, it's a lie. It's not even from my butt-hole."[35]

The same story repeated in 2018, with *Hellraiser: Judgment*. This time, however, the $350,000 film was helmed by veteran franchise make-up designer Gary Tunnicliffe, who made an earnest attempt to get the *Hellraiser* films back on track, based on faithful additions to its mythology he had been proposing since the 1990s. This was still not enough to secure the return of Bradley, who criticized the film as a perfunctory exercise in retaining rights, and balked at a lengthy nondisclosure agreement limiting his ability to speak about the film on the lucrative horror conference circuit.[36] Tunnicliffe's efforts, however, evinced a decades-long struggle behind the scenes to spearhead a well-funded, high-quality reboot of the original *Hellraiser*, which remained frustrated, but not forgotten. There were, after all, more souls to be harvested, and more money too.

The Agony of Friends

"Hell," Barker once remarked, "is reimagined by every generation."[37] In contrast to most of the franchise preceding it, the 2022 *Hellraiser* reboot represents an earnest attempt to reinvigorate the original story, develop its mythology, and say something about the world that produced it. This can be largely attributed to Barker regaining his control of the brand, and now having a say over how his characters are used. The new film also boasts a much larger budget and a cast of young people who my students assure me are celebrity zoomers, plus *Sense8* and *The L Word* actress Jamie Clayton as Pinhead, and the direction of David Bruckner of *Night House* and *The Ritual*. The reboot was produced by streaming giant Hulu for its subscribers, which keeps it off the big screen. This is unfortunate, as the Cenobites in particular look their best in decades—led by an unforgettable Clayton, who recaptures the Pinhead character's breathy androgyny from the novella, breathing uncanny terror into its cosmic dispassion while delivering pitch-perfect aphorisms like: "Enough is a myth."

Set in an unnamed American city, the film follows the alcoholic zoomer Riley McKendry, who struggles to find her footing in the labor market and navigate the impossible demands placed upon her by the world, largely represented by her older brother and sublandlord Matt. Riley works an ill-defined service sector job dependent on tips, and is "really tired of being broke." To help cope, Riley enters into a loveless relationship with fellow addict Trevor, who is casually employed as an art handler (perhaps the most meaningless and despair-inducing of my own many shitty jobs over the years).[38] They live at the fringes of the labor market doing unrewarding jobs, kept in a suspended state of adolescence, and routinely escape this reality through intoxication.

The sex between Riley and Trevor is similarly devoid of any substance or passion; Riley even terminates the act when Trevor incautiously professes his love. To Riley, sex is not enjoyable in itself or part of any meaningful social connection, and doesn't point to any pleasure greater than a temporary distraction. The same goes for companionship; Trevor describes their status as "being lonely together." Riley lives with her brother Matt, his boyfriend Colin, and their roommate Nora, in an all-too-familiar shared apartment where young adults make each other tacos and listen intently to the sounds of arguments and sex pouring through the walls. Far from the queer hedonists anticipated by Barker's Cenobites, the gay couple Matt and Colin are solely depicted in chaste domestic scenes, such as reading poetry to each other in bed, presumably exhausted from work. Otherwise, Matt's principal activity is clamping down on Riley's fun, and demanding she earn more money. Riley, for her part, considers Matt's interest in her to be compensation for his lack of social power or mobility. "You just love having something to fix," she shouts at him, "so you can feel like a big success in this shitty apartment."

So Exquisitely Empty

This points to the most interesting of the reboot's many divergences from the 1987 *Hellraiser*. There is no domestic horror, because there is no terrible house. The rented apartment the siblings share is merely used for some feeble character development, as the story shepherds the zoomers toward their fate in the kind of creepy mansion shopworn in traditional gothic lore. For these young people, property ownership is out of the question; it's difficult enough to make rent. And the dissolution of Julia and Larry's marriage, central to the original film, is already a fait accompli; consistent with trends in England and the US in the years since the original film, nobody in this *Hellraiser* is even married to begin with.[39] And never does the story so much as hint at the siblings' parents. Unlike countless of their teenage horror forebears, the drama of Riley and Matt does not revolve around superseding parental authority and facing the world on their own. They begin their journey already immersed in the harshness of a world that proves almost more than they can bear. And from here, there's nowhere to go but down. It's a universe far meaner than Barker himself could imagine in 1987, even before the Cenobites appear.

This is not to say there's no wealth floating around in *Hellraiser*. Earthly authority is represented by the billionaire Roland Voight, a trader of occult art who is revealed late in the film to be Trevor's secret employer. The consummate boss, Voight is a predator who manipulates and exploits innocent young people, sacrificing them to his own ambition, quite literally. In the rebooted *Hellraiser*, victims of the LeMarchand Configuration are effectively subcontracted out; those who wish to open the box must provide the Cenobites with five unwitting human sacrifices, who are stabbed against their will with a blade protruding from the box. Then, as Riley explains, using an interesting turn of the phrase, the Cenobites "come to collect." Gone is the illusion of free choice for the vast majority of the Cenobites' victims. And the reward awaiting the box holder at the end of this mass murder is not transportation to a realm beyond pleasure and pain, but an audience with the god Leviathan, in which they receive a "gift" said to fulfill their "ultimate desire." In order for one character to be delivered to Leviathan, five must perish. There aren't even enough full-time positions to go around in hell.

As the story unfolds, Riley is marked as a sacrifice by Trevor, working at Voight's behest. (Asked why Trevor would prey upon her this way, Voight remarks: "because this is the best deal of his miserable life.") But Riley inadvertently passes off the box to Matt, who is summarily whisked off by the Cenobites in her place. As Riley struggles to make sense of the supernatural, in classic final girl fashion, she learns that Voight has previously solved the box, and in his audience with Leviathan, requested the gift of "sensation." Like Frank, Voight expected untrammeled sexual gratification, but instead received unending, inescapable pain. Riley thereby learns that the string of sacrifices that ensnare the young roommates amount to Voight's attempt to summon the Leviathan once more and attempt to free himself from their pact. "I sought pleasure," the billionaire explains to Riley, in a telling exchange, "but all they have to give is pain. It's a trick. All of it." Take it from the billionaire: the game is rigged.

The rebooted *Hellraiser* lacks the romance and eroticism of the original, but perhaps that's the point. Julia and Frank, as Sarah Trencansky argues, are "two adults so complacent in their bourgeois lives that they seek out the 'pleasure' promised them by the box as one more capital [sic] attainment."[40] Their zoomer equivalents, by contrast, have long given up on realizing lofty desires, aiming instead for the procurement of basic necessities, or else not to simply become somebody else's lunch. What's more, they have likely seen the promise of desire unchained turned into so much more fodder for marketing commodities or the creation of interest groups for neoliberal politicians to pander to. Voight, the closest character the film has to Uncle Frank, seems out of place in a story populated by young people who believe in nothing and expect less. The flip side, though, is they are not so easily bought.

"There is no retreat once a threshold has been crossed," Pinhead ominously drones, in one of their many classic lines, which constitute the best moments of this film. "All you can do is search for a greater threshold." The zoomers, however, could beg to differ. In an excellent scene, Pinhead asks Nora: "What is it you pray for?" to which she replies: "Salvation." A disappointed Pinhead responds: "There's no music in that." Later, when Pinhead attempts to ensnare Riley in the same old Faustian bargain that has strewn the *Hellraiser* franchise with bodies, she isn't biting. "I've seen your rewards," Riley responds, "I don't want anything from you."

The 2022 *Hellraiser* reboot is a horror film suitable for the so-called Great Resignation and the growing number of zoomers opting to stay out of college if it means a mountain of debt.[41] It speaks to a generation who have precious few illusions of what capitalism can offer them, and must decide whether they will kill themselves pursuing its gilded promise anyway. The viewer is only left wondering where this horror story will go next—on the screen, and more importantly, in the real world it reflects so deviously.

Hybrid Moments

This text first appeared on the *Hard Crackers: Chronicles of Everyday Life* website in September 2022.

■

On September 17, 2022, I witnessed something long believed to be impossible: a reunion of "The Original Misfits," founder, songwriter, and vocalist Glenn "Danzig" Anzalone, bassist Jerry "Only" Caiafa, and guitarist Paul "Doyle" Caiafa. Danzig and Only are well into their sixth decade, with Doyle close behind. They have played a handful of gigs since their 2016 reunion, their first in thirty-three years, but never in my city. It had become tempting to believe the Misfits reunion was just the latest of the strange rumors that have followed the band since the 1970s: they worship Satan, rob graves, and only play on Halloween. Like most punk kids of my generation, I grew up obsessed with this band that had broken up before I was born. Their uncanny death rock anthems, played on a perennial loop and sung together in drunken revelries, reinforced three essential certainties: (1) death (it "comes ripping"), (2) the Misfits are the greatest punk band of all time, and (3) you will never see Danzig and Jerry Only on stage together. But here they were, like the creatures in one of their creations, mythic movie monsters come to life, wreaking havoc on legions of hapless kids.

Too Much Horror Business
The setting was Riot Fest, a latter-day heir to the punk nostalgia package Warped Tour. Riot Fest's marketing draws on the argot of aging

and perennially online millennial hipsters who lost track of the fuzzy border between irony and sincerity sometime in the Bush administration. Its slogan: "Riot Fest Sucks." Get it? It's a place where the kind of "fifteen-foot-high stages" the Dead Kennedys deplored are adorned with the names "Riot," "Rise," "Roots," "Rebel," and "Radicals," decked out with Broadway lighting and fortified by barricades and small armies of bouncers enforcing a barrier that punk is supposed to have overcome. Between bands, patrons pay airport prices for food, drinks, and mountains of merchandise tailored to court the disposable dollars of hipsters-cum-yuppies still sentimental for their salad days. Many wear the shirts advertising previous Riot Fests, or the shirts of bands playing that day—which, in my day, one didn't do.

Riot Fest was founded in 2005, an indoor festival at the Congress Theater in Logan Square featuring dubious lineups of classic punk acts like the Dead Kennedys, the Germs, and a ragtag version of the "Misfits" led by Jerry Only. After hosting such improbable reunions as Naked Raygun, the Replacements, and Jawbreaker, Riot Fest has developed a reputation as the ultimate vendor of punk nostalgia. In the process, it has ballooned into a multimillion-dollar operation with corporate funding and seemingly endless pockets to procure top tier acts. Quickly outgrowing a single club, Riot Fest became a federation of venues, and in 2012, moved outdoors to a central location in Humboldt Park, the center of a working-class, traditionally Puerto Rican, neighborhood on Chicago's West Side.

The move was a massive takeover of public space for private profits, in a historically disinvested but gentrifying nonwhite neighborhood, with scant public space to begin with—all for a fest that draws an overwhelmingly white clientele. Since then, Riot Fest has become a flashing, flaming, blaring beacon emblematizing the long-standing race-blindness of punk, in which largely white devotees from relatively privileged backgrounds cast themselves as the wretched of the earth, draw from Black and brown musicians who are seldom acknowledged, and serve as shock troops for gentrifying speculators, often with little sense of how clueless they appear.

Rainfall at Riot Fest 2014 led to intensive damages to Humboldt Park, some of which remained closed even after the fest declared it repaired. Even when things go smoothly, Riot Fest entails a literal enclosure of the commons, erecting meshed fences to prevent entry or even sight, and shutting down public space for weeks at a time. Public relations outreach through the nonprofit Riot Fest Foundation, including the promise of $500,000 in local donations, the distribution of 600 Thanksgiving turkeys, and free tickets for neighbors, failed to stem opposition.[1] In 2015 Riot Fest was ousted from Humboldt Park and relocated to Douglass Park, in the largely Black, working-class neighborhood of North Lawndale.[2] There, the same protests have been raised ever since.[3] Adding fuel to the fire, a recent investigation discovered, in classic Chicago fashion, Riot Fest has leveraged political connections to avoid paying practically all of the attendant fees for use of the park and subsequent damages.[4]

In short, Riot Fest is corny as hell. But, in an honest assessment, so are the Misfits. And, apparently, so am I.

Possession of the Mind Is a Terrible Thing

In May 2022, Riot Fest announced the Misfits would play their entire album "Walk Among Us" in September. The full album gimmick has become a way for older bands with regrettable latter-day releases to assure the faithful that they will play the hits from back in the day. It also imbues some novelty into the performance of material decades old. Initially I balked; three years living in Chicago have taught me that enjoying Riot Fest is about as cool as preferring the Cubs over the White Sox. I attended a few Warped Tours as a teenager, and swore the whole thing off as a miserable, sunbaked cash-in for musicians whose best days were behind them. Since being initiated into the underground fraternity of DIY punk at fifteen, I have found big concerts impersonal, prefabricated, and way too expensive. Above all, I love the Misfits, but I wasn't sure I wanted to see a bunch of guys my parents' age prancing around in spooky makeup calling themselves teenagers from Mars.

As the summer wore on, however, I found myself, like the protagonist of Spielberg's *Close Encounters of the Third Kind*, drawn irresistibly toward the dayglow terminus where alien invaders promised to touch down and transform my life forever. On Spotify, chunks of Glenn Danzig's infernal hymnal slowly replaced my more responsible choices of college educated post-punk, bebop jazz, first-wave ska, and ambient noise, which I have deemed dignified for a creative professional closer to forty than thirty. I recalled the exhilaration that coursed through me the first time I heard Danzig's voice, levitating over a fuzzy guitar belting out hook after unforgettable hook, propelled by galloping bass and drums, stringing together sentiments I could not believe human minds had formulated, all within the space of two sublime minutes, or less.

As a youngster completely at odds with the known world, the Misfits assured me that the profound disjunction I felt, like a mutated Martian or human fly, was not my burden to bear alone. There were others, including many who had come before me, who had found in this world nothing worth liking, and declared themselves its sworn enemy. They stared the ugliness and cruelty of the world in the face, and refused to be its victims. To survive a world of monsters, they became monsters themselves. If it was shocking or offensive, they would say it. Whatever was disallowed, they would do. They were not beholden to God, family, country, or even the human race. They had found each other, and now, like radio waves from another world, their message had reached me, calling me forth to walk among them. In the summer of 2022, I heard this message once more.

Desperate for a way out, I contacted my ace, cultural critic and ne plus ultra millennial punk Andy Folk, known to the normies as A.M. Gittlitz. He had seen this lineup of the Misfits play a sold-out show at Madison Square Garden in 2019. "Forget about it," I hoped the Folkman would tell me. "They looked and sounded awful. It ruined my teenage years, as if they could get any worse." But to my chagrin, Andy testified that the "The Original Misfits" were actually the second best show he had ever seen—after Iggy and the Stooges. Even in the nosebleed section of MSG, he said, it still felt like an epic punk show. He couldn't believe that Riot Fest allowed attendees to get so close to the band for the cost of general admission, and was already regretting not flying out himself. And with that, like the kind of tortured soul one encounters in Danzig's lyrical landscape, torn hither and thither and ready to turn their soul over to Lucifer himself, I was doomed.

Hybrids Opened Up the Door

The more you think about the Misfits, the less they make any sense. They were a bunch of tough guys from Lodi, New Jersey, known locally as "Land of Dumb Italians" and a popular setting in the Sopranos. "The Misfits were an old school New York guido thing," recalls Necros frontman Barry Henssler.[5] Close enough to New York to absorb the grit by osmosis, but too far away to earn its sophistication or coveted street cred, the Misfits were overeager to prove they "ain't no goddamn son of

HYBRID MOMENTS

a bitch," as one of their most famous lyrics insists. The Caiafa brothers worked in their father's machine shop to finance the band, spending their off hours lifting weights and rooting for the New York Giants. While Danzig was the artist of the bunch, one high school classmate remembers him as "a typical short Italian guy from Lodi with a temper."[6] In the years since, he has proven this reputation countless times, sometimes to his peril, as in the famous viral video in which he steps to another performer and is knocked out cold.

At the same time, these cliché bridge and tunnel goons dressed themselves in an exaggerated version of goth fashion, complete with corpse paint and "devil lock" hairdos, which they invented. Their all-American athletic physiques were repurposed to accentuate monstrosity. At a time when punks still stopped traffic, and were met with casual violence from cops and squares alike, the Misfits took its penchant for shocking images and outrageous antics and upped the ante. In the process, they made themselves into the worst thing someone in a small town can be: an alien.

In short, the Misfits were mutants, estranged not only from the suburban hellscape of their Anytown, USA, home, but from the other freaks and weirdos too—the hippies, bourgeois bohemians, champagne socialists, art school set, and the cosmopolitan punks of New York City. Danzig in particular was far too weird for Lodi, New Jersey. But nobody in a Manhattan coffee house could mistake him for anything but an unrefined hoodlum from the Land of Dumb Italians. As Andy Folk argues, the Misfits are therefore the ultimate suburban band. They are the avatars for us weirdos who grew up close enough to the city to feel its intoxicating allure, and who dreamed of attaining its worldliness and authenticity, but found ourselves hopelessly tethered to the philistine purgatory from whence we came, making us alien to both worlds, like teenagers from Mars. For the Misfits, like so many suburban punks, the harsh fact of this double exclusion became a vendetta against the world. "Singing of pure violence," writes Folk, "the Misfits fantasized about armies of mutants like them overthrowing the normal world they abhorred."

B Movie Born Invasion

Formed by Danzig in 1976, and joined by Only shortly thereafter, the Misfits are technically a '77 punk band. That year they played their first show at New York City's famed CBGB and released the "Cough/Cool" seven inch, an organ-driven otherworldly apparition. Over the next six years, a flurry of singles, two landmark LPs, and a treasure trove of bootlegged and unreleased material, the Misfits built a dedicated cult following across the US. Their efforts at touring spread the devil's gospel, but were financial disasters marred by violence provoked by the crowd and Misfits alike, including a riot in San Francisco, where Doyle knocked someone unconscious with his guitar. They also maintained the "Fiend Club," highly personalized mailers to their growing base of rabid fans, or "fiends." Living the hardcore ethos of the time, the Misfits released their own records and merch, and played small shows across the US.

In contrast to the minimalism and communalism of their hardcore contemporaries, however, who clustered in insular scenes, spurning artifice (and often musicianship) to strip punk down to harsh bursts of sound meant to leave outsiders mystified, the Misfits crafted ornate aesthetics around a sound that was "accessible, strangely familiar, and utterly digestible," in the words of James Greene Jr., author of the Misfits biography *This Music Leaves Stains*.[7] The band remained aloof from the tribal DIY scene on the nearby Lower East Side, with its violent sectarianism and strict code of musical austerity, instead orienting nationally, along with sister band Black Flag. Perhaps this contained the germ of the rock star ambitions the core members would later reveal. Among the many recriminations later hurled between them were claims that Danzig had calculatedly monopolized royalties, at a time when few in hardcore were bothering to even copyright their material, amid his own insistence that the Caiafa brothers would have rather sounded like Van Halen and Judas Priest than a hellish choir of predawn corpses come to life.

On the surface, the Misfits' canon was bubble gum American pop culture: comic books, Top 40 rock and roll, classic Hollywood, and above all, the B monster movies syndicated endlessly on pre-cable television. But this was no fantasy of return to the good old days; as America came apart at the seams in the aftermath of the turbulent 1960s, the Vietnam war, economic crisis, and the beginning of decades of downward mobility, the Misfits ghoulishly perverted the nostalgia for "Happy Days" that terrified suburbanites clung to in the encroaching night of American decline. At their hands, the James Dean imitating greaser of yore, since neutered to become the family-friendly Fonzie, was reimagined as a corpse-painted ghoul out cruising the darkness in search of ultraviolence. The harmless idyll of suburban Halloween was recast as a ghastly terror of mutilation and murder. In short, there was no golden age to return to.

The violence and grotesquery of the present had always been there. The Misfits revealed the fantasy of postwar Americana so cherished in the popular culture to be a thin veneer stretched atop brutality, barbarism, and pornographic violence.

Danzig's legendary baritone vocals tell the whole story. He can intone with the likes of Roy Orbison, the Righteous Brothers, or even the King himself, conjuring the apex of the harmless, American Bandstand rock and roll carefully shorn of its Black roots. But nobody could confuse Danzig's lyrics, like "the maggots in the eye of love won't copulate" or the strange Jaqueline Kennedy sexual fantasy of "Bullet," with those of "Unchained Melody" or even "Burning Love." In Danzig, the stately crooner had gone haywire, like some malfunctioning cyborg from *Westworld* or *THX-1138*, and in the place of coy innuendo and familiar comfort, was spouting almost unimaginable morbidity and filth. And like the Ramones before them, the more these freaks pledged allegiance to American pie, the more grotesque, barbaric, and stupid it appeared. Rock nostalgia was recast as a collection of miniature skulls hung up on some maniac's wall.

The genre of horror was particularly easy pickings. Gothic literature and Hollywood monster movies have become a harmless part of the cultural canon, as young children dress up like zombies, vampires, and Frankenstein's monsters each October. This is because horror is a genre that allows ostensibly normal people to work through their deepest fears, insecurities, and the desires they wish they didn't have, all in a socially acceptable way. It is therefore easy to lose sight of just how grotesque the subject matter of horror actually is—and many fans would be happy to keep it that way. But Misfits listeners were assaulted with the crimson reality of this cultural tradition: murder, disfigurement, rotting flesh, perverse sexual desires.

It was the Misfits' revenge on the world they wanted to destroy, and was not limited to horror. The Misfits took prurient glee in the popular fixations of Patty Hearst ("She"), JFK ("Bullet"), Sid and Nancy ("Horror Business"), Marilyn Monroe ("Who Killed Marilyn?"), and a whole society of voyeurs "blue from projection tubes" ("Static Age"), glued to their televisions, mesmerized by the spectacle of it all. By sharpening the dull edge of Hollywood nostalgia with turbo-speed aural blasts, they effected, in Greene's words, "the ultimate marriage of Ramones and Romero."[8] Unfortunately, they couldn't keep from tearing each other to shreds.

You Bet Your Life There's Gonna Be a Fight

It is often said that tension between band members propels a musical act forward for as long as it can last without being ripped entirely apart. If this is true, as Greene so dutifully chronicles, the Misfits are case in point. By all appearances, the band was simply never big enough for Danzig and anyone with a mind of their own, especially Jerry Only. "When you put two tigers in the cage," Only recently reflected, "it's an issue."[9] These uneasy dynamics, compounded by the band's lack of commercial viability, led to their abrupt 1983 demise. For the better part of the next three decades, Misfits traded petty barbs as they soldiered on in the strange afterlife of performers whose defining moments came in a youth ever receding into the past. Danzig enjoyed some mainstream success as a solo performer, supplemented by the royalties he enjoyed as the sole credited Misfits songwriter. The Caiafas alternated between work in their family's shop and attempts to cash in on the notoriety of their old band, which only seemed to grow with the passage of time.

The Misfits may not have broken into the mainstream in their heyday, but true to form, their walking corpse has haunted nearly every corner of the Earth in the time since. In the early 1990s the so-called alternative scene, built on the foundation of early hardcore, became a worldwide phenomenon. Suddenly the Misfits were being reverentially covered by chart-topping acts like Guns 'n' Roses and Metallica, as Danzig's star rose, in its own right, in the genre of metal. The other Misfits had long disputed Danzig's claim to sole ownership of the band's rights, and this sudden bankability of their recordings led to a legal reckoning. This included the sale of their entire catalog, and the subsequent distribution of royalties to the musicians who had played on Misfits records.

The settlement also enabled the 1995 emergence of a Caiafa-led Misfits *sans* Danzig, which toured extensively and released two pop punk albums featuring a young vocalist named Michale Graves doing his best Danzig impersonation. As this so-called Misfits lineup fought to establish itself outside its creator's shadow, ongoing bad blood with Danzig forced fans around the world to take sides on what is essentially a Lodi, New Jersey, playground beef. For instance, my high school friends and I, who became rabid fans around this time, were happy to cast our lot with Danzig, refusing to indulge "The Newfits" with ticket sales or even a fair listen. (In hindsight, I can now admit: not too bad!)

HYBRID MOMENTS

The Only-led Misfits limped into the twenty-first century, shedding Doyle in 2000 and Graves in 2001. To sweeten the pot for fans, they added stints from marquee punk veterans Marky Ramone, Dez Cadena of Black Flag, and the return of Black Flag and former Misfits drummer Robo, for concerts that increasingly became star-studded exercises in punk rock karaoke. Jerry Only, and whoever was around him at the time, also produced a couple of nominal Misfits records, often featuring himself on vocals, which were inferior to even the recordings with Graves. In a dramatic twist, Doyle effectively switched sides during this period, appearing episodically with Danzig throughout the aughts and into the teens to perform Misfits songs on Danzig tours, which remained commercially viable, even if the heights of Danzig's stardom were behind him.

In 2005, Danzig initiated copyright complaints over Only trademarking several Misfits logos, including a version of the iconic Crimson Ghost, which Danzig had himself taken without permission from the 1946 film of the same name. Only's persistent use of these copyrights led to Danzig's filing a 2014 lawsuit, asserting him to be "the creative force behind the band" dating back to 1977. Characteristically, the filing argued Only's "primary qualification [for joining] was that he had recently received a bass guitar for Christmas."[10] While Danzig's claim was thrown out by the overseeing judge, negotiations between the two camps took a surprising turn: discussion moved from squabbling over forty-year-old intellectual property and trading childish barbs, to ironing out the logistics of a Misfits reunion with Danzig on vocals.[11]

It shouldn't have been much of a surprise; each party had entered the suit seeking to maximize their profits from the Misfits brand, and this was most certainly the way to do it. By 2016, Danzig and Only had agreed to an arrangement that split the profits between them, treating Doyle as a hired employee, along with an unspecified drummer, ultimately Slayer's Dave Lombardo. Putting a fresh spin on Romero, a cynical James Greene Jr. quipped: "When there is no more room in court, the Misfits will reunite."[12]

Come Back and Bite My Face

A longtime fan, like me, who had never seen the Misfits play, Greene nonetheless refused to attend the 2016 reunions. He dismissed the shows as "a legal resolution, an agreement between Glenn and Jerry so they stop dragging each other to court over pictures of skulls they stole from somebody else in the first place."[13] After skipping the first two shows, he explained: "I felt skepticism that any of this would really go down, or that it might veer into disaster if it did. The venue struck me as wrong; the Misfits in their glory days were always a club band.... And, of course, this assembly is not really the original Misfits—it is Most of The Original Misfits Featuring Dave Lombardo." Ultimately, though, he added: "Yes, I feel some regret."[14] (My reasons were less complex: I was broke and legally disallowed from leaving New York City.)

Naturally, massive concerts like Riot Fest trade the supposed authenticity of seedy clubs and extensive touring for a small number of guaranteed paydays, backed by corporate sponsors and financers, drawing large numbers of a band's most affluent fans to one place, flush with cash for high-priced tickets and merchandise. Was it punk? Probably not. But are the Misfits? Hardly. Today they are affluent old men who have been suing each other for decades and cashing in on their past whenever possible. Not that I really blame them. They must be asking themselves how much longer they can go out there and perform, and are likely just saving up for retirement. As a teenager, sheltered in a house financed by my parents' lives of toil, I found it unpardonable that a punk band would compromise their integrity for something so trivial as money. Nowadays, I look at reunion shows, reissues, festivals, and merch as an understandable solution to a problem I now know all too well: paying the bills. And the money appeared to be good. A spate of Misfits shows in different US cities came and went in 2017, 2018, and 2019, crossing the threshold of the ten appearances that Danzig and Only were on the hook to play as part of their legal agreement. This meant they could actually tolerate each other for reasons other than compulsion by the law.

Meanwhile, I was too broke to even entertain the idea of paying more than $15 for live music, much less traveling for it. By 2022, however, my fortunes had improved. Employed as a professor in the Chicago area, I was flush with disposable income, graying at the temples, and increasingly sentimental about punk rock, which now stood for a world of freedom and immediacy from which I had been exiled by the passage of time and my entry into the professional world. In other words: I was the perfect mark for an expensive Misfits reunion at Riot Fest.

Entrance into Heresy

The atmosphere at Riot Fest was surprisingly mellow; the $120 ticket price seems to have kept the rowdiest punks on their barstools cursing the corporatization of it all. The audience ranged from hordes of teenagers—desperate, as I had once been, for an authentic world outside their monotonous suburban life—to a comfortable number of fans who made me feel young. I saw no evidence of protest by locals, save for a wheat-pasted flier: "No Mega Fests in Douglass Park / Parks for Play Not Profit." On the other hand, a number of ostensible locals looking to make the best of the situation posted up on the sidewalks outside the fest selling food and alcohol to attendees, or else just partied bemusedly amid the chaotic swarm of drunken outsiders. I don't drink, and attended alone. This was a solemn occasion.

Inside the confines of the privatized park, I took a carefully engineered trip down memory lane, with a soundtrack provided by Bad Religion, FEAR, Seven Seconds, and the almighty Madball. Looking around, though, it was clear that most people were there for one thing. Some packs of young fans sported corpse paint and even devil locks. The Crimson Ghost was everywhere. Now that this image pops up in films, music videos, and shirts worn by celebrities like Demi Lovato, XXXTentacion, and even Justin Bieber, one can forget just how creepy it is. The Crimson Ghost is the uncanny superimposition of a skull mask over dispassionate, dark-ringed human eyes, flashing a punctuated grin, and effecting thereby the perfect marriage of horror camp and flesh and blood brutality. The result is truly unsettling, and it was ubiquitous. One young woman advertised the Crimson Ghost, alongside an inscription in the Misfits font that took Danzig's most extreme lyrics—"I've got something to say / I raped your mother today" and turned them into the positive affirmation: "I practiced consent today." Another boasted a message far less ambiguous: "Fuck Glenn Danzig."

The Misfits were slated in the headliner spot, running from 8:30 to 10:00 pm. As the clock creeped toward showtime, and the crew toiled in the dark, amplifier stacks stenciled with the Crimson Ghosts amassed where the Misfits would soon play. The stage was framed by two massive jack-o'-lanterns, their faces contorted evilly, belching dry ice, tokens of the band's enduring commitment to Halloween store schlock. This setting was topped off by a massive wall of video screens, black like monoliths from Kubrick's *2001: A Space Odyssey*, but soon to come to life, signaling the Misfits arrival at a twenty-first century corporate rock event. Their stage was bordered to the left by an equally large screen featuring the current band playing on the stage next door, Gogol Bordello, a frenzied Romani-inspired punk ensemble. Concerts like Riot Fest minimize the often-excruciating dead time inherent in the club experience by placing two headliner stages side by side, resulting in nearly no waiting between bands. It is one of the perks of paying a small fortune for punk rock.

In all my strained imaginings of this improbable moment, I had not planned to get anywhere near the stage. I envisioned broken bodies in the death rock dance hall as a mad dash of monster kids responding to Danzig's murdergram pushed and shoved each other for hundreds of feet in every direction. In reality, I was able to politely meander through the crowd, up to within about twenty-five feet of the stage. I had expected to endure a miserable crush, but even after getting close enough to the stage that I could have been seeing the show at a midsized club, standing room was comfortable, and the audience considerate. This just added to the dreamlike quality of an event I increasingly believed could not possibly be real. At last, the lights went dark on Gogol Bordello, and the piped-in sound of forlorn spooky wind signaled that either a Spirit Halloween store had opened nearby, or the hour of the Misfits had come.

This Ain't No Fantasy

I had never laid eyes on any Misfit in the flesh, and seeing them walk on stage was truly a monster movie come to life. Jerry Only, smeared with his football-inspired ghoul makeup, sporting the signature devil lock, and enveloped in his spooky spiked jacket. The corpse-painted behemoth Doyle, shirtless and hulking, more muscular and menacing than he appears in photographs decades old. And Danzig, the olive oil-voiced ringmaster of this devil's carnival, his signature black hair blowing in the wind, and his iconic Samhain belt buckle put to the test by a quarantine fifteen (or two), but holding it all together to make him as formidable a presence in person as in the ethers of punk lore. By this point, if Frankenstein's monster himself had lumbered onto the stage and picked up a guitar, I wouldn't have second guessed the scene. It was intense enough to see them all just standing there, so thrilling, so satisfying, that I momentarily forgot I had come for any other purpose. But then they started to play!

Here is where I wish I could say: "With that first errant note, I realized I had made a tragic mistake. The Misfits appeared old and worn out, bungling their old songs, and bearing no resemblance to the musicians who furnished the soundtrack of my youth. This is when I realized that Johnny Thunders was right, you *can't* put your arms around a memory. What's more, in that moment I accepted that the Misfits were never mine to be nostalgic about; my fascination with them bears no resemblance to an actual band from Lodi, New Jersey, but was instead the product of my own extreme alienation, not just in place, but in time, sufficient for me to ensconce my life with music written before I was born. In reality, I have no real relationship to the Misfits beyond that of a consumer, and a latecomer at that. And anyway, that's for the best, because some of their most classic songs, like 'Die, Die My Darling,' contain troubling themes that today appear hopelessly dated, perhaps offered at the time for adolescent shock, but still boldly trumpeted by their creators long after they have shed the alibi of youth. And what was I doing at the enclosed commons of Riot Fest anyway? Where was my class consciousness? So I promptly turned my back and departed, emboldened by the words of James Green Jr.: 'I never saw the Misfits when Danzig was in the band between 1977 and 1983. I'm keeping a streak alive.' It was the last time I would ever listen to my old friend Andy."

Alas, I cannot say any of this. The Original Misfits is the coolest shit I've ever seen!

At once, the massive metal stage, closed on three sides and sheltered by a protruding roof some seventy feet in the air, lit up to assume the appearance of a great spacecraft landed on a barren field bearing its angel mutant cargo. The Misfits launched into "20 Eyes," conjuring the body horror fantasy of a human mind overpowered by visual stimulation: "When you're seeing twenty things at a time / You just can't slow things down / When you're seeing twenty things in your mind / Just can't slow things down." This is precisely how I felt for the next hour and a half. Where to look? What to do? Sing along? Dance? Feast on human flesh? I leapt in the air and my sunglasses immediately fell out of my pocket and were stomped to oblivion; no matter, I wouldn't be needing those in the crypt! A dusty circle pit opened up and I remembered Folk's insistence that it was a very special thing to be able to mosh to the Misfits, so I alternated between a few goes round, and then rejoining the thousands-strong singalong unfolding all around me. My overloaded ego came tantalizingly close to achieving what Freud once called "that oceanic feeling" attainable only by religious experience or extreme drug use, and I would interrupt these rare and precious moments only to remind myself: I'm actually seeing the Misfits!

The reunited Misfits are heavy and mean, thanks in no small part to Lombardo's relentless propulsion, which only stepped on the songs' toes once or twice, few enough to be forgiven. Their sound bears the hallmark of the thrash metal genre, which spawned in the years following the band's breakup thanks in part to the band's own influence, and now lends all of their music heavier and more aggressive tones. It was tempting to bemoan this souped up Misfits as an inauthentic departure, but following the Caiafas' increasingly corny appropriation of the band's brand over the decades, the present lineup is akin to Wes Craven's 1994 *New Nightmare*, which rescued Freddy Kreuger from the dopey camp of the latter-day sequels, making him faster, more violent, and much scarier, while reminding the audience that corny wisecracks aside, this is the supernatural form of a deceased ghoul who rips children to shreds in their fucking dreams. And in many ways, this was just the Misfits picking up where they left off in 1983; their final record, *Earth A.D.*, traded B movies, comic books, and Ramones beats for visceral scenes of realistic carnage, matched by music far heavier, faster, and darker than anything they'd done before.

The violence of the Misfits' music was not disappointed by their presence on the stage. Doyle, in particular, plays his guitar with such beastly ferocity that he was either out of tune or missing strings by the end of every song, and began a steady rotation between multiple instruments—also explaining the unassuming presence of hired gun Acey Slade, set off in the back left corner, also playing guitar. Only was busy smashing his bass seemingly every ten minutes, and immediately producing an identical one in its place, erasing whatever doubt I had that he is a living cartoon character. Danzig strutted and puffed his chest, never getting winded as he belted out one classic after another at perfect pitch. The trio bounced around the stage, either having a great time or doing a damn good job pretending. They even seemed warm toward each other, which was surprising, but must be easier these days, with no broken-down tour van to return to for endless drives on a shoestring budget. The Misfits rocketed through "Walk Among Us," getting about halfway before Danzig began to complain that they "had to" play those songs, but soon enough they'd play whatever the crowd wanted to hear. And sure enough, they played almost everything I could think of, for nearly ninety minutes. It was so impressive to see these guys thirty years my senior tearing it up for as long as they did; by the halfway point, I was completely exhausted!

Moments Like This Never Last

Cynical as I am about these things, I initially waited for the euphoria to wear off, for me to begin noticing things ugly, shabby, and mean that would shatter my good time. Surely I could have scrutinized Danzig's stage banter, including some dumb quips about the Chicago murder rate and a predictable lament about "cancel culture" (as if he wasn't headlining a massive festival), to cast myself as too politically pure for this problematic affair. Or I could have balked at the elaborate lightshow, including blinking strobes, the unofficial beacon of shitty corporate music. I could have taken further issue with the barricade between the band and the crowd, that primal enemy of punk rockers, or the giant television screen, calling to mind the Misfits' derisive anti-TV dirge "Static Age," or the fact that two of the five men on stage could not be considered "Original Misfits" by any stretch of the imagination. But as the Misfits powered on, I simply became obsessed with the fact that their set would not last forever. Breaks between songs became unpardonable interruptions. Ten o'clock approached like my execution. And finally it came. The speakers went dead, the lights came down, the Misfits returned to being Glenn, Jerry, and Paul, and I was left wandering through a dark field with thousands of other survivors of this beastly bacchanal, our mouths still bloody from the feast, condemned to figure out what had overcome us.

One strange detail I keep returning to in the week since Riot Fest is the T-shirt bearing the détourned lyrics of "Last Caress." It is a defiant retort to one of the most heinous declarations in musical history, words made doubly despicable by their presence in the catchiest, most radio-friendly rock and roll melody of the entire Misfits cannon. The lyrics of "Last Caress" were no doubt calculated to cause maximum shock and revulsion in the listener, as it surely did to me. It would be obvious for someone, especially in today's polarized cultural terrain, to hear this song and denounce its creators and all who would dare hum its tune. But maybe that's too obvious, too predictable, and perhaps playing right into Danzig's hands. So this fan had refused to flinch. She stared straight in the Mona Lisa smile of the Crimson Ghost, and grinned back. The music of the Misfits, the profound sense of alienation from which it sprang, and the belligerent desire to chart one's way out of it, all belong to her just as much as anyone else, including the author of the song himself.

This is nothing new. Since its inception, interactions between many punk musicians and their audiences have been antagonistic, even violent, or else characterized by an uneasy tolerance rooted in the acknowledgment that the role of each requires the other. This detachment comes in handy, because many aging punk musicians like Danzig have grown hopelessly out of touch with the world, but still insist on adopting the contrarian posture that characterized their youthful work. For many fans like me, the most dangerous time at a punk rock reunion show is the dead space between songs, when the vocalist decides to give the audience an offbeat take on current events—which may sound edgy and subversive to the speaker, but usually ends up being a load of reactionary crap.

Ultimately, it doesn't really matter, though, because punk is oedipal; our heroes exist to be destroyed. Far from a coherent musical canon, punk denotes a particular feeling, an out-of-placeness with the world and disrespect for all things holy. Authorities and elders are treated with suspicion and derision, like the father who must be killed, or the fool crowned king. The savviest of all are the ones who are in on the act: the villainous frontman, like FEAR's Lee Ving, who taunts the crowd, using incendiary language and insulting gestures, and is jeered in return, theatrically reenacting the struggles against authority, and for self-determination, which characterize the lives of young (and not so young) people who follow punk rock. In this way, punk is a bit like professional wrestling, though the violence is often real. And reveling in the pettiness, smugness, thin-skin, and Napoleon complex for which he has been known since the 1970s, Glenn Danzig has always been happy to play the role of heel.

If punk has anything clear to say, it can be summarized by some of its most recurrent lyrics: fuck you. Beginning with the Sex Pistols affirmation "no future"—or the Stooges' "no fun," or the Ramones' no anything—punk's strongest suit has been what Hegelians might call "determinate negation": defining itself through being opposed to all that exists. This can be a powerful and necessary posture, an essential rejection of a detestable state of affairs from which the new can spring—that is, assuming the new is affirmed in place of what has been rejected. Otherwise, punk becomes a mere posture, a stale performance

HYBRID MOMENTS

of rebellious promise forever deferred. On the "Rebel" stage at the corporate "Riot" festival so unwanted by its working-class neighbors, we witness the eternal reenactment of the failure to actually rebel. (Hegelians might call this "bad infinity.") Or worse yet, as critic Lester Bangs argued in an essential 1979 essay: "anytime you conclude that life stinks and the human race mostly amounts to a pile of shit, you've got the perfect breeding ground for fascism."[15] In the very least, this seems to have translated to a profound blindness to questions of race, gender, and other ways the suffering and powerlessness of the world so furiously denounced by punk is dealt out unevenly, to some of the people least represented on its stages.

In the end, I have to admit that trying to overly intellectualize this strange music, which gives unhappy young people a means of charting their own offbeat path in the world, feels just as unfair as the demand adult radicals have made of rebellious youth since the 1960s: to solve the social problems grownups can't. "Given the structural powerlessness of working class kids and given the amount of state pressure they have to absorb," write Paul Corrigan and Simon Firth, "we can only marvel at the fun and the strength of the culture that supports their survival as any sort of group at all. If the final question is how to build on that culture, how to organize it, transform resistance into rebellion, then that is the question which takes us out of youth culture and into the analysis of working class politics generally."[16] In this view, punk is something less than many of its leftist adherents, myself included, wish it were, and something more than what its apolitical fans want it to be, "just music." But punk will never be anything on its own—except for an outlet for disaffected people to find community, and just maybe, enjoy brief moments of real, communal transcendence, before returning to the grind of their everyday lives.

"If you're gonna scream, scream with me," Danzig bellows, in his finest legato. "Moments like this never last."

The Future Belongs to the Mad

This text first appeared on the *Hard Crackers: Chronicles of Everyday Life* website in June 2024.

■

"What are the roots that clutch, what branches grow
Out of this stony rubbish? Son of man,
You cannot say, or guess, for you know only
A heap of broken images, where the sun beats,
And the dead tree gives no shelter, the cricket no relief,
And the dry stone no sound of water."
—T.S. Eliot, "The Waste Land"

This summer marks the release of *Furiosa: A Mad Max Saga*, the fifth install-ment of Australian auteur George Miller's *Mad Max* franchise. Since its debut in 1979, the postapocalyptic, diesel-driven desert Wasteland of the Mad Max universe has become one of the most enduring tropes of world cinema, spawning hundreds of imitations ranging from the big budget Hollywood epic *Waterworld* (Kevin Reynolds, 1995) to scrappy microbudget grindhouse films like *1990: The Bronx Warriors* (Enzo G. Castellari, 1982), part of a distinctly Italian analog to the spaghetti western that scholar John Hay dubs the "pasta postapoc."[1] Music videos by artists as diverse as Tupac Shakur and Phil Collins have paid homage to Miller's dystopia, as its reach extends far beyond action cinema to literature, art, fashion, music, comic books, video games, and even that great theater of the American proletariat, professional wrestling. The term "Mad Max" itself has also

THE FUTURE BELONGS TO THE MAD

entered the cultural lexicon, as a metonym for an anarchic postapocalyptic world, evoking what is perhaps the most popular collective vision of the future toward which our present society is hurtling at top speeds.

"The way these stories arise out of the filmmaker is not a conscious thing," George Miller once remarked. "Those of us who did *Mad Max 1* were the unwitting servants of the collective unconscious, we definitely were, and for someone who was fairly mechanistic in his approach to life, for whom everything conformed to the laws of physics and chemistry, it is quite confronting for me to be suddenly made aware of the workings of mythology, and I'm in wonder of it."[2] Miller, who had recently discovered mythology scholar Joseph Campbell and his book *Hero with a Thousand Faces*, was referencing a distinctly midcentury theory of hero stories as transhistorically possessed of deep structural continuity. Setting this curious possibility aside, it is undeniable that Miller was also channeling a collective unconscious highly particular to the time and place in which he was making art. And if the enduring popularity of his vision is any indication, we are still stuck inside the historical morass that produced *Mad Max*, no matter how much we may spin our wheels in an effort to move beyond it.

A Few Years from Now

"Fifi Macaffee: They say people don't believe in heroes anymore. Well damn them! You and me, Max, we're gonna give them back their heroes!
Max Rockatansky: Ah, Fif. Do you really expect me to go for that crap?
Fifi: You gotta admit, I sounded good there for a minute, huh?"
—*Mad Max* (1979)

The original *Mad Max* begins with a breakneck cannonball run toward oblivion. It is, we are told, "a few years from now" and a rapid barrage of images welcomes us to the future: A decrepit industrial building labeled "Hall of Justice," with these very letters hanging askew, seems to crumble before the viewer's eyes. A forlorn highway painted with a skull and crossbones is adorned with a sign announcing fifty-seven road deaths that year alone, on the "high fatality road" monitored by the Main Patrol Force (MPF)—which a vandal has modified to read "Farce." A pudgy, juvenile cop from MPF, known commonly as "the Bronze" for the color of their badges, uses the scope of his sniper rifle to spy on an anonymous couple engaged in some of the only sex we ever see in Miller's dystopia, as his partner dozes off in the car, feet dangling out the window. A quaint wooden road sign indicates we are just three kilometers away from "Anarchie Road." It is a world, as cultural theorist Evan Calder Williams puts it, defined by an "apocalypse that has not *happened* but has been *happening*."[3] Unlike the subsequent films, *Mad Max* is not set after a cataclysmic event like a global nuclear war, but unfolds in the slow downward grind of a society coming apart at the seams.

The MPF cops' lackadaisical idleness is shattered by a call over the radio: a dangerous criminal known as the Nightrider has murdered one of the Bronze and taken off with his V-8 Pursuit Special, the fastest car in their arsenal. A scruffy biker with wild eyes and matching "mama duke" girlfriend riding shotgun, the Nightrider taunts the Bronze over their own radios with manic glee: "I'm a fuel-injected suicide machine!" he bellows. "I am a rocker! I am a roller! I am an out-of-controller!" One MPF squad car after another, painted to resemble flashy race cars, engages him in a raucous chase, tearing through the remnants of a downtown area known only as "population." In the process, these inept and overeager "officers" of some vaguely defined law wreak as much havoc on pedestrians and fellow motorists as does the criminal biker psychotically proclaiming himself "born with a steering wheel in his hand and lead in his foot!" Sometimes indifferent to the damage they're causing, other times celebrating it with sardonic glee, the cops desperately want above all else to keep moving—or "stay in the game" as they put it—as they drive their vehicles into the ground. Before long, though, all are stuck in place. Meanwhile, a disembodied MPF dispatcher cautions fruitlessly: "Remember, only by following instructions can we hope to maintain a successful highway program."

In between shots of the MPF's ineptitude and insanity, we receive glimpses, à la Sergio Leone, of their finest driver, one Max Rockatansky, played by a twenty-one-year-old Mel Gibson, as he cooly prepares to take the wheel of his own Pursuit Special. Max is in no rush, he will get his man. And he does, with almost absurd alacrity; no sooner does Max *appear* on the scene than the Nightrider's mad delusions crash and he is reduced to tears. "There'll be nothing left!" the Nightrider cryptically bemoans as Max closes in on him. "It's all gone." As the Nightrider deflates so too does his mama duke—there is no happy ending for this romantic duo's flight.

THE FUTURE BELONGS TO THE MAD

In fact, there is to be no happy ending for anyone. *It's all gone*, and *there'll be nothing left*. Facing the twilight of the modern world, and oppressed by the imperative to keep going at full speed, the Nightrider runs head-on into another, *unrelated* car accident, meeting the first of the franchise's many fiery demises. Exiting his own suicide machine, which can be counted on for plenty of homicides before reaching its final destination, Max looks on in mock horror, feigning innocence in the grisly affair as only a cop can do, as we see him all put together for the first time. Artistic flourishes aside, *Mad Max* remains a grindhouse affair, and the death of the Nightrider sets off an escalating spiral of vengeance between Max and a gang of menacing bikers that will transform him from a well-adjusted family man to the solitary Road Warrior of the sequels.

All told, there's not much original about Max: he's the sullen, leather-clad progeny of James Dean and Marlon Brando, especially the latter's seminal motorcycle movie *The Wild One* (László Benedek, 1953), visibly tormented by the violence that masculinity requires him to perform on others, and most of all, on himself. His harsh moral universe is largely framed by the law-and-order vigilante genre that gave us *Death Wish* (Michael Winner, 1974), and its overlap with the fascist archetype of the cop forced to break the law in the name of order, exemplified by *Dirty Harry* (Don Siegel, 1971). "Can't you see they're laughing at us!" Max's best friend the Goose wails as another criminal walks free at the hands of slippery lawyers and a broken court system. "I'm not a bad man, I'm sick," one of the film's biker villains insists when Max finally catches up with him. "Psychopathic, you know, personality disorder! The court, man, he said so!"

Predictably enough, when they are denied justice in the failing court system, Max and his cop colleagues find it on the road. "See you on the road, Scag!" one of them taunts a biker who has beaten his charges on a loophole. "So long as the paperwork is clean," McAfee subsequently tells the MPF, "you boys can do what you like out there." "With taglines like 'When the gangs take over the highways, pray he's out there somewhere,' and 'the last law in a world gone out of control,'" writes cultural theorist Travis Linnemann, "the film's narrative emboldens the fear and savagery of a lawless Australian frontier and offers the violent retribution of an unhinged cop as antidote."[4]

Meanwhile, this thin line between lawman and the lawless, often dramatized by morally ambiguous midcentury westerns like *The Good, the Bad, and the Ugly* (Sergio Leone, 1966), provides the primary narrative tension in the first *Mad Max* film. "That rat circus out there," Max warns the MPF chief Fifi McAfee. "I'm beginning to enjoy it. Any longer out on that road and I'm one of them, a terminal crazy. Only I've got a bronze badge to say I'm one of the good guys." As the violence intensifies, Max even quits the MFP and takes his wife and child to the countryside, fleeing the unfolding catastrophe into increasingly improbable and maudlin domestic scenes. But as with the Nightrider, the delusion of escape cannot be sustained; the bikers catch up with the Rockatanskys and brutally strike down Max's wife and son, and with them, his only remaining ties to society. Max then becomes resigned to the sort of nihilistic spectacle of automotive death satirized so deftly in *Death Race 2000* (Roger Corman, 1975) and *The Cars That Ate Paris* (Peter Weir, 1974), fusing eros and thanatos in the explosive cauldron of an internal combustion engine. Mimicking the Nightrider, Max steals a police V-8, wreaks the boilerplate vigilante vengeance that the audiences paid to see, and like the grizzled, world-weary protagonist of *Ultimate Warrior* (Robert Clouse, 1975), tears off into the literal and figurative Wasteland beyond our crumbling world, as the credits roll.

At the risk of stating the obvious, *Mad Max* is not without its clichés, many of them from avowedly right-wing cinema. "He will Lose Everything," jokes journalist Luke Buckmaster, "in a case that This Time is Personal."[5] The original 1979 film can be viewed as a rote and belated entry into a decade of thoroughly *mean* movies representing, in the most exaggerated and often racist terms, the decline of postwar Keynesianism and the advent of a world defined by chaos and secular instability, even for white people living in the imperial core. The whole biker genre launched by *The Wild One*, especially *The Wild Angels* (Roger Corman, 1966), built upon the juvenile delinquent panic cinema of the 1950s to depict society beset by nihilistic fiends aided by every variety of speed. Mimicking the descent of *Death Wish*'s Paul Kersey and countless imitators stripped of their liberal illusions by encounters with such a menacing criminal Other, Max helps bridge the idealism of postwar liberalism to the era in which Margaret Thatcher could proclaim there to be *no such thing* as society—a notion Miller carries about as far as it can go. Not to mention that the sheer virtuosity of the films' thrilling stunts, which render social collapse as an object of prurient consumption, can seem an awful lot like a celebration of antisocial behavior unmoored, at long last, from obligations to others.

THE FUTURE BELONGS TO THE MAD

It is especially tempting to consider the first film as celebrating nascent neoliberalism, as *Mad Max* bucked the traditional Australian model of government-funded cinema and relied solely on private investors—who made a fortune off the surprise international hit, reigning for twenty years as the most profitable movie of all time.[6] There's also the stubborn fact that many of Max's biker enemies seem to be queer, adding an uncomfortable dimension to their narrative role of menacing the nuclear family, and with it, society itself. In short, there is therefore a strong case to be made, along with critic J. Emmett Winn, that the franchise constitutes "Reaganite entertainment," and much cause for concern, first raised by Australian public intellectual Philip Adams, that the nihilism at the film's core makes Miller's dystopian vision little more than "dangerous pornography of death."[7]

All of this, however, requires reading *Mad Max* and its sequels as uncomplicated celebrations of the worldview they present, when they are in fact much more tortured treatments of the breakneck acceleration of capitalist society toward the irreversibility of a catastrophe which is already underway. Surely the postapocalypse often appears sexy and cool, but after all, this is the movies, and neither Miller's craftsmanship, nor the fun he has doing it, should be confused with endorsements of the Wasteland. Instead, the *Mad Max* films embody the deeply unsettling paradox of revulsion and seduction in the face of human disfigurement, destruction, and ultimately, total annihilation; they are faithful to the uncomfortable truth that the end of the world can be taken as an aesthetic object, just as self-destruction, on an individual or social level, can be hopelessly intermingled with extreme pleasure. Most importantly, the *Mad Max* films betray the nagging desire, however blunted by the intoxication of accelerationism for its own sake, to make it all stop, to reverse course, to escape. Central to understanding this profound ambivalence at the center of the *Mad Max* films is the foremost avatar of the suicidal stupidity of capitalist life: the personal motor vehicle.

Fuel-Injected Suicide Machines

"And which driver is not tempted, merely by the power of his engine, to wipe out the vermin of the street, pedestrians, children and cyclists? The movements machines demand of their users already have the violent, hard-hitting, unresting jerkiness of Fascist maltreatment."

—Theodor W. Adorno, *Minima Moralia:*
Reflections from Damaged Life

The industrial revolution and its consequences have been a disaster for the human race in the *Mad Max* films. Arriving at the scene of a grisly car wreck midway through the first film, Chief Fifi Macaffee casually remarks: "The old meat grinder's humming tonight, eh?" It was a common sight, not simply within Miller's fictitious world of "a few years from now," but in the director's own time as well. George Miller grew up in the small Queensland town of Chinchilla, part of a sprawling network of Australian suburbs which, like those in much of America, render the resident hopelessly dependent on the personal motor vehicle. Accordingly, one is also dependent on gasoline, the costly, poisonous, nonrenewable fuel upon which much of the world's infrastructure has been foolishly erected, most often at the direct expense of mass transit. "The main street of town on Saturday night," Miller recalls, was the domain of "just the kids in their cars. By the time we were out of our teens, several of our peers had already been killed or badly injured in car accidents."[8]

Like J.G. Ballard, whose 1973 novel *Crash* comes closer than any other cultural artifact to distilling the startling transformation of human subjectivity by automotive culture, Miller flirted with his craft while enrolled in medical school. Unlike Ballard, Miller actually worked for several years as a doctor, including during the development of *Mad Max.* "Working in the hospital I had developed a morbid fascination with the autocide we practice in our society," he later recalled, "every weekend I'd see so many young people who'd been killed, or maimed for life, on the roads. You'd see the road toll in the paper on Monday morning and it was accepted with a shrug. It was almost like a weekly ritual, with people being randomly selected out as victims, as sacrifices to the car and the road."[9] To help finance *Mad Max*, Miller and his creative partner Byron Kennedy operated a kind of private ambulance service, dealing often with the carnage of car crashes. The experience, in turn, solidified the concept of the film. "In mid-1975," recalled Kennedy, "in one weekend there were about twenty-five people killed on Victorian Roads. You could see that people had come to accept the fact that people could die on the

THE FUTURE BELONGS TO THE MAD   141

road.... So we thought there's probably some sort of basis for a feature film in that."[10]

There was no speed limit in Australia at the time, and a so-called hoon culture predominated, valorizing dangerous driving as a marker of masculinity, in practices similar to American drag races, games of chicken, and most recently, the consumerist spectacle of the "sideshow." And while the autocide Miller witnessed was—and remains—widely considered a fair trade for the supposed convenience and freedom afforded by the automobile, hoon culture demonstrates something far darker, and stupider, than this Faustian pact. This was Miller's great contribution to cinema: a sort of automotive death drive, a pointless celebration of the destruction of bodies and the ecosystems they rely on, which can titillate when it should repulse. It is no coincidence that film scholar Christopher Sharrett finds in Miller the depiction of Western "car culture" as a "collective repetition-compulsion propelling human-ity toward obsessional behavior and, eventually, suicide."[11] But Miller is not interested in scolding individual people for their callousness or ignorance—though there would be plenty of blame to go around. He is concerned rather with the objective reality of a total world, prefiguring and foreclosing alternatives, which leaves individuals with little choice but to play along with the thrilling spectacle of automotive death. A postapocalyptic scenario, then, becomes the perfect vehicle for discuss-ing the here and now.

In this context, it's useful to think back to the car chase that opens the *Mad Max* franchise, in which pedestrians are forced to dart back and forth, dodging madmen and their murderous machines, through a disgusting landscape of garbage-strewn cement. Far from science fiction, this is a common experience in much of the world, and in the US at least, it seems to have become far worse since the COVID pandemic, which apparently transformed stop signs and traffic lights into gentle sugges-tions. Car horns, intended to be tools to warn pedestrians and fellow motorists of danger, are used instead like the lungs of a petulant toddler. Meanwhile, in a sort of ordinary everyday arms race, cars get bigger and meaner every year. It is extremely difficult to opt out of this profoundly stupid world; in Max's universe, as in ours, the only alternative to tooling around in a carcinogenic cage is the still more dangerous and logistically daunting prospect of being caught without one. Such is the freedom afforded by car culture. And this sad paradox is nothing new. Historian

Cotten Selier describes the mass marketing of the automobile as "the crucial compensation for apparent losses to the autonomy, privacy, and agency registered by workers under the transition to corporate capitalism" in the United States. As workers became less powerful, they could feel more so on the highways—in between shifts, of course, and while the jobs lasted. "In contrast to the sensations and structures of the factory floor and the bureaucratic office that reminded workers of the imperatives of control," writes Selier, "driving still felt and looked like freedom."[12]

Today, the collapse of automotive employment, and many of the Steel Belt cities that revolved around it, coupled with the increasingly murderous nihilism of car culture worldwide, and the actually existing-apocalypse of climate change, give us a clearer sense of what promise that purported freedom really contained. This is particularly palpable around the historical conflation of automotive acumen with masculinity. Countless men, following in the footsteps of Max, cram themselves into muscle cars and absurdly large pickup trucks—most often with pristine beds—in an effort to procure, for outrageously high costs inviting all manner of financial predation, that most elusive of all prizes: *being a real man*. And it is unavoidable to note the similarities between Max's iconic 1973 XB GT Ford Falcon coupe and the Dodge Challenger—the car used by a young Nazi named James Alex Fields Jr. to attack a crowd of antifascists in Charlottesville, West Virginia, in 2017—are such that, as a casual internet search reveals, some owners have taken to modifying their Challengers to look like Max's "last of the V-8s."[13]

"Dodge has a bad reputation among car industry watchers," writes the venerable Marxist bard Jasper Bernes, "who believe it 'markets [its] cars to sociopaths.'"

> Ads for the Challenger are adorned with slogans like "Come at Me," "Ultimate Aggression," and tellingly "This Is America, Drive Like It." A reboot of a 1970s muscle car, the Challenger was released at the tail end of a series of nostalgic remakes of 60s and 70s models. Throughout the commodity boom of the 2000s, as oil prices rose on the back of the Iraq War, US automakers put out a number of these retro gas guzzlers, flipping the bird at the new century and its rising temperatures. They hearken back not only to a golden age of American automaking but to the prosperity that accompanied it.[14]

THE FUTURE BELONGS TO THE MAD

Fields, however, had as little of a chance of returning to the world "before" as did Max, no matter how fast he drove his muscle car and who else had to suffer for his macho delusions.

"When the motor vehicle no longer takes a man to and from his place of employment and home," writes gender theorist Ezekiel Crago, "acting as the means for him to prove his worthwhile masculinity as breadwinner for his family because the road no longer connects places of production, where wage labor is performed, and reproduction, where labor power is produced, it becomes a meaningless path. It is then reinscribed with meaning by becoming the only place left where a man can prove he is the master of his own destiny."[15]

This is, of course, a lost cause. "It's a town full of losers," belts Bruce Springsteen in the paean to automotive autonomy "Thunder Road," "and I'm pulling out of here to win!" The belligerence of this resolution is betrayed by its futility; there is, after all, nothing left to do "except roll down the window and let the wind blow back your hair." The inevitable outcome of the characters' "one last chance to make it real / to trade in these wings on some wheels," is that they will eventually run out of gas, road, or free time, and be forced, like the Nightrider, to face that "It's all gone."

It is here that the automotive fetish of the *Mad Max* franchise cuts to the heart of our society's breakneck dash toward annihilation. "The more you drive," remarks Miller in Alex Cox's 1984 punk rock epic *Repo Man*, "the less intelligent you are." The subjectivity that has arisen around the personal vehicle is the purest distillation of the suicidal myth of the monadic individual, at war with the world, obsessively locked in a high-octane death race toward the vanishing point of ultimate gratification. Communal bonds and the well-being of others, represented by crosswalks, climate accords, and other suspiciously feminine encumbrances to gasoline-powered libidinal discharge, are unacceptable checks on the autonomy of the driver. Essential components of life—water, air, soil—are fouled, sometimes irreversibly, in the name of freedom, autonomy, and other cliches that mean nothing without strong communal ties and an ecosystem to support them. Automotive culture thus bridges the selfish, self-mutilating, sociopathic predation of capitalist subjectivity, especially the masculinity that has coevolved with the gas-guzzling death machine, with capitalism's intractable push toward the destruction of life on a global scale.

"We declare that the splendor of the world has been enriched by a new beauty: the beauty of speed," wrote Italian philosopher F.T. Marinetti in the 1909 "Manifesto of Futurism," part of the avant-garde of incipient fascism in Italy. "A racing automobile with its bonnet adorned with great tubes like serpents with explosive breath ... a roaring motor car which seems to run on machine-gun fire, is more beautiful than the [Greek sculpture] Victory of Samothrace."[16] Before long, the world would see just what that exaltation of mechanized speed, as an end in itself, would mean for the soft bodies of living beings, and the Earth they rely upon for sustenance. And today the consequences of this "new beauty" weigh heavily on any possibility of the future, and, increasingly, its impossibility.

Despite his distinction as perhaps the greatest director of automotive action, remarkably little of this is lost on George Miller. Reviewing *Mad Max*, film critic Jonathan Rayner cites multiple instances where cars are, far from the vehicles of boundless freedom, traps in themselves—as seen in the films' multiple crash victims consigned to perish within them.[17] "The motorcycles and autos of Mad Max," argues Sharrett, "signify a technology that has found little use but to be placed on a circular unproductive course, simply to be used up and destroyed."[18] It's not a stretch to say that the dead-end fate of automobile dependency structures the entire franchise. "It's a lot of stuff that is clearly exaggerated from the present," Miller remarked in 1982. "There was petrol rationing in Australia then, and it was surprising how quickly things degenerated. After just three or four days there was always some kind of aggression in the petrol queues. People's normal lifestyle was threatened, and they were suddenly going after each other. We had a lot of fun exaggerating that."[19] Such biting satire was, however, lost on many viewers from the start. Following the film's 1979 debut, Australian filmgoers sat in the parking garage above the theater, revving their engines.[20]

The Corpse of the Old World

> "One day cock of the walk, next, a feather duster.... So much for history!"
>
> —Auntie Entity, *Mad Max: Beyond Thunderdome*

The two *Mad Max* sequels of the 1980s take us beyond a society in decline and into the Wasteland following its complete collapse. *Mad Max 2: The*

THE FUTURE BELONGS TO THE MAD

Road Warrior (George Miller, 1981) begins with a narrated montage heavily inspired by the rise of Reaganism, the Iranian Revolution, and lingering insecurity held over from the OPEC oil embargo of 1974. "For reasons long forgotten," the narrator intones, "two mighty warrior tribes went to war and touched off a blaze which engulfed them all. Without fuel they were nothing. They'd built a house of straw. The thundering machines sputtered and stopped. Their leaders talked and talked and talked but nothing could stem the avalanche. Their world crumbled, the cities exploded. A whirlwind of looting, a firestorm of fear." We are also informed, in an act of creative retroactive continuity, or "retconning," that the original film was actually set in the *aftermath* of a great, singular catastrophe, rather than offering a more interesting (and realistic) glimpse of a gradual one unfolding in slow motion.

The *Mad Max* franchise has come to exemplify fallout cinema, and enduring radiation is a central theme of the later films, beginning with *Beyond Thunderdome*. But as in the original, overt nuclear themes are absent from *The Road Warrior*. Even the film's opening narration never suggests a nuclear war has taken place. Instead, Miller curiously blends footage of World War II with images of gasoline infrastructure, and global scenes of social unrest from the late 1960s. Significantly, the original script called for the pivotal events to be "A MOB OF ARAB STUDENTS storm a heavily fortified embassy and raise the Iranian flag," and "U.S. SOLDIERS LAND ... on a beach in the Persian Gulf and fight their way across the sand."[21] *The Road Warrior* is nonetheless underwritten by these events, understood however stupidly, as it imagines the world as an increasingly tribal battleground, in which bands of poison belching predators vie to expropriate the nonrenewable resource upon which it was built.

Simultaneously, and more intelligently, the film invites us to pay close attention to how social crisis transforms the individual human beings subjected to its cruel whims. "In this maelstrom of decay," the film's narrator continues, "ordinary men were battered and smashed. Men like Max, the warrior Max." Postapocalyptic stories are, of course, never really about the future. *Mad Max* was a distinct product of its historical moment, posing the problems of the downward grind of liberal democratic societies, increasingly irreversible ecological degradation, and the near-complete subsumption of human social activity into the commodity market. How, the films ask, are these extraordinary, objective shifts changing the ordinary people who are forced to inhabit them? Or, in the words of a latter-day Miller creation, the First History Man: "As the world falls around us, how must we bear its cruelties?"[22]

The Road Warrior finds Max already fully nomadic, tearing up the Wasteland's dirt roads in his "last of the V-8s," living simply to fill his gas tank. His MPF leathers have tattered and his hair grown shaggy, eliminating whatever distinction persisted between Max and the bikers at the end of the first film. It was in *The Road Warrior* that Miller and costume designer Norma Moriceau perfected the signature look of the *Mad Max* universe, fusing punk and BDSM gear with a distinctly orientalist treatment of tribal garb and other symbols of the mythic American and Australian frontiers. Whereas the bikes in the original had been superficially modified to appear appropriately futuristic for "a few years from now," the vehicles of *The Road Warrior* are gleefully pastiche abominations. And so too are the bad guys.

Led by the outrageous Humungus, nicknamed the "Ayatollah of Rock and Rollah"—the specter of crisis in the Middle East is never far from this film—Max's nemeses are tougher, meaner, and significantly *gayer* than even the most flaming of his foes in the original film, which is no mean feat. While Vernon Welles, the actor who plays Max's pink-mohawked nemesis Wez, has since denied any homosexuality in the film, it is difficult to otherwise explain why his character keeps a gorgeous young twink named "The Golden Youth" on a leash, and spends much of the movie avenging his death in a lover's fury—much less why the tribe is divided into two divisions, the "Gayboy Berserkers" and the "Smegma Crazies."[23] (What seems to be the lone heterosexual couple in the gang, we learn, even does it with the woman on top.) Befitting Max's own descent into depravity, however celibate, the Gayboy Berserkers appear as a squadron of uniformed cops who ride their cruisers into battle, sirens blaring. The film's misanthropic core is captured best by a prominent piece of graffiti on a broken-down truck rig: "The vermin have inherited the Earth."

The Road Warrior is largely based on the classic American western *Shane* (George Stevens, 1953), and, accordingly, a traumatized and self-exiled Max spends most of the film trying to avoid the social entanglements imposed on him by a small settler community that needs his help.[24] Led by one Pappagallo, the settlers have established a small defensive fort, built from the twisted metal of the past, around a small oil pump. But unlike the genocidal sociopaths who settled the

American and Australian frontiers, these settlers have made only the most perfunctory gestures toward building any sustainable community, and like the zombie shoppers of George Romero's *Dawn of the Dead* (1978), are stuck absentmindedly reenacting their petroleum-dependent lives from "before." This time, however, the community is forced to live in the nasty environs immediately surrounding an oil rig, as the distance between extraction and consumption is abolished and oil dependence is revealed as an utterly disgusting addiction. It's also a curse; possession of this resource makes them natural prey for the tribes of Humungus, who lay constant siege to the fort, circling it endlessly in an unsubtle evocation of the Indian raids of western lore.

Max, of course, just wants a tank of gas and to be left alone. But society nags him. "You're happy out there, are you?" Pappagallo scolds Max. "One day blurring into another? You're a scavenger, Max. You're a maggot. Did you know that? You're living off the corpse of the old world." In contrast to the leather-clad deviants outside their gates who howl with laughter when one of their ranks loses his fingers, Pappagallo's tribe appears dressed in white, care for each other, and speak of the future with hope. "We're still human beings with dignity," Pappagallo insists. But the horizon for their deliverance is quite literally a tattered old tourism brochure. "Paradise!" one of them tells Max, proudly brandishing its glossy depictions of improbably exotic climes. "Two thousand miles from here. Fresh water. Plenty of sunshine. Nothing to do but breed!" To their white surprise, holding onto the Wasteland is simply not worth the trouble. In a turn of events all too rare in the crimson annals of settler colonialism, this tribe wants to flee the outback, toward the coast whence their ancestors came.

The cheap moral binary posed by the bikers and settlers is simple enough, especially the part about breeding. Pappagallo's tribe is intended to set up Max at a crossroads common to the western, between working for a common good, or remaining one of the vermin he once fought, but has now become. But if this is George Miller's way out of the nightmare he has evoked, he can scarcely believe in it himself, and Max doesn't have a chance. In a tantalizing twist, Pappagallo's tribe detonates their oil well, and seemingly every vestige of the old world with it, and flees to the mythic north. While the film's culminating car chase furnishes us with twenty of the finest minutes of film to ever grace the silver screen, it offers precious few answers about how the settlers came to live otherwise once they escaped. For his part, Max cannot be persuaded to accept a ride in the film's literal deus ex machina, a small gyrocopter that we have already seen crash (anticipating the real helicopter crash which would, two years later, claim the life of adrenaline junkie Byron Kennedy). Whereas the opening montage had teased Max's incipient journey as that of "a man who wandered out into the Wasteland, and ... learned to live again," ninety minutes later, this promise is forgotten. Unchanged, except maybe for the worse, Max remains in the Wasteland, along with Miller, and the rest of us.

And this is where we find him in *Mad Max: Beyond Thunderdome*: a sunbaked Bedouin wandering the desert in a camel-powered wagon. No more interested in sociality than he had been before he "learned to live again," Max is compelled against his will to enter another conflict, this time over the future of a trading outpost called Bartertown. Founded by the charismatic Auntie Entity (played by the inimitable Tina Turner) under the banner "Helping build a better tomorrow," Bartertown is the closest thing to the old world we see in any of the *Mad Max* films. There's a legal system, a rudimentary money economy, leisure activities, and even an alternative source of electricity, based on methane from a small army of pigs who live beneath the town. "Where there was desert, now there's a town," Auntie Entity tells Max. "Where there was robbery, there's trade. Where there was despair, now there's hope. It's civilization."

Aunty Entity's leadership is, however, threatened by the man who controls the power grid, a dwarf named Master who rides on the shoulders of a simple-minded hulk named Blaster. The duo are imposing "embargoes" on Bartertown's energy. Max, dubbed "the Man with No Name" in an homage to the films' great debts to Leone, bumbles around Bartertown palace intrigue long enough to fall out of favor with Auntie Entity and be banished into the desert. There he encounters a group of white youths *gone native*. They have survived a plane crash, taken refuge in a small oasis, and created a tribal society premised on the messianic return of the plane's captain, who they now believe to be Max, who will lead them to a promised land. The film's convoluted plot leads Max and the children back to Bartertown, where they forge an alliance with Master, who is now held prisoner, and in the process of helping him escape destroy most of the town. Another chase ensues. Another flight to some ill-defined better world—this time, the bombed-out remnants of Sydney. Again, Max is left behind. And so are we.

THE FUTURE BELONGS TO THE MAD

"One might even ask," ponders journalist James Newton, "what right do Max and the Lost Children have to come and destroy Bartertown?"[25] At face value, there's really no good answer. The town's justice system leaves much to be desired—it relies on the literal spin of a wheel—and all conflicts are handled with fights to the death in the titular Thunderdome. But this isn't any worse than anywhere else in the Mad Max universe, and the existence of basic infrastructure, especially a distinct kind of renewable energy, seems a whole lot better. Quite frankly, it's unlikely that Miller thought much about the question, because the film never bothers to try to explain itself. It could merely be a side effect of his close emulation of *The Cars That Ate Paris* and *High Plains Drifter* (Clint Eastwood, 1973). But a better answer seems right under our noses.

Bartertown is Auntie Entity's best attempt to reconstitute the old world, rooted in commodity exchange and the *bellum omnium contra omnes* codified into civil law. Everything has a price, and human life is only as valuable as its owner can afford to be. Auntie Entity has made these ideas a reality in an impressive way. And that is *precisely* why Bartertown must be destroyed. While Miller is never clear how to move beyond the world he has created, he understands on some level that the reconstitution of capitalist society is a dead end. It is, he decides, better to simply destroy Bartertown before it can grow, than to treat it as the "left wing of the possible" which Max and the children can help reform. We are, after all, invited by the film's title to imagine a world *beyond* the Thunderdome. And as Tina Turner put it in "We Don't Need Another Hero," a song written especially for the film: "Out of the ruins / Out from the wreckage / Can't make the same mistake this time." Dare we venture that, in the explosive denouement of Bartertown literally caving in on itself, we can faintly hear the righteous demand, from which any imagination of a liberated future must proceed: "Death to Amerika!"

Lost in the Australian Wasteland

"Where must we go ... we who wander this Wasteland in search of our better selves?"

—The First History Man, *Mad Max: Fury Road*

The story goes that Miller first got the idea for *Fury Road* while crossing the street in Los Angeles.[26] It's easy enough to believe; watch enough of these films and it is difficult to not see them playing out all around you in the United States. Whereas *Beyond Thunderdome* had alienated critics and fans alike for taking Max out of his car and into a wasteland of sluggish melodrama, *Fury Road* is one big, loud, epic car chase evenly clocking two unforgettable hours of cinema. Besides being widely hailed among the greatest action movies ever made, and netting six Oscars, *Fury Road* is perhaps most notable for Max being something of a bit part. If Mel Gibson hadn't conclusively aged out of the role, his racist and antisemitic rants—first disclosed after, what else?, an arrest for drunken speeding—disqualified him as a leading man by the time Miller made the film. (This, despite the best intentions of that great fascist auteur, S. Craig Zahler.) Rather than center the film on a new Max, Miller gave the franchise its first real heroine: Imperator Furiosa Jabassa (Charlize Theron), a warrior truck driver serving the autocratic warlord Immortan Joe. In an archetypal enclosure of the commons, Joe's monopoly over fresh water, which he calls "Aqua Cola," ensures his absolute sovereignty. Immortan Joe thereby rules the Wasteland.

Fury Road is a story of defection and flight. Before we meet Furiosa, she has decided to abscond from Immortan Joe's heavily fortified, towering Citadel, along with five of his impressed wives who Joe has conscripted into sexual slavery in the seemingly fruitless effort to bear a child untainted by nuclear fallout. Her plan is to escape to the fertile land from which Furiosa was taken as a youth, the Green Place. Under the pretense of a routine supply run, the women sneak out of the Citadel with Furiosa at the wheel, one of them leaving behind the message: "Who killed the world?" What follows is an earnest attempt to escape the dead world by fleeing its core and building an alternative society on its periphery.

When Furiosa diverts her heavily armored "war rig" away from the ordinary supply route, one of Immortan Joe's "war boys"—radiation-poisoned men guaranteed short lives, organized into a death cult around worship of the automobile—asks where they are going. "It's a detour," Furiosa replies. This will prove truer than she realizes. Furiosa's exodus is fraught from the start, foiled by a double cross and overwhelmed by Joe throwing the entirety of his empire's resources into catching up with her. (In what would have been a clever topical joke if the film hadn't taken years to complete, Joe's cannibal accountant, the People Eater, scolds: "You, sir, have stuck us in a quagmire!") All the while, Max, captured by a war boy and stripped of his V-8, is largely along for the ride, though

THE FUTURE BELONGS TO THE MAD

his driving skills eventually earn him Furiosa's respect and he becomes an important member of yet another improbable and tenuously assembled team.

There is only one problem: the Green Place, that great Gaian refuge from the parched patriarchy of the Citadel, simply does not exist. All that remains of the Vuvalini, the tribe of Furiosa's youth, are a small band of grizzled nomads roaming the desert on motorcycles. Whereas Furiosa had promised the wives that these "Mothers" of the Green Place preserved a caring feminine alternative to macho brutality of the Wasteland, they are shocked to learn that these survivors simply kill anyone they encounter, like any other of its vermin. Like Max, who is still wandering in a traumatized semifugue state, there is no home waiting for Furiosa anywhere. Exiting the Wasteland is a sad fantasy. Evading the empire to live on its margins is impossible.

At this realization, and upon the urgings of Max, who finally emerges as the film's hero, the war rig turns around, headed *back* to the Citadel, to make war on Immortan Joe. *Fury Road* ends with Furiosa and Max returning triumphant, announcing the death of the great tyrant, and Furiosa assuming leadership, letting the water flow freely. The raggedy peasants outside cry "Let them up! Let them up!" as Furiosa and the wives are raised into the heights of the Citadel, where power resides and resources are hoarded. Max, as ever, cannot be compelled to stick around.

And why would he? "Miller," writes scholar Bonnie McLean, "creates a seemingly happy ending that reveals an uncertain future with no way to actually solve the world's problems."[27] Befitting the great hype around *Furiosa* being a "feminist" movie, perhaps we are to assume that Furiosa will be more benevolent than Joe, and that should be enough for us. If, as a popular meme at the time insisted, the answer to the film's central question is that "toxic masculinity" killed the world, perhaps Furiosa's "female masculinity" contains the seeds of a just society.[28] But the behavior of arrogant and callous men didn't kill the world, the capitalist mode of production did, and decades of "diversity, inclusion, and equity" initiatives have shown that the ruthless administration of a suicidal global order is remarkably flexible with regards to the race and gender of the individual technocrats. Given the objective limitations she faces, hemmed in by ecological collapse and the need to brutally ration what sustenance remains, it's unclear how Furiosa will be much different from her predecessor. Philosopher Sarah Kizuk therefore calls the Furiosa story "*Wonder Woman* with cars and leather harnesses and stuff."[29]

Furiosa is correct to conclude that liberation cannot be realized at the margins of a total world. But this insight remains a far cry from substantive social transformation. "We are unlikely to ever see a sequel to *Fury Road* where Furiosa's regime, like the 1917 Russian Revolution, has caused even more [sic] instability and oppression than Immortan Joe's," Newton concludes, "and now has to also be smashed and ruined in order for a better world to materialize."[30] This would, of course, be an almost necessary progression, in Miller's world as in ours. But Furiosa's assumption of power is a fitting end to a films that can be situated—alongside *Midsommar* (Ari Aster, 2019), *Poor Things* (Yorgos Lanthimos, 2023), and most recently Nathan Fielder's 2023 HBO miniseries *The Curse*—in the annals of powerful male directors obsessing over the purportedly waning relevance of men in the upper tiers of the American workforce. And by making the latest film a prequel, Miller opted to set aside, in classic Hollywood fashion, the problem of the day after Furiosa's seizure of power, allowing *Fury Road* viewers to savor her victory, provided they don't think too hard about it.

A marked departure from the frenzy of *Fury Road*, *Furiosa* is a sprawling visual poem of doomed deliverance, failed escapes, and tracks in the sand vanishing only to be followed anyway. Sniper fire rains down on unsuspecting victims, ending their lives before they even see what's coming. A pair of motorcycles are set aside for a romantic flight to a Green Place that we already know doesn't exist, or won't in the near future, but Furiosa and her lover don't even get the chance to use them and find out. Gasoline and fugitive supplies are spread across the desert sand as tokens of another foreclosed line of flight. We even glimpse the Green Place of Furiosa's youth in all its solarpunk splendor, knowing that within the space of two decades it will be reduced to a gray and lifeless bog. As the story begins, a young Furiosa picks an improbable fruit, signifying her permanent banishment from this paradise and its impending disappearance. "There is nowhere else," she is later warned, when plotting her return to the Green Place. "This is the Wasteland. Wherever you thought you were going doesn't exist."

While *Furiosa* is Miller's most ambitious effort at world-building yet—exploring the rudimentary division of labor between Gastown, the Bullet Farm, and the Citadel, and introducing a host of compelling new characters, like the First History Man, who serves up "wordburgers" of factual information from the world before the fall—more compelling than the story itself is the growing mood of claustrophobic enclosure that hems in young Furiosa, and everyone in her world, including Immortan Joe himself, on all sides. We know what is coming in *Fury Road*, and we see, time and again, how it could never have been any other way. Even Max himself is further reduced to a pure spectator; in a brief cameo, he simply watches the action unfold from afar, alongside his "last of the V-8s," which we know he is about to lose yet again.

"My childhood, my mother, I want them back," Furiosa demands. "You are never gonna get anything close to what you want," remarks the cruel warlord Dementus, who has taken these away, and knows better than anyone that he cannot return them. There is no recapture of an earlier time, no escaping the Wasteland. The film's final word is a particularly sour morsel of nihilism, as Furiosa declares: "Each of us in our own way will vanish from this earth. And then, perhaps, some uncorrupted life will rise to adorn it."

"One criticism that has been made of the Mad Max movies," writes Buckmaster, "starting with the first, concerns a perceived logical gap in the core premise. If they are based in a futuristic world where the scarcest, most precious commodity is petrol, why do the characters spend so much time hooning around in fuel-guzzling machines? Why not use methods of transportation that don't squander petrol, their most valuable resource—and the currency most important to their survival?"[31] Even the ordinarily astute critic Evan Calder Williams is too intoxicated with his own intellectual superiority to the films' premise—"one needs gasoline in order to drive around and kill others to steal their gasoline, but in doing so, one consumes the gasoline that one had"—to appreciate that this just might be the point.[32]

"Despite—or more likely because of—the focus on cars, speed, meta-morphoses, and escape," writes scholar Claire Corbett, who worked as an extra on the set of *Beyond Thunderdome*, "one of the main themes in these stories thus emerges as circularity, leading to an enduring sense of stasis despite the exhilaration of the long chase sequences."[33] *Furiosa* brings this into sharp relief. Befitting a prequel that culminates in the beginning of a long, circular chase, it bends the *Mad Max* franchise into a neat ouroboro. In the most extreme of anticlimaxes, the film concludes with the final of many returns to the start, with true escape never possible.

Surely George Miller, the great action auteur who has conjured the essence of car culture with the hallucinatory mania of Hieronymus Bosch, the problematic grandiosity of Leni Riefenstahl, and the urgency of an apocalypse already underway, does not lack imagination. The stuckness in place of *Mad Max*, then, however its colorful ensemble of characters can spin their wheels, is a far more profound reflection of the historical cul-de-sac in which even the most strident critics of advanced capitalist societies find themselves. Miller's characters can't go any further, because Miller can't go any further, because, simply put, virtually nobody can. Diagnosing such "crisis cinema" back in 1990, Sharrett observed: "contemporary culture is now at the stage of recognizing the bankruptcy of capitalism and patriarchy, but validates them anyway."[34] Decades later, not much has changed, except the tenor is more hopeless than ever. So what's left to do, besides race in circles?

Beyond the Citadel

"The world is already apocalyptic and ... there is no event to wait for, just the zones in which these revelations are forestalled and the sites where we can take a stand."
—Evan Calder Williams, *Combined and Uneven Apocalypse: Luciferian Marxism*

"Mad Max has effectively become a synonymous substitute for 'post-apocalyptic,'" writes John Hay. "But what other post-apocalypses have thereby been closed off?"[35] Hay's proposed alternative is positively puerile: the return of American chauvinism, via Kevin Costner's 1997 mawkishly patriotic film *The Postman*, which exalts the return of the US from an end-times scenario through the labors of a lowly postal worker. In reality, the presumed death of the United States of America is one of the few silver linings to be found in Miller's dystopia, and is also completely deserved, as the US has done far more than any other nation-state to make *Mad Max* real. To rescue Americanism from the ashes of an apocalyptic event, as Hay proposes, would be a giant step backward—and this, recall, is why Bartertown must be smothered in its crib. But what if Hay is closer to the answer than it might seem? What if the solution could be found in that which is simultaneously hidden and ubiquitous, in both the films of George Miller, and the societies whose death drive they represent so viscerally?

THE FUTURE BELONGS TO THE MAD

Taking a step back from the sheer enjoyment that the *Mad Max* films demand of the viewer, it is more than a bit jarring to realize how effectively Miller has crafted an entire mythology around tribal life in the Australian outback completely devoid of actual Indigenous people. As Claire Corbett writes, "images and references to Indigenous people in the Mad Max world are so evanescent as to be dreamlike, and yet they're unmistakably and critically present."[36] Token symbols like boomerangs and didgeridoos, and settler tropes like forts under siege by savage Indians, are nonetheless inhabited by white settlers reduced to "purposeful savagery," as Furiosa's love interest remarks of her in the latest film. *Beyond Thunderdome* is the most explicit in its simultaneous fetishization of Indigeneity and disavowal that it has any history in Australia predating colonization. "These images of white 'tribal' children with their corn-rowed and dreadlocked hair, dressed in skins, leaves, armbands, and loincloths, Corbett concludes, "seem to be almost mocking, adding the insult of parody to the injury of absence."[37]

This is hardly innocent. *The Road Warrior* was funded in part by billionaire mining magnate Lang Hancock, a far-right firebrand who publicly campaigned to end Indigenous rights to mineral-rich land, and even called for the "race" of Indigenous "half-castes" to be eliminated through eugenics.[38] The franchise has also figured in the broader cultural campaign to recast white settlers as *real* Australians. It offers "a mythic trajectory for Australia," argues scholar Delia Falconer, "in line with our emergent 'new nationalism,' in which historical relations must be ignored in order to facilitate a productive future, and settlement can be rewritten and authenticated as 'Indigenousness.'"[39] But it seems that what fuels the Indigenous erasure in *Mad Max* is a more banal, but no less destructive, function of the ordinary everyday ignorance that settler societies require of their adherents. And it helps explain the fundamental *stuckness* within which the series finds itself, and which it shares with the societies it represents. Unable to chart a way forward, and chauvinistically ignorant of alternative modalities of being in the world, all that's left to do is clutch firmly onto to the reins of the fuel-injected suicide machine.

"The Mad Max franchise constructs a collective national nightmare for non-Indigenous Australians," write anthropologists William S. Chavez and Shyam K. Sriram, "a society built by transported convicts and colonizers gone 'savage' following global catastrophe."[40] But does it have to be this way? Why, in the face of existential destruction wrought by capitalist modernity, should the turn toward indigeneity in settler societies be a *nightmare*? Is not the very problem of *Mad Max* the destruction of the Earth and debasement of its people by a society that has reduced life and land to so many interchangeable objects of exchange, to be depleted and destroyed as a matter of intrinsic, individual *right*? What else leads out of this morass but a new communal politics, grounded in an alternative spirituality capable of restoring true dignity to life? What would be so wrong with making a resource like gasoline sacred, to be used only on the most special of occasions, as part of a social system organized toward preserving the planet for generations to come? It is a sad irony, though supremely appropriate, that the very ways of being omitted from Miller's dystopia likely offer the elusive keys to moving beyond it.

"Land is the terrain upon which all our relations play out," writes Indigenous scholar Mike Gouldhawke, and it can even be seen as a living thing itself, constantly shaping and being shaped by other life forms. Land isn't just a place, it's also a territory, which implies political, legal, and cultural relationships of jurisdiction and care. Settler claims to sovereignty and private property are also relational—that is to say, transactional. They reflect the relationship between an individual citizen and their state, as well as a particular way of relating to one another and to the world—social and economic systems of domination, individualism, competition, and exploitation.[41]

The contrast is stark, and immensely practical: one world must be defeated, the other made to thrive. And it is all connected. "There will be no end to these wars of empire," wrote the recent student occupiers of Cal Poly Humboldt, in the indispensable publication *CrimethInc.*, "if the struggles in 'first world countries' don't develop teeth and begin to embody solidarity and 'land back' as more than symbolic gestures."[42] What this means concretely remains to be worked out in collective practice, but cannot be achieved with the same old fetishism of piggish imperialist "luxury," *automated* and *communist* or not. The necessary cessation and reversal of genocidal projects like American exceptionalism and Zionism must be accomplished alongside social practices that respect all land and life, and place their inherent value above whatever possibility for profit, or opportunities for antisocial "leisure," they provide.[43] This imperative will demand we develop more profound relationships with the world and each other, unmoored from the imperative

THE FUTURE BELONGS TO THE MAD   157

to constantly consume, traverse great spaces, and make a big mess in
the process, while also putting to rest the vapid valorization of luxury
consumption that has sadly come to transcend the class line. The solution for moving forward, then, is far closer to a politics of "degrowth."[44]
But it has likely yet to be given a suitable name, much less articulated
coherently.[45]

In his criminally understudied masterpiece *Heman Melville*, Marxist
intellectual Loren Goldner tarries extensively with another doomed
voyage straight to oblivion: that of the *Pequod* and its crew in Melville's
Moby Dick. Goldner situates the *Pequod*'s voyage within a crisis of a
bourgeois society deprived of the myths which once sustained it, and
therefore no longer able to believe in itself, but simultaneously unable to
accept that its only possible supersession is that of worldwide communist society. *Moby Dick*, Goldner argues, thusly follows "Ahab's demonic
self-destructive quest, the crackup of a whole civilization built on the
isolated bourgeois ego," as a grand parable in which a motley crew unified
by capital is unable to collectively reverse its suicide mission.[46]

The book's final hope, however dim, does not come from Ishmael,
the kind of disaffected, functioning-depressive intellectual who writes
wan and overlong scholastic reflections not unlike the present one, while
secretly coveting submission to strong men like Ahab who he claims to
disavow. Instead, Goldner argues, Melville invites us to consider that
the modern capitalist subject must rediscover the "antemosaic cosmic
men," harpooners Queequeg, Tashtego, and Daggoo, representative of an
older world of cosmological unity predating the divergence of logic from
mythology. These figures embody a communal metabolism with nature
that stands in sharp relief to Ahab's compulsive courtship of acceleration
unto death.[47] In contrast to the linear "great leap forward" wanly awaited
by Billy Bragg in song, this theory of history understands social change
as operating in a "'helical-vorticist' fashion, wherein elements of earlier
mytho-historical modes 'return' in higher modes."[48]

This is not a call for the vulgar appropriation of "Indigeneity"; there
are already enough white yoga teachers burning sage in the strip malls
of America as it is. Instead, Goldner invites us to formulate, within
advanced industrial societies, a profound engagement with *antemosaic,
cosmic* forms of life, which reject the reduction of life on Earth to so many
objects of manipulation and destruction. In place of the dead letters of
our blood-caked religious texts, a new spirituality is in order which sets

aside the psychosis of unseen worlds in the hereafter—a doctrine which, perhaps more than anything else, explains the popular apathy toward environmental destruction here on Earth—and places the preservation of the real world at the center. This should not be a set of "beliefs," in the common sense of being divorced from sensuous practice, but must be rooted in a practical engagement with existence that treats life and land as sacred.

And where better to start than the simple mantra of the 2016 antipipeline movement at Standing Rock, "water is life," under which a motley crew of rebels fought for a future worth inhabiting? "Whereas past revolutionary struggles have strived for the emancipation of labor from capital," writes Indigenous scholar Nick Estes, whose *helical-vorticist* titled book, *Our History is the Future*, draws clear lines from Standing Rock to the necessity for mass struggle: "we are challenged, not just to imagine, but to demand the emancipation of the earth from capital."[49] And at the center of this existential struggle is the unavoidable necessity of global communism. Any time spent clarifying this vital political convergence will be almost certainly well spent.[50]

At a recent memorial for Goldner, who died this past April, his long-time comrade Amiri Barksdale reflected on the enduring significance of *Herman Melville* for understanding our historical conjuncture. "Now that capitalism has well and truly swallowed the world," Barksdale remarked, "we are now all aboard an aluminum and carbon fiber *Pequod*, sailing a spectacular sea of lies, word salad, and AI generated content. Though it is now helmed by blinkered technocratic billionaires, they still believe their own lies, and are hoist on their own petard of arrogance and ignorance. Who else is aboard? What fires their passion for freedom? What do they want?" To chart a way forward, Barksdale concluded, it is imperative to "see the future in the present and in the past. That's the only way that Marx can be right in the 1844 manuscripts when he writes, from the future, that 'man returns to himself not as he began at the origin of his long history, but finally having at his disposal all the perfections of an immense development, acquired in the form of all the successive techniques, customs, religions, philosophies whose useful sides were—if we can be permitted to express ourselves in this way—imprisoned in the zone of alienation.'"[51]

Which brings us back to Max, hopelessly stuck in a distinctly deranged zone of alienation, awaiting the return of humanity to itself as a matter of bare survival. "The science fiction of a communist society is inspiring not when it is most outlandish and fantastical," write revolutionary scholars Phil A. Neel and Nick Chavez, "but when worlds fundamentally different from our own are shown to be nonetheless constructable from the mountain of bone bequeathed to us."[52] Such is the challenge to which we are invited by the *Mad Max* universe and its persistent failure to conjure a way out of George Miller's dystopia—as the need for real deliverance becomes a simple matter of survival. How much worse, one wonders, does our own world need to get, before this becomes common sense? "Who'd have thought 20 years ago," Miller observed back in the halcyon days of 1999, "that people would one day be nostalgic for the apocalypse?"[53]

Dedicated to Loren Goldner, a road warrior who hated cars.[54]

PART 4
LOOKING RIGHT

Three Months Inside Alt-Right New York

This text first appeared in issue 1 of *Commune*, Fall 2018, under a pseudonym.

During my three months inside New York's alt-right, the Daily Stormer Book Club never got around to reading any books. Instead, they plotted their move off the internet and onto the streets, drank beer, and shot the shit. Through the Book Club I entered a network of far-right activists integrating the old guard of white nationalism with millennial internet trolls while drawing new recruits from the websites and podcasts of online youth culture. Much of their shadowy organizing happens openly in New York City bars, sometimes within earshot of the normies.

This was early 2017. Trump's victory gave white nationalists a boom akin to what Occupy did for the left. In the year and a half since, the alt-right has been beaten back by the combined pressure of antifascist streetfighters, PR-conscious tech companies, embarrassing internal scandals, the disaster in Charlottesville, and most importantly, a critical mass of ordinary white people rejecting openly espoused white chauvinism—for now. But if the alt-right has demonstrated one thing, it's that ideological white supremacism, ingrained as it is within American society, can be remarkably versatile. When pushed back to the shadows, it won't stay there forever.

I didn't infiltrate the alt-right as a writing project. I wanted to do whatever I could to inhibit its transition from the internet to the streets, and decided I could help best by gathering information on the ground

THREE MONTHS INSIDE ALT-RIGHT NEW YORK

level. Looking back on this bizarre experience, I hope to provide a sketch of the people I met and the social world they inhabit. For brevity's sake, I've condensed ten meetups stretching over forty hours into a basic narrative that omits dozens of minor characters, focusing instead on the guys I got to know best. While it's impossible to abstain entirely from debate surrounding the origins of, and remedy for, the resurgent far right, my intent is rather to present this outré world to the reader faithfully.

I first became aware of the alt-right after the 2015 massacre in Charleston, South Carolina. The shooter, Dylann Roof, frequented an online hub for neo-Nazi news and social networking called *The Daily Stormer*. What surprised me most about the *Stormer* was its novelty. Irony-soaked meme culture flowed neatly into serious fascist treatise by an angry everyman named Andrew Anglin. Just below the surface of Anglin's humor lurked a ghastly bitterness and visceral disgust with politicians, celebrities, commercialism, and every imaginable sacred cow of liberal society. The *Stormer* offered a nihilistic rejection of daily life, to which Nazi politics almost seemed an afterthought. And in a way, it makes sense. As Sid Vicious demonstrated by donning a swastika, once you've become the sworn enemy of all that is holy, what's left to do but declare yourself a Nazi?

The *Stormer* led me to The Right Stuff (TRS) network of podcasts. Its expansive roster covers a variety of niche topics—*The Fatherland* for fathers, *The War Room* for veterans, *Fash the Nation* for policy wonks, *The Convict Report* for Australians, and so forth. TRS is a subcultural hothouse for memes and loyalty-cultivating in-jokes, such as the practice of placing three parentheses around a Jewish name, which extend far beyond the network's more than 100,000 listeners. Steeped in bittersweet nostalgia, TRS flagship *The Daily Shoah* harks back to '90s shock jocks like Opie and Anthony and pranksters like the Jerky Boys. The *Shoah*'s juvenile humor, with polished song parodies like "Summer of '88" (the code numbers for "Heil Hitler") set to the tune of the Bryan Adam's hit "Summer of '69," provides a cloak of irony for politics that have become sharper and more activist-oriented in the four years since it debuted.

I had encountered neo-Nazis before. They lurk on the fringes of every punk scene, kept at bay only by violence. But the alt-right movement, though no less contemptible, was different from the old guard of self-serious skinheads and Nazi costume players. Their podcasts sounded like my dorky high school lunch table, with many of the same jokes repeated verbatim. These were not historical reenactors. They were the kind of ordinary guys I grew up with in a downwardly mobile, opioid-soaked, white-flight wasteland. I could picture my old friends, numbing themselves to the banal brutality of the world with liquor and gallows humor, enraged at having been fucked out of a quality of life their parents had known, which itself wasn't that great to start. Now they are getting mad as hell, and who is helping them give their problems a name?

The Book Club

I spent two months on the *Stormer* message board, first posting a spate of generic comments, and only later inquiring about meetups. I was contacted privately by Tom, a thirty-something weed dealer living with his father on Long Island, who vetted me with basic questions about my background and intentions. Tom shared with me his vision for building a sophisticated neo-Nazi subculture, with study groups, weightlifting, fight training, and "something to do every night of the week." It would start with the Book Club, to which I was now invited.

In the end Tom didn't even show up, but the small group cackling at the edge of the bar was easy to spot. The meeting took place in a favorite spot for the Book Club, Williamsburg's Barcade, a haven for millennial transplants yearning for the return of bygone days. A deindustrial interior of exposed brick, reclaimed wood, and sparse furnishings aestheticizes the urban poverty largely evacuated from the surrounding area along with the working-class Puerto Ricans who once called it home. Archaic arcade games, invoking nostalgia for the days of Reagan, line the walls. Squarely in the center of liberal Williamsburg, Barcade may seem like an unwelcoming location for a neo-Nazi meetup, but Matt Philips expressed to me his confidence that "the white people moving to Brooklyn can be won over."

"The 1980s was a good time to be a white kid," he told me, taking the place in. "The pink and blue, the Miami Vice shit. It's coming back!" It was March 2017, and Matt had cause for optimism.

A goofy stoner in his mid-thirties, Matt is a dead ringer for Woody Harrelson. He had recently relocated from Alabama to the spot-gentrification surrounding the Jefferson Street L stop in Bushwick to work as a set designer. Matt showed me photos of trips to the Arizona desert, where his friends looked like the garden variety blend of hipster and hippie one encounters in North Brooklyn. Matt fit right in.

Matt never took much interest in politics before Trump, and his artistic sensibility put him at odds with his conservative father. The

THREE MONTHS INSIDE ALT-RIGHT NEW YORK

Trump movement kindled Matt's interest in politics, however, and brought him and his dad together. Through right-wing trolling Matt discovered the *Daily Stormer* and began participating in its forum. Gradually the political stakes of the alt-right got serious. He helped establish the local Daily Stormer Book Club, one of dozens of meetups like it across the country. By the time I met him, he was a man about town in the alt-right social scene.

For almost three decades, Matt's role model was Pete "Maverick" Mitchell from *Top Gun*. But that changed with the rise of Donald Trump. Matt loves Trump not because he's a serious leader, but because he's ridiculous: the hair, the orange complexion, the outrageous statements. Matt reposts the memes his liberal friends share ridiculing Trump. Chuckling, he showed me one of Trump in a child's car, honking the horn. But Trump isn't a joke to Matt. A president comes and goes every four to eight years, he told me, but a real hero is for life.

"That's what people want. It's why they love pro wrestling, and it's why they love Trump."

Eric Rajala, a hulking fast talker in his mid-thirties with a close-cropped "fashy" hairdo, and a lifelong wrestling fan, agreed. At eighteen Eric left an affluent New Jersey suburb to attend the University of Michigan, where he enjoyed sexual conquests thanks to "feeding women Long Island iced teas." After college, he complained, women stopped letting him get them drunk, and even worse, preferred the affections of nonwhite men. Eric researched new "pick up" tactics, discovering the Chateau Heartiste and My Posting Career. He began blaming his problems on biological differences between men and women, and soon enough, biological differences between races. Eric soon realized he had always been antisemitic, but lacked the vocabulary to express it.

"It was like taking a shit," he told me, "getting it all out."

Even after becoming a full-blown neo-Nazi, Eric continued to work at a liberal tech office and lives in Greenpoint. Despite his cushy job, fancy haircut, and soft hands, he represents himself as "blue collar." A sharp facilitator, Eric led our discussions, returning the most obscure tangents back to racial politics.

Paul Schmieder from Middle Village, a bald and stocky Queens native in his early thirties, matched Matt with exotic vacation photos of his own. Paul was an ordinary *Fox News* conservative until Trump came along and a coworker showed him the *Daily Stormer*. Paul found shock-driven laughs, and, increasingly, a new vocabulary to express his fears about a world changing all around him. For Christ's sake, he reported grimly, his neighborhood pizza shop was being replaced with "The Taj Mahal!"

Paul once ran a trucking company. But he was too young, he told me, and took risks. With twenty trucks in mortgage, Paul thought the growth would last forever. But in 2008 his mortgages abruptly changed hands, the premiums went through the roof, and he was finished. Paul now lives modestly, managing a concrete company in Brooklyn. He arrives fifteen minutes early, so nobody can give him any shit, and is happy just to smoke cigarettes in his office and take off for the day when his work is done. Paul also enjoys tweeting abuse at left-leaning politicians and media figures using his real name. Growing up in New York, Paul met plenty of Jews, including a childhood friend he still gets along with. "Sure," he admitted, "they're not all a part of the Zionist-Occupied Government." He admires that they take care of each other, and are serious about their customs. But none of this stopped him from getting the vanity license plate GTKRWN: "Gas the kikes, race war now."

Paul recalled a visit from his nephew, a college undergrad. After righteously lecturing Paul about his racism, the kid boarded the wrong train and wound up at Van Siclen Avenue in East New York. He called Paul scared out of his mind, stammering "you need to pick me up, I don't feel safe!" Paul replied "Why not? Those are your people!" But Paul was just teasing. Fearing for his nephew, Paul picked him up. He's a good kid, Paul reiterated, he's just had his head mixed up by college. Eric recalled his sister, who's an astrophysicist but "is stupid about a lot of things" because she spends all her time in the classroom with the "exceptions that prove the rule." How will she be handled if she isn't won over by arguments? He has clearly given this issue a lot of thought.

Eric then changed the subject to the alt-right's patron saint, Shia LaBeouf. LaBeouf's postelection "He Will Not Divide Us" project facilitated a kind of unity LaBeouf never could have imagined. HWNDU was intended to be four years of piously chanting "he will not divide us" on a livestream outside Long Island City's Museum of the Moving Image. Led by the self-serious LaBeouf, an affluent pretender easily provoked to rage, HWNDU was the perfect target for alt-right trolling, and its livestream became a place of convergence. Many from the notorious 4chan image board made their "IRL trolling" debut at HWNDU, networking with IRL fascists who held court openly at nearby bars. "Alt-lite" groups like the

Proud Boys mixed with the likes of Identity Europa. LaBeouf was forced to move the project out of New York, but the trolls followed him, and HWNDU was eventually abandoned. Thanks to HWNDU, Eric told me, "the New York City alt-right is completely cross pollinated at this point." Eric had even become friendly with a few Proud Boys, "who aren't as gay as Gavin [McInnes] ... but they're still pretty gay."

Emboldened by the crew they'd gathered, and lubricated by alcohol, the Book Club began to speak quite freely. It was an uncomfortable scene for me, sitting within earshot of other patrons and the Black bouncer. Eric gushed: "I know this is the same story every guy has, but it's just so nice to be able to hang out with guys and say stuff like 'nigger.' It's cathartic to just say it: 'nigger.'"

The Boys

Whiskey Trader on 55th Street is a cool cave of finished wood and flatscreens indistinguishable from countless overpriced Midtown bars. Perhaps homogeneity appeals to the alt-right groups who prefer these haunts, but in this case it is Whiskey Trader's proximity to Trump Tower that brought the Proud Boys there for a March 5 "Pro-Trump Bar Crawl."

The Proud Boys are a "Western chauvinist fraternal organization" comprising followers of *Vice Magazine* cofounder Gavin McInnes. They crib their worldview from McInnes's rants and *The Death of the West* by Pat Buchanan. Though McInnes cites prominent nonwhite Proud Boys against accusations of racism, Proud Boys spout ultranationalist, anti-Muslim, antiwoman, and antitrans rhetoric, sporting matching Fred Perry polos in the tradition of blue-collar hooligan culture. Long before street fighting erupted in Berkeley and Charlottesville, the Proud Boys embraced violence against leftists as a central tenet of their group.

This time I brought my friend Max from Long Island. Two uniformed cops guarded the door of Whiskey Trader when we arrived. The event's organizers, Chris Minervini and Sal Cipolla, paced around inside. Chris, in his late thirties, lanky and soft-spoken, works for Goldman Sachs. If he's been in a fistfight, I doubt he won. Sal is short and obese, always fidgeting, stammering when he talks, and supremely anxious to impress. An unlikely player in white nationalist circles, Sal is not "white," he's Latino. Recently fired from his office job after a Proud Boys exposé by antifascists, Sal was living off crowdfunding, hopscotching the country and starting up Proud Boys chapters.

Max and I introduced ourselves as working-class Trump supporters. After five minutes of macho man talk about fistfights, truck driving, and laying heavy pipes, they were sold. I mentioned my connection to the Book Club, and in order not to disrupt my cover story, identified myself as a neo-Nazi to every Proud Boy I met. That's fine, they all told me. Gavin has a strict policy: no Nazi imagery or language is allowed in public, and *especially* when you talk to the press. There's a pinned message in their private Facebook group stating this policy, they told me. Otherwise, you can believe and say whatever you want among other Proud Boys.

I mentioned I'm a fan of the *Shoah*, and Sal excitedly showed me his text messages with its host, TRS founder Mike "Enoch" Peinovich. "Mike and I text all the time" Sal beamed proudly, showing me dozens of messages as evidence. Sal claimed Peinovich and the rest of the TRS "pool party," their euphemism for meetup groups, were on the way. They never showed.

As the hours wore on, many Boys, and even a few women, marched into Whiskey Trader. They were mostly white-collar shitlords testing the waters of trolling in real life. I met one, among dozens, who worked with his hands. Their pristine "Make America Great Again" hats, displayed boldly in a pack, showed little evidence of prior wear. Matt from the Book Club showed up unexpectedly, and lots of people in attendance knew him. Despite their questionable racial composition, Matt later told me, the Proud Boys are an important bridge between normie conservatives and fascists. Additionally, he added, partying with them is lots of fun.

The bar crawl meandered through Midtown, a sea of red MAGA hats two-dozen strong chanting pro-Trump slogans along the sidewalk. We stopped at Faces and Names on West 54th Street, and then the Irish Pub across the street. There a uniformed cop approached Sal smiling and requested he stop tweeting our location, to avoid trouble from antifascists. Sal obliged. Later, a plainclothes cop approached a heavily intoxicated Sal, flashing his badge, and asked if the Proud Boys were having fun. Sal slurred yes, and the cop replied:

"Let us know if you need anything."

I shot an inquiring glance at Sal, who explained the police contacted him *before* the crawl, due to "insane" amounts of threats on his Twitter. When I checked Sal's Twitter, however, I didn't see many. A police escort trailed us throughout the night, even as the Proud Boys grew belligerently drunk, chanting "build the wall!" on the sidewalk, to thumbs up from

THREE MONTHS INSIDE ALT-RIGHT NEW YORK

tourist families and finance bros. At the Irish Pub, new Proud Boys were initiated by reciting:

"I am a Western chauvinist who refuses to apologize for creating the modern world!"

Cheers resounded from the other patrons. I took the pledge myself, amid applause from all corners of the Irish Pub, formally joining the group. (I suppose now is a good time to tender my resignation.)

The Proud Boys were also joined by young trolls from the "Politically Incorrect" (/pol) forum of 4chan. Their striking nonwhite composition does not stop them from terrorizing the opponents of fascism and white nationalism and otherwise spewing racist venom. I told a few of the /pol kids I had a bone to pick with them, namely the recent doxing of Mike Enoch. After antifascists revealed he was Manhattan software developer Michael Peinovich, /pol disclosed he was married to a Jewish woman, and the ensuing scandal almost killed TRS. "Mike is a Jew!" Tom had told me in confidence, months later. Mason, a chanlord in his early twenties with shaggy hair and timid eyes, defended the dox, explaining that his own politics are in line with those of Julian Assange: "Mike was living a lie, and he deserved to have it exposed."

Seeing this exchange, a Proud Boy hastily pulled me aside and cautioned: "Man, don't fuck with 4chan, they'll ruin your life!"

The crawl degenerated into a slither and wound up at Trump Tower, where the Boys breezed past Secret Service with a friendly wave. At the Trump Bar I learned the price a man impersonating the champion of the forgotten American charges people impersonating that American for a beer. I was then offered cocaine in the Trump Tower bathroom by one of the Boys. I befriended John, a Bushwick hipster and accountant in his late twenties. John and his girlfriend had been ordinary conservatives until recently. The "Western chauvinism" of the Proud Boys appealed to them, however, and here they were already mixing with open fascists. John's pristine white MAGA hat was adorned with an enamel pin of Pepe the frog—until Sal walked over, plucked the pin off John's hat, and put it on his own. Sal then walked away, without a word exchanged.

The Forum

Playwright Tavern is a three-story Irish pub on 49th Street. A visitor ensconced in its polished wood bowels, surrounded by nostalgic New York memorabilia, might be surprised to learn it has only existed since

1995. The bar's old-time charm is calculated to snare tourists searching for authenticity lost. Its third floor offers a private dining room for functions, and on March 6, 2017, was the setting for the New York Forum.

The Forum is a semiregular gathering of alt-right organizers and ideologues sponsored by Counter-Currents, a publisher on the movement's intellectual side. Matt is a friend of its founder Greg Johnson, and got me on the list. The pseudonymous Johnson is an openly gay phenomenology scholar who stomachs the locker room homophobia of the alt-right, and is in turn tolerated, even appearing on *Shoah*. This time Johnson was on vacation, with the Forum left to the care of Margot "Metroland" Sheehan, a fifty-eight-year-old Manhattanite writer. Sheehan greeted me at the door, collecting my $40 entry fee. I thanked her for putting the event together.

"Don't thank me," she replied, "thank Mike Enoch."

Seated beside me was Chris, a sexagenarian New York native with a bright red face and snow-white hair. Chris boasts long-standing ties to Jared Taylor and his *American Renaissance* journal and conference. Across sat Joel Marasco, a charismatic family court attorney from Jersey City in his early forties, and member of the Council of Conservative Citizens (CoCC). A group dating back to the 1960s, CoCC's website collecting "Black-on-white crime" stories was an essential part of Dylann Roof's politicization. At the front sat long-standing *Stormfront* personality Robert "BoyHowdy" DePasquale, a sexagenarian Manhattanite whose decades-long tenure as webmaster and internet troll earned him a profile by the Southern Poverty Law Center. DePasquale squints through tinted glasses entangled in curly salt-and-pepper hair, speaking softly and nasally. He is sure to get the name and contact information of everyone who crosses his path. Joel calls him the godfather of New York City's white-nationalist circles.

Across the aisle sat Identity Europa's "Eli Mosley," real name Elliot Kline, a former Proud Boy until just months prior. Kline bragged to me about his proximity to Richard Spencer, whose sartorial style and iconic hairdo the significantly shorter and wider Kline was striving to imitate. Kline had rapidly risen up the ranks of the alt-right since Trump's inauguration by hopping from city to city, agitating and organizing at every alt-right demonstration he could get to. Kline built his reputation on his experience in Iraq, passing himself off as an expert on combat tactics. Later it all turned out to be a lie. Kline mixed with the Stuyvesant Goys

Club, TRS's local pool party, composed of young, awkward internet geeks whose slender bodies vanished into oversize dress shirts, giving them the appearance of nebbishy office temps. I could only imagine what lions they are when behind keyboards. The strategic coup of projects like the Forum is forging a link between these two worlds, the self-serious old guard and the irony-saturated shitlords of the new generation.

At the head table sat Mike "Enoch" Peinovich, a dour hulk in his early forties. Two months prior, Peinovich received his fifteen minutes of fame as the Upper East Side's neo-Nazi media kingpin with a Jewish wife. It was, undeniably, quite a story, as he admitted to me. But Peinovich is no novelty act. He and a few internet friends built the TRS podcast network, turning a small circle of libertarian Facebook trolls experimenting with edgy racist humor into an international organizing platform for millennial neo-Nazis. As Trump's star rose, TRS moved from edgy fun and games to a serious organizing project, and its guests increasingly became street-oriented activists. TRS now exists largely to funnel disaffected young men into local pool parties, where they can plug into overtly fascist organizing projects. TRS organizers, including Peinovich and Kline, played a central role in organizing "Unite the Right" in Charlottesville, for which they are now being sued. For a white person living in America, it takes precious little time to tumble down the slippery slope from edgy racist humor to outright fascism. Just ask Peinovich, who woke up one day to find himself an Upper East Side neo-Nazi with a Jewish wife.

Matt arrived at last, flanked by Paul, the two of them laughing about skits by alt-right comedian Sam Hyde they'd listened to on the ride. Matt introduced me to Peinovich, who greeted me graciously, listening intently when I spoke, wisecracking in his unmistakable, husky, soothing radio voice, and often invoking the *Shoah*'s house response: "*oh gawd!*" in the caricatured voice of an old New York Jew. As a long-time listener, I have to admit, it was a bit of a thrill to meet Mike. Though melancholy and downcast even in moments of enthusiasm, Peinovich speaks with profound self-assurance, peppering his remarks with historical referents, facts, and figures, most of which are just made up out of thin air. I expressed my sympathy for his recent doxing and insisted on buying him a beer as a small token of appreciation for his show "red-pilling" me. He accepted, telling me he loves it when guys tell him that. (I knew that from listening.)

I asked how he'd been doing since getting doxed. He told me he was forced to move after the publication of his address, but was able to stay in the area, and while he was fired, he was able to sue his employer for discrimination and win a small settlement. It wasn't much, only enough to live off for a few months, but he savors the moral victory. I asked how he found a lawyer, and he confided there's an alt-right lawyer in NYC who prefers to remain anonymous. Peinovich chuckled, recalling how flummoxed his boss was when a Nazi threatened to sue for discrimination, and the law was on the Nazi's side! As for his wife, he told me, they were going to split anyway. She saw this coming. When he started the show, neither of them could have guessed he was going to become famous. Who could have? He then excused himself. Against all odds, he was now the master of ceremonies.

Peinovich introduced the first speaker, Counter-Currents author Jef Costello. The mustachioed Costello had barely introduced himself, however, when a young, brown-skinned waiter appeared in the glass door behind him, eliciting a collective gasp. The waiter made it two steps into the room before a surprisingly agile Peinovich sprang to his feet and stopped the man in his tracks, wagging a scolding finger to gales of laughter from around the room.

The waiter stammered, "I just need to . . . ."

"Just come back later!" Peinovich barked. The waiter turned on his heels and vanished, and Peinovich pantomimed locking the door behind him. Laughter intensified.

"I hate niggers!" a TRS pool partier exclaimed, to emphatic cheers.

Costello continued where he left off. His talk compared the alt-right to the League of Shadows from Batman movies. With Trump in power, he claimed, the left's "resentment, in the Nietzschean sense" is driving it to become more prone to violence. Today's left is "even worse than Stalin, Lenin, *and* Mao," because these leaders had a vivacious will to power and were unashamed of their strength, in contrast to SJWs, who attack because they are weak and resentful. In response, he concluded, the alt-right must be principled, prudent, and always prepare for the battle ahead, like characters from the Batman movies. Costello concluded his remarks by advocating that everyone present spend a bit more time at the gym.

The second speaker was Hunter College adjunct professor Joseph Salemi, one of those "anti-PC professor" types. He carried on for close to forty-five minutes along those shopworn lines, blaming some of our society's most powerless people for his failure to become a successful poetry professor.

The Forum adjourned to another Times Square hellhole I had thought reserved for tourists. I chatted with Stuart Sudekum, a TRS pool partier recently fired from the Bushwick Tarot Society after an exposé by antifascists. "I was fired for trying to bring a little racial consciousness into my classes," he told me bitterly.

The Hike

The Hate Hike is a national custom among *Stormer* and TRS meetup groups looking to get back to nature. I met Paul outside Fortunato Brothers cafe in Williamsburg to catch a ride to Blydenburgh County Park in Hauppauge, New York. I climbed uneasily into his Dodge Ram, noting the vanity plate "GTKRWN." Paul acted like he's proud of the plates, but his fiancé told him he's an idiot for getting them, and he was clearly on the fence. "Nobody knows what it means besides us," he reasoned. During our two-hour ride to Blydenburgh, the subject of race only came up briefly, when Paul described his neighborhood. Middle Village residents, he told me, are dedicated to keeping the neighborhood "the way it is," and will shun anyone who rents their property to nonwhite tenants. An old lady Paul knows, ostracized after violating this covenant, replied that it wasn't her fault—no white people had applied!

Tom was waiting for us in the parking lot, with Eric, Rich, and Nicky. Rich is a twenty-something from Long Island with slicked-back, greying hair and a goofy smile. A fresh recruit to TRS, Rich was only recently allowed to the pool parties after a year of intensive Skype-vetting by their gatekeeper, the pseudonymous D'Marcus Leibowitz. He gave me his Twitter handle, @OrwellHuxley, adding sheepishly, "it's from before I got red-pilled." Nicky is a slight, dark-skinned teenager from Brooklyn, who clearly has most of his social interaction online. He used to be in the NYC pool party, but was kicked out for being an "agecuck," unable to drink at bars, "among other reasons." Nicky complained that TRS guys are aging yuppie barflies. They don't do physical training together like they do in Cascadia, a large TRS group in the Pacific Northwest. Nicky assured me that the *Stormer* group can expect more guys like him, looking for action and not riding bar stools.

The Hate Hike meandered through a web of wilderness trails and creaky wooden bridges straddling picturesque swamplands. Tom sucked on his vape pen and waxed nostalgic about a youth spent in these woods. Eric complained about the "autistic nerds" in TRS, who had recently given him a hard time for his lax security measures in bringing new guys around their gatherings. Tom bristled at the mention of TRS. He tried to join, but after his initial audition via Skype, Leibowitz told him he's too fat. Tom replied, "I'll kill you if I ever see you in person." Since then, Tom isn't welcome at TRS events.

The sun had begun to set when we completed the seven-mile loop around Lake Hauppauge. On the long ride back to Brooklyn, Paul and I discussed the video of Spencer getting punched in the face. Paul admitted it's pretty funny, not in the least because Spencer's such an uptight preppy. Paul told me that Spencer had been invited to appear on CNN, which he could barely believe. Sharing his astonishment, I replied that the antifascists may be right—the only way to stop Spencer is to take away his platform. Paul agreed completely:

"They think they'll give him enough rope to hang himself with, but he won't."

The Vanguard

Jack Demsey's is an overpriced Irish pub on 33rd Street like all the rest. After the Forum, Joel invited me to this "little monthly gathering" he hosts there. It was April 10, Trump had just bombed Syria, and spirits were low in the alt-right. I texted Matt making sure he wasn't too "blackpilled," meaning nihilistic about the prospects for the movement.

"I've been snorting black pills like a motherfucker," he replied.

By the time I got there, everyone was seated for dinner. Sixteen men—and zero women—turned and froze like deer in headlights, before Joel popped up and shook my hand, and everyone relaxed.

I asked about Trump bombing Syria. Joel replied: "Listen, Trump is a cuck. His kids married Jews. He went to a Jewish wedding, with a guy with one of those beards there, and was OK with it." He never harbored illusions about Trump, but Trump was the "least antiwhite candidate" and he doesn't regret voting for him. Joel talked excitedly about his plan for building a white "city-state" and wonders what that would entail. "Maybe a dozen of us running for office?" I remarked that the demographic shift in NYC makes that possible, but Joel was not sure the white people moving to the city are willing to "take their own side," since they love helping out "NAMs" (non-Asian minorities).

THREE MONTHS INSIDE ALT-RIGHT NEW YORK

White liberals, Joel said, are the most "white supremist" of all, since they think minorities need so much special help to advance. White liberals are the most racially aware people around, he reiterated, "even more than us!"

Across from me sat Phil from Identity Europa, talking incessantly. Phil is short and skinny, balding with cropped blonde hair, resembling Kip from *Napoleon Dynamite*. He joked that he's thirty and looks fifty, and if he's really thirty, that's true. As a young man he joined the navy and was deployed in Iraq, and when he returned he was disenchanted with US interventionism. He began to hang out in antiwar circles, including Iraq Veterans Against the War. But his major issue became corruption of the banks, which naturally led him to thinking about Jews.

As for Trump, Phil was never fooled. "Trump never builds a casino without Chinese investors." Still, he concluded, "it's a good moment for us. His movement is not the same as ours, but he helped us."

Struggling to get a word in edgewise were Tim, Deacon Gerard, and a different Joel, all from Vanguard America (VA). Deacon and Joel, both in their early twenties, had recently left the army, where Deacon was part of a popular online comedy troupe called Terminal Boots. After discharge the two relocated to "the Jewish side" of Crown Heights from their native North Carolina. They are thin and handsome, sharply dressed in tight fitting slacks and button-down shirts, sporting Hitler-youth haircuts, impeccably gelled and matching. They assured me of their eagerness to "realize the fourteen words," a reference to the white nationalist pass-code: "we must secure the existence of our people and a future for white children."

Tim is about ten years older and more slovenly. He hails from central Jersey and clearly spends a lot of time on the internet. He complained VA was losing members to an offshoot of the Iron March Forum who position themselves as hard-core revolutionaries, but only troll other groups for not being militant enough. They talk a big game about being a paramilitary organization, Tim told me. "Call me when you're robbing banks and blowing shit up" is his attitude.

VA's main organizing activity is hanging up racist flyers in the dead of night. The three of them had recently flyered Prospect Park, but complained it didn't get any media attention, which they rely on for recruiting. I asked what they had planned next, and Tim replied sheepishly that they were going to flyer another college.

"I know it's been done a lot," he sighed, "but it's the only thing that works. We tried other places—"

"The museum, the park ..." Deacon interjected.

"And nothing!" Tim continued. "The beauty of colleges is there's always some aspiring journalism student looking for a scandal. It works every time."

Black-Pilled

There was another New York Forum on May 20. By this point, I was ready to throw in the towel. Something about the alt-right's self-mutilating meanness, its defiance of empathy in the face of the horrors of the world, and its embrace of cruelty cloaked in lighthearted humor had been profoundly *black-pilling* me. I was becoming resentful and mean-spirited, even more pessimistic about the future than usual. I could talk for longer and longer with the *Stormer* guys without feeling like I was even in character anymore. It was time to get out.

This New York Forum was much of the same as before, with ten or fifteen more guys. Peinovich was the main speaker, and turned his segment into an endless training on how to argue with leftists on the internet. He invited the crowd to offer up "common leftist arguments" for him to refute with his much-vaunted, battle-honed skills. This pettifoggery amounts to refusing to accept the premises of a question, sidestepping the question altogether, and adopting an offensive, rather than the anticipated defensive, posture. I suppose it's a good skill to have, if you enjoy spending your finite time on Earth engaged in bad faith online arguments with total strangers.

But as a longtime *Shoah* listener, I had often fantasized about the opportunity to stump Peinovich with the perfect question, one that brings his house of cards tumbling down. I patiently waited for my turn, as he shot down strawman after strawman offered up by his loyal devotees. At last, my time came.

"If you like white culture so much," I asked, smirking assuredly, "what's your favorite novel, poem, and symphony?"

"Metallica," he replied.

Looking Back

Many observers now wish to write off the alt-right as a media bugbear, a "movement where thirty people with cheap tiki torches can seem like an

THREE MONTHS INSIDE ALT-RIGHT NEW YORK

army in the echo chamber of social media," as a *Times* journalist recently put it. I am more inclined to the argument Leonard Zeskind offers in his magisterial *Blood and Politics*. "Convinced by the history of the early civil rights movement that small groups of determined individuals could influence and change the world around them," he writes, "I believed that racists could turn the wheels of history as well as antiracists could."[1] This holds true only if the conditions are right for radical change. Which, in the US, they are.

Persistent economic and political crisis in the United States, amid a long downturn for wages, job security, and basic human dignity, promise no happy return to the political center anytime soon. The alt-right did not emerge in response to the stupidity of marginal internet liberalism, as Angela Nagle suggests in *Kill All Normies*.[2] Rather it is a response to decades of decline in standards of living for working people, amid the proliferation of unemployment and meaningless, dead-end jobs. Moreover, no coherent leftist movement exists through which everyday people can make sense of this world and collaborate across lines of race and gender to build a better one. As a result, many of those who reject the status quo blame their problems on immigrants, feminism, trans rights, and other bogeymen, rather than the capitalist social relations from which the problems facing working people inevitably proceed.

The real threat today is not that small pockets of white-supremacist ideologues exist. It's that their vision of society might become the only one that makes sense to ordinary white people, for whom reality increasingly seems like a battle between racially defined interest groups for slivers from a shrinking pie. These same working-class white people face a dilemma as old as our country itself: whether to choose to be human, or choose to be white. One path leads to human liberation, another to planetary ruin. Who is helping them give their problems a name?

Thankful for President Trump: Thanksgiving with Stop the Steal

This text first appeared on the *Hard Crackers: Chronicles of Everyday Life* website in November 2020.

On Thanksgiving morning supporters of President Trump's doomed reelection effort descended on the Loop neighborhood of Chicago to raise the battle cry "stop the steal!" The "steal" in this tortured locution is the purported Democratic Party theft of the November presidential election, chronicled in a convoluted conspiracy theory that one conservative federal judge recently compared to "Frankenstein's Monster," as it is "haphazardly stitched together."[1] As Trump and his personal lawyers continue to dig in their heels and spin an ever more preposterous narrative justifying his defeat—seeking to disenfranchise Black voters in particular by focusing on "corruption" in cities like Detroit and Philadelphia—Stop the Steal rallies have proliferated across the United States. The campaign is not new; notorious Republican operative Roger Stone registered the first Stop the Steal website in 2016, planning to wage a similar effort should Trump lose that election.[2] Nonetheless, today's Stop the Steal rallies offer a glimpse into the state of Trumpworld's activist edge in the transitional period between his presidency and whatever comes next.

There is of course no chance that President Trump, his Pythonesque legal team, or even his most ardent supporters assembled en masse will overturn the results of the 2020 election. But that's not the point. With his legal options exhausted and his eye on the next chapter in the Trump

THANKFUL FOR PRESIDENT TRUMP

saga, the president is keeping the ruse of overturning the 2020 election going to save face—he's no loser, after all—and to keep his most loyal supporters activated for however he decides to use them next.[3] Similarly, lesser grifters than Trump who have monetized MAGA for upwards of five years have no intention of getting real jobs, and continue to feed off Trump's carnage like pilot fish trailing a great white shark. Nor will organized power blocs like the US police and border patrol, whose unions endorsed Trump almost unanimously, give up flexing their political muscles on the national stage, as they have done with Trump's encouragement, especially in response to the George Floyd Rebellion and the resurgence of Black Lives Matter.[4] The same goes for local petty bourgeoisie, who share with the police the desire to conduct their business as they see fit, free from state and federal oversight, and with as little taxation and regulation as possible. Their organized political blocs often overlap with organizing against gun regulations, which have dovetailed almost seamlessly into anti-public health protests, and the two share grounding in local right-wing churches, which organize members around preserving local power through these issues and others, like controlling women's bodies by fighting access to abortion. And here and there you just might find ardent Trump loyalists motivated by honest-to-God ideological dedication to white supremacy, Christian supremacy, xenophobia, patriarchy, and all the rest, but people rarely take action based on ideas alone.

Though national in scope, Stop the Steal rallies are local affairs, syncretizing with state-specific, right-wing organizing, especially campaigns against COVID-related business and school closures. They also build on the success of Trump motorcades, Trump boat parades, and the ongoing pro-cop, anti-Black Lives Matter demonstrations held under the banner "Back the Blue." The largest of these rallies was the so-called Million MAGA March in Washington, DC, on November 14, which grew out of a broad coalition of right-wingers from ordinary conservatives to outright fascists, who traveled from around the country for a large and violent romp in which local symbols of the Black Lives Matter movement were vandalized and destroyed, and numerous anti-fascists attacked, including multiple stabbings.[5] For his part, Trump made good on a Twitter promise and drove through the crowd and waved en route to playing golf, consistent with most of his public appearances since November 3.

Of course, the Stop the Steal movement has a looming expiration date. Two days before the Thanksgiving rally it was dealt a near-lethal blow by the president himself, who reversed course and formally allowed for the transition process to begin. Luckily, Stop the Steal organizers had emphasized a local grievance—Chicago's COVID safety regulations, dubbed the "Lightfoot lockdown" after Mayor Lori Lightfoot, who has generated considerable publicity advocating for masks, social distancing, and other basic public health measures meant to mitigate the lethal spread of COVID. Thanksgiving morning, organizers claimed, was chosen in defiance of Lightfoot's toothless suggestion to limit Thanksgiving gathering to ten guests, which they claimed constituted the mayor "cancelling Thanksgiving." National Stop the Steal organizer Ali Alexander, who has organized a number of these protests, including an armed march on an Arizona election office, announced that to protest Lightfoot's imaginary "cancelling [of] Thanksgiving" he would skip his family dinner to protest in Chicago.[6] Alexander predicted "over a thousand strong" departing from Trump Tower, and requested the attendees be "mostly men ... because women should be cooking."[7]

Nothing like Alexander's "over a thousand strong" materialized in the Loop. The streets were sleepy, with a light police presence for the rally and sporadic businesses still boarded up—either leftover from the summer's looting, the postelection civil war that never came, or anticipating whatever chaos is supposed to come next. When I arrived there were two dozen or so demonstrators milling around on a small slab of sidewalk on the northeast corner of North Wabash and East Wacker, across the Chicago River from Trump Tower. There was roughly one journalist for every two people in attendance, including a duo from the pro-Trump, Chinese-dissident *Epoch Times*, who enthusiastically interviewed rallygoers. The rest had a distinct "who did I piss off to get this assignment" look about them. I must confess, a little voice inside my head remarked "So this is the fucking coup I've been hearing about for years on end!" The rally would reach about fifty participants at its height, replete with MAGA hats and Trump flags flopping around in the wind. It was opposed by a lively counterprotest about half that size, relegated to the opposite side of Wacker, who made as much noise as they could to drown out the speeches. Several vehicles plastered with anti-Trump slogans periodically drove by, blaring their horns. And contrary to Alexander's wishes there were in fact a fair amount of women, including the core local organizers.

THANKFUL FOR PRESIDENT TRUMP

The rally was emceed through a tinny megaphone by Ashley Ramos, organizer of local pro-cop "Back the Blue" rallies.[8] At Ramos's side was speaker and fellow Back the Blue organizer Emily Cahill, who disseminates far-right, pro-cop, and race-baiting propaganda through the Facebook page "Protest the Protesters." Back the Blue rallies like those organized by Ramos and Cahill have helped build a base of civilian support for the political power of local police—already organized, for over half a century, by their powerful unions and connections to "law and order" politicians like Trump—while simultaneously allowing far-right activists and more traditional conservatives to openly mix and mobilize against the Black Lives Matter movement and the more general state of rebellion that has heralded its 2020 redux. Vociferous on social media, Ramos and Cahill struggled to be heard over the counterprotesters blaring sirens and banging pots, and the latter's hands shook as she attempted to read brief prepared remarks largely drowned out by the noise.

Back in September, Ramos and Cahill rallied in support of Kyle Rittenhouse outside the juvenile detention center where he was held following his murderous attack on multiple protesters in Kenosha, Wisconsin.[9] Looking on as Cahill attempted to speak Thursday morning was Carl Arriaza who organized the Rittenhouse rally under the banner "Self Defense Is Not a Crime."[10] Arriaza also serves as president of Illinois Gun Owners Together, itself something of a nexus of far-right militias like the Three Percenters, the Back the Blue crowd, and the local Proud Boys.[11] He also appears to spend a great deal of time on Twitter harassing and threatening antifascists half his age. The trio of Ramos, Cahill, and Arriaza may succeed in passing themselves off as ordinary conservatives due to their avowed interests in the Second Amendment and sticking up for the cops. But they are key organizers in a dynamic, if small, far-right activist ecosystem that, intentionally or not, provides a conveyor belt from ordinary conservative issues into the fascist corners of the local right.[12]

Also milling through the crowd was Edgar "Remy Del Toro" Gonzalez, president of the local Proud Boys. Though implicated in the chaos of Charlottesville—Unite the Right organizer Jason Kessler had even been a member—the group survived the demise of the alt-right, and even gained steam in the vacuum it left behind, due in no small part to their multiracial makeup and emphasis on national chauvinism over white racial purity.[13] The mere sight of nonwhite Proud Boys like Gonzalez is enough to stymie the novice observer, who expects all US fascists to look like Richard Spencer. The Proud Boys served as a point of entry for more traditional conservatives into overtly fascist politics, offering beer-swilling camaraderie and rowdy street battles with antifascists as enticement to alienated young men eager to perform masculinity and experience homosocial belonging. For the Proud Boys, the protofascist milieu of Back the Blue is both the ideal recruiting ground and a place to operate in broad daylight.

Similarly harking back to the salad days of the alt-right was featured speaker Mike Coudrey. Back when he went by the name Mike Tokes, Coudrey was openly affiliated with the alt-right, associating with unapologetic antisemite Tim "Baked Alaska" Gionet, gleefully Sieg heiling on camera, and taking part in the Unite the Right rally in Charlottesville.[14] Many in the alt-right believed that Trump's victory meant they could soon openly espouse their white supremacist politics, and Charlottesville was supposed to solidify the unbroken link between mainstream US conservatism and the fascist fringes that Trump's campaign had opened up, hence the name Unite the Right. After it accomplished the opposite, leaving much of the alt-right publicly disgraced, hobbled by lawsuits, and embroiled in embarrassing infighting, Coudrey successfully rebranded, peddling baseless conspiracy theories about the California wildfires, COVID cures suppressed by the fake media, and most recently, aligning closely with Alexander and hopscotching the United States claiming that Trump's resounding electoral defeat was the product of a vast conspiracy.[15] In keeping with the disjointed premise of the rally, Coudrey's brief and unenthusiastic remarks—perhaps he expected a larger crowd—soldered the usual Trump talking points about election fraud onto an anti-public health message emphasizing the plight of small businesses. He made no attempt to bridge these issues.

The rally also featured Pastor Steve Cassell, who unsuccessfully sued the State of Illinois over the shuttering of his Beloved Church in Lena, Illinois, as Governor J.B. Pritzker struggled to contain surging COVID cases earlier this year.[16] Since COVID precautions began last spring, protests against "the lockdown" have provided an ongoing base for far-right street mobilizations, encouraged by the president himself. Cassell's initial defiance of the state made him something of a hero in

THANKFUL FOR PRESIDENT TRUMP

local libertarian circles, and his remarks to the crowd underscored the publicity victory his federal lawsuit scored for the anti-public health movement, while downplaying the fact that it lost. To the untrained eye, the soft-spoken man of God may have seemed something of the odd man. But Christianity has long been the basis of white nationalist and protofascist organizing in the United States, if not just as a base of power for the local petty bourgeoisie, and where the alt-right failed to mobilize along lines of racial purity and antisemitism, a fascist movement that embraces Christianity as a common denominator might just succeed. Additionally, Cassell represented the grievances of small business owners who have been crushed by the US government's failed response to COVID, but have organized against public health regulations instead of against a social order that made their hard work so disposable in the first place.

Ali Alexander was the rally's headlining act, arriving fashionably late and flanked by an armed security detail. Despite his boyish looks, Alexander has been a controversial figure on the fringe-right since at least 2006, when he went by his given name, Ali Akbar.[17] Thanks in large part to his harnessing the momentum of the Tea Party movement against Barack Obama, Alexander has managed to become something of an arch grifter, even receiving funds from megadonor and Breitbart's guardian angel Robert Mercer. This, despite dual convictions for theft and fraud, a consistent simmer of scandal surrounding his handling of funds, and a habit of falsely designating his groups "nonprofits." Alexander also generated controversy as a McCain election staffer, by suggesting their presidential campaign engage in none other than ... election rigging![18]

The notoriety Alexander earned in his early years seems to have spurred his name change. And despite being Black himself, cutting his teeth as a writer at the now-defunct *Hip-Hop Republican*, Alexander was very comfortable with the alt-right in its heyday, even in its most explicit neo-Nazi form.[19] Alexander keeps company with fellow grifters Alex Jones, Jacob Wohl, Laura Loomer, and has been pictured with the late Andrew Breitbart and Donald Trump himself.[20] It's unsurprising, then, to find Alexander at the center of the ultraright issue du jour and its complex web of funding, since, in the immortal words of Willie Sutton, "that's where the money is!"[21] In chasing Stop the Steal funding Alexander joins fellow grifters Jack Posobiec, Mike Cernovich, and a string of lesser lights who have long monetized MAGA. And since getting involved,

Alexander has already come under fire for falsely claiming in fundraising material that the Trump campaign has endorsed his organizing.[22]

Alexander, who often spends hours at a time livestreaming his meandering rants, delivered the rally's most memorable remarks. "The Republican Party is MIA!" he declared provocatively, as the crowd booed the name of RNC chair Ronna McDaniels. "That's why we have Lin Wood, that's why we have Sidney Powell, that's why we have Rudy Giuliani!" He bragged about phone calls from the capitulation faction within Trump's White House, who told him to stop rocking the boat. To this he said "If *we the people* didn't take the streets, Trump would have already conceded!" Similarly, he claimed, when "a top Trump advisor" told him to stop saying "stop the steal," he flatly refused. By his estimation, the fate of Trumpism was now in the hands of Stop the Steal and the activist base upon which it has been built. "The day after the election we were really fucked," and it was only the action of the grass roots that kept Trump's chances alive. In short, Alexander is more than prepared for a clean break between Trumpism and anything resembling orthodox conservatism. And as he bragged repeatedly, truthfully in this case, against all odds Alexander seems to retain deep ties to far-right donors, and will not stop organizing any time soon.

Toward the end of his remarks Alexander finally lost patience with the counterprotesters, and taunted that they were out doing the bidding of "a billionaire" (likely Soros—Alexander has a long history of anti-semitism) who didn't care about them.[23] The irony of this formulation seemed lost on those dedicating their Thanksgiving morning to Donald J. Trump as he played golf, just as it did when a young white man in a MAGA hat derided the counterprotesters for not being at home with their families.

Besides Alexander, the speakers largely lacked the charisma and confidence to project their voices over a boisterous counterprotest and the commotion that ensued as a few young Black counterprotesters crossed the street to antagonize the crowd up close. Rallygoers increasingly divided their attention between these skirmishes and the reheated conspiracy theories served up by the speakers, with many deciding it was more fun to hurl thinly veiled racist abuse at the enemy than listen to boring speeches nobody could really hear anyway.

"Trump lost! Y'all are a bunch of losers!" the counterprotesters would say.

"You're racist! Black babies matter!" one reply ran, evoking a common antiabortion trope.

"Obama built the cages ... Biden's 1994 crime bill locked up 90% [?!] of Black people!" ran another, drawing on the particularly Trumpian tactic of outflanking interlocutors on the left, from a position that's undeniably hard-right.

"You corona bitch!!" a young Black woman, separated from the Trumpers by three high-ranking, on-duty policemen, shouted to a man without a mask.

"Get off of welfare and America will be great!" an older white woman shot back.

"Do you kiss your pimp with that dirty mouth?" came another retort.

Two vocal Trump supporters, one Black and one identifying as Latino, held up an American flag, the latter taunting: "Get triggered Marxists! Get triggered lefties! You can't stand minorities holding the flag!" Another Black man, waving a Trump flag, yelled: "You don't have any Black people! Where are the Black people?"

There were of course a number of Black people counterdemonstrating, including a few who banged pots and pans, hurled insults, and mixed with rallygoers until police ordered them to back off. One young man in particular kept demanding to use the megaphone. A Stop the Steal organizer told him he couldn't, and an argument ensued. Finally the exasperated organizer said "He just wants to get on here and say 'Fuck America.' Why don't we let him?"

"Fuck America!" the young man shouted into the megaphone.

And so on.

After standing around on the sidewalk for over an hour listening to swapped insults and a string of lousy speeches, Ramos announced at last: "We're going to march to Millennium Park, but before we do I want to play a song in honor of our president!" After a slight pause, her mobile speaker blared "YMCA" by the Village People—a disco song celebrating gay cruising culture in 1970s Manhattan, harried in its time by constant police harassment and violence, and gentrified out of existence by Trump and his fellow developers. It was a nice reminder that in contemporary mass politics, nothing means what it used to, if anything even means anything at all. Ramos then led the rally on a short sidewalk march, Trump flags waving, closely pursued by the counterprotest on the other side of the street, with the latter hemmed in only by a line of bicycle cops. Stop the Steal chants typically put right-wing spins on some left classics: "Hey, ho, lockdown Lori has got to go! … When I say lockdown you say sucks! When I say legal votes you say matter! When I say Donald you say Trump! When I say stop the you say steal!"

As counterprotesters chanted "No Trump, no KKK, no MAGA here today!" they were met with retorts of "USA" and of course: "Back the blue!"

Thus, as Trump prepares to vacate the White House, albeit kicking and screaming, he leaves in his wake an interconnected web of small-time hucksters, politicized police and border patrol, Christian chauvinists, ideological white supremacists and xenophobes, and local petty bourgeois prone to representing themselves as "the white working class." While it might seem obvious to predict the impending collapse of such an unstable compound, it is worth remembering that Trumpworld has been through the fire for almost five years, and its collective parts, however incongruous with one another, seem to know a good thing when they see one, and don't seem to have much interest in giving it up. And while Charlottesville constituted a setback for the ideological operators hoping to pull conservatives rightward, the kind of indistinct borderlands between conservatism and outright fascism is once again populous, thanks in no small part to projects like Back the Blue, Stop the Steal, and of course the greatest gift to American fascists in a generation, Trump himself.

At this point the reader might be imagining the above as something of a joke: a couple of two-bit hucksters, used car salesmen, cop-loving Karens, gun nuts, and wannabe fascist street thugs walk into a bar, proud of the fact they're not wearing masks, and the bartender says: "Who gives a shit?" This is fair enough. But after some 73 million Americans threw in their lot with Trump, after watching him in action for four long years, I wager that it's worth mapping the contours of the activist base his presidency leaves behind. While they do not pose any particular danger stemming from intelligence, ability, or even coherence, Trump managed with none of these qualities to summon a massive movement we will be stuck with for a long time. Especially after 2016, there's nothing saying a shameless huckster can't spin hot air into a substantive base of support, and real political power—especially when they are willing to throw in their lot with the latent white supremacy, xenophobia, and outright cruelty built into American social life.

As COVID ravages the US alongside protracted austerity and the reality of deindustrialization that no populist politician can reverse, a strident antiestablishment message offered by purported enemies of the existing social order poses a particular threat of gaining adherents—especially when it comes cloaked in the garments of homespun Americanism and speaks the language of civic myths drilled into our heads in public schools. The lack of a viable anticapitalist left current cedes this ground, and left support for the kind of "diversity" on offer in the Biden administration will only make it easier for the far right to hang the neoliberal Democrats around the necks of all who fight for real human emancipation. On the most basic level, with the Democrats back in the White House, the MAGA movement now becomes the resistance, which compared to actually wielding power is easy and fun. The hat worn by one rallygoer Thursday betrayed not just the self-aware futility of Stop the Steal, but how little it matters when compared with keeping the MAGA machine going: "Impeach Biden."

The march ended in the tourist hell of Millennium Park. The police corralled counterprotesters away from the rally, and they continued their noisy disruption as Alexander orchestrated a group photo in front of the park's big Christmas tree. An older woman in a surgical mask approached Pastor Cassell and explained that she wasn't wearing it to prevent the spread of COVID, but to protect everyone from a nasty cold she recently contracted. "The left is a social movement," Coudrey declared, "but the right is a family." And before parting ways, this family joined together to recite the Lord's Prayer—save for a few, who ignored the praying and continued to trade insults with the counterprotesters, as East Asian tourists looked on with great confusion. Meanwhile, all across Chicago, families large and small were sitting down to eat their Thanksgiving dinner.

The Big Takeover

This text first appeared on the Hard Crackers: Chronicles of Everyday Life website on January 7, 2021.

On January 6 a determined mob from across the United States descended on Washington, DC. They rumbled with police, overturned barricades, breached the perimeter of the United States Capitol, and smashed their way into the building itself—all while both houses were in session. Inside, the insurgents played cat and mouse with police and federal agents, gleefully traipsing the evacuated halls of Congress and the Senate, and marauded through the offices of high-level politicians, who escaped a direct confrontation by a matter of minutes. The scene at the Capitol was replicated in miniature across the US, with large crowds menacing state houses in Washington state, Georgia, Arizona, Oklahoma, and others.[1] But nothing compared to the spectacle playing out in the nation's capital.

Mike Davis aptly cites the surrealist dictum that "no idea or image that might lend itself to a rational explanation of any kind would be accepted."[2] In fact, many of the images emerging from the Capitol render the word "surreal" banal. "Where's Pence," shouted a shirtless man clad in furs topped with Viking horns from atop the dais of the United States Senate. "Show yourself!" Elsewhere a grinning man put his feet up on a desk in House Speaker Nancy Pelosi's office while others ransacked Pelosi's and other offices, snapping selfies and livestreaming all the while. Another man clad in furs, and a bulletproof vest and riot shield taken from police, rested on a wooden staff looking bewildered and bereft of a plan before simply taking a seat on an ornate leather bench. In some scenes, the insurgents appear as spectators in the Capitol's halls, respecting the velvet rope stanchions installed to marshal guided tours, while one waved at the camera, grinning ear to ear while attempting to loot the lectern of the House of Representatives.

Davis, however, is too quick to dismiss the insurgents, who he claims "didn't have a clue." For each absurd or risible image we can cite to write them off, there is another that demonstrates tactical militancy and seriousness of purpose. An armed demonstrator in military fatigues and tactical gear stormed the floor of Congress with zip ties, indicating intent to take hostages or even perform summary executions akin to a foiled plot in Michigan late last year.[3] The breech itself required a serious fight in multiple locations, with participants clearly equipped for street confrontations, and many appearing to be armed. At some point within the Capitol a small crowd attempted to smash through a barricade, and the first over the hill was shot and killed, thirty-five-year-old Ashli Babbitt, a veteran of the endless wars in Iraq and Afghanistan, and an ardent supporter of Trump and the QAnon conspiracy theory movement. Babbitt traveled from San Diego to engage in violent direct action. "Nothing will stop us," she tweeted the previous day, "they can try and try and try but the storm is here and it is descending upon DC in less than 24 hours … dark to light!"

Babbitt met death doing exactly what she came to DC for. The siege had been planned for weeks in tandem with a large pro-Trump rally, promoted by the president himself.[4] "Big protest in DC on January 6," Trump tweeted in mid-December. "Be there, be wild!" Heeding the call for another revolution in the vein of 1776, armed rightists traveled from across the United States to stop the certification of Biden's electoral victory by any means. Trump himself headlined a massive rally outside the White House, whipping up his supporters for a march on the Capitol he falsely claimed he would personally lead, before vanishing back into the White House, not interested in physically leading a coup after all. But it turned out the crowd didn't need him to find its way to the Capitol. In a sign of things to come, Trump's involvement became largely irrelevant, as the movement that has operated in his shadow took on a life of its own in the streets.

Violent revolution was a consistent theme throughout the day's events. A reporter for Glenn Beck's Blaze TV bragged of his participation in "the current revolution" in a since-deleted tweet claiming: "I am inside Nancy Pelosi's office with the thousands of revolutionaries who have stormed the building."[5] Trump may not have been serious about an armed coup—allegedly he has long given up on retaining power, and is simply keeping his base fired up and his name in the news.[6] But plenty of his followers were deadly serious. Chants of "storm the Capitol" and "1776" echoed before the march even arrived at the building.[7] A hanging scaffold, complete with a noose, was erected outside the Capitol, and a pipe bomb was planted outside the office of the Republican party.[8]

While Biden's victory was ultimately certified amid a barrage of maudlin platitudes, the siege of the US Capitol was nonetheless a massive victory for the insurgent far right in the US, akin to the siege of the Third Precinct in Minneapolis that helped catalyze and set the militant anti-cop tone of the George Floyd Rebellion last summer. The militancy of the siege is a bellwether of the changes that the US far right has undergone in the five years since the Trump movement gave it renewed life. The siege also provides the movement a much-needed opportunity for self-clarification, which will unfold in the coming weeks and months among the ragtag movement of US rightists who have hitched their wagon to Trump's falling star. Above all, at the risk of engaging in the "crystal ball" thinking Davis rightly warns us against, when the history of this period is written, the siege of the Capitol is likely to mark the beginning of a new chapter in the US far right.

Back in the halcyon days of 2015, the alt-right rose to prominence on the back of the Trump electoral campaign, using media savvy to carve out an oversized role for itself in the national discourse, as Trump rallies and related street battles brought a variety of young reactionaries off the internet and into the streets.[9] The alt-right's major strength was the zone of indistinction the Trump movement created between the mainstream conservative movement and its fascist fringes, which enabled alt-righters to operate in broader conservative circles and pull so-called normies toward their emergent brand of fascism. This strength was also the movement's weakness, however, as the alt-right was itself indistinct, and never achieved sufficient clarity about whether it was system-loyal or system-oppositional, to use the helpful framework furnished by *Three-Way Fight*.[10] Led by Richard Spencer, alt-right leaders pursued a strategy of militant reformism, seeking to mainstream white nationalist views within civil society as a means of transforming it. Setting aside their

THE BIG TAKEOVER

191

ghastly view for how society should run, they didn't have much of a clue how to get there besides convincing white people to support them and running candidates for office.

For the most part, alt-right politics were eclectic and held together by mutually held enmity, not a clear political analysis or vision. This was a product of the movement's novelty, but was not sufficiently overcome. Even when the Proud Boys sought out violent encounters with antifascists and were often arrested, they swore allegiance to the US police and branded antifascists "terrorists" who must be fought in the name of the country they love. In early 2017, I watched Proud Boy leader of yore Sal Cipolla carted off by NYPD for attacking a journalist. The Proud Boys made no moves to resist or antagonize the cops, and Cipolla gushed to the arresting officers over and over that he supported them! In another telling scene, a frequent cohost of The Right Stuff's flagship program *The Daily Shoah*, the *Chapo Trap House* of the alt-right, pranked his comrades by calling the show and asking: If the United States is controlled by the Jews, why do you support it? The hosts were completely stumped! After an awkward silence the joke was revealed, and amid nervous laughter the program continued, never returning to a question they weren't prepared to answer.

The alt-right didn't have much more time in the sun to think the question over. The public relations disaster of Charlottesville was meant to "unite the right" in the alt-right's favor and solidify their entry into mainstream conservatism, but turned instead into what some fascists called "the Altamont of the alt-right." While heaps of public scorn, infighting, and a crippling lawsuit contributed greatly to the movement's demise, the decisive factor was its inability to choose between a movement of respectable law-abiding citizens, and a movement of political violence—in other words, it remained stymied at the crossroads between system-loyalty and system-opposition. Without a clear sense of what they were, they buckled under the pressure. It's no coincidence that the only group to see its star rise in the aftermath of Charlottesville was the Proud Boys, who were at peace with their pursuit of political violence and had sufficient clarity among themselves to persevere beyond Charlottesville, while dodging accusations of white supremacism thanks to prominent nonwhite members.

The Proud Boys style of street violence survived Charlottesville and fused with similar groups like the neofascist Patriot Prayer, and emissaries of the decades-long US militia movement like the Three Percenters. These groups helped engender a culture of carnivalesque brawls in Berkeley, Portland, and other cities, nurturing a street fighting culture among right-wingers and fringe weirdos dedicated to political violence and/or bored and craving the next adrenaline rush. Fighting the antifascists who dutifully countermobilized became something of an extreme sport, the way summit-hopping was for leftists of the alter-globalization movement. "The thing that happened today [at the Capitol] was a part of a trajectory of right-wing street actions that have been happening since 2017 in Berkeley," wrote journalist Shane Bauer. "A bunch of the same people. Same stupid costumes. Same worldview."[11]

Open conflict with police, however, was never part of these rightists' horizon. In fact, these rallies often demonstrated considerable overlap with police organizations under the banner of Blue Lives Matter, especially after the George Floyd Rebellion. We must never forget how Kenosha killer Kyle Rittenhouse, a celebrated product of this rightist milieu, was encouraged by the police before the shooting, and subsequently allowed to leave.[12] This same milieu also produced "anti-lockdown" protests against public health measures taken in the face of COVID, which in turn dovetailed into pro-Trump rallies, motorcades, boat parades, and finally "Stop the Steal" rallies against the purported theft of the election.[13] All of these rallies had a strong component of support for the US police, whose unions had overwhelmingly—and singularly, among US unions—thrown in their support behind Trump.

In the weeks leading up to the Capitol siege, however, this began to change. Proud Boys antagonized the cops at their "Million MAGA March," a previous DC romp, demanding to be let through a police line separating them from a much smaller detachment of antifascists.[14] A large group of rightists subsequently attacked symbols of Black Lives Matter, including burning a banner stolen off a historically Black church. In late December, rightists in the orbit of Patriot Prayer and the Proud Boys attacked the State House in Salem, Oregon, clashing with police in the process, including spraying cops with chemical irritants.[15] In early January, the scene was repeated in the streets of Salem, which saw some rightists make a big show of stomping on a thin blue line flag.[16] The night before the January 6 rally, police and rightists openly clashed for control of the streets of DC.[17] Thus a movement that had built itself in large part as supporters of US police against BLM and antifa began planning for armed encounters with not antifa or the Democrats, but the cops themselves. This profound ambiguity is best captured by the storming of a police line in DC by an insurgent waving a thin blue line flag.

This is not to say there haven't been small pockets of revolutionary rightists all along, especially in the militia movement or isolated and largely stuck online. But they have largely been isolated, and effective only at lone wolf–style attacks. By contrast, the mayhem in DC demonstrates that a considerable segment of US rightists are beginning to unambiguously embrace a system-oppositional framework. In doing so they are aided in no small part by Trump himself, who has spent the better part of the last two months crowing that the government is not legitimate and its laws are therefore not to be respected. But this is also due to the working out of contradictions in their own theory and practice through struggle, toward an extraparliamentary fascism, the same way moving beyond reformism is essential for a leftists' coming to political maturity, and is often achieved only through concrete engagement.

Ironically, Trump's departure leaves the wind at the backs of US fascists to a degree unparalleled since his arrival. There's no longer an incumbent to wring hands over supporting; it's back to the joys of being the deposed opposition. And this coming on the eve of a Democratic presidency that even mainstream Republicans do not consider legitimate is a massive boon for the coming years of rightist organizing. The comrades at *Three-Way Fight* are correct to point out that the way the state responds to these rightists in the coming months will play a large part in whether an antipolice common sense ossifies.[18] Seen through the lens of the siege of the Capitol, which left a wildly careless trail of digital evidence, it is hard to imagine the coming months will see anything but a widespread crackdown that splits the system-loyal and system-oppositional rightists in an enduring way, helping to outline the contours of the movement post-Trump. Chief among the dividing issues will be the role of the police: friend, or foe?

Most commentary so far has been limited to the eternal stating of the obvious that right-wing white men have a comparatively easy time with the police, which functionally amounts to a plea for the proportional use of brutal state violence against *everyone*. And while the right-wing conspiracy theory mill is already claiming the insurgents were antifascists in disguise, the garden variety leftist analyses aren't much better.[19] A single video showing some cops abandoning a barricade without a fight has been circulated alongside a clip of some bemused cops inside the Capitol taking selfies with the insurgents to support the conspiracy theory that the Capitol police let this happen on purpose. It won't matter that the journalist who shot the former video has claimed it is being portrayed all wrong.[20] It seems that no amount of footage of hot conflict between police and rightists, including scenes of great courage that many leftists would hesitate to imitate, matters to those determined to lean on this analysis. And this is not to say that cooperation on an individual or even concerted level between the rightists and the cops is outside the realm of possibilities, or that the Capitol was equally equipped for an assault as it would be, had the rally been leftist. But the burden of proof for people making claims of conspiracy, presently almost nonexistent, must be raised exponentially.

More broadly, such conspiracy narratives are preferable to confronting the fact that an explicitly revolutionary rightist tendency is very likely enjoying an auspicious moment of recomposition, unafraid of meting out violence or meeting it, even to the point of death, and should therefore be respected as formidable foes, equally capable as leftists of opposing the US state, or worse yet, appearing as the only visible alternative to neoliberalism, as Trump did in the 2016 election. With Donald Trump quickly fading into irrelevance, what we are seeing is almost certainly the birth of something new coming into existence that we'll be contending with for years to come, defined by the experience of the Capitol siege, and the ideological and practical lines it will both expose and draw. Moreover, the conspiracy narrative allows people to sidestep facing the challenge that a comparatively small, focused, and courageous group of people can do a whole lot once it lets go of its fear and preoccupations with appeasing polite society or stepping on the toes of anyone who claims to represent large groups of people.

In a country where the majority of eligible citizens do not vote, rampant interpersonal violence, addiction, routine mass shootings, and suicide epidemics testify to a profound hopelessness that anything can be done to improve daily life. The nonsensical, logic-proof theories of QAnon don't demonstrate the stupidity of their adherents as much as the desperation people feel for communal belonging, to find a theory that makes sense of the desperation and misery of their lives, and to take actions into their own hands, acting in concert. Collective actions like the siege of the Capitol, no matter how ephemeral, register in the minds of millions of people the idea that drastic measures can be taken by ordinary people. Forget how risible or horrific it may seem to professional pundits or social media celebrities who shed tears for the sanctity of the "hallowed halls" where imperialist wars and austerity programs are hatched. The sight of gate-crashers angrily storming the Senate demanding that Mike Pence reveal himself, a man in proletarian dress with his feet up on a desk in the office of the multimillionaire powerbroker Nancy Pelosi, and the perverse fun most of them seemed to be having doing it, furnish powerful political images that speak to the widespread disgust with US life that's just about the only thing everyone agrees on.

What is our alternative?

Iowa Bluffs

This text first appeared on the *Hard Crackers: Chronicles of Everyday Life* website in October 2023.

"Indeed, we are all implicated in Iowa."
—Heather Anne Swanson, "The Banality of the Anthropocene"

Crossing the Mississippi River from Illinois into Iowa by car is an almost effortless glide, eliding entirely the forceful pull of the Great River and the centuries of violence greater still that harnessed its bucking current into an engine of commerce unsuitable for fishing, swimming, or drinking. It's difficult to imagine that this momentary glimpse of blue in my peripheral vision was once the artery from which fortunes gushed or trickled, the playground where the nineteenth century's Saint Hucks found death and adventure, and the vanishing horizon for the freedom of enslaved people sent ever-southward as the human traffic on which this nation's wealth was built drew the entire southern social order into its own death spiral. Comfortably burning nonrenewable fuel high above the Mississippi's churn, it becomes all too tempting to consider this the distant past.

On the fuzz-drenched wasteland of AM radio, eerie voices emerge and dissolve once more like messages from the beyond. The mind-numbing banality of sports radio alternates with glad tidings of life after death through the salvation of Christ, before at last synthesizing into their logical conclusion, a man's voice narrating the deadening ritual of

IOWA BLUFFS

an unfolding baseball game, punctuated by the Good Word proffered in the time between pitches. A few clicks down the dial, an old man's molasses drawl laments Fulton County's indictment of Donald Trump, declaring it to be unconstitutional, according to the studious insights of a constitutional expert, one Edwin Meese.

On the channel next door, a woman with a nasal twang waxes exasperated at the state of a conservative movement poised to defend conspiracy theorist Russell Brand against a slew of sexual assault allegations. Lamenting the cults of personality that have taken the place of conservative principles, the host declares that Donald Trump has led the movement so far into chaos and disarray that it is time to inquire whether he is a "deep state" asset, propped up by the CIA. Then, at once, an invisible line is crossed, and this fading voice in the wilderness gives way to harsh static, quickly replaced by a still more ethereal Christian choir simulating ascent through the great pearly gates.

CIA asset or not, Donald Trump is coming to Dubuque, Iowa. The four-times-indicted, twice-impeached, two-time Primetime Emmy-nominated former president of the United States of America and current World Wrestling Federation Hall of Famer has chosen the riverside Rust Belt enclave of Dubuque, Iowa, for one of his increasingly rare public rallies. With the fabled company bearing his name on the verge of court-ordered dissolution, and ninety-one felony indictments hanging over his head, the seventy-seven-year-old has cut far less of an imposing figure on the campaign trail than he did in in previous election cycles, when he taunted his adversaries with dastardly relish, furnishing classic sound bites and instant memes, as he danced across the stage drunk on adulation, hopped up on amphetamines, and clearly having loads of fun.

Today, the network TV star, who has found far more success portraying a thriving businessman than actually being one, tramps glumly into what promises to be his final leading role, on the boldest reality programming since *Survivor*: either he becomes president of the United States once more, or he spends the rest of his days under house arrest, or even in prison. Yet, if the polls are to be believed, even as he skips Republican debates, and spends his days issuing unhinged rants on his own (also failing) social media platform, lacking all the humor and verve which once made him the unofficial king of Twitter trolls, Donald Trump is still, somehow, against all odds, poised to win the Republican nomination and face off against an even older, less coherent, and potentially more vulnerable nemesis next fall. Trump is therefore tasked with an increasingly perfunctory exercise in rallying his troops to make America great again, again, in what he insists is the most important election in the history of our country, again. And in the arcane annals of US presidential politics, all roads lead to Iowa.

Little Cloud's Big Claim

The setting of the latest Trump carnival was once peopled by numerous Indigenous tribes, including the Sauk, Meskwaki, and Ho-Chunk, in advance of European colonization, which arrived in the late eighteenth century in the person of one Julien Dubuque. As recounted in Franklin T. Oldt's *History of Dubuque County*, the Quebecois adventurer was drawn to the area by rumors of lead mining, a disastrous process for miner and consumer alike, already begun by natives acculturating themselves to trade with the ever-encroaching Europeans. Dubuque constructed lead furnaces and ingratiated himself with the locals sufficient to receive written permission from a Meskwaki chief, dated 1788, to mine and settle an ill-defined plot of land surrounding a small complex of mines. It was the beginning of Euro-American private property in the region, according to which distinct plots of land belonged irreversibly to individual people engaged in an effective state of war with the world outside of it, theirs to destroy along with the rest of the planet should they see fit.

The natives lacked the legalistic conception of landed property that accompanied the rise of capitalism in Western Europe and now transformed the vast expanses of Turtle Island into a continental jigsaw puzzle of private holdings. They almost certainly meant to allow Dubuque, who they affectionately dubbed Little Cloud, to simply make use of the land, likely in exchange for serving as a conduit to settler traders. Nonetheless, equipped with their written agreement, Dubuque approached colonial authorities and claimed the writ as title to a large and ill-defined territory of Meskwaki on the eastern bank of the Mississippi, centering around the county that today bears his name. Dubuque also went into the real estate business, selling off a portion of his holdings, and taking on a business partner to capitalize on the ever-appreciating riverfront property and its poisonous bounty of blue-gray shimmering lead.

It was a time of remarkable flux, even for the Heraclitean order of private property in the New World. In the fifteen years following

IOWA BLUFFS

Dubuque's supposed land purchase, claimants to the territory beneath his feet shifted from the Spanish Crown to France, and finally to the United States under the Louisiana Purchase—to say nothing of a number of Indigenous tribes who already lived there. The Louisiana Purchase also added the Mississippi River to US territory alongside a massive westward expanse, and redoubled both the river's importance to commercial traffic and the centrality of ports like the one that would soon stand on Dubuque's claim.

Following the Louisiana Purchase, Dubuque petitioned the nascent US government to legally sanctify his holdings. The curious writ caught the attention of US Secretary of Treasury Albert Gallatin, who introduced onto the record his belief that Dubuque had simply received permission to mine the land and was now misrepresenting this as a property claim. Further complicating matters, Dubuque's agreement with the Meskwaki lacked the precision of even the most rudimentary land title; simply put, Gallatin observed, there was no title at all. Against these objections, Dubuque's claim was upheld by the federal government, based in large part on the fact of his already having taken charge of it. Possession, as the old saw goes, is nine-tenths of the law. For their part, the natives bolstered Gallatin's case significantly when, upon Dubuque's 1810 death, they burned Little Cloud's house and erased all signs he had ever mined there to discourage further European incursion on land they were happy to populate and mine themselves.[1]

Another noteworthy dissent to the land treaties of this period emerged in the person of Sauk warrior Ma-ka-tai-me-she-kia-kiak, also known as Black Hawk. Black Hawk had watched in disgust as an 1804 delegation of Sauk and Meskwaki chiefs had signed away a massive tract of land just east of the Mississippi, including Black Hawk's birthplace of Saukenuk in present-day Illinois, to the nascent United States. In his 1833 memoir, *An Autobiography*, Black Hawk recounted how these chiefs, who lacked the authority to sell tribal land should they have even intended to do so, had set out to St. Louis to petition for the freedom of an imprisoned tribesman. In the process, they were plied with alcohol and manipulated into making a sale they did not understand. As insult added to injury, the man was released from prison—only to be shot in the back as he fled. Such treatment by the US led to the Sauk fighting against the US, on the side of the English in the War of 1812, where Black Hawk distinguished himself as a warrior.

Between 1829 and 1832, as settlers increasingly populated the land ceded in 1804, Black Hawk led numerous incursions eastward across the Mississippi to reverse the course of colonization. He commanded a squadron of Sauk and Kickapoo warriors and their families known as the British Band, because they flew an English flag, less out of enduring loyalty to the English than defiance of US sovereignty. Engaged in a series of escalating conflicts with settlers and militia troops, the British Band failed to sufficiently rally neighboring tribes and soon experienced forceful retaliation by the US government.

Thus, the ill-fated Black Hawk War ended in a massacre of British Band troops and their families. The tragedy afforded the US federal government the chance to clear up some ambiguity surrounding some of its new holdings west of the Mississippi. The Sauk and Meskwaki were forced to the table to negotiate a "peace" that included the cession of vast stretches of land, including the holdings claimed by Dubuque, effectively ending the Indigenous contestation of US settlement in the Midwest. All tribes, including those who had nothing to do with Black Hawk, were pushed ever westward at gunpoint, to clear the way for Euro-American settlers to lay claims to their very own plot of private property.[2]

The Key City

Violence and duplicity had laid the foundation for law and order on the prairie and beyond. But controversy surrounding Dubuque's land claim lingered for decades following his 1810 death. Namely, prospective settlers questioned what role the state would play in the distribution of this land. While a number of claimants declared themselves the owners of the land, the prudent homesteader remained skeptical the US government would honor their claims. This ambiguity populated the area with the kind of rough and rapacious mining town familiar to viewers of the HBO series *Deadwood*. It was a mode of settlement geared around maximizing exploitation of the land's resources with no regard for long-term sustainability.

Following the so-called treaty with Black Hawk in 1832, some of the most desirable Dubuque land was unceremoniously claimed by settlers who camped on the ceded land on the wager that the US government would rule against Dubuque's claim. Initially they were run off by federal troops, including those commanded by one Jefferson Davis, who were charged with ensuring the orderly dispersal of territory by the federal

IOWA BLUFFS

government. Some were undiscouraged, however, and opted to bide their time east of the Mississippi, or else camped out on the river's islands, crossing the border illegally when the soldiers departed, and seizing the land in explicit violation of federal law. Within a year, the troops tired of this game of cat and mouse, and conceded the settlers' de facto right to the Dubuque land based, again, on possession. The settlers chartered their own city in 1837, named Dubuque after the man whose claim they had usurped by force.

It was a gamble, but the settlers' wager paid off; in 1846, Iowa formally joined the United States, and the Dubuque claim was nullified by the federal government. The land was aggregated with the rest of the state's holdings, and precedent for ownership was given to those who were already living on it. Settlers who had seized the land benefited immensely from the illegality at the center of the law, as their property was now sanctified by the same rule of law they had violated to secure it. Julien Dubuque's inheritors pushed the matter all the way to the Supreme Court, which ruled in 1854 that the natives did not have the right to sell Dubuque the land in 1788, since it had been already claimed by the Spanish Crown, whether they knew it or not. More to the point, the court ruled, by 1854, the land was undeniably inhabited by thousands of settlers, who had effectively taken possession of it, and for all intents and purposes, it belonged to them. Almost overnight, brick replaced wooden structures; the settlement was here to stay.[3]

The lead mines, which had laid the foundation for colonialism, were soon exhausted. Due to its proximity to the Mississippi, and later, railroads, however, Dubuque became in the nineteenth century a thriving mill town, revolving around the export of raw lumber, shipbuilding, brewing, and meatpacking. Intensive government investment in a modern port and railway infrastructure earned Dubuque the moniker "the Key City," establishing a strong twentieth-century industrial economy embodied in a large John Deere manufacturing plant that opened in 1947. As documented in the booster publication *Encyclopedia Dubuque*, Dubuque's city government played a key role in lobbying for federal investment in promoting Mississippi River modernization to facilitate competition with railroads and alternative transit routes like the Panama Canal. But industry in Dubuque suffered nonetheless under capital flight and deindustrialization in the 1970s, and by the 1980s the city faced a depression common to the region as the steel belt turned to rust.

In 1985, faced with a collapsing tax base and high unemployment, the city government turned to city-sponsored gambling as a source of tax revenue. The city opened the Dubuque Greyhound Park, which morphed, with the 1995 legalization of casino gambling in Iowa, into a full-fledged casino, known today as the Q. In Dubuque, and elsewhere in Iowa, such arrangements have paved the way for a much-heralded comeback from the scourge of deindustrialization. Revenue from gambling serves to finance local infrastructure investments, and, as local politicians are quick to point out, keep taxes low.[4] This kind of revenue is of course a far cry from manufacturing. From an economic perspective, the money that flows into Dubuque's coffers through gambling does not represent newly created capital, but merely the siphoning of revenue from players. It is a voluntary form of financing governance by fines and fees that has made towns like Ferguson, Missouri, notorious, though losing your money in Dubuque seems at least marginally more fun.[5] Which is not to say I saw anyone smiling.

Casino Capitalism

Trump was headed for the Grand River Convention Center, in a Port of Dubuque that has been significantly overhauled in the past two decades. Whereas in the golden age of Mississippi River commerce the Port of Dubuque was a nexus of manufacture and trade, today its most prominent feature is a cluster of new development, bordered by an ornate river walk, geared toward the extraction of tourist dollars. The new river front also includes a hotel complex and water park called Grand Harbor, the National Mississippi River Museum and Aquarium, a brewery, and the financial engine driving the project, the Diamond Jo Casino. Unlike Q, Diamond Jo is privately owned and operated—though, like the Q, the nonprofit Dubuque Racing Association, a public/private body composed of local politicians and business leaders, controls the license. While both arrangements benefit the city budget in Dubuque, Q is the bigger cash cow. As long-time city manager Mike Van Milligen once remarked: "Whoever owns the facility, gains the most."[6]

This massive redevelopment was spearheaded in the late 1990s by the Dubuque Historical Society, using local funds from gambling and other city revenue, its own America's River Project, and state funds from the Vision Iowa project.[7] Vision Iowa was funded by selling hundreds of millions of dollars of bonds to the private market, backed by the state tax

IOWA BLUFFS

on gambling. By the alchemy of gambling local economies on the financial market, Vision Iowa leveraged a state investment of $200 million into some $3 billion in infrastructure improvements supporting local commerce.[8]

The Diamond Jo casino is accessed by an arched viaduct that connects the Port to downtown Dubuque across the busy Route 61. On a weeknight, parking is not difficult to come by. Seniors passing each other in the dayglow parking lot greet by waving cans. The doors are deeply tinted, either to keep the daylight outside, or to keep the neon in. Even low-end casinos like Diamond Jo are meticulously designed to disorient the guest and rob them of their sense of time. Mesmerized by importunate light flashes and tinkling sounds and chilled awake by excessive air conditioning, the gamblers are pumped full of endorphins as they vainly chase the all-but-impossible dream of getting rich quick, and the slight, more probable but still unlikely, possibility of leaving with a bit more money than they walked in with.

I hesitate in crossing this threshold, taken aback by the obnoxious technicolor on the other side, a bit like the entrance to Toontown in *Who Framed Roger Rabbit*. Sensing my apprehension, an old white woman waiting for her taxi home tells me the place is no good. She had just lost all her money. It was her mistake, she continues, for going to Diamond Jo at all. She would have been better off at the Q, which she identifies as an Indian reservation casino down the street. There, she tells me, the odds are better. It's actually not true that the Q is Indian owned. But it's likely that the tiny elite of Indigenous people who profit off reservation gambling do in fact benefit from the persistent belief among Euro-Americans that whatever they have managed to cling to is still ripe for the taking.

A novice in the world of gaming, I quickly learn that this so-called casino is basically a video arcade for baby boomers. Even casino staples like blackjack are mostly played electronically, with no chips, but plastic cards with value added to them on stationary machines. Most of the floor is lined with flashing video gambling consoles of impressive height, looming above the player as the arcade console imposes itself on the child, and this is likely no coincidence. The game's control panels are strewn with ashtrays; this is an indoor smoking casino, and those who desire a "nonsmoking section" can take refuge in a tiny corner room with a dozen or so games crammed into the corner, connected to the smoking area by a large, breezy, and completely open ingress. There's a small cluster of human-operated tables in the center of the room, most of which are closed during my multiple visits over two days. This means there are few employees to be found in Diamond Jo besides those serving drinks and keeping an eye out for trouble. Even the roulette wheel has been automated.

Outside, in the parking lot abutting the convention center, large trailers full of merchandise boast their contents: memorabilia celebrating the deranged political career of Donald J. Trump. Smirking smugly, larger than life Trump likenesses smile and point their fingers across the largely vacant parking lots of the Port of Dubuque. He is a fitting idol. A decade before Dubuque staked its future on a roulette wheel, and decades before the much-heralded revitalization of the port, Donald J. Trump stood at the forefront of the movement known today as neoliberalism. In the mid-1970s, when Ronald Reagan was still largely considered too fringe for national office, Trump was hard at work capitalizing on the New York City fiscal crisis and putting "trickle down" economics into practice.

As recounted in Samuel Stein's *Capital City*, Trump took great advantage of the city's postindustrial economic hardship, and was a key part of a cadre of developers and financiers who effectively redefined the priorities of city government from crisis-laden Keynesianism to the explicit operation of the public sector for the generation of private profits. In the process, New York's postindustrial life has been defined by the dominance of the Finance, Insurance, and Real Estate (FIRE) sector of the ruling class, rooted in service-sector employment, tourism, and the private financialization of public funds.[9] The Port of Dubuque is a far cry from Times Square, but has effectively followed the same formula. Trump's coming, then, as many of his followers generally believe, could be seen as nothing short of Providence.

Among the Goblins

Outside the Grand River Center the following day, the line to see the big man stretches blocks, dotted with MAGA hats and patrolled by peddlers hawking Trump merchandise, including a custom shirt made only for this event, at bargain basement prices. The cheaply made imported goods contrast sharply with Trump's legendary rhetoric about revitalizing American manufacturing, but the supporters who have stuck with him this far are immune to contradiction. One man even proudly boasts five-dollar Make America Great Again hats, "made by Creole Chinamen," to the general amusement of all within earshot, though even a fairly thorough Google search has failed to explain this particular racist joke to me. And as the dark clouds looming in the Iowa sky give way to rain, the lesser hucksters hawking the image of their leader enthusiastically peddle ponchos to the faithful, who weigh whether they'd rather part with five dollars or get wet. Meanwhile, a dozen or so anti-Trumpers straight out of central casting brandish signs mocking Trump's hair and comparing him to a Cheeto.

As I check into the hotel across the street, the white boomer woman working the register asks if I'm there for "that *thing* next door," a slight lilt indicating mischievous disapproval. I say yes, and ask what she thinks of Trump. "I voted for him the first time, but never again," she tells me. "I thought he was going to change things, but he just makes everything about himself."

At this moment a balding millennial man clad in a T-shirt, cargo shorts, and long skateboarder socks with Vans to match walks in, completely drenched from the drain, and asks to use the bathroom. The clerk tells him he can't, since he's not a paying customer. Dejected, he slinks out without a word, and I follow. He asks if I'm here for the rally. I say yes, adding I am excited to see Trump, because he "always puts on a good show." He squints at me incredulously. "*Comedically* I guess that's true, but ..." He trails off, wincing. Maybe it's the rain, the overfull bladder, the long line—or maybe Trump is losing him. I ask if he's seen Trump before, and he says no, but he did see Obama when he came through here in 2008. Lowering my voice, I ask if he voted for Obama. Sure, he says, but he forgot to sign the ballot so it wasn't counted. Nonetheless, "I would have!"

Meanwhile, a local YouTube duo amateurishly aping the late *All Gas No Brakes*, jockeying for the market share surrendered by its disgraced host Andrew Callaghan, trawls the crowd for the craziest people they can find to interview. They represent themselves as an advocacy group seeking to raise awareness that Earth-born goblins are in fact piloting UFOs. A man who has been yelling various QAnon-adjacent theories is an obvious mark. He does not disappoint, ranting about goblins and UFOs as they egg him on. The people around him roll their eyes. "They're just trying to make Trump supporters look stupid," one woman cautions. Knowingly taking this bait, the e-girl steps in and delivers an impassioned speech about the existence of goblins. Afterward she remarks that of course they are going to edit the video to try to make her look bad. But, simply put, this denizen of chanworld will not be out-trolled. All the while, a chorus of listeners incredulously exclaims, in the ever-charming Great Lakes dialect, "Gahwblins? Did he say gahwblins?"

I speak at length with a white boomer woman who was in the crowd on January 6. She assures me it was not violent. She describes a convivial atmosphere, notable for the curious lack of security surrounding the building, which, in hindsight, confirmed her suspicion that the Trump supporters walked into a trap. She did not breach the building, but freely admits she would have if given the opportunity. Instead, her section of the crowd was packed shoulder to shoulder around the inauguration scaffolding immediately in front of the building. Having watched hours of footage of violence in that area, I ask for a second time if she is sure she didn't see any scuffles. She concedes that there were provocations by a handful of *outside* actors. "Antifa? Deep state?" I ask. "I think they were CIA," she responds.

I then try to reconcile this claim with the high-profile convictions of some of these very same provocateurs, who have been identified as established right-wing activists and appear to be serving very real jail time. She waves it all off, saying the trials make her so sad she can't bear to watch them. She also noticeably winces at the mention of the word "footage," surely a sore subject among J6 protesters. I can relate.

A few minutes earlier, the e-girl had declared to a small audience that Trump was likely removed from office on purpose to show us how bad things are without him. My new friend agrees. He was even late on January 6, by a numerically significant time, to send a message. He communicates using numbers, she tells me. He is in control of things. I ask what she thinks of DeSantis and the other challengers. Is Trump in danger? Absolutely not, she tells me. Trump and the "people working with him" are "twenty-five steps ahead of everyone." She pauses. "Or at least I hope he is!" At this, she laughs nervously, her eyes widening at the realization this might not be the case at all. I begin laughing too, she laughs back, and we both drag it out for a bit too long, staring at each other, laughing in the face of the insanity of 2023.

At this, a woman behind us, another white boomer, interjects, saying that surely Trump will win, but this is precisely why "they" won't even let the election happen. "Maybe there will be another pandemic."

Hunkering Down

Long before Trump arrives, the Grand River Center has been heavily fortified by the Secret Service, state and local cops, and private security guards, who compensate for their lack of badges and guns by walking around in skintight polo shirts, tattooed arms flexed to the point of physical discomfort, sporting black leather gloves and looking extremely eager to connect them with someone's face. The Exhibit Hall, a sparsely furnished trade show floor resembling a processing center for victims of a natural disaster, is packed to less than half of its 2,500 capacity. In a classic case of "hurry up and wait," those who dutifully arrived at 11 a.m. or earlier, and stood in a slowly winding line pelted by rain, will now stand back and stand by until well after 3 p.m. just to hear Trump speak. There are a few hundred chairs, many roped off for VIPs. Everyone else has to stand.

This is the third time I've seen Trump speak and the furthest I've seen him stray from his ostentatious airplane, Trump Force One. This gaudy global-warming machine has long enabled the former president to pull up to lonely airstrips in counties like Dubuque, where he last appeared on the runway of the regional airport in 2020, rant for ninety minutes or so within a hundred steps of his plane, and be back in the air before most of his fans have made it back to their cars, which often takes hours. This time, however, Trump is quite late. Chasing the thrill of yesteryear, die-hards try to get classic Trump rally chants going—"We love Trump" and "USA"—but the lion's share of the crowd isn't in the mood. There's something meaner and more sour in the air; the Stones' foreboding "Gimme Shelter" would be the perfect soundtrack, assuming of course that their label, BMI, hadn't already served Trump with a cease and desist order for using Stones music at his rallies in the past.

As the crowd silently shuffles around shaking out the pain of interminable standing, a middle-aged white woman with a prosthetic leg begins to give a speech about our duty to love America. The crowd around her cheers. At this, she raises her voice to a shriek, her entreaties becoming ever-more deranged. High above the piped-in music and chatter of the crowd, she exhorts the crowd to defend America in a desperate wail most befitting someone fighting for their life. Those around her grow quiet, stepping away and looking elsewhere, embarrassed by the grim spectacle. At last, she is summarily escorted out of the auditorium by the Secret Service, a private security guard trailing close behind, obviously salivating for a piece of the action as she shouts at him to keep back.

All the while the PA system has been blasting the uncanny soundtrack of Trumpworld, fusing the quintessential Manhattanite's love of show tunes and disco with the songs he imagines his fans want to hear. Toby Keith's sappy right-populist temper tantrum "Angry American" giving way to Abba's "Dancing Queen," for no good reason besides that it's a Trump rally. Large monitors astride the stage flash the logo of the Trump campaign, episodically interrupted by video accompaniment for exactly two songs: Elvis performing "If I Can Dream" from his 1968 comeback special, and the title track of The Who's rock opera *Tommy*, with footage taken from the film. Each time it seems to the weary crowd like some kind of pivotal moment in the event, an introduction—undoubtedly a strange one—that will nonetheless herald Trump, or else something, *anything*, besides more standing around.

But the songs end, Elvis leaves the building, the screaming mods carry Roger Daltry and his comically oversized oxblood Doc Marten boots out of the auditorium, the screen fades back to the Trump logo, and the crowd's energy continues to wane with each false alarm. This sense of interminable waiting is made worse by a truncation of the usual Trump rally playlist, likely due to just about every musician played at his rally threatening him with legal action, so that roughly seven songs are looped over and over again for hours, giving the distinct impression of an entire auditorium of people being collectively left on hold.

The emcee is Iowa's native son Matthew Whittaker, Trump's controversial one-time acting attorney general and part of an ever-shrinking club of Trump administration hacks who will have anything to do with their former boss. Notoriously enough, Whittaker got that job by campaigning for it on cable news via questioning the legality of the Mueller investigation, but was promptly returned to the world of private-sector grifting when he failed to gain the support of the Senate. As hype man for Trump in Dubuque, Whittaker warms up the crowd by introducing a panel discussion with local politicians and a local sheriff. Their topic is the unholy apocalypse that Joe Biden has supposedly unleashed on the Mexican border, ushering in an explosion of crime, gangs, terrorism, and drugs, namely fentanyl, which we are supposed to believe is trafficked across the border by asylum seekers clutching only what they can carry.

This discussion will set the tenor of the entire event, and one moment in particular says it all. Quoting a popular saying among the hard right, the sheriff declares somberly that nowadays, "Every town is a border town." The crowd goes wild. They've likely heard this many times before, but it strikes right to the heart of what has brought them to this COVID-soaked dungeon of gloom. (Author's note: I got COVID.) This is not a congenial political gathering in a bland convention center at the center of a sleazy redevelopment scheme in corn country. It is a bunker besieged, from all sides, by a slew of monstrous enemies. Sideways glances cast in my direction suggest that some may even be in the room. And the master of ceremonies is a man who has raised insecurity, paranoia, and the desperate search for scapegoats to a veritable art form.

Let Loose from the Noose

An hour or so passes from the conclusion of the panel discussion, with no other programming on the menu save for waiting for Trump. Moments like these are a good reminder that Trump campaigns have always been shoestring operations, where staffing is sparse and loyalty is prized above experience and skill. As sighs proliferate, Whittaker reemerges in a huff, accompanied by the fanfare of AC/DC's crotch rock anthem "Back in Black." Received with polite applause, Whittaker doesn't actually have much to say. He tries to hype the crowd but this is not his strong suit. He stalls for a while, noticeably wilting on stage, and ultimately beats a hasty retreat, assuring the crowd that Trump is "on the way" and will be there in "a few minutes." A half hour goes by. A large section of seats in the front have been reserved for those who made a special donation, and these have sat empty for hours. "Donald Trump doesn't need my money," one man mutters, explaining the scheme. "I need some of his!" The emergence of VIPs from a private room is the first credible lead in hours that the event is actually moving along. "Here come the important people!" someone jeers. This heralds the anticlimax to end all anticlimaxes.

Abruptly and without fanfare, after hours of collective anticipation, Trump is hastily announced and plods out from behind the curtain, before his theme song, Lee Greenwood's maudlin, flag-fondling "God Bless the USA" can even begin playing. Instead of strutting up and down the stage waving and pointing as he has done in the past, or breaking into his signature dance that resembles above all else a person masturbating two men at the same time, the former president stands awkwardly in one spot, hands by his sides, looking lost and defeated, as Greenwood warbles on and on about how he'd sure have liked to serve his country but never got around to doing it. Trump's broad shoulders curve downward into a distinct slump, and his suit, so expertly tailored to mask his obese frame, now seems overlarge, like the man is melting before our very eyes. Meanwhile, the screens alongside the stage display the latest Fox News poll showing cratering support for Ron DeSantis, formerly Trump's chief opponent, but increasingly just a political has-been with whom Trump has an axe to grind. And Trump has a lot of axes to grind in Dubuque.

As Greenwood fades out, Trump takes a few labored steps to the rostrum, where he will remain for the duration of the event. Caked in more makeup than usual and wincing under the lights, he props himself up with one hand, leaving the other free to gesticulate, albeit weakly and without conviction. And then, no doubt riding high from the fleeting rush of the speed that has fueled his motor-mouthed persona for decades, he put his strongest muscles to work—those animating his jaw. They don't stop moving for nearly eighty minutes straight. All the while, everything about Trump betrays desperation, vulnerability, creeping and inevitable mortality—all that his tough guy mythos seeks to deny. "This is a big crowd," he declares, harping on a favorite obsession. "You got a lot of people outside, trying to get in." Just about everyone in the crowd must know that the number of people waiting outside is exactly zero. And with this, Trump is off to the races.

Gone are the camp, irony, and self-aware humor that constitute Trump's bizarre yet undeniable charisma, and once distinguished him from a ranting and raving old crank like the one tossed out of the rally before it even began. Bitterness, vengeance, and retribution are the order of the day in Dubuque. As the standing crowd shifts from one foot to the other, Trump weaves a complex demonology of America at the brink of annihilation, beset on all sides by the forces of evil from a comic book rendering of Revelation. These are not new themes for Trump, but their exposition is darker, meaner, and positively Boschian in detail. At this very moment, Trump drones ominously, "lawless mobs of unscreened, unvetted illegal alien migrants are stampeding across the border by the millions and millions, including hordes of criminals, terrorists, human traffickers, child smugglers, and inmates emptied out of their prisons and insane asylums and mental institutions."

Without taking a breath, he adds: "And that sounds bad, but it's actually worse than that!"

Going for Broke

Perhaps Trump is saying much the same as always, with a bit more of a dramatic flair. But the tone is more sinister, increasingly unhinged, and with the twinkle gone from his eyes, its pure ugliness stands denuded. The "American carnage" of "factories scattered like tombstones" now seems rosy by comparison. All the while, Trump's deceptively disorganized remarks effectively walk the listener through an extended exegesis of the good old boy sheriff's earlier remarks, crafting a complete worldview around the notion that "every town is a border town."

The *umwelt* Trump outlines with such fanatical gravity is essentially this: The American frontier was once claimed with brute force. A settler democracy was founded on love of commerce, the nuclear family, and Christian, Euro-American supremacy. The hostile natives were supposed to be dead, but it turns out, we didn't kill them all. Like the all-American Freeling family of the *Poltergeist* films, the Indian graveyard on which we've settled has come back to life. With it, the frontier has returned, and now it is everywhere; the immigrant crime statistics are written on the walls in blood. And the guns that good Americans so desperately need to fight back are being stripped from them, along with the rough masculine values that make guns any good in the first place. The police and border patrol are handcuffed by politicians like Joe Biden. These fiends are not just senile, feeble, wimpy, incoherent, and incompetent to stop the threats (though Trump emphasizes numerous times that Biden, his three-year senior, is all these things), but are actively working in league with the globalists who put America last, an ill-defined cabal that verges into *The Protocols of the Elders of Zion*, seeking to overrun America's borders and destroy the country for good. Shadowy enemies like "Chinese Communists" blur seamlessly into Islamist jihadists and refugees seeking sanctuary, to form an amorphous brown blob threatening to absorb all that is good and holy in the United States until it is gone.

But this is not all. All the while, American society is being simultaneously undermined by "enemies within," like Black Lives Matter rioters, "critical race theory" teaching that the settlement was unjust, gender theory undermining the heteropatriarchal basis of the family, and countless other tentacles of the nefarious "woke" menace threatening to demoralize the young and convert them to the cause of America's enemies. Trump's blistering attacks on the enemies within receive some of the most thunderous applause of the day, perhaps especially his vow for an improbable ban on "communists and Marxists entering the country." Similar hosannas accompany Trump's promises to defeat so-called transgender ideology and defund schools mandating vaccines. In these fleeting moments, the languid assembly truly comes alive.

In this grim spectacle, Trump offers his most faithful a worldview that equally balances imminent doom and opportunistic denial. Any crisis that cannot be saddled on an abject scapegoat—climate change, COVID—must be denied altogether. The mere articulation of these social facts as problems is treated as an enemy assault, so much confusion injected into the pleasing sureties of Fox News bedtime stories for patriotic, God-fearing children. The power of collective denial, and the outrage that must be stoked to keep it simmering, ranks among the strongest political forces that exist. This is because it cuts to the heart of the one thing most people fear most, powerlessness in the face of their own mortality, and invites them instead to collectively hallucinate a world where all is in fact well, save for the naysayers, a Heaven where everything's fine. And in this same seductive manner, Trump soothes the bad conscience of white Americans, who *all* understand at some level that the system has been rigged in their favor, inviting them to shed the guilt and shame and to simply embrace this as their birthright, while insisting, with a wink, that white supremacy doesn't exist at all.

At the center of Trump's meandering path of doomsaying and denial lies the realm of pure fantasy. Trump invites us to a world where his first crack at the presidency in fact made America great again: where he defeated ISIS, built the wall, and drained the swamp. Not only did Trump build the wall, he adds, but Mexico did in fact pay for it, by sending millions of soldiers to the border, whose salaries were certainly not paid by the United States! And Trump also would have single-handedly prevented the Russian invasion of Ukraine had he not been removed by a rigged election. Similarly, his return to office is now plagued by "election interference" in the form of multiple felony cases. Even these indictments are a testament to how great Trump made America, he insists, which earned him the backlash of his foes. Practically affixing himself to a cross, he bellows "I'm being indicted for you!"

Along the way, Trump makes exactly two boasts that even brush against reality. The first comes when he claims that after fifty years of pro-life activism, he single-handedly ended *Roe v. Wade* through his Supreme Court nominees. The room explodes. Dubuque is a Catholic stronghold, after all. In the eyes of the American church, Trump's many sins might just be forgiven if he is willing to focus on the handful of "culture war" issues that have effectively turned American Catholicism into a single-minded advocacy organization aimed at limiting the rights of women and LGBTQ people at all costs, all the while standing in broad daylight as a real-life pedophilic cesspool, which QAnon has quite unnecessarily invented out of thin air. (Author's note: I grew up Catholic.) The second truth comes in his claim to be the first president in decades to not start a new war. Trump surely did not sow peace on the global stage, but the popularity of his isolationist views should not be overlooked. Growing up in the shadow of 9/11, I must register the uncanny feeling of standing in an auditorium full of the hardest-right elements of the Republican Party, draped in cheap reproductions of flags, eagles, and all that is holy, roaring with approval as their standard bearer promises to *stay out of wars.*

As the show winds down to the final "Make America Great Again!" Trump's presentation has run about fifteen minutes shy of the other times I've seen him. The energy is low. He seems closer to Nixon in his final days in office than to William Jennings Bryan, the populist orator to whom Steve Bannon rightfully compared him when this whole crazy adventure first began. Back then, Trump was having fun thumbing his nose at the so-called establishment, relishing the high that draws all the biggest narcissists to politics. Seven years later, he is a desperate man, painting a desperate picture of the world. Worst of all, the consummate showman is now guilty of a crime far graver than any of the felonies for which he stands accused: Donald J. Trump is boring.

All Bets Are Off

In the classic study *Renegades, Mariners, and Castaways,* written in immigration detention on Ellis Island, C.L.R. James examines Melville's *Moby Dick* as an enduring study of American society, and the disastrous, and seemingly intractable, end toward which it surges. Weighing the carnage of mid-century life, James argues that Melville foresaw the great totalitarian figures of the twentieth century, whose obsession with mastering nature and imposing their monadic will on the world promised to become, like Ahab's mad quest, a suicide mission for themselves and everyone else. The main question raised by the fate of the *Pequod,* then, is not what Ahab is after or why it consumes the ship, but why, after numerous warnings that the ship's disastrous fate looms largely on the horizon, does the crew not rebel?[10]

Donald J. Trump is such a figure as Melville's Ahab. He is a parasite and predator economically, politically, socially, sexually—a vile and unserious man who serves his most base impulses at all costs, but lacks any sustained sense of self-preservation, much less a drive to protect those around him. Instead, the realization of his base desires ensures disorder and pain for everyone in his path. He uses people until there's nothing left, until they're consumed by the fires he can't stop setting in his own house, and he seems to have no control over this, much less any wish to make it stop. Instead, he is uniquely adept at capitalizing on the chaos he wreaks, turning each catastrophe into a new opportunity for profit, on the way to the tragic culmination of his ego-fueled suicide mission.

But just as *Moby Dick* does not concern itself with the singular figure of Ahab, all of this is not said of just one man. Trump is the perfect avatar of his class fragment of footloose financiers possessing no plan for anything but maximum profit extraction in the here and now, hopscotching the planet from one self-inflicted disaster after another, skimming a little here, scamming a little there, speculating on the dividends of whatever hope still exists and capitalizing that too, as leverage to ensure the next calamity. He has no plans to fix anything or save anyone except himself, for as long as he can until he becomes his own final victim. To Trump's credit, however, unlike the rest of the FIRE sector scumbags who think what he says while preaching diversity and inclusion and saving the planet, he has really never pretended to be anything other than Donald J. Trump. And among his many sins, nobody can ever accuse Trump of not knowing his audience.

Landlocked in their own tiny *Pequods*, Trump's enduring supporters are lesser Ahabs, morbidly obsessed with defending the homeland, the purity of the family, the sanctity of landed property, and the pitiable fairy tale of eternal life after death. Despite his entreaties to "Make America Great Again Again," this Trump does not speak to those who have been "left behind." He is talking explicitly to people with something to hold onto. Gone is the talk of manufacturing work; he didn't bring those jobs back and they're never coming back. The blue-collar Trumper of 2016 lore was not a complete fabrication, but was just as likely to be the shop's boss, dressed in crisp Carhartts and driving a cartoonishly large Ford pickup with a pristine bed. The forgotten American is back to being forgotten. Trump stands in Dubuque as a globe-trotting, border-smashing, hedonist polyglot of the big bourgeoisie, binding small men of local fiefdoms into a cross-class alliance under the ridiculous premise that he represents land-bound capital, closed borders, and traditional values.

Surely these people have real problems and grievances—the famous "economic insecurity" and other symptoms of a social order in decline. The crunch of austerity, capital's crisis of profitability, and the social chaos of an untenable world order have been defining features of decades of mass movements waged to build a just world for all, and have driven many in the so-called middle class into the streets, often with more alacrity than those worse off. In contrast, however, Trump's little Ahabs seek only to save themselves, their families dissolved by capital's shifting bases, and their communities poisoned by unregulated industry, in the name of some imagined ideal of America that never really existed. And Trump's enduring popularity is proof positive that they will go down guns blazing, Rittenhouses of the spirit, on the suicidal quest to make fantasy real again. Perhaps there's a dark pleasure to be found in willing one's own annihilation, realizing the violent end foretold by America's violent beginning. But I saw no evidence of this, only a miserable rage, the self-mutilating glorification of tearing the fabric of asunder.

Trump, for his part, doesn't give a shit about these people or their problems, any more than he cares about abortion, American factories, or transgender ideology. "It's amazing how strongly people feel about that," he remarked incredulously last summer. "I talk about cutting taxes, people go like that [polite applause], I talk about transgender, everybody goes crazy. Five years ago you didn't know what the hell it was." Standing at the Port of Dubuque, a public/private monument to the world remade in his image, Trump bears a message from the future. It is a garbled harangue drenched in cynicism, despair, paranoia, and hopeless self-destruction, spoken by a pathetic man driven mad by selfishness, resentment, and fear. He slouches, sweating and panting, at the intersection of settler colonialism's enduring violence and the electronic roulette wheel of twenty-first century statecraft, bellowing invectives against the world's most powerless people, as he and the social order he so deftly represents career heedlessly toward total destruction. And this time, he doesn't even have any good jokes.

PART 5
EVERY FIRE NEEDS A LITTLE BIT OF HELP

Every Fire Needs a Little Bit of Help

This essay first appeared in "That Summer Feeling," a 2022 special issue of *Endnotes* commemorating the two-year anniversary of the George Floyd Rebellion.

■

> Dedicated to the slain and imprisoned heroes of the George Floyd Rebellion.[1]

On May 30, 2020, thousands of people descended on downtown Chicago for a raucous daytime march. The gathering was part of a nationwide crescendo of rebellion that began in Minneapolis five days prior in response to the police murder of George Floyd. After being cooped up for months amid the uncertainty of the COVID pandemic, fearful of everyone as a potential carrier of disease, we had been set free by the images of Minneapolis's Third Precinct aflame. Hitting the streets that day was something akin to a religious experience. From the onset it was clear that the crowd would not follow the shopworn "peaceful" Black Lives Matter protest script. I watched with glee as teenagers scurried through the crowd graffitiing every conceivable surface with anti-cop slogans like ACAB and Fuck 12, alongside their own confrontational reappropriation of "Black Lives Matter," a long stalled out movement which many of them were too young to have participated in. An American flag was summarily lowered and burned, and after some spirited debate involving sentimental locals, the Chicago flag was similarly put to the torch. Chicago police cars were attacked, their windows smashed with

EVERY FIRE NEEDS A LITTLE BIT OF HELP

the skateboards preferred by many young people, or whatever else people could get their hands on. Multiple CPD cars were set on fire. The cops themselves were outmaneuvered by a massive crowd swarming a sprawling downtown grid, and formed defensive lines unprotected from behind, wantonly swinging clubs and deploying pepper spray with no clear purpose save perhaps their proximity to particularly valuable sites of potential looting.

In response, Lori Lightfoot—the city's Black lesbian mayor, who often postures as a police reformer—ordered the hulking drawbridges connecting Chicago's iconic loop with the rest of the city to be raised. This dramatic scene, which would recur episodically throughout the summer, effectively cut off the heart of Chicago's affluence from its largely Black and brown working-class outer ring, revealing the subtle counterinsurgency mapped onto the stark racial segregation of the city's terrain. On May 30, raising the bridges also functioned, alongside the closure of the subway and parts of the city's main artery, Lake Shore Drive, to trap protesters downtown, and a hastily announced 9 p.m. curfew served as the pretext for mass arrests numbering in the hundreds. As the sun set, Chicagoans who had escaped this net hit the streets in an explosion of looting that seemed generalized throughout the city's otherwise disjointed neighborhoods. Affluent areas like the chic Wicker Park, and working-class neighborhoods like South Shore, were similarly cleaned out. These expropriations continued into the next day, as the cops guarded the big money retailers, leaving grocery stores and other targets deemed low value to be stripped bare by leisurely crowds operating in broad daylight. Before the weekend was over, CPD would arrest at least a thousand people, and hundreds of cops would claim to be injured.[2]

By the standards of the summer of 2020, this was not a particularly remarkable turn of events. Cops were outflanked and overrun in cities across the United States all summer. They were confounded by the ferocity of the riots, the abuse rained down on them by even the so-called peaceful protesters, and perhaps most shockingly, the people whom they ordinarily harass and intimidate with impunity defending themselves—and even going on the attack. Perhaps some cops were surprised by the realization that tens of millions of Americans hate their guts and want them to quit their jobs or else just die. If they were honest with themselves, though, they'd admit this was all a long time coming. The biggest surprise of the George Floyd Rebellion is how long it took to arrive.[3]

The rebellion unfolded amid a protracted capitalist crisis exacerbated by a global pandemic that laid capital's most brutal contradictions bare. It came after decades in which stubbornly low rates of profit and the violent instability of the global market had wrought an enduring state of "churning and flailing," as David Ranney put it. The stagnation of capital, lacking steady outlets for acceptable levels of protracted valorization, has created a protracted global instability with disastrous consequences in the lives of working people made to endure the worst of the chaos. But, as Ranney argues, working-class people are not simply acted upon by the turbulence of capital's contractions; on a terrain largely configured by forces outside their control, they are forced to constantly react, and sometimes go on the offensive.[4]

As production and circulation are reconfigured at a breakneck pace, cutting the legs out from underneath any inherited sense of what it means to be a political actor or part of a larger polity, the disorder of what is glibly called "late capitalism" has spurred on churning and flailing within the political identities and forms of association necessary for proletarian struggle. Working-class Americans have been compelled to struggle against the disastrous form of life capital has engendered for them, and to replace this hellish world with a new one, while it is nowhere clear how to rectify the disjunction between the particular and the universal. In the magisterial *American Civilization*, C.L.R. James argues that the gulf dividing the belligerently "autonomous," freedom-loving American individual from their broader social world has been the fundamental problematic of American politics since the colonial period.[5] And the vociferous American individual, stubbornly irreducible to the universality for which they nonetheless strive in religion and politics, is also defined by profoundly different experiences of capitalist exploitation—so-called race, gender, national belonging, sexual identity, and an almost infinity of differentiating criteria. Thus the very constitution of American subjectivity is in constant tension with the necessity, objectively imposed upon exploited and oppressed people, for working political unity sufficient to create a world where *the free development of each is the free development of all.*

This formulation may seem abstract, but its implications are pressingly practical. American proletarians, like working people across the world, are compelled by the circumstances of their daily lives to engage in struggle. But once they are activated, key questions present themselves:

EVERY FIRE NEEDS A LITTLE BIT OF HELP

who are we, what are we fighting, and what are we fighting for? Absent coherent answers, few will struggle for long. In recent decades in the United States, these questions have been addressed by two main answers, alternately rooted in race or class. Polemicists insist that one must choose one or the other, as if they even can be disentangled, let alone counterposed. But the recent American experience demonstrates something more profound is going on in the streets: a churning of struggles which are advanced under the aegis of a coherent identity—class in Occupy, race in Black Lives Matter—which posits a tentative reconciliation of particular with universal, before this identity becomes a reified, meaningless abstraction, and an obstacle to the further unfolding of the movement. The only thing left to do in those moments is break these abstractions apart. The George Floyd Rebellion was the latest of such eruptions.

Assault on Precinct 3

"Heard about the guy who fell off a skyscraper?" asks the young Hubert in Mathieu Kassovitz's 1995 film *La Haine*. "On his way down past each floor, he kept saying to reassure himself: So far so good ... so far so good ... so far so good."

Most of May 2020 was a sustained downward plummet. After nearly two months of stay-at-home orders, whatever novelty "the lockdown" originally held had decidedly worn off. The realization was setting in that COVID-19 was not going away fast, and whatever "normal" we eventually returned to would be irreversibly shaped by the virus. For the luckiest workers, disproportionately white and college educated, this meant working from home, doing some of the most alienating and pointless jobs in world history, while battling depression, substance abuse, and a profound despair further amplified by the collective nervous breakdown known as social media. But this was only some 42 percent of American workers; the majority of the workforce faced grimmer prospects still, either losing jobs outright (33 percent), or being forced to risk the virus as a condition of continuing employment as so-called essential workers (26 percent).[6] Service and transportation workers, suddenly deputized as unwaged enforcers of public health codes, tangled with customers refusing to wear masks, leading to countless acts of humiliation and abuse, a spate of assaults, and multiple murders of workers simply requesting that a customer cover their nose and mouth.[7] Prisoners were largely left to fend for themselves in their squalid petri dishes, as COVID ripped through US carceral facilities, briefly making New York City's Rikers Island penal colony the worldwide epicenter of the virus.[8] Accordingly, carceral facilities became early sites of struggle in 2020.[9]

Even in the months before the pandemic, some 10 percent of Americans could not afford their monthly bills at all, while 39 percent would be unable to cover an unexpected expense of $400. A quarter of Americans skipped medical care because they could not afford it. By May of 2020, upwards of 25.4 million people were counted as out of work entirely, for increasingly long stretches of time. The unemployment rate was highest among Black and brown Americans, who made up 16.8 percent and 17.6 percent of the unemployed, respectively, compared to 12.4 percent for white people. Even among the employed, a quarter of Black and brown adults who desired full-time jobs were forced to work part-time. The demographic hit hardest by the COVID recession was teenagers, who comprised 29.9 percent of those looking for work and unable to find it, and who would go on to play an outsized role in the rebellion.[10] Only a national moratorium on evictions prevented an avalanche of sudden homelessness. This policy, along with the temporary suspension of student debt payments, represented state intervention to stem the most brutal immediate consequences of capital's austerity regime, in order to keep it intact in the long term. This approach to governance would define the public relief under COVID. Many laid-off workers found temporary relief in a one-time stimulus check, alongside unemployment benefits that enabled those many to keep afloat, or even live better than before while avoiding a return to shit jobs. But the rent would eventually come due, benefits would dry up, and anyone brave enough to face the future in May 2020 knew that the picture was exceedingly bleak.[11]

The often-overlooked events that set the George Floyd Rebellion in motion in the first place paint a grim portrait of the desperation that defined working-class life in the early days of the pandemic. It all began in the Cup Foods bodega in South Minneapolis, when George Floyd, a forty-six-year-old precariously employed Black man recently laid off and freshly recovered from COVID, bought a pack of cigarettes with a twenty-dollar bill that may or may not have been counterfeit. The Black teenage cashier who sold the cigarettes suspected Floyd's money was counterfeit, but accepted it anyway. But as Floyd exited, the young cashier changed his mind, and decided he had to get the cigarettes back.

EVERY FIRE NEEDS A LITTLE BIT OF HELP

Who cares about a lousy pack of cigarettes, least of all an exploited teenage cashier? In this case, loyalty to private property or bourgeois law did not play a part. Like so many proletarians kept on the worksite during COVID, the employees of Cup Foods had been christened "essential" and tossed to the frontlines of the pandemic as cannon fodder to keep capital circulating. And just like the clerks in other places being thrown to the front lines as unwaged enforcers of mask mandates, Cup Foods workers had also been deputized as unwaged currency inspectors, forced to determine on the spot whether the money customers like Floyd handed them was real or fake, and to then engage in a potentially explosive confrontation with the customer. If a Cup Foods cashier allowed a counterfeit bill to slip by, they would have to cover it out of their own meager wages. Twenty dollars, which would come out of this cashier's pocket, translates to a lot of time laboring for free in a city where the average cashier makes roughly $12 per hour, before taxes.

The cashier consulted a manager, who dispatched him to Floyd's car to demand the cigarettes back, and then commanded another clerk to call the cops.[12] The needs of capital accumulation had thrown this young service worker into the miserable situation of policing other working-class Black people like George Floyd, who had long survived on the margins of the labor market, alternately used and discarded as capital saw fit. These were two Black men struggling to keep their heads above water in a country where the odds were against them. Thanks to the machinations of management science, their personal struggles to navigate the bottom rungs of the labor market were turned into direct conflict with each other. And to make matters worse, the cops were on the way.

"I've never seen a situation so dismal," the Irish republican Brendan Behan once remarked, "that a policeman couldn't make it worse." When Minneapolis cops arrived, the low-stakes conflict between Floyd and the cashier turned deadly almost immediately, thanks to America's infusion of police violence into nearly every facet of life for working-class people otherwise left to fend for themselves.

Shortly after Floyd's murder, the Minneapolis Police Department (MPD) released an account of his death entitled "Man Dies After Medical Incident During Police Interaction." It is a remarkable example of the magical rhetoric US cops deploy to hide their atrocities, most often parroted with great fidelity by the press. "[Floyd] was ordered to step from his car," the press release claimed. "After he got out, he physically resisted officers. Officers were able to get the suspect into handcuffs and noted he appeared to be suffering medical distress. Officers called for an ambulance."[13] The millions of people who have viewed the footage of George Floyd's murder have beheld a dramatically different scene. It is impossible to say how many times such a fabrication has passed for the truth, as cops can often command the very nature of reality to obey. But this time, video evidence of Floyd's murder, shot by a Black teenager named Darnella Frazier, quickly crisscrossed the internet. In the stifling hell of locked-down America, with hundreds of millions of people cooped up and facing an uncertain future, the image of a man slowly choked to death by the repressive agents of US capitalism soon found resonance far beyond its local context.

The following afternoon, thousands gathered in the intersection where Floyd was murdered. Marches snaked through Minneapolis streets as demonstrators hurled rocks at cop cars. Much of this crowd soon arrived at the Third Precinct, where the killer cops had suited up the day of Floyd's murder. The precinct's windows were smashed and its walls graffitied, along with the windows of every cop car and personal vehicle they could get their hands on. A liquor store was looted and its goods redistributed. Professional social movement "organizers," equipped with safety vests and megaphones to assert their authority, attempted to stop the action. But they were outnumbered—the momentum belonged to the rebels, who shouted that nobody got to decide when things ended. The people returned the following day with redoubled ferocity. Looting spread, providing food and liquor to sustain the growing crowd, but the main target remained the Third Precinct. By the following evening, it would be sacked and set afire, after the cops were forced to beat their ignominious retreat.[14] Images spread across the country of a determined multiracial crowd fighting the police, destroying cop infrastructure, taking what they wanted without paying, and above all, undertaking bold and decisive actions at a time when trepidation ruled the land—and winning. The heat was on.

Forty Years in the Desert

The George Floyd Rebellion capped off a decade of struggles through which the decomposed and disoriented US proletariat struggled to articulate and assert itself on a social terrain defined by decades of

EVERY FIRE NEEDS A LITTLE BIT OF HELP

retrenchment and "class war in which only one side was fighting."[15] The struggles of the late twentieth and early twenty-first centuries were drenched in the long shadow of the 1970s, when the US postwar boom ran aground amid a global crisis of overproduction, and a diminishing profit rate in manufacture, led capital away from large-scale industrial employment and toward both the dramatic automation of production and increasingly ethereal speculation in the finance sector. Capital proved time and again unable to break the tendency, long heralded by Marx, of surplus capital, lacking a productive outlet, amassing alongside surplus populations of proletarians, for whom there is no place in a market they have nonetheless been forced to depend on.[16] In the United States, the rate of profit, difficult as it is to calculate conclusively, fell from anywhere between 25 percent to 33 percent in the years between 1948 and 2015.[17] Nostalgia for the good old days have long abounded—fueling the popularity of both Donald Trump and Bernie Sanders—despite more time having elapsed since the postwar boom ended than the boom itself lasted. Meanwhile, jobs have become less stable, lower paying, and more demanding, while pensions have vanished, and employment in the "gig economy" now resembles the frenetic drive of capital from one outlet to another, never satisfied and never sitting still.

Capital's turn to intensive financialization in the final decades of the twentieth century has driven an intensive project of global urban recapitalization known as gentrification, which has unfolded alongside the dismantling and privatization of essential public services like water, garbage collection, and education. Not only do the reinvestment in neglected land and the subsumption of previously public goods provide outlets for surplus capital desperate to valorize itself, these brutal forms of expropriation also represent a ruling-class offensive against entitlements hard-won by twentieth-century working-class struggle. This is especially true among Black and brown people in the US, whose decades of militancy had, by the late 1960s, begun to procure auspicious inroads into the labor force and housing market. Beginning with great intensity in the 1970s, however, the restructuring toward what is commonly called neoliberalism hit working-class Black and brown people especially hard. The crisis of 2008, which demonstrated the objective economic limits to neoliberal policy alongside the ruling class's unwillingness, or inability, to change course, also occasioned the particularly devastating liquidation of Black-owned wealth.[18]

Today's ruling class has only managed to stave off disastrous crises by sowing small-scale disasters all across the globe, especially in the daily lives of a growing number of proletarians. Among the chief global laboratories for austerity, the United States has undertaken a dramatic restructuring of working-class life, defined by the shifting of state functioning away from the welfare state and toward police, prisons, and military expenditures. This arrangement provides outlets for capital in the construction of carceral and military infrastructure, while cops protect real estate investments and other private property, prisons discipline proletarians to accept abysmal wages, and surplus populations are housed in prisons and military barracks. Geographer Ruth Wilson Gilmore has dubbed this arrangement "the prison fix"—a stopgap measure overseen by a state increasingly reduced to deploying its immense capacity for violence to mitigate the most egregious symptoms of a protracted crisis it cannot end.[19] Brutal state-sponsored crisis containment, with no horizon for resolution, constitutes part of the "holding pattern with a gradual loss of altitude" that characterized the post-2008 years.[20]

This transformation of labor and life on a global scale was not uncontested. In particular, the antiglobalization movement of the 1990s represented an attempt at an internationalist mass movement politics, albeit three steps behind the global hopscotch of capital long freed from the strictures of the nation state. With influences dating back to the militant activism of groups like ACT UP around state inactivity amid the AIDS epidemic, the antiglobalization movement was also the debut on the world stage of a profoundly fragmented amalgamation of people, grasping to articulate a positive conception of politics amid great disorganization and a decades-long crisis of universalist political identity. Lacking any substantive platform in production or circulation, dedicated and courageous activists took to the streets in spectacular confrontations with riot cops at trade summits where attendance became something of an extreme sport. The September 11 attacks, in turn, channeled this momentum into ill-fated attempts to block the US warfare state's decades-long imperialist misadventures in the Middle East, where capital's search for valorization in oil fields and arms dealing generated profits for some at the expense of untold carnage and irreversible social instability.

"In order to continue its philosophy of full employment," autoworker James Boggs wrote in 1963, "organized labor has become part and parcel

EVERY FIRE NEEDS A LITTLE BIT OF HELP

of the 'American way of life.' It has become partners with the military in establishing and maintaining a war machine the only purpose of which is to threaten the destruction of humanity."[21] The same could be said about the buildup of the police and prison apparatus in the decades that followed: far from the enemies of the working-class they were once considered, cops' and guards' unions—whose primary demands are freedom from consequences of their brutality—became some of the most powerful unions in the American Federation of Labor and Congress of Industrial Organizations, the largest labor federation in the United States.[22] It is small wonder then that attempts to contest the new regime of globalizing capital were characterized by an isolation of mass movement politics from the point of production. Even in the salad days of the postwar boom, as Boggs argued, most American unions surrendered control over conditions of production in exchange for higher wages and other benefits that could be revoked once worker power was decisively stemmed. Now that the proverbial carrot has been withdrawn from a significantly weakened labor movement, and it is mostly the stick that remains, recapture of the point of production has proved elusive, thanks in large part to unions remaining thoroughly institutionalized as the junior partners of capital and the eager accomplices of America's prison and police boom taking the place of its vanished welfare state.

The despondency produced in the early 2000s by the failure of the antiwar movement, the rightward drift of US politics, including its labor movement, and a general downward grind of working-class life across the country, can help the contemporary youthful observer make sense of the curious cult of Barack Obama, a tepid neoliberal technocrat on whom millions of Americans were all too willing to project their yearning for "hope and change." Before Obama even took office, however, the 2008 crisis made it clear that any change would be for the worse. It was the culmination of decades of accumulation fueled by fictitious capital, as diminishing profits led investors to increasingly ethereal financial schemes.[23] Some $10.2 trillion in the United States alone was revealed to exist nowhere except the imagination of feverish speculators.

Considerable sleaze and malfeasance throughout the ruling class prepared the ground for the worst of 2008. And thanks to bailouts overseen in part by Obama himself, the lion's share of the suffering was kicked to the bottom of the social ladder. There it wreaked havoc in proletarian life in the form of persistent unemployment and cuts to most social spending outside military, prisons, and cops. Black homeowners, who were disproportionately targeted by predatory loans at the center of the housing bubble, were particularly devastated. More than 240,000 lost their homes. Overall, white families lost 28.5 percent of their total wealth to the crisis, while Black families lost 47.5 percent—dramatically exacerbating long-standing trends in wealth inequality and home owner-ship dating back to slavery.[24] The ravages of the crisis, initially met with meager resistance from unions, capped off a demoralizing decade of retrenchment and defeat. But as Loren Goldner would later reflect, "the sky is always darkest just before dawn."[25]

Don't Call It a Comeback

On September 30, 2011, rumors ricocheted across social media that the English rock band Radiohead was set to play a surprise show at the Occupy Wall Street encampment in Manhattan's Zuccotti Park. The movement had originated with a call by the politically ambiguous "anti-consumerist" publication *Adbusters* to descend on Wall Street on September 17, but it was quickly taken up by a variety of local actors, and soon escaped any coordination or control by the magazine. Local Occupy movements had important predecessors, like the 2009 protests in Oakland against the police murder of Oscar Grant, and the 2009–10 student movement, which had considerable influence in New York and California, perhaps especially the clarion call: "Occupy Everything!" As the Radiohead rumor spread that day, thousands of New Yorkers descended on the tiny park, spilling into the street in every direction and exponentially increasing the protest movement's record crowd. The concert was all a hoax, but it didn't matter. The energy was electric; in the crush of the crowd, I sensed that something truly new was happening. Best of all, just about everyone could be part of it by virtue of just showing up.

The massive crowd brought traffic to a standstill as it meandered through the financial district, landing at last on the doorstep of One Police Plaza, NYPD's home base. Communicating through the human microphone, a crowd-based amplification technique used to circumvent the city's aggressive ban on unauthorized amplification, speakers echoed the movement's populist themes of "the 99%" versus "the 1%," peppered with a new grievance: police brutality. The previous week, a Staten Island cop gained international notoriety for emptying his pepper spray on a

EVERY FIRE NEEDS A LITTLE BIT OF HELP

crowd of young women for seemingly no reason at an Occupy protest. This scene has greatly increased sympathy for—and participation in—the Occupy movement. The day after the Radiohead stunt, another massive crowd descended on the park, marching across the Brooklyn Bridge's vehicle lane, and directly into an NYPD kettle that netted seven hundred arrests. If it was the cops' intent to stem the movement with violence and arrests, this backfired. Occupy Wall Street was just getting started.

Occupy was the largest and most intense wave of struggle in the US that my generation, which came to politics around the antiglobalization and antiwar movements, had ever seen. But it was not unprecedented. In December 2001, Argentinians took to the streets in large numbers, blocking roads, banging pots, and raising a resounding cry: *Que se vayan todos!*, "they all must go." This wholesale and belligerent rejection of Argentina's neoliberal political establishment was accompanied by assemblies on the hyperlocal level, experiments in building a new conception of politics from the ground up. Its starting point was the imperative to wipe it all clean and start from scratch.[26] These movements could be called "antiformist" as, in contrast to reformist or conformist movements, which work within established modalities of political engagement, they sought a radical remaking of the social order, predicated on the delegitimization of existent politics almost altogether.[27]

Argentina's *piqueteros* were a harbinger of things to come, perhaps befitting the country's early and intensive adoption of neoliberal governance, which by 2001, had transformed life in a way deemed untenable by a critical mass of people. The movement augured a wave of massive public space occupations that rejected the entire social order root and branch—albeit with no clear conception of what was to take its place. This global wave of struggle, which crashed into ground zero of American finance capital with Occupy Wall Street, would come to be called "the movement of the squares."[28] Beginning in 2011, similar scenes recurred throughout the Middle East and North Africa as part of the Arab Spring, the Occupy movement across the United States, and in Greece, Spain, and Portugal.

Occupy encampments were places where participants, drawn by a wholesale rejection of the capitalist status quo, sought to replicate in miniature new forms of social relations and democratic participation, through mutual aid and direct democratic rituals inherited from the antiglobalization movement. At their best, Occupy camps were experimental sites for common life outside of commodity exchange. They brought together great ingenuity and collective action, albeit among a tiny fraction of their city's population. In one instance, a city ban on gas generators was quickly circumvented by some ingenious Occupier fashioning a battery powered by a stationary bike, which was itself banned under some flimsy pretext or another in short order. But camps also inherited many of the social problems US official society has largely given up on addressing, including mental illness, substance abuse, and sexual assault.[29] And while many of us who upheld the radical horizontalism of the antiglobalization movement as an article of faith went into the movement believing in the ideology of direct democracy, like most desires, its fulfillment was a nightmare; endless self-aggrandizing assemblies proved to be the last place where decisive action could be taken. Initiative taken outside of these bodies by affinity groups and other ad hoc micro-groupuscules gave flesh to the Invisible Committee's imperative: "*Abolish general assemblies.*"[30]

Thus, the fragile ecosystems of many Occupy encampments struggled with social problems that could only be adequately remedied by structural social transformation. By looking inward toward problems of social reproduction that no monadic community can solve under capitalism, much less in an open-air downtown encampment besieged by police, the camps ossified into ends in themselves, failing to realize their potential for serving as the basis of a class offensive. Reproducing the camps and defending them against increasingly violent cops organized on a national level to crush the movement became the movement's sole horizon. The spatial location of the movement wasn't just an element of its strategy; it was the strategy. This was perhaps best encapsulated by the fate of the human microphone. Originally a clever tactic that circumvented New York City's prohibition on unpermitted public amplification, it became divorced from this context, and was used needlessly, when amplification was available, or else everyone could hear the person speaking. This produced a creepy, cult-like mass of core activists, dead-eyed and drained of enthusiasm from months of intensive struggle, chanting banalities in a frightful deadpan unison, for no reason other than that's what they thought they were supposed to do. As temperatures dropped in many cities, evictions were likely welcomed by more than a few occupiers as relief from a situation that was increasingly chaotic, violent, and lacking direction.

At the risk of stating the obvious, Occupy failed to penetrate "the glass floor" separating street demonstrations from sites of production, and was exiled from any strategic leverage save for blocking traffic.[31] In the United States at least, the public character of the movement was often celebrated as a strength, the return of the elusive commons buried beneath the atomization of capitalist society. But in reality, this really just represented the widespread evacuation of movement politics from workplaces, schools, and other social institutions, leaving people quite literally pedestrians in the politics of their daily lives. The most promising solutions to this problem, which has dogged US mass movements since the 1960s, came from Occupy Oakland's putative general strike and West Coast port blockade alongside dissidents in the International Longshore and Warehouse Union, who naturally had to oppose their union leadership to make this happen. But these were exceptions proving the rule; by and large, Occupy encampments were places people went in their off-hours and on their way home, a form of politics removed from workplaces and the neighborhood where people lived.

Who Is the 99%?

My favorite part about Occupy Wall Street was that just about anyone claiming membership in a political entity predating September 17, 2001, was treated with suspicion when they expected to be able to throw their weight around. While the antiformist Occupy movement was based on the profound fragmentation of traditional political coalitions and identities, and the rejection of much of the old world outright, including its oppositional politics, Occupy's political subject was actually a quite coherent one, assumed in advance. The movement was, its faithful argued, the struggle of "the 99%" against "the 1%," who hold a quarter of the nation's wealth, and still more political power. In some of the movement's most clever propaganda, participants photographed themselves holding signs explaining their struggles. The typical story ran something like: I followed society's rules as I understood them, went to college because I was told that was the path to prosperity, worked hard, sacrificed, and so forth, but now I am a low-waged or precarious laborer in considerable debt, and the future looks grim. The messages almost always concluded with: "I am the 99%."

While these narratives no doubt reveal a process of proletarianization across the middle tiers of the US labor market, stagnating the career trajectories of many eager young professionals who expected to exceed their parents, of course nowhere near 99% of the country has been proletarianized, nor is the proletariat itself without divisions. Despite the incessant chant to the contrary, Occupy *never was the 99%*. A case in point was the growing presence of otherwise homeless people in Occupy camps. Many occupiers sought to exclude them from the movement altogether. This evinced not only the real divisions within the so-called 99%, but the unwillingness of downwardly mobile young people to let go of their class chauvinism.[32] The main reason the 99% failed as a class analysis is largely because it wasn't one. Class is a social relationship of exploitation and domination, not a demographic fact. Many enemies of the working class, like the cops who guarded the Occupy camps, could conceivably make less money than unionized blue-collar workers. This would not change the fact that the cops are structurally opposed to the assertion of working-class politics. By reducing class to how much money a person makes, Occupy didn't just cast the homeless people in its camps in league with many of the bankers who served as its bête noir. The movement also prevented a serious treatment of what exactly class is, and how it can therefore be overcome.

Accordingly, the question of the social role of the cops was a recurring roadblock to Occupy developing a clear sense of itself. They were surely in the 99% as a purely economic category, but what sense did it make to say that the 99% was cracking its own heads? As cops clamped down on camps across the US with a degree of brutality most of the white participants had never experienced, many occupiers struggled to rectify this particularly glaring evidence of the shallowness underlying the 99% identity, with many anarchists and communist participants happy to challenge the movement's soft stance on the cops with a deeper structural analysis of the role cops play capitalist society. Looking back from the comfort of 2021, when ACAB—"all cops are bastards"—has become a movement shibboleth even among many liberals, the degree of vocal support cops enjoyed from the heart of the Occupy movement may seem like a bad dream. But the cop love was real, representing the limitations of a populist analysis reducing class to income categories. While many occupiers came to despise the cops in the course of that struggle—thanks, in large part, to the brutality and belligerence of the cops themselves—this issue remained contentious even as Occupy's wave crested.[33]

EVERY FIRE NEEDS A LITTLE BIT OF HELP   233

But the central division within Occupy emerged around the question of race. While the 2008 crisis had hit Black and brown people worst of all, and three short years later Black people would be out in force for the Black Lives Matter movement, Occupy encampments remained overwhelmingly white. This could be in part attributed to the location of many Occupy camps far away from segregated neighborhoods where many working-class Black Americans live. But it must also be attributed to the movement's populist flattening of racial difference into an abstract signifier of class. In the United States, where structural racism, especially in the years immediately following Obama's election, often comes cloaked in an ideology of "color blindness," failing to explicitly address race can be tantamount to endorsing the racial order. Michelle Alexander's *The New Jim Crow* is importantly subtitled *Mass Incarceration in the Age of Colorblindness*, and deftly explores the unique moment of color blindness that immediately followed Obama's election.[34] Above all, many Black people in the United States, especially in working-class communities, are constantly reminded that they are Black; if the geography of segregation and differential access to wealth, education, employment, and health care are not sufficient objective reminders, landlords, teachers, bosses, cops, and strangers on the street are happy to do it subjectively. Why, then, would a challenge to US society, waged by a critical mass of Black people, be first couched in anything else besides the particularity of the Black experience? All the critiques in the world of Black particularity, no matter how correct on paper, cannot abstract away from this visceral fact of American life.[35]

Many nonwhite protesters who took part in the movement challenged its flattening of racial difference. These encounters, which challenged Occupy's conception of class as a demographic category, were typically taken up using theory from middle-class academic and nonprofit settings, where postmodernist and "intersectional" theories, valorizing the irreducible singularity of all people, had flourished for decades without any truth-testing in mass movement activity. These theories of difference tend to be less geared toward mass movement politics, and more toward winning classroom debates, discrediting professional nemeses, and beating out other competitors for scant resources like funding and employment by distinguishing oneself as the sole authentic voice of an oppressed community. Surely there were instances in Occupy's debates over the relationship between race and class where all participants involved did not talk past each other, but I wasn't present for them. In the years following the movement, however, a number of critical engagements with intersectionality theory in particular wrestled with the tension between individual subjects and collective political struggle, particularly as it relates to questions of race and class. Many people emerged from Occupy with these questions in the front of their minds.[36]

In short, the simplicity of the 99% figure reaped its successes up front in the form of broad popular appeal, but the downsides came quickly enough. As was observed in these pages, "the fact that the 2011 movements presented themselves as already unified, as already beyond the determinations of a horrible society, meant that their internal divisions were usually disavowed. Because they were disavowed, they could only appear as threats to the movement."[37] Meanwhile, the tactical horizons of square occupations served as an apt metaphor for an initially dynamic movement that reified its own self-understanding almost immediately, and became, both figuratively and quite literally, fixed in space. This hackneyed class-first approach of course did not make very real divisions go away, any more than a judge's orders to allow occupiers back into Zuccotti Park in the days after the eviction, pathetically brandished by hardcore activists demanding readmission in the encroaching winter cold, were respected by NYPD cops who simply shrugged and kept the park closed indefinitely. Nonetheless, Occupy put the issue of class—and dormant practices of mass collective struggle—front and center in American life. And the turbulence of daily life compelling Americans to take action, and take these questions seriously in the process, would not cease.

This Stops Today

On December 4, 2014, a large crowd gathered in Sarah D. Roosevelt Park on Manhattan's Lower East Side for a march called by the Trayvon Martin Organizing Committee. The previous day, a Staten Island grand jury had declined to indict the cop who murdered Eric Garner. Convergences called by dinosaur Marxist-Leninist parties and autonomous leftists alike had quickly escaped the control of the organizers, paralyzing much of Manhattan with snake marches tens of thousands strong. The major challenge for organizers in this setting was getting the ball rolling; cops would do everything in their power, including brutal arrests, to keep

EVERY FIRE NEEDS A LITTLE BIT OF HELP

marches in parks and on the sidewalk, but once a critical mass of people took the street, cops had to beat a tactical retreat and prepare the next assault. On this particular night, the anarchists and communists who had called the convergence milled through the growing crowd, plugging people into a text message-based alert system, and letting them know that as soon as they heard "I can't breathe," it was time to march. A lone speaker announced he would be sharing the final words of Eric Garner, which featured the heartbreaking repetition of the words "I can't breathe" eleven times. At the final iteration, the crowd surged forth through a weak spot in the police line and into the street, catching the cops off guard and easily gaining the upper hand. Within minutes, the raucous snake march ran into another massive crowd, fusing together with great exaltation, to crisscross city streets ordinarily guarded so jealously by the cops, chanting the names of their victims as it blocked tunnels and bridges, parading up and down the West Side Highway, surging forth intractably toward nowhere in particular.

Shortly after the evictions of Occupy camps, a Black teenager named Trayvon Martin was murdered by a Latino neighborhood watch volunteer in Sanford, Florida. Demonstrations popped up across the country, including among the remnants of Occupy. In North Miami Beach, dozens of students capped off their high school's walkout by ransacking the local Walgreens pharmacy, and in New Orleans, three Confederate monuments were defaced, with a message proclaiming the action to be "for Trayvon."[38] Agitation around the movement that would soon be commonly known as Black Lives Matter continued through a spate of killings of Black people by US police and white vigilantes, including Jordan Davis, Renisha McBride, and Johnathan Ferrell. The downward grind of daily life for working-class Black people, whose recovery from 2008 was even worse than the sluggish progress of their white counterparts, surely drove some of the anger at these deaths. But the hegemonic political narrative that emerged from these campaigns emphasized the poor treatment of Black people by US police, arguing for greater procedural justice against vigilantes and the cops.

Despite the steady drumbeat of disastrous publicity throughout 2014, US cops could simply not stop killing Black people long enough for the movement to blow over. "Martyrs drive this movement," writes Tobi Haslett, "they are its origin and blazing emblems."[39] One such martyr was Eric Garner, who had long been harassed by police as he plied his trade of selling untaxed cigarettes on New York City's Staten Island. When, in mid-July 2014, a gang of cops accosted him after he had broken up a fight, Garner stood up to them, saying enough was enough. "This stops today!" he declared. For his defiance, Garner was attacked and placed in a choke hold that slowly drained the life from his body. As would later recur with George Floyd, Garner's final words, "I can't breathe," immediately found resonance among large swaths of proletarians hemmed in on all sides by austerity and violence. Similarly, the killing of the Black teenager Michael Brown in Ferguson, Missouri, was widely compared to a lynching. Like Garner, Brown was killed for refusal—while walking in the street, Brown ignored a Ferguson cop's orders to "get the fuck on the sidewalk."[40]

The reader may recognize this scene, the inscription of one's social role by a cop on the street, from the famous example of interpellation, or subject formation by an external authority, proffered by philosopher Louis Althusser. In Althusser's example, the cop calls "Hey you there!" and the addressee, by turning around, establishes themselves as the "you" who is subject to the police authority.[41] But just as the police encounter is one where a subject position is imposed, so too can it be resisted. The cop who killed Brown later claimed that Brown responded "Fuck what you have to say," and refusing to be pushed off the street, taunted him: "What the fuck are you gonna do?" Whether or not he made up this detail to make Brown appear more menacing, it is a telling feature of his justification for the latter's killing: Brown's act of refusal, no matter how trifling the original offense, posed a serious threat in the cop's mind.[42] His colleagues apparently agreed that Brown had to be made an example of; Brown's body was left uncovered on the street for over four hours, in the hot sun, for all to see. As Ferguson Committeewoman Patricia Bynes later observed, the display "sent the message from law enforcement that 'we can do this to you any day, any time, in broad daylight, and there's nothing you can do about it.'"[43]

Garner and Brown had not just refused police orders; they had refused their ordained role in a social order where their lives did not matter, where the stagnation of capital offered them little in the way of employment or public relief to keep them afloat, and where their daily life was managed by armed custodians who treated them like inmates of an open-air prison, allowing them not even the pretense of dignity. The contrast between Althusser's "hey you there!" and "get the fuck on the

EVERY FIRE NEEDS A LITTLE BIT OF HELP 237

sidewalk" furnishes a handy testament to how nakedly and belligerently the racialized class order in the US is enforced by the cops.

Doing well by the martyrs who gave the movement impetus, the antiformist spirit of refusal which underlay these incidents would also define the public response to them, as a critical mass of people refused to be intimidated into submission by the gruesome spectacles, and heeded instead their spirit of defiance. Adding to the threat these acts of refusal posed to police power, many white people subsequently refused the silent complicity in Black death demanded of them by their historical role in their privileged strata of the US workforce. This was significant, since a critical mass of white workers have, since America's colonial period, been reliably willing to uphold a cross-class alliance with white elites, against everyone else. This alliance, between working-class whites and the ruling class, is especially important to the latter in the powder keg environment engendered by capital's austerity regime. But beginning in 2014, prominent cracks emerged in this unholy pact. Their source was not the world of ideas, but material changes afoot at the bottom tiers of the US labor market, long home to Black workers, and to which a growing number of whites (including those like the archetypal Occupier, who once imagined a bright future for themselves) were being consigned.

The movement that would come to be called Black Lives Matter originated as a much broader rejection of this entire social order—albeit one defined negatively, in opposition to killer cops. In Ferguson, this resistance took the form of widespread protests defying the heavily armored state security forces, episodic looting, and as the movement wore on, arson and sporadic gunshots in the direction of cops. Images of courageous Ferguson rebels confronting cops hiding behind *RoboCop* riot gear purchased with their tax and fine money inspired protests all across the US. Successive announcements of nonindictment—first Brown's killer on November 24, then Garner's on December 3—served as fuel to the fire. The memetic forces of such images, as Adrian Wohlleben argues in the remarkable essay "Memes Without End," in their viral transmission via images broadcast on social media and TV news, was more compelling than any stated political ideology or analysis of the situation in the short term. Instead, militant tactics and a general spirit of belligerent refusal were viewed and replicated throughout the US.[44]

Solidarity actions largely consisted of large, unpermitted snake marches, defaulting to the blockading of highways, bridges, and other transit infrastructure. Some commentators at the time attempted to argue that this constituted attacks on the circulation of capital. No matter how exciting a thought, however, it was a hard pill to swallow for this participant; it seemed more accurate that we blocked these sites because we had a whole lot of people willing to cause a big public disruption, and nothing better to do. We were, in a word, all dressed up with nowhere to go.[45] This is not to say that it was worse off than open-ended occupations. Some organizers even tried to root the movement down by planning space occupations, but the state is always ready for the last class offensive, just as many activists are loathe to repeat it, and the combination of police aggression and popular apathy saw these projects come to naught. The relationship to space that ensued was frenetic, almost an experimental praxis of reclaiming terrain tightly regulated by the cops. But it soon regained the clear limitations consistent with being quite literally out in the street.

On the one hand, the blockade tactic, which emerged organically in many places, evinced a degree of courage and assent to illegality that surprised many of us so-called revolutionaries, who had expected to lead these actions. Like the Occupy camps before it, however, this tactic quickly ossified, and became a limit to the heightening of militancy. Standing in the middle of the street with no plan was exhilarating at first, given that an all-consuming tactical objective of most street mobilizations in the recent past had been simply getting marches "off the sidewalk and into the street," as the chant goes. But this dynamism soon grew stale, its victories increasingly shallow. Direct clashes with cops, let alone attacks on them and their infrastructure, were rare and largely unpopular. Looting was similarly rare and discouraged. Anti-cop chants were routinely shut down. A gesture as harmless as toppling a trashcan was militantly opposed by so-called peace police among the protesters, who even resorted to assault, in the name of nonviolence!

Those of us who caught legal cases for actions outside the canon of "nonviolent civil disobedience" found little support in a broader movement that was quickly becoming dominated by nonprofits with direct ties to Wall Street and local Democrats. Self-styled "founders" and "leaders" of Black Lives Matter fell over each other to bathe in oceans of foundation money and denounce anyone to the left of the Ford Foundation. While the memetic nature of tactics accounted for their early success, autonomous leftists failed to popularize politics connecting them with

EVERY FIRE NEEDS A LITTLE BIT OF HELP

a conception of who we are and what we were doing, while all the old party formations could do little better than recite passages from Trotsky, Lenin, and Mao. This ground was seized by liberals, who recast the rebellion in the familiar trappings of civil rights ideology and the unfinished struggle for inclusive capitalist democracy, thus the initial dynamism of the movement coagulated once more.

This was, however, not exactly co-optation. The first Eric Garner march had been called by none other than Al Sharpton, and the movement enjoyed earnest support from its inception up and down the class ladder of Black America. Such "vertical mediation" meant that the steering of this protest activity into reformist channels was not the victory of an outside entity, but the resolution of struggle intrinsic to the movement. Under the aegis of the liberal wing of what is today called the civil rights movement, career movement politicians like Sharpton posited a monolithic Black identity transcending the class stratification of Black America. Whereas Occupy had flattened its self-conception in the name of an undialectical and thoroughly reified conception of class, the mainstream currents of the Black Lives Matter movement, which ultimately won the day, similarly defaulted to a one-dimensional conception of collective unity, this time in the name of a cross-class conception of race.[46] Race is a category fundamental to the ordering of US society since its colonial period, specifically with regards to the structure of America's division of labor.[47] It is also viscerally felt in daily life by anyone lacking the luxury to ignore it. Occupy had very likely remained disproportionately white for the very reason that it did not take race as a central category to how austerity is experienced. But it is also possible to bend the stick too far in the other direction.

The invocation of race as a fixed concept, rather than the social processes by which vastly different people are lumped together in a pseudoscientific unity, often assumes the quality of what Karen and Barbara Fields call "racecraft." A play on the term witchcraft, racecraft describes the magical thinking which begins with the real premise of America's racial disparities, and the uniqueness of how racialized capitalist exploitation is experienced. Racecraft assumes race itself to be a meaningful and unchanging attribute of human beings. When racecraft is in play, the assumed existence of race becomes the sole factor for sundry phenomena in social life. Under racecraft, any issue involving Black people in particular is reduced to a so-called racial issue. Poverty that impacts Black people becomes Black poverty, an issue distinct from the economic structure of US society. Mass incarceration in the United States, which impacts millions of non-Black people, must be discussed as a distinctly Black issue. So-called races are depicted as having distinct histories, hermetically sealed from each other, and irreducible to any total social picture. Most importantly, racecraft assumes that racial categories are fixed, and inherent in individual people. By contrast, the Fieldses argue, race itself is an ever-changing social relation, and above all, it is not an explanation for anything; it is the creation, reproduction, and stubborn perseverance of race, they argue, which must be explained.[48] America's contemporary racecraft is doubly pernicious as political traditions like "identity politics," which originated in the context of class struggle as a recognition of real and dynamic differentials of experience structured by capitalist exploitation, have become counterinsurgent reifications of difference, and comfortably at home in the Clinton wing of the Democratic Party, which uses its jargon to attract the left.[49]

In the movement that became Black Lives Matter, the problem of composition that bedeviled Occupy was thus solved with another overlarge abstraction, a singular Black identity. This contained within it a diffusion of class interests and antagonisms sufficient to make the president of the United States and homeless people harassed along Pennsylvania Avenue part of the same oppressed group. Meanwhile, the only acceptable role for non-Black people became the spineless "ally," destined to blindly follow the leadership of any nonwhite person they encountered—who were all, according to these allies, completely interchangeable.[50] The racecraft structuring American politics reduces people to abstract categories, which social movement managers are eager to map onto a complex nexus of rules for who is allowed to say what, stand where, or even count themselves among those who are struggling. To this day, it remains a controversial proposition in the US left, sometimes even among self-identified revolutionaries, that white people can have any grievance against capitalist society that isn't simply evidence of their sense of entitlement. What better gift could be imagined for the far right?

But the churning of the individual and the universal was able to escape these strictures for largely practical reasons. Of course in practice, most "allies" conveniently "follow the leadership" of people who they already agree with politically. But even the most earnest "white ally,"

EVERY FIRE NEEDS A LITTLE BIT OF HELP

chock-full of antiracist training, who encountered a heated argument
between two Black would-be snake march leaders, would have to choose
which to follow when they parted ways in opposite directions. In short, it
was all but inevitable that political affiliations based on racecraft would
begin to give way to those based on political affinity.

There were some other noteworthy developments in the post-
Ferguson period. Plenty of people who hadn't attended enough
activist-led "de-escalation trainings" to know better took it on themselves to antagonize and physically engage the cops. Toward the end
of the movement in New York City, protesters began marching into
high-end Manhattan stores, interrupting business, leading chants—and
promptly marching out. A comrade reported at the time that the valuable
merchandise seemed so near, but yet, so far. Looking back on this tactic
from the vantage of the large-scale looting of lower Manhattan's luxury
retail stores during the George Floyd Rebellion, it is tempting to think
of it as a kind of testing of the waters, however unconsciously, inch-
ing toward a heightened illegality. The same can be said of the protest
encampment outside Minneapolis's Fourth Precinct, which lasted for two
weeks following the late 2015 police murder of Jamar Clark. Protesters
massed outside the precinct of killer cops, as they would five years later a
mere six miles away, and were menaced by armed vigilantes, who opened
fire.[51] But the horizon of this action remained fixed on reforming the
system to better ensure police accountability.

Thus, while this upsurge demonstrated a qualitative leap forward
in the intensity and illegality of struggle, everywhere lagged behind
Ferguson. Serving as an exception proving the rule once more, Oakland
in particular did its best to follow suit, with more than two weeks of
riots characterized by looting and skirmishes with the cops. Riots in
Baltimore in 2015 following the death of Freddy Gray also bucked against
the movement's "nonviolence" fetish, and were accordingly contained by
the city's Black establishment with remorseless violence. However, such
a clear display of the limits of race as a reified political category bespoke
the antagonistic churning within a movement predicated on a cross-
class conception of Blackness, but which could no more abstract from
the instability of flattening dynamic class relations in the name of race,
than Occupy could by flattening race into class. Following the 2015 riots
in Baltimore, which pitted working-class Black kids against a largely
Black city government, Keeanga-Yamahtta Taylor observed: "When a

Black mayor, governing a largely Black city, aids in the mobilization of a military unit led by a Black woman to suppress a Black rebellion, we are in a new period of the Black freedom struggle."[52]

As much of Black Lives Matter coagulated into a reservoir for foundation money, with self-identified founders monetizing the movement in the receiving line of its own wake, a crucial segment of young activists refused to be quietly folded into the Democratic Party. Instead, they bristled against the limitations of a class-blind conception of race, laid bare in the streets of Baltimore. Infused with ever-sharpening critiques about the interrelations of race and class in US history and society, a new generation of activists grasped toward connecting the figures of austerity, the primary thrust of Occupy, and the country's behemoth punishment system, the driving force behind Black Lives Matter. Groups like Black Youth Project 100 and Movement for Black Lives developed analyses tying together mass incarceration and the disinvestment of Black and brown communities. They issued ambitious programs for wealth redistribution under the banner of "divest/invest": divesting funds from the carceral state, and redirecting them to the communities most impacted by mass incarceration.[53]

Among a growing number of young organizers, the problem was no longer conceived as greed run amok, the wrongdoing of individual cops, or racism understood as the bad ideas of individual people, but was instead a matter of the material distribution of wealth and power in a society where, as Stuart Hall observed, "race is the modality in which class is lived."[54] Their understanding of who they were and what they were doing began to ever more reflect the reality of living in a class society structured by race. Police departments and prison systems were no longer seen as the sum total of individuals—as was the case in early BLM, or Occupy, when someone could derail a meeting by crying about their cop dad—but were coherent political forces structurally hostile to working-class Black life by virtue of their position in class relations. An important influence in this political development would be a growth in popularity for the politics of abolitionism, a distinctly American tradition rooted in the purported linkage between slavery and mass incarceration. Black revolutionary figures like Angela Davis and Assata Shakur, and abolitionist groups like Critical Resistance and INCITE! Women of Color Against Violence, became important political touchstones among young people politicized by BLM. This would also

EVERY FIRE NEEDS A LITTLE BIT OF HELP

occasion a rectification within the movement of the long-standing male chauvinism and homophobia characterizing civil rights politics. And even as movement activity in the streets ebbed, the ravages of capitalism surely were not making these figures, or their ideas, any less relevant.

Love in the Time of COVID

Gunfire rang out in Chicago's Garfield Park neighborhood as looters grabbed whatever they could from the liquor store and adjacent businesses. Looted liquor bottles were being passed around, so was the shooting celebratory? An ATM rolled by on a shopping cart and the crowd cheered its driver on. Could a baseball bat open it up? One man attempted to find out, stopping only to gesture toward us with the bat, as if to say we better keep moving. Tear gas wafted in the air as Chicago cops blocked an intersection for no clear reason, seeming unsure of their next move. It was August 10, 2020. The previous night, in response to a police shooting in Englewood, Chicago's posh Magnificent Mile was ransacked by a massive car caravan of looters who clashed with the cops who tried to stop them. It was part of a new sensibility in 2020, akin to the customary rights chronicled by E.P. Thompson in eighteenth-century England. Whereas in those days, prices above the commonly accepted maximum engendered marketplace riots deemed socially legitimate, in the summer of 2020, police shootings were met by large-scale expropriation and attacks on the cops almost as a reflex.[55] As Garfield Park followed suit that day, the police scanner announced there were too many calls for looting in progress for squad cars to cover. The local Black Lives Matter chapter, flush with foundation money meant to prevent exactly this sort of disorder, bucked its funders and refused to denounce looting. One spokesperson went as far as to call looting reparations.[56]

If COVID did not break the holding pattern entirely, it certainly provided sufficient turbulence for a critical mass of passengers to flip the fuck out. By the end of the summer there had been over eleven thousand protests in almost three thousand distinct locations. While the vast majority followed the predictable script—marching and chanting ad infinitum overseen from the top down by organizers connected to local machine politics, nonprofits, or decrepit revolutionary parties—hundreds descended into violence (if only on the side of the cops), property destruction, and looting.[57] Even the lawful protests were lent impetus and a radical outlook by the actions driving the rebellion, direct attacks on key components of the carceral state: courthouses, police stations, cop cars, and the cops themselves. Courthouses and police stations were attacked in Nashville, Dallas, Denver, Phoenix, Portland, and New York City, among others, in the early days of the rebellion. Later, the Kenosha County Courthouse would serve as a target following the police shooting of Jacob Blake and, in the subsequent rebellion, Kenosha's probation office was burned to the ground.[58] The siege of the Third Precinct and the acts of great courage and ferocity that followed its lead demonstrated a deep-seated conviction that the cops and courts were not to be reformed or bargained with, but represented an enemy force inextricable from the immiseration of austerity and its amplification by the COVID crisis.[59]

Protest largely took the form of roving street demonstrations ranging from orderly demonstrations in the traditional script, to fiery riots characterized by looting, arson, and attacks on carceral infrastructure and the cops themselves. The car, a staple of American social life, became a versatile tool in illegal street tactics—and, recalling the 2017 murder of Heather Heyer by a fascist in Charlottesville, a deadly weapon.[60] In the early days of the rebellion there was not a hard and fast distinction between law-abiding protesters and rebels, as tactics like graffiti, defense against cops, and even looting and other property damage were generalized across large crowds of protesters in key sites of struggle like New York City, Minneapolis, and Seattle.[61] In the early days, it was difficult for counterinsurgent liberals to parse the respectable from the deplorable forms of revolt. Even the tamest protests, New York rebel Tobi Haslett argued, were *"propelled, made fiercely possible, by massive clashes in the street—not tainted or delegitimized by them, nor assembled from thin air."*[62]

This climate of illegality was abetted by the introduction of "frontliner culture," pioneered in Hong Kong, Chile, and other sites of open contest around the world. This blend of tactics, equipage, and above all, a division of labor straddling so-called "peaceful" protesters with the most militant street warriors, provided a rich toolbox for US rebels in pitched battles against the cops. Police tactics and technologies are international; so too is the resistance against them.[63] Frontliner culture also bears the indelible mark of Standing Rock, a struggle that drew militants from across the United States and fostered a high degree of tactical militancy rooted in the building of trust not simply across the lines of so-called race, but in the willingness to engage in collective risk-taking against

EVERY FIRE NEEDS A LITTLE BIT OF HELP

considerable state violence.[64] Before long, the iconic frontliner umbrella—a defensive tool against pepper spray, projectiles, and the prying eyes of the press, to name a few—popped up across the US. Networks like Vitalist International helped spread memes around tactics across social media, including polished guides on the basics of street tactics, and pithy slogans meant to solidify tactical commitments, which appeared on walls across the country as they whizzed across the internet. Perhaps the most effective of these was: "No good cops, no bad protesters," six little words that drew the battle lines of the movement, and amounted to a pledge not to engage in the work of movement policing long practiced by "peaceful" protesters.

One curious tactic that gained traction as street conflicts waned represented at once the rejection, by a critical mass of Americans, of the dead weight of their past, and how this rejection can itself become still more weight of dead generations. Across the US, crowds attacked statues representing the old guard of American white supremacy. Statue topplings could be festive and intense affairs bringing together diverse crowds to engage in shared illegality and trust building.[65] But these tactics also risked succumbing to the belief that the statues had intrinsic qualities beyond shaped metal and stone; it soon became a symptom of the movement's increasing fixation on fighting symbolic warfare within the popular discourse of official society, rather than class war on its streets.

As in 2014, these courageous maneuvers were largely conducted on the run. Unlike the movement of the squares—and continuing trends established in 2014—the George Floyd Rebellion largely did not produce permanent space occupations. Notable exceptions included the Capitol Hill Autonomous Zone (CHAZ) in Seattle and the City Hall Autonomous Zone in New York City, the occupied Wendy's where Rayshard Brooks was murdered by cops in Atlanta, and Jefferson Park in Louisville, outside the courthouse where the wheels of justice turned slowly—and fruitlessly—for Breonna Taylor. Phil Neel called CHAZ a "tactical regression" to an earlier form long superseded.[66] It was as if the problems bedeviling the space occupations of 2011, which soon became quagmires, had been forgotten, or perhaps never learned in the first place. If, as has been suggested, the CHAZ came as an alternative to burning a police station abandoned by retreating Seattle cops, it is most certainly true that the return of Occupy's misadventures in prefigurative politics, supplanting the zeitgeist of open attack on the carceral state, was atavistic and lamentable.[67] To the extent that open-ended space occupations served as staging areas for outward-focused activities, as they appeared to do in New York City, they served the rebellion's dynamism. But when they became ends in themselves, these occupations became dangerous dead ends.[68] By and large, however, the movement stayed out of space occupations.

While the George Floyd Rebellion did not enter into the hidden abode of production, it is also unfair to say that the relationship to space and sites of struggle remained unchanged since 2014. Widespread looting brought confrontational politics into sites of capital circulation, and represented a pointed disavowal of the necessity to procure commodities with the money earned through wage labor. Even more promising was the movement's relationship to carceral infrastructure: cop cars, courthouses, and the famous Third Precinct were directly attacked, and even entered, in the case of several state buildings. This was an offensive relationship to the street-bound movement, in which people were united by their opposition to a common foe, which was then identified and attacked. Some even made forays into coordinating the reproduction of these attacks through the expropriation of commodities; a Minneapolis rebel describes how the Target near the Third Precinct was used to supply the crowd laying siege, sustaining the intensity of the attack over a long period of time.[69] Reproducing a Minneapolis Commune for weeks and months would have, of course, required a more complex engagement with local supply chains, necessitating a sympathetic presence within numerous nodes on the complex logistical chains that keep cities functioning. Ultimately, these chains trace back to the point of production. While this prospect may seem far-fetched in 2022, the reader should recall how far off the summer of 2022 seemed in the spring.[70]

Treason and Treachery

Perhaps the most striking aspect of the movement was the diversity of its composition. The urban rebellions of the 1960s had been largely Black and brown affairs. Key offensives in the George Floyd Rebellion were led by Black proletarians, including the events in Minneapolis, and the militancy and dedication of Black and brown proletarians continued to fuel the rebellion throughout the summer. Alongside them, however, were millions of white people risking police and right-wing vigilante violence. In a profound sense, the outpouring of white participation was not itself a change, but a sign that beneath the surface of the monolithic categories of race that structure the US political discourse, a profound change has been taking place.

To say that these white people were simply "allies" of Black Americans, and did not recognize their own liberation as bound up in the Black struggle against police violence, implies that they were simply fighting for Black people to enjoy the same quality of life that they enjoy as whites. Given the carnage capitalism has wrought throughout American life, including much of white America, this is a tough proposition to swallow. Coming nearly a decade after Occupy eulogized the golden age of upward mobility for white youths, and amid a downward slide of quality of life for white working-class people, perhaps the white youths who took to the streets in 2020 represent a generation averse to "dying of whiteness" and determined instead to fight austerity and state violence as part of a multiracial movement.[71] "Rather than killing themselves with drugs," wrote Shemon Salam and Arturo Castillon in a must-read essay on the topic, "a section of white proletarians heard the battle cry of Black Lives Matter and joined the rebellions."[72]

Footage of the burning of the Third Precinct shows a remarkably diverse crowd working together to accomplish a common task, in a setting that is perhaps best described as celebratory.[73] Similar images proliferated of great multiracial unity in the face of police violence and white vigilantism. Simultaneously, clear divisions emerged within the monolith of the US Black identity, as militants and liberals made their political differences known, and the rift between the old guard of the civil rights movement and a new generation of more radical, street-savvy militants deepened.[74] For a short time, the composition problem that bedevils all movements in the era of advanced fragmentation was tentatively overcome in the unity of practical action against an external foe: the carceral state and all who defended it. But the honeymoon of this happy union, defined negatively as it was, was therefore not to last.

Before long, the rebellion found itself hobbled by distrust, particularly against white participants. Cops and politicians, aided by Twitter-addled talking heads like Northwestern University historian Kathleen Belew, spread reckless rumors, tantamount to outrageous and unsubstantiated conspiracy theories, about "outside agitators" and undercover white supremacists secretly guiding the hands of young Black rebels—who could not, of course, undertake militant acts on their own volition.[75] "The mere existence of last summer's rumors, and whom those rumors accuse, tells us everything we need to know," writes militant Tim Bruno. "You see, the real bad actors, ops, provocateurs ... never take action, only prevent it."[76] Worse yet, poor information discipline among even the most sincere activists led to breathless rumors proliferating of impending attacks by right-wingers, making the white rebels putting themselves on the line in the streets increasingly suspect, and sowing distrust in moments that could have been characterized by communal letting go of fear.[77]

"For all the rumors about supposed provocateurs," writes Bruno, "less has been said about those real bad actors: the stylized Instagram militants, armed to the teeth yet who never pull the trigger, settling instead for a collaborative photo-op with a white-shirted lieutenant; the petty activist functionaries barking orders through megaphones, conveniently dividing the crowd into smaller and smaller marches, perfectly sized for kettling; the peace police enforcing order on a rally by handing over rowdy radicals to the real police."[78] And as the fires smoldered, traditional social movement managers, spurned in the early days of the rebellion, regained their grip on the movement and encouraged divisions along the lines of race.[79] Racial animosity was not strictly Black and white; on Chicago's Southwest Side, Latino vigilantes attacked Black people they claimed to be prospective looters.[80] As incisively noted by Idris Robinson in the early days of the rebellion, a more pernicious trick came from many US liberals who didn't seek to discredit the rebellion's militancy as much as redefine the rebellion such that it never even existed.[81] But the greatest barrier to multiracial solidarity was something far more concrete than the mythical Belew Brigades of Nazi ninjas planting "bait bricks" and distributing incendiary devices to guileless Black teens to pick up and throw. It was the US color line itself.

W.E.B. Du Bois furnished us this evocative concept in his 1903 work *The Souls of Black Folk*, where he argued "the problem of the twentieth century is the problem of the color line."[82] Unfortunately, by all indications, the same could likely be said about the twenty-first. At the end of the day, American society is deeply stratified along the lines of race, which is a biological fiction but an enduring social fact. Long-standing historical segregation in housing, employment, education, worship, and just about every other feature of life, in addition to widespread ideological racial chauvinism among individual white people, have combined to engender a visceral dividing line between working-class Black and white people in particular, but also between all so-called races. Marx, as David Roediger and Elizabeth Esch argue, may have been correct to predict that high concentrations of workers from different backgrounds would break down dividing lines such as race. But he did not anticipate how effectively capital could erect *new* dividing lines in their place, while weaponizing the old ones as part of a nascent science of management.[83]

While it is perhaps consoling to white radicals to imagine that racial prejudice is simply a trick played on their friends and family by the ruling class, it is hard to argue with a straight face that prejudice and chauvinism are foisted on guiltless white workers by their social betters.[84] Instead, belligerent differentiation along the lines of race, ethnicity, national belonging, and so forth, often comes from below, with working-class white people as enthusiastic participants. While this pact with the devil doesn't reflect well on the moral character of these individuals, it tells us far more about the predictable result of a race to the bottom for US proletarian quality of life, amid the absence of any effective multiracial movement to reverse this course.[85] (The absence of such a movement, of course, in the face of enduring racial prejudice, becomes something of a chicken or egg question.) The color line structuring US society is of course not a static thing; the intense white participation in the rebellion can be taken not so much as a sign of "allies" pledging allegiance to a cause that is not their own, but rather the possibility of new alliances being formed in the growing ranks of the American labor market's lowest tiers. But the racecraft that structures American life cannot be undone by common economic suffering alone, or else the US south would have long been a site of harmonious multiracial class struggle.

The appearance of multiracial crowds engaging in mass illegality together during the summer of 2020 has led to a welcome resurgence of interest in the concept of "race treason," drawing on the work of Noel Ignatiev and the now-defunct journal he coedited with John Garvey, *Race Traitor*. Drawing on W.E.B. Du Bois, Ignatiev and *Race Traitor* argued that race in the United States revolved around a cross-class alliance between white workers and the white ruling class, and the corresponding relegation of Black workers to the bottom tiers of the labor market. Race has not always existed, and only came into being as a hierarchical ordering principle. Thus, they argued, dismantling white supremacy is not a matter of achieving equality between the so-called races, but detonating the social category race itself. With regards to whiteness in particular, this means, as the journal put it: "to dissolve the club, to break it apart, to explode it."[86]

In the wake of the rebellion, the concept of race treason has been deployed by a number of writers reflecting on the lessons of 2020. This is not an intellectual trend but rather a reflection of transformations in how people live, and struggle, that were profoundly felt by participants in the rebellion. The influx of white participants in the rebellion, engaged in dangerous and illegal acts alongside Black people in particular, made for experiences that defied the received political wisdom. As a result, a number of participants in the rebellion turned to the theory of race treason to make sense of what they had lived through. These accounts, hard-won by courageous participation in the rebellion, represent positive contributions toward what should be the primary goal of US revolutionary praxis: chiseling away at the walls between the so-called races.[87] But just as they point toward the possibility of struggle overwhelming these walls, these accounts also tend to overemphasize the profundity of fleeting moments of tenuously common struggle, which appeared as a drop of water in the vast desert of US social life.

"These white insurrectionists fail to grasp," writes an anonymous collective of Black anarchists, "how their own whiteness continues to exist within and beyond the riot, instead opting to believe that race is magically transcended when they smash a window."[88] While it is hackneyed and incorrect to label all proponents of this position white, this is nonetheless a point worth making. No matter how auspicious the sight of Black and white people fighting the cops together, the long-standing and well-earned mistrust of white people, or the ornate stratification between all so-called races, cannot be expected to simply vanish through spontaneous struggles—just as they remained present even in these much-heralded moments of overcoming. In my own experience, and that of other militants I have spoken to, the visceral reality of race was not absent from a single second of struggle in summer 2020, including some instances I have seen cited as multiracial crowds overcoming the color line. And even in the best moments of the rebellion, cooperation against a clearly identified enemy is one thing, but transcending the strictures of race is another altogether. Ultimately, the risk these analyses run, likely against the intentions of their incisive authors, is positing the moment of riot as the sole horizon for overcoming race. But most

EVERY FIRE NEEDS A LITTLE BIT OF HELP

of the time we are not rioting. What can we do, during these times, to challenge the racial order permeating so much of daily life?

American Revolution

On August 25, 2020, a call went out for "patriots willing to take up arms and defend" the small Wisconsin city of Kenosha, following two nights of intense rebellion. While the Kenosha County Courthouse was the primary target, it was defended by militarized cops who then propelled the crowd into the streets. Dozens of businesses were looted and put to the torch. In response, armed militia clad in paramilitary gear and ornately outfitted in shiny new gear swarmed in to stand guard outside businesses and menace protesters, alongside local and state cops and a sizeable detachment from the National Guard. Military Bearcat vehicles prowled the dark and otherwise deserted streets. But the rebels were undaunted. At the corner of 60th Street and Sheridan Road, four blocks from the courthouse, a Bearcat pelted the crowd with plastic pellets filled with pepper spray, receiving bricks from a nearby construction site in response. Meanwhile, militia guarding the Ultimate gas station were taunted by rebels who got in their faces and forced them to step backward as they anxiously eyed each other. The armed men seemed scared and surprised that their guns were not sufficiently intimidating.

Part of the crowd took off headed south, wearing dangerously thin. Before we knew what hit us, shots rang out. First one burst, then another, punctuated by sporadic pops seeming to emanate from all directions. Adding to the confusion, in the middle of it all, a car pulled up and its passenger sprayed a few of us with a fire extinguisher. The cloud of noxious white dust cleared to reveal a crowd of Black teenagers screaming and crying around the lifeless body of Joseph "JoJo" Rosenbaum. Meanwhile, another volley of shots up the street signaled the death of Anthony Huber, who had pursued the gunman, armed only with a skateboard. The rebels were dispersed in all directions, pursued down lonely suburban streets in a game of cat and mouse with Bearcats, National Guard, and vigilantes like the shooter, who would soon become a hero to the US far right.

Somewhere in the chaos of Kenosha it struck me: this is how heightened struggle was always going to look in the United States, where people can barely resolve disputes over a parking space without armed conflict. These movements have been spurred by the casual violence of everyday life in the US, and for the short term, at least, seem capable of only deepening it. The stagnation of capital has dramatically increased interclass competition, while making large parts of the population expendable in the eyes of the market and state. It is a world where life is cheap, defined by everyday violence—including mass shootings with no discernible purpose—and the now increasingly routine murders of activists, with a mixed but nonetheless remarkable blessing from some US courts. Through the eyes of 2020, what's remarkable is not the degree of violence permeating the vestiges of American civil society, but how much remains peaceful. In the not-too-distant future, the present moment, with its soul-crushing barbarism, just might be considered the "good old days" before American society really went off the rails.

Since at least 2008, an armed movement of extraparliamentary rightists, most famous for their forays into insurrection on January 6, has broken with the fetters of legalism to constitute an armed challenge to liberal democracy.[89] Between shootings, cars ramming street protests, and the extraparliamentary murder of antifascist Michael Reinoehl by US marshals acting under orders of President Trump, 2020 provided clear signs that the unfolding of struggle in the United States will be dark, dangerous, and armed to the teeth.[90] While some white leftists in New York City complained of the discursive violence of "NYPD suck my dick!"—"the impossible demand,"[91] and chant of choice among working-class Black youth—rebels in many places across the US took our lives into our hands each time we left the house, entering settings that were increasingly disordered and anything but harmless and safe. It's hard to imagine that social revolution in the United States would be any better; in all likelihood, it will be much worse.

The month after Kenosha, Kentucky Attorney General Daniel Cameron announced that of all the cops responsible for Breonna Taylor's death, only one would be charged—for shots that were fired into a neighboring apartment. In advance of the announcement, downtown Louisville had been placed under nothing short of a military occupation; National Guard and heavily armed cops from multiple jurisdictions locked down roads and surrounded Jefferson Park with a massive show of force. Armed vigilantes positioning themselves at gas stations and other businesses seemed a bit redundant, as their lazy demeanor suggested they were well aware. Meanwhile, the protesters themselves, who had faced down vigilantes for months at Jefferson Park, brought considerable firepower of their own to the streets. At one point, wedged in the middle

EVERY FIRE NEEDS A LITTLE BIT OF HELP

of a shouting match between cops and angry protesters, I realized I was in the small minority not openly brandishing a firearm. I felt at once like a traveler from another time, hurled into a grim future I was not at all prepared to face. And that's probably what I was. A feeble attempt to march out of the square was crushed by competing jurisdictions of cops seemingly tripping over each other to bring the hammer down on the outnumbered protesters, who never managed to mount a substantive challenge. Later in the night, a great racket erupted, as cop cars and helicopters flew by at top speeds. I later learned that frustrated and hemmed in at all sides, one protester had emerged from a march and fired his gun at the cops. It is hard to shake the feeling that this repressive environment, and the desperate resistance it engendered, furnished a snapshot of long, hard days to come.[92]

This is not to say everything is bad, as Michel Foucault once remarked, only that everything is dangerous. The spiral of violence that faced the rebellion in its later days isn't a proposition that one can simply be for or against; it presented a new reality, which pressed novel questions of how the movement relates to armaments and violence, and how these choices will in turn reshape the movement.[93] This is only one part of a total world picture. As the stagnation of capital and its attendant churning and flailing erodes the quality of proletarian life, it has engendered a decomposition of liberal democracy that can move at a breathtaking speed. Enduring support for Donald Trump and his imitators, though by no means constituting a majority of Americans, demonstrates a solid base for authoritarianism, and enables a smaller but no less important vanguard for extraparliamentary rightist politics. One of the most serious rightist groups, the Three Percenters, derive their name from the belief that only 3 percent of colonists fought in the US Revolutionary War, which they purport to demonstrate that Lenin's *dedicated few* can make a decisive impact at the right moment.[94]

Perhaps they're right. But the images of January 6 that have aided US liberals in making a bugbear of "political extremism" of all sorts pale in comparison to the millions who took part in the George Floyd Rebellion. In fact, the biggest threat facing the rebels of 2020 is not the resurgent right as it currently exists, but the massive boom the right would enjoy if autonomous leftists were to forfeit the terrain of extraparliamentary politics in the name of building united fronts with liberals and so-called democratic socialists against impending fascism in the

United States. This is not to discount the reality that America is ripe for authoritarianism, but to dispute the idea that a woke variant of neoliberalism will appeal to Americans more than a hard-right repudiation of it. The danger in the present is that, as Americans join people across the world in rejecting the capitalist status quo with great disgust, the extraparliamentary right will become the only visible organized antisystem movement.[95] As the flimsiest pretenses of civil society are blotted from much of the planet, and politicians race to outdo each other in their blatant incompetence, political extremism does not present us with a yes or no question, but a crossroads: will it be our extremism that carries the day, or that of the far right?

Abolishing Ourselves

By the end of the summer of 2020, the rebellion had largely run its course. This was surely due in part to the work of counterinsurgents, clad both in police uniforms and "social movement" garb, and the versatility of the color line eroding the tenuous trust won in the hottest moments of struggle. But the ultimate limit on which the rebellion ran aground was its inability to articulate a positive conception of what it was, and where it was going, capable of keeping things moving. The mimesis of tactics celebrated by Adrian Wohlleben, initially spurring the rebellion, soon stalled out as actions taken in the street became stale repetitions devoid of any dynamism. But this was not simply due to the failure of militancy to escalate and thus produce more and better images; people cannot live on memes alone. Nor do tactics necessarily suggest a politics underlying them. American history is riven with instances of riots, street battles with the cops, and even attempts at insurrection, most recently the Capitol takeover of January 6, 2021, which actively oppose human liberation in their political content, but to the naked eye, might resemble many of the crowning moments of the George Floyd Rebellion.

Wohlleben's radical faith in the active "gesture" as a form of political expression, then, is capable of addressing its audience more effectively than a rhetorical entreaty, and provides an ingenious framework for understanding the wildfire spread of tactics across great expanses of space in short windows of time. But images can only carry politics so far; people in sustained revolt thirst for meaning. The memetic gesture, which in practice is largely a reformulation of the centuries-old anarchist "propaganda of the deed," was no substitute for a cogent and easily digestible

EVERY FIRE NEEDS A LITTLE BIT OF HELP

assessment of what the rebellion was, who its partisans were, and where it was all headed—desires irreducible from the desperate quest for meaning, and ultimately, human community, so endemic to our age. Beneath the fiery negativity of the rebellion, through which it was defined by aggressive acts conducted against an external foe, was a subtle and inchoate, yet nonetheless urgent, striving for a positive politics. Accordingly, for partisans of the meme to accuse other political tendencies of co-optation is to lament losing a game they never really played. The spread of images memetically is not an alternative to deliberate and coherent political organizations, no matter how frustrated many of us have become with the maddening and often fruitless efforts to bring them into being.

Accordingly, the political tendency that met this need most effectively was a loose national network organized under the banner of abolitionism, the product of decades of deliberate political organization. It drew upon the momentum of the rebellion to craft local campaigns to defund police departments, largely through electoral mechanisms. While US abolitionists often trace their lineage back to the antislavery agitators of the nineteenth century, the present movement is more directly related to the antiprison activism that arose from the prisoners' rights and Black revolutionary movements of the 1960s and 1970s, typified by Angela Davis, who bridges that era with the present. Today's abolitionists consider police and prisons to be structural foundations of the racialized division of labor intrinsic to US society. Many consider the US itself to be irredeemably racist. They do not believe in reforming police or punitive institutions, but seek to eliminate them, as part of radically remaking the world to meet the needs of all.[96] In short, abolitionists offer a politics that speaks at once to the need to replace the present world with a better one, while providing a clear sense of who people are and what they are doing. And as much as abolitionism represents a sophisticated body of theory, more fundamentally, it is today a name given by many young people activated by the George Floyd Rebellion to their striving, within the present, for a liberated future.

But what, concretely, is the world abolitionists are actually building? What this means in concrete terms ranges considerably from the wonkish technocracy of Alex Vitale, who pushes for electoral measures to create a postabolition system akin to Northern European capitalism somehow devoid of cops, to the overt revolutionary politics upheld by scholars like Joy James and militants like the Revolutionary Abolitionist

Movement.[97] The campaign to defund the police represented the uneasy tension between the movement's liberal and revolutionary wings, who achieve working harmony by squaring the circle of campaigns like Defund by calling them "nonreformist reforms"—strategic interventions that point toward broader, largely inchoate, structural transformation in the future.[98] While the theory linking these campaigns to revolution is undeveloped, it would be a mistake to discount the reality that many people engaged in these activities believe they are working toward a postcapitalist society, and do so with great enthusiasm. Nonetheless, the persistence of this divide has engendered a profound indistinction within abolitionism, where those pushing a kinder, gentler capitalism work alongside those seeking its overthrow.

This ambiguity at the heart of US abolitionism, between reform and revolution, sometimes seems to be by design. Many abolitionists are primarily interested in working together on practical projects they consider nonreformist. This includes prisoner support, opposing jail and prison construction, and otherwise pushing for a lessened role of police and courts in social life. Abolitionists are generally organized in small locally situated groups and campaigns, equipped with extensive public-facing propaganda.[99] A notable tendency within contemporary abolitionism originated in the anti-domestic violence movement, and came to the framework of abolition through practical experience with the failure of cops, courts, and prisons to mitigate the social fallout of interpersonal violence.[100] This means many abolitionists are intimately acquainted with the harsh realities of proletarian life, and have, through sustained practical activity, experimented in building a better world, while remaining rooted in a clear-eyed assessment of the present one.

The nonsectarian, action-oriented impetus of abolitionism pays off. It was partly their organization within national networks of locally oriented projects, and their accessible critiques of police and the punishment system, that allowed abolitionists to seize on the ideological vacuum left vacant by the more insurrectionary partisans of the George Floyd Rebellion, thus creating a large freshman class of self-identified abolitionist activists enlivened by the events of 2020 and longing to replace this world with a better one. With their large body of theory and a number of concrete political projects, abolitionism has furnished an outlet for young rebels to think through racial questions in terms of class, and class questions in terms of race, thus superseding the morass of Occupy's class-first color blindness and the cross-class alliance of race posited by Black Lives Matter. Abolitionism also came equipped with decades of praxis around the persistent problems of gender- and sexuality-based chauvinism and violence, which had sown considerable divisions within the great monoliths of race and class.

Abolitionism won the consciousness of a critical mass of people engaged in the George Floyd Rebellion, but winning material gains has proven more difficult. Initiatives to defund the police have largely come to naught across the United States.[101] This casts considerable doubt on the viability of abolition's electoral ambitions, which were purported, especially in the writing of the deft theoretician Kay Gabriel, to be the strategic application of radical politics in a modality in which they could actually win.[102] The present morass facing abolitionism, coming as it does amid a great influx of interested partisans, should give the movement sufficient cause to evaluate its own internal contradictions. In a period when carceral infrastructure is attacked and set afire in response to police shootings, the invocation of "nonreformist reforms" can no longer suffice to defer the question of reform or revolution. This is not an intellectual question, but a practical matter of how people orient struggles already underway: to save capitalism from its contradictions, or to push them to the breaking point? Unless the political terrain of the US changes dramatically, a viable revolutionary current in the United States is as likely to emerge from abolitionism as from anywhere else. If this is the case, revolutionaries do not have the luxury of being against abolitionism (or even lazily *for* it), but must push the contradictions within it, to help sharpen its focus toward an extraparliamentary politics that seeks abolition through the overcoming of class society.

Perhaps the most helpful metric for mapping this dividing line can be found in a central figure of contemporary abolitionism: "abolition democracy." This notion comes from W.E.B. Du Bois's masterpiece *Black Reconstruction in America*. In it Du Bois reinterprets the Civil War to cast slaves, who he calls "the Black workers," at the forefront of a "general strike," the mass abandonment of plantations and desertion to the Northern army, sufficient to win the war and establish Reconstruction, which tended toward a "dictatorship of the proletariat."[103] Du Bois gives the name "abolition democracy" to the unsteady political coalition of Reconstruction in the postwar South, that sought to considerably democratize large areas previously under the rule of the plantocracy, including through the creation of public schools and the thwarted attempts to collectivize much of the slaveholder land seized during the war. Reconstruction was defeated, as Du Bois argues, to the great detriment of Black and white southern working people alike. The figure of "abolition democracy" was subsequently adopted by Angela Davis to argue that contemporary abolitionism is concerned with completing the work of Reconstruction, as a radical democratizing project that can demolish the color line and build a society meeting the needs of all.[104] Many contemporary abolitionists have followed Davis to pick up this concept as a central lens for interpreting abolitionist political engagements.[105] But the imperative to take up the "unfinished revolution" of Reconstruction, as historian Eric Foner has characterized the period, begs the question of how we understand the work of Reconstruction in the first place.[106]

This is precisely the problem raised in a 1991 response to Foner by the historian and lifelong revolutionary Noel Ignatiev. A close student of Du Bois, Ignatiev concurs with Foner's characterization of Reconstruction as a pivotal revolutionary moment in US history, uniquely constitutive of our own. But Foner, Ignatiev argues, has completely misinterpreted just what kind of revolution Du Bois had in mind. For Foner, the work of Reconstruction was that of a bourgeois revolution, extending the promise of free labor under capitalism, and the realization of the rights of formal equality once denied to Black people by their position as slaves. In this liberal conception of Reconstruction, its remaining work could unfold within a class society, effected by the cross-class cooperation toward the realization of the formal equality enjoyed by the wage laborer in a society otherwise defined by social classes. Not so fast, says Ignatiev; Du Bois, who reinscribed the story of emancipation in the argot of proletarian revolution—casting the slaves as workers, their abandonment of plantations as a general strike, and likening Reconstruction to the dictatorship of the proletariat—understood the real stakes of Reconstruction, namely, the attack it attempted on private property. It is here, Ignatiev argues, that the real unfinished business of Reconstruction can be found: the abolition of class society.[107]

While this may seem like a scholastic debate, its implications are practical. People are already struggling against the present world and toward a new one. The name of this struggle, in the minds of some of the boldest and most dedicated among them, is abolitionism. But where is their struggle headed? Practices of mutual aid, popularized by

EVERY FIRE NEEDS A LITTLE BIT OF HELP

abolitionists, are welcome palliatives to the suffering of daily life under capitalism, but scarcely point toward a revolutionary offensive, when they aren't simply charity by another name.[108] Similarly, building small, isolated lacunae against the worst symptoms of capitalism in decline, dedicated to simply reproducing themselves in a gentler way than life on the outside, is not a viable strategy for going on the attack.[109] Similarly, opposition to prisons and cops is a negative unity; even the category Adrian Wohlleben counterposes to prison abolitionism, "prison demolitionism," does not escape this trap.[110]

Striving toward a positive vision, abolitionists have created daring programs for redistributing wealth and building autonomy on the local level, following the model of Divest/Invest.[111] Even this horizon, however, amounts to making demands of the state to work against its own interests. History instructs us that the US ruling class would happily hand the state to outright fascists before ceding any substantive ground in the class struggle, much less reconfiguring society to such an extent that prisons and police will be obsolete. Likewise, realizing even the modest economic program of US Senator Bernie Sanders would in all probability require militant class struggle to a degree unseen in over a century, including the public beheading of about half of Wall Street. If the tenets of abolitionism are to be taken seriously, organizers and theorists in the present must engage head-on with the question of extraparliamentary conflict with capitalism and its supporters, which will be, by necessity, a violent and thoroughly dangerous affair nonetheless essential to escaping the death spiral of capitalism. It is no longer enough to talk about abolitionism as an "imagination" or a "dream," as its more poetic adherents often insist. Abolition must be a coherent practical approach to abolishing class society through mass struggle, or else it is just that: a dream. "Linking together struggles that affect working class people is at the heart of the anti-capitalist abolitionist vision," writes Zhandarka Kurti, "because it can help concretize community, an otherwise amorphous term shaped by identity politics around a set of concrete political demands that can build political power and challenge the very ills that police power manages. Otherwise, abolition will simply be a rhetorical politics, a fad among the most woke elements of the academic left, or worse, a liberal pathway into building a more efficient and brutal social order."[112]

A new world organized according to the righteous principles abolitionists uphold will not just require alternatives to conflict mediation and responding to antisocial behavior. It will also require the collectivization, on a mass scale, of the means by which we labor and live. This is not something to be prefigured on paper. It will be the result of struggles to take possession of workplaces, neighborhoods, and above all else, the means by which commodities are produced and circulated. And however exciting and auspicious, the struggles that have defined the past decade in the United States have been limited in their capacity by their exile from these strategic sites of production and reproduction. As struggles tend to create their subjects, and not vice versa, reclaiming these locations as sites of struggle is not only essential for the strategic purposes of sustaining revolt, it will also determine the very political subjectivities who remake the world. In a very concrete sense, abolition will mean the destruction of the subjectivities foisted upon us by the dictates of capitalist society, including subject positions like race, that presently serve as the basis for solidarity. Just as the final victory of the proletariat will come not in its attainment of power but in its self-abolition as a class, creating the people who will inhabit the new world will require abolishing ourselves.

Above all, in order to satisfy even its most modest aspirations, then, the greatest hurdle facing abolitionism in the present remains the archrival of a half century of social movement activity: the separation of mass level left politics from both the point of production and the networks of circulation and massified social reproduction that crisscross advanced capitalist societies. Undoing the world that has made the violence of police, prison, and war necessary on the barbaric scale we see today will be a planetary exercise in reconfiguring how people live, labor, and distribute the plenty of the planet we share. The direct, extralegal appropriation of vast expanses of private property for communal use is not simply the outcome of abolition, but the only means by which it can be achieved. And the politics that prove adequate to these tasks may not bear the name abolitionism in the end, but it will share the desire to bridge struggles in the present to an emancipated future, which has characterized abolitionism in the present and earned it the support of a new generation of rebels. This is a massive undertaking but it must be done. Nothing short of the survival of life on the planet Earth depends on the defeat of capitalism and the creation of a new world suited to the needs, dignity, and free development of all. And as abolitionists are typically the first to admit: nobody said remaking the world would be easy!

AFTERWORD

Toward Something Else

The essays in this volume span a decade of experimental political engagement driven by the convictions that "the emancipation of the working classes must be conquered by the working classes themselves," and that this demands "not a struggle for class privileges and monopolies, but for equal rights and duties, and the abolition of all class rule."[1] Invoking the multipolar First International here is deliberate. In my political life I have consistently proven too anarchist for the self-styled communists flying flags leaden with *the weight of dead generations*, and too Marxist for the anarchists with whom I almost always end up aligning in moments of concrete struggle. Nonetheless I have striven to set these historical distinctions aside in pursuit of a political orientation that benefits from the strengths of both traditions and seeks to recapture the spirit of their common genesis in the pursuit of *everything for everyone*. I can only hope that future readers will puzzle at my suggestion that these late, great, political orientations ever found themselves intractably at odds.[2] As a start, my friend Liz Simmons suggests that the antiauthoritarian left set these labels aside and simply call ourselves "ultras." I think she might be onto something.

Like many in my now graying generation, I became aware of left politics around the alter-globalization movement, via punk rock, only to become utterly demoralized by the failure of the antiwar movement to stop the madness of post-9/11 carnage in the early aughts. I subsequently wandered for some years in the hazy realm of nihilism, depression, intoxication, and capital T Theory, before the student movement of 2008–10 and Occupy Wall Street in 2011 forced me to think seriously about mass politics as a potential vehicle for revolutionary social change.

I emerged from that wave understanding myself as part of a distinct political tradition that rejects rigid programmatism and direction from above, and values instead the autonomous action of so-called everyday people as both an important catalyst, and the primary impetus driving revolution. Working in street-level activism also acquainted me very quickly with the central role the police and other uniformed agencies, including jail guards, play in the social reproduction of US society.[3]

During this time I have found particular affinity with the traditions of autonomism, Black radicalism, left communism, insurrectionary anarchism, and the so-called communization current. I have drawn particular influence from the Johnson-Forrest Tendency of the postwar years, in particular, the Trinidadian Marxist C.L.R. James, as well as the Sojourner Truth Organization (STO) of the 1970s–80s, especially though my friendships with Noel Ignatiev, John Garvey, Kingsley Clarke, Mike Morgan, and Dave Ranney, and over a decade of correspondence with Don Hamerquist. I also studied closely with the late left-communist thinker Loren Goldner, and found him to be as brilliant as he was generous with his time. The theoretician Arya Zahedi, who I first met as a contrarian teenager in the Boston hardcore scene, introduced me to the ultraleft, including the milieu around the 2008 occupation wave in New York—may he be praised or blamed accordingly. Today, my favorite revolutionary publication is the almighty *Chaos Star*. Taken in sum, these traditions emphasize the necessity of proletarian self-activity, including independence from social movement bureaucracies like labor unions, and taking the color line and other social divisions head-on toward a decisive break with legality and the revolutionary transformation of society. These are commitments that I hope show through in the writing collected here.

Despite these allegiances, and hopefully in service to them, I have always considered myself, above all, a writer. I have organized my entire adult life around the practice of writing, which absorbs most of my free time. I type with two fingers, so it takes some time. While there will always be another mountain to climb, I remain thankful every day that *anyone* is reading the stuff, much less publishing it. Even when one name goes on the byline, my writing has never been a solo effort; the essays in this volume benefited immensely from a number of organizing projects, interpersonal relationships, and long-term exercises in writing and thinking collectively, especially a near decade of collaborative writing

AFTERWORD   **263**

with Zhandarka Kurti and a number of study groups organized with the
prison scholar Abby Cunniff, including the reading of all three volumes
of *Capital* out loud.

At its best, my work is grounded in the concrete struggles playing out around me, large and small, with a general attentiveness to the
profound political potential of "everyday life"—from the contradictory
interpersonal relationships unfolding in the lowliest jail cell, to the
Olympian heights of popular culture. This is the methodology of *Hard
Crackers: Chronicles of Everyday Life*, a publication I cofounded with a spirited band of castaways in the post-STO milieu, and edited between 2016
and 2024. Most of the essays in this book come from that project, and
bear the influence of its editors and contributors. My own decidedly
more bohemian approach fuses the mantra of "recognize and record"
offered by C.L.R. James and Grace Lee Boggs, with the cosmodemonic
methodology of that great American Nietzschean, Henry Miller, who
advocated the pursuit of extreme experiences alongside rigorous, omniv-
orous study, and skepticism toward any custom, law, or authority that
stands in the way.[4] In the process, I have also indulged episodically, and
perhaps to excess, in what renegade rock critic Lester Bangs once called
"the vast vacuous beauty of this crap culture we're fryin' in."[5]

The result is a body of work undertaken under circumstances ranging from sheer euphoria to great bodily risk, sometimes simultaneously,
and driven by the imperative to lean into complexity, ambiguity, and
contradiction, setting aside rote slogans and activist clichés to simply
tell the truth as it has been revealed to me. "If you are squeamish," writes
the Greek poet Sappho, "don't prod the beach rubble."[6]

One of the most rewarding (and infuriating) parts of writing is, if
done properly, it lays bare limits of the author's knowledge and thinking
that are ordinarily easy to ignore. As I struggled to conclude the essay
"Three Months Inside Alt-Right New York," I ran into this wall. Following
an utterly draining and potentially dangerous experience infiltrating
that strange and yet oddly familiar movement, I hoped to express some
profound truth of our political conjuncture, and the rightward turn of
so many young men who reminded me a whole lot of me and my friends,
growing up in the suburbs south of Boston. My conclusion, however, was
rushed and fairly weak. I felt hung up on the distinctly 2016 belief that
the new generation of fascists were "working-class" men who had turned
to Trump out of disgust with the Democrats. Did this really apply to the

tech workers and college-educated fascist intellectuals who made up the core of the alt-right? I was stuck.

Critics on the left were largely generous; the worst rebuke I received came from my pointing out that these supposed warriors of the master race were mostly quite out of shape (body negativity). But I remained haunted by my failure to develop a more nuanced class analysis of the core demographic of the alt-right. Why was this so difficult? How much more Marxist theory did I need to read? At last, it dawned on me: this was because it was basically *my own class position*, what we might call "white lower middle-class." And this was a distinct subjectivity that I had spent years running away from, thanks in part to my (temporary, in hindsight) exile into the miserable world of blue-collar wage labor, and my presence in political milieus that typically refuse to conduct honest assessments of their own race and class composition, ignore the prevalence of generational wealth, and describe just about everyone on our side as a "proletarian." Of course, it is the fundamental nature of the middle class to mask its social position, as a means of its mediating function between labor and capital—just as most white Americans downplay the comparative privileges they enjoy. And here I was, replicating the very tendencies I long believed myself to be taking apart.

Wrestling with these doubts, I recalled a critique raised by Don Hamerquist of "The Old Mole Breaks Concrete," the first essay that appears in this volume, at the time of its publication. "I question this phraseology," Hamerquist wrote, "'the US working class is on the move,' 'this is the class groping towards a form of militant action.' This language avoids the contradictions and internal dynamics that a radical intervention should clarify—e.g., the issues raised by marginalization and precarious labor—and it substitutes consideration of the real problems of mass, intermediate, and revolutionary organization and the work needed to sustain and build from near-insurrectionary moments with a fetishism of militancy and a spontaneism that assumes a too easy path ahead."[7]

Noel often said: "I've won every argument I've ever had, but I never changed anyone's mind." Don might say the same thing; at the time of his writing this, I simply wasn't ready to hear it. In hindsight, of course, he was correct; my schema of "the class" in action was a classic case of *avoiding the contradictions and internal dynamics that a radical intervention should clarify.*[8]

AFTERWORD   265

In recent years I have attempted to grapple more seriously with a
nuanced assessment of racialized class composition, without succumbing to the kind of vulgar Marxist sociology that turns dialectics into
butterfly collecting.[9] I feel that this should begin with revolutionaries
making an honest assessment of their own position. For instance the
notion, popularized around the George Floyd Rebellion of 2020, that
rioting somehow abolishes or suspends racialization, however tempo-
rarily, has been occasionally bandied under the mantle of "race treason,"
when it is in fact the same old race blindness in a shiny new package.
Moving beyond these dangerous illusions is imperative; the work of
clarifying the evolving contours of class in US society and beyond is as
difficult as it is necessary, and I can only hope, in the very least, to no
longer stand in the way of it.[10]

In the process, I have been forced to confront another topic I was
socially conditioned to ignore: the settler-colonial nature of US society.
The need to redress this deficiency came to me in the composition of
another frustrating writing experience, in which I reflected on attending a Trump rally in Mosinee, Wisconsin.[11] Staring at a blank page,
desperate to redeem an arduous round trip drive from Chicago made
all the more dystopian by binging on the It Could Happen Here podcast, I
simply could not come up with compelling reasons for Trump's enduring
appeal, besides the racism and xenophobia that isn't exactly lacking
under the surface of most Democrats, including Joe Biden. The best
answer I could muster was the appeal of celebrity and spectacle, which
are surely factors of the Trump phenomenon, but hardly explain it.
Again, I was stuck.

I was never happy with the essay, which I quietly released and moved
on, and in 2023 I decided to travel to Iowa and take another crack at
it. Having recently read Patrick Wolfe's Traces of History and J. Sakai's
magisterial polemic Settlers, I decided to focus instead on Trump's unique
appeal to the ideology of settler colonialism.[12] This lens opened up an
entirely new vista, resulting in the essay "Iowa Bluffs," contained in this
volume, in which I feel I finally begin to understand a thing or two about
the country I have lived in all my life. I further explored these themes in
"The Future Belongs to the Mad," also in this volume, in which I argue
that any serious communist politics must center a spiritual relationship with the Earth, and engage especially with received Indigenous
traditions. I can only hope this project amounts to more than a "land

acknowledgement" at the beginning of some otherwise cliché white ultraleftism, but I will leave it to readers to make that judgment.

I have compiled this collection in the shadow of the racist apartheid state of Israel undertaking genocide in the Gaza strip, as part of its historical mission to liquidate the Indigenous Arab population "from the river, to the sea" and beyond. This year I had the privilege of taking part in multiple pro-Palestine university encampments, linking up with the Lake Effect crew in Chicago, and serving as the faculty advisor for the first chapter of Students for Justice in Palestine at the university where I work, alongside a new generation of activists with a fierce anti-imperialist analysis and an internationalist outlook.[13] This has made me realize how little of my own work engages seriously with the global picture, especially the relationship of US imperialism to domestic life.

I have always jokingly referred to myself as a "townie internationalist," concerned with the struggles playing out right in front of my face as a concrete step toward affecting change in the broader world. This is not exactly incorrect, in vulgar practical terms, but it is a recipe for myopic analysis that borders on national chauvinism. And on the most basic level, as we today see the state of Israel fighting counterinsurgent warfare against pro-Palestine American citizens through a variety of institutions ranging from law enforcement and higher education, to the very halls of Congress, I have witnessed firsthand how foolish it is to erect a line of demarcation between struggles in my own nation-state and the rest of an increasingly shrinking world.

During the composition of *States of Incarceration*, I organized an encrypted video chat for partisans of the George Floyd Rebellion to give feedback on draft chapters.[14] Two comrades from the same city seemed to describe totally different events. The first, a cis man, celebrated the heroism of pitched battles with the police, designer stores looted, and nights of joyous partying on the barricades, waxing poetic in the argot of ultraleft high theory. The second, a cis woman, recounted the trauma of police violence, sleepless nights spent doing jail support, and the pervasive burnout experienced by her comrades. Of course, these could both be true, but I was struck by how gendered these experiences were.

The contrast stuck with me, and I began to fear that my own writing has valorized a particularly macho aspect of the struggle, while downplaying the difficult and necessary work of social reproduction that remains largely feminized. I reflected about how much I had benefited from jail

AFTERWORD

support, street medics, and endless hours of proverbial (and sometimes literal) shoulders to cry on, and how little these roles figured into my analysis of moments of rupture. In case it is not clear in everything I have written: mutual aid, jail support, street medicine, interpersonal care, and other movement tasks that unfold in the shadow of spectacular street confrontations are just as valuable as the more confrontational militancy—and in fact, *enable* it to sustain itself across time. Treating intense moments of street combat as more important than these necessary tasks reproduces the devaluation of feminized labor that characterizes capitalist society. What's more, alternative forms of social reproduction will be a necessary ingredient to a new society, and are innovated not only in moments of rupture, but the time between them.

This is, of course, not to say that those who do feminized labor don't also throw down in the streets. Instead, it means that the movement work that disproportionately falls to these comrades in the aftermath is a central part of the story of any mass struggle, and ought to be treated that way—as part of breaking down the gendered division of labor in movement work altogether. This includes writing, which, as I am fully aware, I do more of than anything else. Beth Henson of STO and *Race Traitor* recently punctuated an excellent reflection on a Gaza solidarity movement with the observation: "I was surprised that most of the campers were women and trans people. Despite the years I've been lurking on the fringes of anarchist movements, I did not expect that, because nearly all the writers are men. I won't name names and I love my comrades, but women, trans folks—please—step up. Writing is a way of thinking things through, don't let the cis men do it all."[15] As one of the names graciously omitted, I wholeheartedly agree, and I think those of us cis men who write must to do more to help make it happen—whether this means sharing resources, socializing skills, or just encouraging people to write down the things they say and work them out in a systematic way.

I am well aware that some readers might find all of the above self-criticism to be an instance of, as we say in Massachusetts, "light dawning on Marblehead." That's fair enough; those who foolishly believe themselves to have risen above the ordinary prejudices of their historical moment are actually the most susceptible to them. I have certainly not been immune to the chauvinism, arrogance, and unearned confidence one would expect of a white American man from my time and place, and I thank everyone in the movement who has believed that I have the potential to leave at least some of this baggage behind. Anyway, I've never taken for granted that those of us willing to fight for a liberated society will be fit to live in it.

Two more notes are in order. The first concerns my use of the three-way fight framework, especially in my analysis of January 6, "The Big Takeover." This essay was written in response to comrades pushing conspiracy theories about that day's events, especially the notion, subsequently debunked, that Capitol police were part of the attack. I find narratives in which we ordinary people are the helpless pawns of unseen forces to be boring and borderline politically useless. I also respect the agency of people who take risks in the name of their politics, even when I don't agree with them, or, in this case, they're my overt enemies. I therefore found the impulse to deny the January 6 insurrectionists the agency to carry out the Capitol attack to be reactionary and defeatist, especially given that I'd like to see our side do far more things like this, and believe it's possible. But my overemphasis of the autonomy of the insurrectionists, and their "antisystem" intentions, also demonstrates the weakness of applying the three-way fight perspective to Trumpism.

Contrary to what I wrote at the time, keeping Trump in power as president of the United States was in fact the center of January 6. Following his departure from office, Trump remained a near hegemon in the US right, and, in many cases, has integrated "system loyal" and "system oppositional" elements of the US right to a point of virtual indistinction, which he personally embodies. Following Trump's 2024 electoral victory, the system-oppositional right is nowhere to be found in the streets, as the alt-right was in 2016, and much of it can likely be working for, or otherwise supporting, Trump's version of the system. In this light, I believe the three-way fight analysis to be an essential corrective for liberal and *faux*-radical antifascism, which calls for dead-end popular fronts with pro-capitalist, pro-imperialist, and other chauvinist forces antithetical to human liberation. But it is not an analysis that can simply be applied ready-made. Instead, the three-way fight approach offers a clearing of bad politics, upon which good politics can be built, along with a set of tools to help do so. The recent *Three-Way Fight* anthology, in which I am honored to appear, is a trove of empirical and methodological insights.[16] But with Trump's return to the White House, it is clear that we're on new terrain.

AFTERWORD   **269**

Similarly, in the essay which gives this book its name, I express the view that abolitionism is the most favorable political tendency for cultivating revolutionary politics in the United States. Granted, this is a fairly low bar. But since the great rebellion of 2020, which raised the possibility of abolition as an insurrectionary act, I have watched with great frustration as most self-styled abolitionists have refused to engage in substantive revolutionary praxis of any kind, and have instead dug in their heels on stale sloganeering and reformist campaigns to which they append the qualifier "nonreformist" in a sleight of linguistic alchemy. Meanwhile, decades-old arguments soldier on like the siege of the Third Precinct never happened. Abolition, I often hear, is a *dream*, an *imagination*, an *ethics*, a *poetics*—and just about everything but a concrete revolutionary project guided by clear strategic lines bridging actions in the here and now to an actually liberated world. I was recently informed, by the editor of a popular abolitionist publication, that since abolition will not happen during our lifetime, there is no reason to draw political lines within it now. This is simply not serious.

If abolitionism means the practical supersession of class society through eliminating the organized institutions of racialized class violence that prop it up, and creating a communist society in place, consider me an abolitionist. But if abolitionism is just a wishy-washy, radical-liberal rebranding of left-Keynesianism, furnishing radical chic verbiage for the left wing of the nonprofit sector, abstruse academic treatises, and social media influencers building their brands, please accept my apology for leading readers astray and consider my naivety a cautionary tale. The answer will be determined, in the coming years, by what abolitionists do.[17]

As I write, I am preparing to turn forty, have recently become a father, and am settling into a fairly gratifying and otherwise comfortable job as a university professor. While these factors should probably combine to make me renounce my youthful radicalism and embrace the pragmatism of slow and patient work, lately I suspect the opposite: that I, and *we*, are not nearly radical or *extremist* enough, are not taking enough bold and courageous actions, and will likely have to explain to future generations why so much infrastructure of misery and death was left standing, and so many elites were allowed to die of natural causes as they ravaged the planet beyond repair and degraded humanity to the point where the Donald Trumps of the world are deemed fit to lead.

Upon reading this book, my daughter might one day ask me why I was writing think pieces about *Hellraiser* and *Mad Max* instead of forming an underground people's army to stop climate change and end capitalism. I suppose I'll tell her, as Lenin remarks somewhere, that you can only be as radical as the times you live in. Perhaps, she'll tell me, that sentiment has always just been "cope."

Approaching middle age and starting a family, I am struck with the growing sense of being a character of the distant past, a great-grandfather whose entire life plays out in the first thirty pages of an epic novel, after which time he is intermittently remembered, before being forgotten altogether. Politically, I think this means understanding our present not as the terminus of a received political history, but as the prehistory of a new one. A future reader of the indispensable edited collection *The George Floyd Uprising*, for instance, will probably look upon its contributors, myself included, the same way we view the historical curiosities populating the opening chapters of E.P. Thompson's *The Making of the English Working Class*: so many millenarians and zealots of vanishing traditions, inhabiting a social terrain changing far more quickly than they can change their own ideas, yet nonetheless preserving "heroic culture" on which future struggles will be built.[18] I believe today's most urgent task is to take this as a serious prospect and act accordingly.

This is not a call for quietism or fatalism, but simply understanding that the inherited political categories are largely inadequate to the struggles ahead. This requires ruthless, self-searching critique and courageous experimental praxis, undertaken with no illusions about the difficulties to be faced, to forge and articulate a new politics already crying out from the tumult of our chaotic present—a bit like the baby screaming in my ear as I try to complete this essay, though probably much less cute, and even more annoying.

Ultimately, the book you have just read is, most of all, a chronicle of the end of its author's youth. "Youth is itself intrinsically falsifying and deceitful," writes Friedrich Nietzsche.

> Later, after the young soul has been tortured by constant disappointments, it ends up turning suspiciously on itself, still raging and wild, even in the force of its suspicion and the pangs of its conscience. How furious it is with itself now, how impatiently it tears itself apart, what revenge it exacts for having blinded

itself for so long, as if its blindness had been voluntary! In this transitional state, we punish ourselves by distrusting our feelings, we torture our enthusiasm with doubts, we experience even a good conscience as a danger, as if it were a veil wrapped around us, something marking the depletion of a more subtle, genuine honesty. And, above all, we become partisan, partisan on principle against "youth."—A decade later, we realize that all this—was youthfulness too![19]

But enough from that old blowhard, and enough from this one. Thanks to the inimitable Prole for the sick ass cover art, to PM Press for making this book happen, and to you, for taking the time to read it. Free the land, fuck the law!

Jarrod Shanahan
Chicago, 2024

Notes

Introduction
1   Upon release, Jarrod began studying the history of the building where we spoke, spur-
     ring a years-long project that turned into the 2022 book *Captives: How Rikers Island
     Took New York City Hostage* (Verso, 2022). Earlier this year, Jarrod turned the project
     into a trilogy with the publications of his furious Rikers journals as *City Time* (NYU
     Press, 2025), a book length ethnography of the jail coauthored with the antifascist
     and former political prisoner David Campbell, and his analysis of an abolitionist
     movement in New York, *Skyscraper Jails* (Haymarket, 2025), written with fellow *Hard
     Crackers* editor Zhandarka Kurti.

The Old Mole Breaks Concrete: The Ongoing Rupture in New York City
1   See "The Holding Pattern: The Ongoing Crisis and the Class Struggles of 2011–2013,"
     Endnotes, no. 3 (2014): 12–54, https://libcom.org/library/holding-pattern-ongoing-
     crisis-class-struggles-2011-2013.
2   The reader at the time would have understood this reference to be indebted to the
     Fire Next Time collective's seminal pamphlet "The Flatbush Rebellion," which, for
     better or worse, colored my thinking on these questions at this time—and probably
     still does. See Fire Next Time, "The Flatbush Rebellion," March 25, 2013, https://
     eastcoastrenegades.wordpress.com/2013/03/25/pamphlet-on-the-flatbush-rebellion.
3   The reader at the time would have recognized this as a reference to the journal *Endnotes*.
4   This section reflects the influence of the Marxist intellectual Loren Goldner, with
     whom I was studying closely at this time.
5   I have no idea what happened in Oakland that day, but it was probably a riot.

Noel Ignatiev, 1940–2019
1   Sojourner Truth Organization, "Theses on Workplace Organizing," 1974, http://www.
     sojournertruth.net/theses.html.

Days Spent Doing Too Much of Fucking Nothing
1   Hannah K. Gold, "From Inside Rikers Island, A Harrowing Look at the Torture of Solitary
     Confinement," *The Intercept*, October 3, 2015, https://theintercept.com/2015/10/03/
     from-inside-rikers-island-a-harrowing-look-at-the-torture-of-solitary-confinement.
2   United States Department of Justice, "CRIPA Investigation of the New York City
     Department of Correction Jails on Rikers Island" (USDOJ, 2014).
3   "Capital Construction," in *Progress Through Crisis 1954–1966*, ed. DOC (DOC, 1956), 365.

NOTES

The Secret Lives of Rikers Island Jail Guards
1   United States Department of Justice, "CRIPA Investigation"; New York City Department of Investigation (DOI), "New York City Department of Investigation Report on Security Failures at City Department of Correction Facilities" (DOI, 2014); New York City Department of Investigation, "Report on the Recruiting and Hiring Process for New York City Correction Officers" (DOI, 2015).

The Surreality of Rikers Island
1   Blaine Harden, "Framed and Forlorn at Rikers; Coffee-Stained Dalí Awaits a New Chance Among the Prisoners," *New York Times*, March 20, 2001; John Marzulli and Tracy Conor, "Rikers Art Theft: It's Goodbye, Dalí," *New York Daily News*, March 2, 2003; Susan Sauly, "A Dalí Vanishes from Rikers Island," *New York Times*, March 2, 2003; Robert Tanner, "Salvador Dalí Original Hangs in N.Y. Rogues Gallery," *Los Angeles Times*, May 10, 1998; Murray Weiss, "Laughing Art-ily—Rikers Dalí Theft Began as a Joke," *New York Post*, September 30, 2003; Paul von Zielbauer, "Art Too Tempting at Rikers; Plot to Steal a Dalí Was Far from a Masterpiece," *New York Times*, October 4, 2003; James Fanelli. "The Great Rikers Island Art Heist," *Esquire*, October 11, 2018.
2   United States Department of Justice, "CRIPA Investigation."

Death to the Walking Dead
1   C.L.R. James, *American Civilization* (Blackwell, 1993), 123.
2   Brian Cronin, "Was *The Walking Dead* Originally on Another Planet?" *CBR*, October 31, 2017, https://www.cbr.com/walking-dead-dead-planet.
3   Brian Cronin, "Comic Legends: The Big Lie that Launched *The Walking Dead*," *CBR*, October 23, 2017, https://www.cbr.com/walking-dead-big-lie-image-comics.
4   C.L.R. James, *The Black Jacobins* (Random House, 1989), 12.
5   Elizabeth McAlister, "Slaves, Cannibals, and Infected Hyper-Whites," in *Zombie Theory: A Reader*, ed. Sarah Juliet Lauro (University of Minnesota, 2017), 71.
6   Steven Shaviro, "Contagious Allegories: George Ramiro," in Lauro, *Zombie Theory*, 7–14.
7   Roger Ebert, "The Night of the Living Dead," *Chicago Sun-Times*, January 5, 1969.
8   Gilles Deleuze and Félix Guattari, *Anti-Oedipus: Capitalism and Schizophrenia* (University of Minnesota, 1980), 335.
9   Craig Elvy, "Why *The Walking Dead* and *28 Days Later* Have Such Similar Openings," *Screen Rant*, April 24, 2020, https://screenrant.com/walking-dead-28-days-later-same-opening-rick-jim-explained.
10 Leslie Goldberg, "Robert Kirkman Reveals His Biggest 'Walking Dead' Regret," *Hollywood Reporter*, November 25, 2014, https://www.hollywoodreporter.com/tv/tv-news/walking-deads-robert-kirkman-reveals-751988.
11 Meredith Woerner, "Why George Romero Rejected *The Walking Dead* to Make *The Zombie Autopsies*," *Gizmodo*, October 19, 2011, https://gizmodo.com/why-george-romero-rejected-the-walking-dead-to-make-the-5851502.
12 Eric Deggans, "Diversity on 'The Walking Dead' Wasn't Always Handled Well," *National Public Radio*, November 28, 2014, https://www.npr.org/2014/11/28/366655295/diversity-on-the-walking-dead-wasnt-always-handled-well.
13 Neil Smith, "Giuliani Time: The Revanchist 1990s," *Social Text* 57 (Winter, 1998), 1–20.
14 Olivia Lawrence-Weilmann and Cloee Cooper, "Blue Lives Matter and the U.S. Counter-Subversive Tradition: A Q&A with Authors Jarrod Shanahan and Tyler Wall," *Political Research Associates*, January 4, 2022, https://politicalresearch.org/2022/01/04/blue-lives-matter-and-us-counter-subversive-tradition.
15 Andy Battle and Jarrod Shanahan, "The Second Time as Farce," *Jacobin*, April 13, 2018, https://jacobin.com/2018/04/death-wish-eli-roth-michael-winner-crime.
16 Michelle Alexander, *The New Jim Crow: Mass Incarceration in the Age of Colorblindness* (New Press, 2010).

17 Travis Linnemann, Tyler Wall, and Edward Green, "The Walking Dead and the Killing State," in Lauro, *Zombie Theory*, 339.

18 Sherryl Vint, "Abject Posthumanism," in Lauro, *Zombie Theory*, 177.

Zoomers Go to Hell

1 Brian B., "Clive Barker Writing *Hellraiser* Remake!" *Movieweb*, October 21, 2006, https://movieweb.com/clive-barker-writing-hellraiser-remake.

2 Michael Kennedy, "Why the *Hellraiser* Reboot Has Been Taking So Long to Make," *Screen Rant*, February 10, 2020, https://screenrant.com/hellraiser-movie-reboot-long-production-delay-why.

3 Eriq Gardner, "'Hellraiser' Writer Reclaiming U.S. Franchise Rights After Lawsuit Settlement," *Hollywood Reporter*, December 1, 2020, https://www.hollywoodreporter.com/business/business-news/hellraiser-writer-reclaiming-u-s-franchise-rights-after-lawsuit-settlement-4098688.

4 Giorgio Paolo Campi, "S/M, Splatter, and Body Modifications in the Early Clive Barker: Birth of a Political Aesthetics," *Whatever: A Transdisciplinary Journal of Queer Theories and Studies* 5, no. 1 (2022): 73–96.

5 Mark Derry, "Clive Barker Interview," *Carpe Noctem*, no. 13, (1998), https://www.clivebarker.info/ints98.html; Lúcio Reis Filho, "Demons to Some, Angels to Others: Eldritch Horrors and Hellbound Religion in the *Hellraiser* Films," in *Divine Horror: Essays on the Cinematic Battle Between the Sacred and the Diabolical*, ed. Cynthia J. Miller and A. Bowdoin Van Riper (McFarland, 2017), 113.

6 Clive Barker, *The Hellbound Heart* (Harper Paperback, 2006), n.

7 Clive Barker, *Hellraiser* (original screenplay), October 1986, https://www.dailyscript.com/scripts/Hellraiser.txt. All subsequent references to the screenplay refer to this source.

8 Barker, *Hellbound Heart*, 5.

9 Barker, *Hellbound Heart*, 29.

10 Barker, *Hellbound Heart*, 5.

11 Paul Kane, *The Hellraiser Films and Their Legacy* (McFarland, 2006), 23.

12 Barker, *Hellbound Heart*, 7–9.

13 Carol J. Clover, *Men, Women, and Chain Saws: Gender in the Modern Horror Film* (Princeton University Press, 1992).

14 Sarah Trencansky, "Final Girls and Terrible Youth: Transgression in 1980s Slasher Horror," *Journal of Popular Film and Television* 29, no. 2 (2000): 63–73.

15 Matthew Sautman, "Domestic Bodies in Hell: The Significance of Gendered Embodiment in Clive Barker's *Hellraiser*," *Body Studies Journal* 2, no. 7 (2020), 72.

16 Levi Ghyselinck, "Clive Barker's Hellraiser Mythology: A Critical Analysis," (master's thesis, University of Gent, 2009), 57.

17 Kane, *Hellraiser Films*, 31.

18 Gina Wisker, *Horror Fiction: An Introduction* (Bloomsbury Academic, 2005), 151.

19 Kane, *Hellraiser Films*, 31.

20 Robin Wood, "An Introduction to the American Horror Film," in *Robin Wood on the Horror Film: Collected Essays and Reviews*, ed. Barry Keith Grant, (Wayne State University Press, 2018), 98.

21 Keri O'Shea, "'Demons to Some, Angels to Others': Celebrating 25 Years of Hellraiser," *Warped Perspective*, September 11, 2012, https://warped-perspective.com/index.php/2012/09/11/demons-to-some-angels-to-others-celebrating-25-years-of-hellraiser.

22 Derry, "Clive Barker Interview."

23 Scott Jeffrey, "Sadomasochists from Beyond the Grave," *Nth Mind*, February 28, 2013, https://nthmind.wordpress.com/2013/02/28/sadomasochists-from-beyond-the-grave.

NOTES   **275**

24   Kane, *Hellraiser Films*, 92.
25   Congressional Research Service, "Real Wage Trends, 1979 to 2019," updated December
      28, 2020, https://sgp.fas.org/crs/misc/R45090.pdf.
26   Alex J. Pollock, "Long-Term Home Ownership Trends: The US, England, and Canada,"
      American Enterprise Institute, March 26, 2014, https://www.aei.org/articles/
      long-term-home-ownership-trends-the-us-england-and-canada; Prudence
      Ivey, "Millennials Are Buying Fewer Homes—We Wouldn't Have to Care if the
      Alternatives Were Better," *The Standard,* April 5, 2022, https://www.standard.co.uk/
      homesandproperty/property-news/millennials-buying-homes-property-affordable-
      housing-policy-house-prices-b992410.html.
27   Patricia Allmer, "'Breaking the Surface of the Real': The Discourse of Commodity
      Capitalism in Clive Barker's *Hellraiser* Narratives," in *Space, Haunting Discourse,* ed.
      Maria Holmgren Troy and Elisabeth Wennö (Cambridge Scholars Publishing, 2008),
      19.
28   Sautman, "Domestic Bodies in Hell," 74.
29   "The Logic of Gender," *Endnotes* no. 3 (2014): 56–90, https://endnotes.org.uk/
      translations/endnotes-the-logic-of-gender.
30   John D'Emilio, "Capitalism and Gay Identity," in *The Gay and Lesbian Studies Reader,*
      ed. David M. Halperin, Henry Abelove, and Michele Aina Barale (Routledge, 1993)
      467–76; Derry, "Clive Barker Interview."
31   Allmer, "'Breaking the Surface of the Real,'" 15.
32   Lúcio Reis Filho, "Demons to Some, Angels to Others," 13.
33   Katie Rife, "Watching All Nine Hellraiser Movies Is an Exercise in Masochism," *AV
      Club,* October 30, 2014, https://www.avclub.com./watching-all-9-hellraiser-movies-
      is-an-exercise-in-maso-1798273640.
34   Steve Barton, "Hellraiser: Revelations—Doug Bradley Speaks Out! Will NOT
      be Returning!," *Dread Central,* August 21, 2010, https://www.dreadcentral.com/
      news/19101/hellraiser-revelations-doug-bradley-speaks-out-will-not-be-returning.
35   Clive Barker (@RealCliveBarker), August 21, 2011. https://x.com/RealCliveBarker/
      status/105189711416524800.
36   Zachary Paul, "Doug Bradley Speaks (Again) About Hellraiser: Judgment," *Halloween
      Love,* February 9, 2017, https://halloweenlove.com/doug-bradley-speaks-again-about-
      hellraiser-judgment.
37   "It's Finally Time to Say Goodbye to Hellraiser's Pinhead," Geek's Guide to the Galaxy,
      Wired, May 23, 2015, https://www.wired.com/2015/05/geeks-guide-clive-barker.
38   Jarrod Shanahan, "Chicago: The Very Best of Judy Chicago, Reviewed by an Art
      Handler," *Art Handler,* no. 1 (2016), http://art-handler.com.
39   Laura Mowat, "Marriage Rates for Opposite-Sex Couples Drop to Lowest on
      Record," *Sky News,* May 19, 2022, https://news.sky.com/story/marriage-rates-for-
      opposite-sex-couples-drop-to-lowest-on-record-12616647; United States Congress
      Joint Economic Committee, "U.S. Marriage Rate Hits New Recorded Low," April
      29, 2020, https://www.jec.senate.gov/public/index.cfm/republicans/2020/4/
      marriage-rate-blog-test.
40   Trencansky, "Final Girls and Terrible Youth," 68.
41   Anne Kim, "Generation COVID: Record Numbers of Youth Opt Out of College, Work,"
      Newsweek, September 28, 2022, https://www.newsweek.com/2022/10/07/generation-
      covid-record-numbers-youth-opt-out-college-work-1746793.html.

Hybrid Moments
1   Matt Pollock, "A Complete History of Riot Fest 2015's Troubles," *Chicago,* September
      9, 2015, https://www.chicagomag.com/arts-culture/September-2015/A-Brief-
      History-of-Riot-Fest-2015s-Troubles.
2   Stephanie Lulay and Darryl Holliday, "Riot Fest Moved to Douglas Park After Tensions

in Humboldt," *DNAinfo*, May 19, 2015, https://www.dnainfo.com/chicago/20150519/humboldt-park/riot-fest-talks-about-moving-douglas-park-alderman-says.

3   Elvia Malagón, "As Riot Fest Crews Set Up in Douglass Park, Little Village, Lawndale Residents Push for Music Festival to Leave," *Chicago Sun-Times*, September 14, 2022.

4   Kelly Garcia, "Donations, Violations, and Fees," *The Reader*, September 15, 2022, https://chicagoreader.com/news-politics/donations-violations-and-fees.

5   Steven Blush, *American Hardcore: A Tribal History,* 2nd ed. (Feral House, 2001) 201. The historical account that follows is largely indebted to Blush and Greene.

6   James Greene Jr., *This Music Leaves Stains: The Complete Story of the Misfits* (Scarecrow Press, 2013) 8.

7   Greene, *This Music Leaves Stains*, 3.

8   Greene, *This Music Leaves Stains*, 30.

9   Luke Morgan Britton, "Misfits Explain that Recent Lawsuit Helped Them Reform," *NME*, May 15, 2016, https://www.nme.com/news/music/misfits-5-1198438.

10   James Greene Jr., "Glenn Danzig Sues Jerry Only for Trademark Infringement in Latest Misfits Lawsuit," *JG2Land*, May 6, 2014, https://jgtwo.com./2014/05/06/glenn-danzig-sues-jerry-only-for-trademark-infringement-in-latest-misfits-lawsuit.

11   James Greene Jr., "The Misfits Almost Settled Their Latest Lawsuit with a Reunion," *JG2Land*, March 14, 2016, https://jgtwo.com./2016/03/14/the-misfits-almost-settled-their-latest-lawsuit-with-a-reunion.

12   James Greene Jr., "When There Is No More Room in Court, the Misfits Will Reunite," *JG2Land*, May 12, 2016, https://jgtwo.com/2016/05/12/when-there-is-no-more-room-in-court-the-misfits-will-reunite.

13   James Greene Jr., "Dave, Dave My Darling," *JG2Land*, August 29, 2016, https://jgtwo.com/2016/08/29/dave-dave-my-darling.

14   James Greene Jr., "It Actually Happened Again," *JG2Land*, September 19, 2016, https://jgtwo.com/2016/09/19/it-actually-happened-again.

15   Lester Bangs, "The White Noise Supremacists," *Village Voice*, April 30, 1979, https://www.villagevoice.com/the-white-noise-supremacists.

16   Paul Corrigan and Simon Firth, "The Politics of Youth Culture," in *Resistance Through Ritual: Youth Subcultures in Post-War Britain*, ed. Stuart Hall and Tony Jefferson (Routledge, 1976), 238.

The Future Belongs to the Mad

1   John Hay, "The American *Mad Max: The Road Warrior* Versus *The Postman*" *Science Fiction Film and Television* 10, no. 3 (Autumn 2017): 315.

2   Sue Matthews, *35mm Dreams: Conversations with Five Directors about the Australian Film Revival* (Penguin, 1984), 234.

3   Evan Calder Williams, *Combined and Uneven Apocalypse: Luciferian Marxism* (Zero Books, 2011), 24.

4   Travis Linnemann, *The Horror of Police* (NYU Press, 2022), 89.

5   Luke Buckmaster, *Miller and Max: George Miller and the Making of a Film Legend* (Hardie Grant Books, 2017), xv.

6   Buckmaster, *Miller and Max*, 36, 98.

7   J. Emmett Winn, "*Mad Max*, Reaganism, and *The Road Warrior*," *Kinema* (Fall 1997); Philip Adams, "The Dangerous Pornography of Death," *The Bulletin*, May 1, 1979.

8   Quoted in Buckmaster, *Miller and Max*, 4.

9   Matthews, *35mm Dreams*, 236.

10   Quoted in Buckmaster, *Miller and Max*, 25.

11   Christopher Sharrett, "The Hero as Pastiche: Myth, Male Fantasy, and Simulacra in *Mad Max* and *The Road Warrior*," *Journal of Popular Film and Television* 13 (1985): 84.

12   Cotten Selier, *Republic of Drivers: A Cultural History of Automobility in America* (University of Chicago Press, 2009), 13, 66. A key exception to this is the liberation of adolescent

NOTES

sexuality from the strictures of the nuclear family, in which the automobile proved a key setting. This likely could have been accomplished, however, in ways that did not permanently warm the planet past habitability.

13 Buckmaster, *Miller and Max*, 39.

14 Jasper Bernes, "Our Streets," Verso Books (blog), August 24, 2017, https://www.versobooks.com/blogs/news/3371-our-streets.

15 Ezekiel Crago, *Raggedy Men: Masculinity in the Mad Max Movies* (Peter Lang, 2020), 67.

16 Reprinted in James Joll, *Three Intellectuals in Politics* (Pantheon, 1960), 181.

17 Jonathan Rayner, *Contemporary Australian Cinema: An Introduction* (Manchester University Press, 2000), 43.

18 Sharrett, "Hero as Pastiche," 83.

19 David Chute, "The Ayatollah of the Moviola: Interview with Dr George Miller," *Film Comment* 18, no. 4 (1982): 29.

20 Buckmaster, *Miller and Max*, 91.

21 Terry Hayes, George Miller, and Brian Hannant, *Mad Max II*, April 13, 1981, https://imsdb.com/scripts/Mad-Max-2-The-Road-Warrior.html.

22 *Furiosa: A Mad Max Saga*, directed by George Miller (Warner Bros. Pictures, 2024).

23 "Interview with Vernon Welles," *B&S About the Movies*, June 6, 2020, https://bandsaboutmovies.com. Miller also disagrees with Welles. See Matthews, *35mm Dreams*, 245.

24 For a detailed examination of the western origins of the *Mad Max* franchise, see Martin Holtz, "Mad Max and the Western," *Studies in Australasian Cinema* 17, no. 3 (2023): 141–53.

25 James Newton, *The Mad Max Effect: Road Warriors in International Exploitation Cinema* (Bloomsbury Academic, 2021), 96.

26 Buckmaster, *Miller and Max*, 261.

27 Bonnie McLean, "'Who Killed the World?': Religious Paradox in *Mad Max: Fury Road*," *Science Fiction Film and Television* 10, no. 3 (2017): 427.

28 Jack Halberstam, *Female Masculinity* (Duke University Press, 1998). For the cringe memes, see https://www.tumblr.com/feministmadmax.

29 Encrypted Signal correspondence.

30 Newton, *Mad Max Effect*, 95–96.

31 Buckmaster, *Miller and Max*, 29.

32 Williams, *Combined and Uneven Apocalypse*, 26.

33 Claire Corbett, "Nowhere to Run: Repetition Compulsion and Heterotopia in the Australian Post-Apocalypse, from 'Crabs' to *Mad Max: Beyond Thunderdome*," *Science Fiction Film & Television* 10, no. 3 (2017): 348.

34 Christopher Sharrett, ed., *Crisis Cinema: The Apocalyptic Idea in Postmodern Narrative Film* (Maisonneuve Press, 1993), 5.

35 Hay, "American Mad Max," 309.

36 Corbett, "Nowhere to Run," 338.

37 Corbett, "Nowhere to Run," 339.

38 Buckmaster, *Miller and Max*, 144; William Finnegan, "The Miner's Daughter," *New Yorker*, March 18, 2013.

39 Delia Falconer, "We Don't Need to Know the Way Home," in *The Road Movie Book*, ed. Steven Cohan and Ina Rae Hark (Routledge, 2002), 262.

40 William S. Chavez and Shyam K. Sriram, "'What if We Were Savage?': Mad Max Transmedia as Speculative Anthropology," *Journal of Religion and Popular Culture* 35, no. 1 (2023): 28.

41 Mike Gouldhawke, "Land as a Social Relationship," *Briarpatch*, September 10, 2020, https://briarpatchmagazine.com/articles/view/land-as-a-social-relationship.

42 "From Redwood Trees to Olive Groves, the Commune Grows a Statement from the Tree Occupation at Cal Poly Humboldt," *CrimethInc.*, April 29, 2024, https://

crimethinc.com/2024/04/29/from-redwood-trees-to-olive-groves-the-commune-grows-a-statement-from-the-tree-occupation-at-cal-poly-humboldt.

43   This is not a simple matter of replicating the existing lifestyles of advanced capitalist societies with different technologies. Electric vehicles (EVs), for instance, are not a practical alternative to the gas guzzlers they are heralded to replace. From the disastrous mining practices that extract their necessary elements like lithium, to the outsized wear and tear they put on roads and other infrastructure, while continuing to foul the air with brake particulates, rubber, and other pollutants, and of course, relying on electricity, most of which comes from polluting sources. In short, EVs continue the environmental harm of gas-powered cars while simultaneously functioning to stand in the way of the only serious solution: the elimination of personal motor vehicles and their replacement with public transit infrastructure that allows everyone, especially people with mobility issues, to get around comfortably and sustainably. And just imagine what beautiful public spaces we could create if there weren't cars everywhere, spreading their filth and danger while turning their operators into homicidal maniacs. See James Warren, "Electric Cars Won't Save Us, They'll Make Our Cities Worse," *Human Centric Design*, July 22, 2022, https://www.humancentricdesign.org/blog; Nina Lakhani, "Revealed: How US Transition to Electric Cars Threatens Environmental Havoc," *The Guardian*, January 24, 2023, https://www.theguardian.com/us-news/2023/jan/24/us-electric-vehicles-lithium-consequences-research.

44   See Kohei Saito, *Slow Down: The Degrowth Manifesto* (Astra House, 2024).

45   A fascinating project I am still wrapping my head around goes by the name of *Decomposition* and seems to deserve close attention: https://decompositions.noblogs.org.

46   Loren Goldner, *Herman Melville: Between Charlemagne and the Antemosaic Cosmic Man* (Queequeg Publications, 2006), 5.

47   Goldner, *Herman Melville*, 116–18.

48   Goldner, *Herman Melville*, 25. We can set aside, for now, the question of whether the mode of life that has enabled the real possibility of planetary extinction can be deemed "higher" in any possible connotation.

49   Nick Estes, *Our History Is the Future* (Verso, 2019), 257.

50   For a good starting place grounded in concrete struggles, see the interviews collected in Peter Gelderloos, *The Solutions Are Already Here* (Pluto Press, 2022). Additionally, Mike Gouldhawke has assembled an invaluable compendium of writing at the intersection of Marxism and Indigenous radicalism. See "Marxism & Indigenous People," archived at https://web.archive.org/web/20250204115038/https://mgouldhawke.wordpress.com/marxism-indigenous-peoples.

51   Courtesy of the author, used with permission.

52   Phil A. Neel and Nick Chavez, "Forest and Factory," *Endnotes*, December 2023, https://endnotes.org.uk/posts/forest-and-factory.

53   Quoted in Adrian Martin, *The Mad Max Movies* (Currency Press, 2003), 47.

54   Much of the life's work of Loren Goldner can be found on his website *Break Their Haughty Power*, https://www.breaktheirhaughtypower.net. Besides the indispensable Melville book, Goldner's unique and invaluable theory of American politics, history, and culture can be found in the essay collection *Vanguard of Retrogression* (Queequeg, 2001), which, as the young people say, *goes so hard it's unreal*, beginning right on the cover.

Three Months Inside Alt-Right New York

1   Leonard Zeskind, *Blood and Politics: The History of the White Nationalist Movement from the Margins to the Mainstream* (Farrar, Straus and Giroux, 2009), xiii.

2   Angela Nagle, *Kill All Normies: Online Culture Wars from 4Chan and Tumblr to Trump and the Alt-Right* (Zero Books, 2017).

Thankful for President Trump: Thanksgiving with Stop the Steal

1   Jan Wolfe and Tom Hals, "U.S. Judge Calls Trump Claim Challenging Biden Win in Pennsylvania 'Frankenstein's Monster,'" *Reuters*, November 21, 2020, https://www.reuters.com/article/us-usa-election-pennsylvania/u-s-judge-calls-trump-claim-challenging-biden-win-in-pennsylvania-frankensteins-monster-idUSKBN2810WR.

2   Rob Kuznia, Curt Devine, Nelli Black, and Drew Griffin, "Stop the Steal's Massive Disinformation Campaign Connected to Roger Stone," *CNN*, November 14, 2020, https://www.cnn.com/2020/11/13/business/stop-the-steal-disinformation-campaign-invs/index.html.

3   Philip Rucker, Ashley Parker, and Josh Dawsey, "Trump Privately Plots His Next Act—Including a Potential 2024 Run," *Washington Post*, November 21, 2020.

4   Alice Speri, "Police Unions Reject Charges of Bias, Find Hero in Donald Trump," *The Intercept,* October 9, 2016, https://theintercept.com/2016/10/09/police-unions-reject-charges-of-bias-find-a-hero-in-donald-trump; Abigail Hauslohner, Mark Berman, and Aaron C. Davis, "As Police Unions Endorse Trump, Some Worry Officers Displaying Bias Could Be Intimidating at the Polls, Affect Voting," *Washington Post*, October 31, 2020.

5   Andrew Beaujon, "Saturday's Pro-Trump Events in DC Have a Very Real Potential to Turn Violent, According to Experts Who Track Extremism," *Washingtonian*, November 12, 2020, https://www.washingtonian.com/2020/11/12/saturdays-pro-trump-events-in-dc-have-a-very-real-potential-to-turn-violent-according-to-experts-who-track-extremism; Youth Liberation Front, "'Antifascism Doesn't Start by Confronting Fascists in the Streets, It Starts Way Before That': A Report from DC," *It's Going Down*, November 26, 2020, https://itsgoingdown.org/dc-analysis-maga-march.

6   Paul Blest, "An Armed Mob of Trump Supporters Tried to Shut Down an Arizona Election Office," *Vice*, November 5, 2020, https://www.vice.com/en/article/z3vxbj/an-armed-mob-of-trump-supporters-tried-to-shut-down-an-arizona-election-office; Ali's announcement came in a since-deleted post on Twitter.com.

7   Ali Alexander (@TheRealAliA), Twitter.com (deleted).

8   Paige Barnes, "'Black Lives Matter' Counter-Protest Causes Friction with 'Blue Lives Matter' Demonstration," *Columbia Chronicle*, July 26, 2020, https://columbiachronicle.com/metro/Black-and-blue-lives-meet-in-grant-park.

9   Shield Wall Chicago, "'Self Defense Is Not a Crime': Blue Life Rally in Support of Kyle Rittenhouse Outside the Juvenile Detention Center Where He Is Held," September 7, 2020, https://shieldwallchicago.noblogs.org/post/2020/09/07/self-defense-is-not-a-crime-blue-life-rally-in-support-of-kyle-rittenhouse-outside-the-juvenile-detention-center-where-he-is-held.

10   John Lopez, "'Self Defense Is NOT a Crime' Rally Starts at 11AM in Front of Lake County Juvenile Complex Center," *McHenry County Blog*, September 4, 2020, archived at https://archive.ph/LyfGh.

11   Anne Frank Army, "Chicagoland Alt-Right Militias: Explore pro-2nd Amendment orgs 'We The People' III%ers, IGOT, Patriot Front Illinois, & Proud Boys," n.d., https://annefranksarmy.noblogs.org/a-look-inside-chicago-alt-right-militias; Anne Frank Army, "Let's Meet the 'We The People' III% Militia!" *Idavox*, November 10, 2020, https://idavox.com/index.php/2020/11/10/lets-meet-the-we-the-people-iii-militia.

12   Shield Wall Chicago, "The Suburbs Are Rising Up," October 21, 2021, https://shieldwallchicago.noblogs.org/post/2020/10/21/the-suburbs-are-rising-up.

13   Luke Barnes, "Proud Boys Founder Disavows Violence at Charlottesville but One of Its Members Organized the Event," *Think Progress*, August 24, 2017, https://archive.thinkprogress.org/proud-boys-founder-tries-and-fails-to-distance-itself-from-charlottesville-6862fb8b3ae9.

14   Since-deleted posts on Twitter.com from @IGDnews.

15   Ali Breland, "Meet the Right-Wing Trolls Behind 'Stop The Steal,'" *Mother Jones*, November 7, 2020, https://www.motherjones.com/politics/2020/11/stop-the-steal.
16   Amanda Vinicky, "Judge: Stay-at-Home Order Doesn't Violate Religious Rights," *WTTW*, May 3, 2020, https://news.wttw.com/2020/05/03/judge-stay-home-order-doesn-t-violate-religious-rights.
17   Matt Osborne, "The National Bloggers Club and Their Super PAC Friends," *Crooks and Liars*, September 12, 2012, https://crooksandliars.com/matt-osborne/national-bloggers-club-and-their-supe.
18   Eric Dondero, "John McCain Staffer Allegedly Discussed Using Voter Fraud Tactics," *Libertarian Republican*, December 17, 2007, https://archive.fo/KIPeC#selection-935.1-935.67.
19   Jared Holt, "'New Right' Activists Pivot Backwards, Share Laughs with 'Unite The Right' Demonstrator," *Right Wing Watch*, October 19, 2017, https://www.peoplefor.org/rightwingwatch/post/new-right-activists-pivot-backwards-share-laughs-with-unite-the-right-demonstrator.
20   Project Veritas Exposed, "Ali 'Akbar' Alexander," n.d., https://www.projectveritas.exposed/ali-akbar-alexander.
21   David Armiak, "Operatives Tied to Council for National Policy Organizing Protests Alleging Voter Fraud," *Center for Media and Democracy*, November 6, 2020, https://www.exposedbycmd.org/2020/11/06/operatives-tied-to-council-for-national-policy-organizing-protests-alleging-voter-fraud/stopthesteal.
22   Roger Sollenberger, "Right-Wing Trolls Launch Stop the Steal PAC to Cash In on Election Lies," *Salon*, November 18, 2020, https://www.salon.com/2020/11/18/right-wing-trolls-launch-stop-the-steal-pac-to-cash-in-on-election-lies.
23   Shane Croucher, "Twitter Founder Jack Dorsey Says Ali Akbar, Hard-Right Figure Behind Anti-Semitic Tweets, Makes 'Interesting Points,'" *Newsweek*, January 18, 2019.

The Big Takeover

1   Morgan Lee and Ben Nadler, "Protesters Swarm Statehouses Across US; Some Evacuated," *Associated Press*, January 6, 2021, https://apnews.com/article/joe-biden-donald-trump-georgia-coronavirus-pandemic-evacuations-e81e82d4c6d3db6bc45a68ae0124c85e.
2   Mike Davis, "Riot on the Hill," *New Left Review*, January 7, 2021, https://newleftreview.org/sidecar/posts/riot-on-the-hill.
3   Adam Gabbatt, "How the Domestic Terror Plot to Kidnap Michigan's Governor Unravelled," *The Guardian*, October 9, 2020, https://www.theguardian.com/us-news/2020/oct/08/michigan-governor-gretchen-whitmer-kidnap-plot.
4   Jane Lytvynenko and Molly Hensley-Clancy, "The Rioters Who Took Over the Capitol Have Been Planning Online in the Open for Weeks," *Buzzfeed News*, January 6, 2021, https://www.buzzfeednews.com/article/janelytvynenko/trump-rioters-planned-online.
5   Maxwell Tani, "Glenn Beck Employee Boasts of Breaching Nancy Pelosi's Office Alongside 'Revolutionaries,'" *The Daily Beast*, January 6, 2021, https://www.thedailybeast.com/glenn-beck-employee-brags-about-breaching-nancy-pelosis-office-alongside-revolutionaries.
6   Anita Kumar, "Trump Privately Admits It's Over, but Wants to Brawl for Attention," *Politico*, January 5, 2021, https://www.politico.com./news/2021/01/05/donald-trump-election-challenge-455233.
7   Marisa Peñaloza, "Trump Supporters Storm U.S. Capitol, Clash With Police," *NPR*, January 6, 2021, https://www.npr.org/sections/congress-electoral-college-tally-live-updates/2021/01/06/953616207/diehard-trump-supporters-gather-in-the-nations-capital-to-protest-election-resul.
8   Rachel E. Greenspan, "A Pipe Bomb was Reportedly Found at RNC Headquarters and Destroyed by Authorities, and a Suspicious Package Arrived at DNC

Headquarters," *Business Insider*, January 6, 2021, https://www.businessinsider.com./pipe-bomb-reportedly-found-at-rnc-headquarters-dnc-evacuated-2021-1.

9   See Jarrod Shanahan, "Three Months Inside Alt-Right New York," in this volume.

10   See *Three Way Fight: Revolutionary Politics and Antifascism* (PM Press, 2024).

11   Shane Bauer (@ shane_bauer), January 6, 2021, https://x.com/shane_bauer/status/1347026941459632129.

12   "Kenosha Shooting: Video Shows Suspected Gunman Kyle Rittenhouse Being Allowed to Leave Scene," *CBS Chicago*, August 26, 2020, https://www.cbsnews.com/chicago/news/kenosha-shooting-video-shows-suspected-gunman-kyle-rittenhouse-being-allowed-to-leave-scene.

13   See Jarrod Shanahan "Thankful for President Trump: Thanksgiving with Stop the Steal," in this volume.

14   N'dea Yancey-Bragg and Joshua Bote, "At Least 23 Arrested as Crowds Turn Unruly after Pro-Trump Rally In Washington, DC," *USA Today*, December 12, 2020.

15   Tom Tapp, "Armed Protesters Break into Oregon State Capitol Building, Break Windows, Assault Journalists, Hit Police with Chemical Agent," *Deadline*, December 21, 2020, https://deadline.com/2020/12/armed-protesters-enter-oregon-state-capitol-building-assault-police-chemical-agent-1234660385.

16   Mathieu Lewis-Rolland (@MathieuLRolland), January 1, 2021, https://x.com/MapProtests/status/1346945429330485249.

17   Aaron Mak, "On Eve of Congress' Certification, Pro-Trump Protesters Fought with D.C. Police—and One Another," *Slate*, January 6, 2021, https://slate.com/news-and-politics/2021/01/proud-boys-and-pro-trump-protesters-clash-in-d-c-on-tuesday.html.

18   "Broken Windows Fascism," *Three-Way Fight*, January 7, 2021, https://threewayfight.org/broken-windows-fascism.

19   Jordan Williams, "Some on Right Blame Antifa, not Trump, for Mob at Capitol," *The Hill*, January 7, 2021, https://thehill.com/homenews/news/533088-conservatives-blame-antifa-not-Trump-for-violence-at-capitol.

20   Matt Cannon, "Capitol Police Didn't Open Gates for Rioters, Says Man Behind Viral Video," *Newsweek*, January 7, 2021.

Iowa Bluffs

1   Franklin T. Oldt, *The History of Dubuque County, Iowa* (Western Historical Co., 1880).

2   Black Hawk, *Autobiography of Ma-ka-tai-me-she-kia-kiak, or Black Hawk* (J.B. Patterson, 1882).

3   Oldt, *History of Dubuque*.

4   Encyclopedia Dubuque, https://www.encyclopediadubuque.org, accessed September 2023.

5   United States Department of Justice, Civil Rights Division, *Investigation of the Ferguson Police Department* (DOJ, 2015).

6   Jennifer DeWitt, "Dubuque Model Keeps Money Local," *Quad City Times*, October 16, 2012, https://qctimes.com/dubuque-model-keeps-money-local/article_24fe74f2-1775-11e2-872c-0019bb2963f4.html.

7   Convergence Design, "Success Story: America's River Project, Dubuque, Iowa," March 2013, https://engg.k-state.edu/CHSR/outreach/tab/workshops/docs/07b-SuccesStoryDubuqueIA-s.pdf.

8   Randy Evans, "Vision Iowa Was a Smart Investment in Communities: The State Should Bring it Back," *Iowa Capital Dispatch*, September 9, 2020, https://iowacapitaldispatch.com/2020/09/09/vision-iowa-was-a-smart-investment-in-communities-the-state-should-bring-it-back.

9   Samuel Stein, *Capital City: Gentrification and the Real Estate State* (Verso, 2019).

10   C.L.R. James, *Renegades, Mariners, and Castaways: The Story of Herman Melville and the World We Live In* (Dartmouth College, 1953).

Every Fire Needs a Little Bit of Help

1   For more information on ongoing legal cases and how the comrades can be supported, see the prisoners support clearinghouse Uprising Support (https://uprisingsupport. org).

2   Claudia Morell and Becky Vevea, "Lightfoot Reports 1,000 Arrests Amid 'Heart-Wrenching' Weekend Violence," *WBEZ Chicago*, June 1, 2020, https://www.wbez. org/politics/2020/06/01/lightfoot-reports-1-000-arrests-amid-heart-wrenching-weekend-violence.

3   My analysis of the George Floyd Rebellion was developed, as it unfolded, in collaboration with Zhandarka Kurti. See our essay, written in the first two weeks of the rebellion, "Prelude to a Hot American Summer," Field Notes, *Brooklyn Rail*, July/August 2020), and subsequent book, *States of Incarceration: Rebellion, Reform, and America's Punishment System* (Reaktion Books / Field Notes, 2022).

4   David Ranney, *New World Disorder: The Decline of US Power* (CreateSpace, 2014), 9–10.

5   C.L.R. James, *American Civilization* (Blackwell's, 1993).

6   May Wong, "Stanford Research Provides a Snapshot of a New Working-from-Home Economy," *Stanford News*, June 29, 2020.

7   Clarissa Lan-Jim, "The Other Victims of the Pandemic: Workers Killed in Fights Over Masks," *BuzzFeed News*, July 15, 2021, https://www.buzzfeednews.com/article/clarissajanlim/workers-killed-fights-masks.

8   Miranda Bryant, "'Coronavirus Spread at Rikers Is a 'Public Health Disaster,' Says Jail's Top Doctor," *The Guardian*, April 1, 2020, https://www.theguardian.com/us-news/2020/apr/01/rikers-island-jail-coronavirus-public-health-disaster.

9   David Campbell, "Stick-Up on Rikers Island," *Hard Crackers: Chronicles of Everyday Life*, May 1, 2020, https://hardcrackers.com/stickup-on-rikers; *Perilous Chronicle*, "First 90 Days of Prisoner Resistance to COVID-19: Report on Events, Data, and Trends," *Perilous Chronicle*, November 12, 2020, https://perilouschronicle.com/2020/11/12/covid-prisoner-resistance-first-90-days-full-report.

10 US Bureau of Labor Statistics, "Impact of the Coronavirus (COVID-19) Pandemic on the Employment Situation for May 2020"; US Bureau of Labor Statistics, "Report on the Economic Well-Being of US Households in 2019, Featuring Supplemental Data from April 2020," 1–3.

11 For a magisterial treatment of US society on the eve of the rebellion, see Richard Hunsinger and Nathan Eisenberg, "Mask Off: Crisis & Struggle in the Pandemic," *Cosmonaut*, June 8, 2020, https://cosmonautmag.com/2020/06/mask-off-crisis-struggle-in-the-pandemic.

12 Nicole Norfleet and David Chanen, "Testimony at Derek Chauvin Trial Triggers Talk of Expectations for Retail Workers to Stopping Theft," *Star Tribune*, April 1, 2021. Salary data for Minneapolis cashiers comes from the wage aggregate website *Glassdoor* (www.glassdoor.com).

13 John Elder, "Man Dies After Medical Incident During Police Interaction," *Inside MPD*, May 25, 2020.

14 "The World is Ours: The Minneapolis Uprising in Five Acts," *It's Going Down*, June 12, 2020. This excellent summary now appears, along with other texts on the rebellion, in Nevada, *The Abolition of Law* (Minneapolis, 2022).

15 Loren Goldner, "The Sky Is Always Darkest Just Before the Dawn: Class Struggle in the US from the 2008 Crash to the Eve of the Occupations Movement," *Insurgent Notes* 2, January 2012, archived at https://libcom.org/article/sky-always-darkest-just-dawn-class-struggle-us-2008-crash-eve-occupations-movement-loren.

16 Karl Marx, *Capital*, vol.1, trans. Ben Fowkes (Penguin, 1976), 762–876.

17 Michael Roberts, "The US Rate of Profit 1948–2015," *The Next Recession* (blog), October 4, 2016, https://thenextrecession.wordpress.com/2016/10/04/the-us-rate-of-profit-1948-2015.

NOTES

18   Christopher Famighetti and Darrick Hamilton, "The Great Recession, Education, Race, and Homeownership," *Economic Policy Institute* (blog), May 15, 2019, https://www.epi.org/blog/the-great-recession-education-race-and-homeownership.

19   Ruth Wilson Gilmore, *Golden Gulag: Prisons, Surplus, Crisis, and Opposition in Globalizing California*, (University of California Press, 2007), 87–127.

20   *Endnotes*, "Holding Pattern."

21   James Boggs, *The American Revolution: Pages from a Negro Worker's Notebook* (Monthly Review Press, 2009), 53. For an excellent discussion of this classic study in the context of the George Floyd Rebellion, see Jason E. Smith, "The American Revolution: The George Floyd Rebellion, One Year Out," *Brooklyn Rail*, July/August 2021.

22   Rebecca Hill, "'The Common Enemy Is the Boss and the Inmate': Police and Prison Guard Unions in New York in the 1970s–1980s," *Labor: Studies in Working Class History of the Americas* 8, no. 3 (2011): 65–96.

23   Karl Marx, *Capital*, vol. 3, trans. David Fernback (Penguin, 1981), 525–42. I first encountered these ideas in Loren Goldner, "The Remaking of the American Working Class: The Restructuring of Global Capital and the Recomposition of Class Terrain," 1999, https://files.libcom.org/files/Loren%20Goldner-%20The%20Remaking%20of%20 the%20American%20Working%20Class.pdf.

24   Nathalie Baptiste, "Staggering Loss of Black Wealth Due to Subprime Scandal Continues Unabated," *American Prospect*, October 13, 2014, https://prospect.org/justice/ staggering-loss-Black-wealth-due-subprime-scandal-continues-unabated.

25   Goldner, "Sky is Always Darkest."

26   Colectivo Situaciones, *19 & 20: Notes for a New Social Protagonism* (Autonomedia, 2011).

27   "Onward Barbarians," *Endnotes*, 2020, https://endnotes.org.uk/other_texts/en/ endnotes-onward-barbarians.

28   "The Holding Pattern: The Ongoing Crisis and the Class Struggles of 2011–2013," *Endnotes*, no. 3 (2014): 12–54, https://libcom.org/library/holding-pattern-ongoing- crisis-class-struggles-2011-2013.

29   Rust Bunny Collective, "Under the Riot Gear," *Sic* 2, 2014, https://libcom.org/article/ under-riot-gear-rust-bunny-collective.

30   Invisible Committee, *The Coming Insurrection* (Semiotext(e), 2009), 121.

31   "The Glass Floor," in *A Théorie Communiste Reader* (2009), https://cooltexts.github.io/ sources/theoriecommuniste.pdf.

32   Craig Hughes, *Occupied Zuccotti: Social Struggle, and Planned Shrinkage*, (WarMachines. info, 2014).

33   Ari Paul, "Occupy Wall Street's Dilemma: Are the Police Part of the 99%?" *The Guardian*, November 1, 2011, https://www.theguardian.com/commentisfree/cifamerica/2011/ nov/01/occupy-wall-street-dilemma-police.

34   Michelle Alexander, *The New Jim Crow: Mass Incarceration in the Age of Colorblindness* (New Press, 2010).

35   The brilliant scholar Adolph Reed has for almost a half-century advocated a form of socialist politics forswearing Black particularity, which has to date found little traction. See Adolph Reed, "Black Particularity Reconsidered," *Telos*, no. 39 (1979).

36   See especially Croatoan, "Who Is Oakland? Anti-Oppression Activism, the Politics of Safety, and State Co-optation," *Escalating Identity*, April 2012, https:// escalatingidentity.wordpress.com. A lengthy reading list compiled by writer Abby Volcano of critiques produced by this period has vanished from its original host but survives on—where else?—Tumblr: https://undercommoning.tumblr.com/ post/85228193397/critiques-of-intersectionality-privilege-and-identity.

37   *Endnotes*, "Holding Pattern," 47.

38   Brian Hamacher, "Trayvon Martin Protesters Ransacked North Miami Beach Walgreens," *NBC Miami*, March 27, 2014, https://www.nbcmiami.com/news/local/ trayvon-martin-protesters-ransacked-north-miami-beach-walgreens/1919382/; Katy

Reckdahl, "3 Defaced New Orleans Monuments Are Cleaned by Volunteers," *Times-Picayune*, March 30, 2012.

39   Tobi Haslett, "Magic Actions," *n+1* 40 (2021), https://www.nplusonemag.com/issue-40/politics/magic-actions-2.

40   The State of Missouri v. Darren Wilson, Grand Jury, Volume IV, September 10, 2014, 45.

41   Louis Althusser, "On Ideology," in *The Reproduction of Capitalism: Ideology and Ideological State Apparatuses* (Verso, 2014) 191–92.

42   United States Department of Justice, "Department of Justice Report Regarding the Criminal Investigation into the Shooting Death of Michael Brown by Ferguson, Missouri Police Officer Darren Wilson," March 4, 2015, 12–13.

43   Julie Bosman and Joseph Goldstein, "Timeline for a Body: 4 Hours in the Middle of a Ferguson Street," *New York Times*, August 23, 2014.

44   Adrian Wohlleben, "Memes Without End," *Ill Will*, May 16, 2021, https://illwill.com/memes-without-end. Wohlleben's analysis comes in part from close observation of the Yellow Vests movement. See Paul Torino and Adrian Wohlleben, "Memes with Force: Lessons from the Yellow Vests," first published on *Mute*, February 26, 2019, https://illwill.com/print/memes-with-force.

45   Jarrod Shanahan, "The Old Mole Breaks Concrete," in this volume.

46   "Brown v. Ferguson," *Endnotes* 4, 14–24.

47   For the historical centrality of the color line to the US economy see W.E.B. Du Bois, *Black Reconstruction in America: 1860–1880* (Free Press, 1999 [1935]); Edmund Morgan, *American Slavery, American Freedom* (Norton, 1975); Theodore Allen, *The Invention of the White Race: The Origin of Racial Oppression in Anglo-America* (Verso, 1997).

48   Karen E. Fields and Barbara J. Fields, *Racecraft: The Soul of Inequality in American Life* (Verso, 2012).

49   Salar Mohandesi, "Identity Crisis," *Viewpoint Magazine*, March 16, 2017, https://viewpointmag.com/2017/03/16/identity-crisis.

50   For the best critique of the racist drivel of "white allyship," see Croatoan, "Who Is Oakland?" As was recently pointed out on social media by the Midwest Peoples' History Project, after a decade of critique following its disastrous mass movement debut in Occupy, the term "ally" has now been replaced by "accomplice," but means virtually the same thing. The source of this rebrand is the 2014 zine "Accomplices Not Allies: Abolishing the Ally Industrial Complex" distributed by Indigenous Action Media. This essay is quite critical of allyship and deserves consideration on its own merits, not the connotation that "accomplice" has assumed thanks to its subsumption into the antiracism industry.

51   Sarah Kaplan, "Minn. Man Accused in Black Lives Matter Shootings Reportedly Subscribed to 'Sovereign Citizen' Subculture," *Washington Post*, December 1, 2015.

52   Keeanga-Yamahtta Taylor, *From #BlackLivesMatter to Black Liberation* (Haymarket, 2016), 80.

53   Movement for Black Lives, *A Vision for Black Lives: Policy Demands for Black Power, Freedom, and Justice*, 2016, archived at https://griid.org/wp-content/uploads/2020/05/a-vision-for-Black-lives.pdf; Center for Popular Democracy, "Law for Black Lives," https://populardemocracy.org/news-article/news-and-publications-law4Blacklives-statement-support-justicefortamir; and Center for Popular Democracy, Law for Black Lives, and Black Youth Project 100, "Freedom to Thrive: Reimagining Safety and Security in Our Communities," 2017, https://search.issuelab.org/resource/freedom-to-thrive-reimagining-safety-security-in-our-communities.html. It occurs to me that these organizations receive foundation money. But receiving it, and using it the way it was intended, can be very different. Above all, young people are often attracted to these groups because they are the most organized projects visible, and sometimes can even pay them to participate. But organizations that court revolutionary-minded

NOTES 285

young people to practice counterinsurgent politics are unstable compounds. See Jarrod Shanahan and Zhandarka Kurti, "The Shifting Ground: A Conversation on the George Floyd Rebellion," *Ill Will*, September 20, 2020, https://illwill.com/the-shifting-ground-a-conversation-on-the-george-floyd-rebellion.

54   Stuart Hall, Chas Critcher, Tony Jefferson, John Clarke, and Brian Roberts, *Policing The Crisis: Mugging, the State, and Law and Order* (Macmillan, 1978), 394.

55   E.P. Thompson, *The Making of the English Working Class* (Penguin, 1968).

56   "Black Lives Matter Holds Rally Supporting Individuals Arrested in Chicago Looting," *NBC Chicago*, Monday, August 10, 2020, https://www.nbcchicago.com/news/local/black-lives-matter-holds-rally-supporting-individuals-arrested-in-chicago-looting-monday/2320365.

57   Armed Conflict Location & Event Data Project (ACLED), "A Year of Racial Justice Protests: Key Trends in Demonstrations Supporting the BLM Movement," May 25, 2021, 1–2, https://acleddata.com/2021/05/25/a-year-of-racial-justice-protests-key-trends-in-demonstrations-supporting-the-blm-movement.

58   Fran, JF, and Lane, "In the Eye of the Storm: A Report from Kenosha," *Hard Crackers: Chronicles of Everyday Life*, September 7, 2020, https://hardcrackers.com./eye-storm-report-kenosha.

59   "The Siege of the Third Precinct in Minneapolis: An Account and Analysis," *CrimethInc.*, June 6, 2010, https://crimethinc.com/2020/06/10/the-siege-of-the-third-precinct-in-minneapolis-an-account-and-analysis.

60   Shemon Salam and Arturo Castillon, "Cars, Riots & Black Liberation," *Mute*, November 17, 2020.

61   New York Post-Left, "Welcome to the Party: The George Floyd Uprising in NYC," *It's Going Down*, June 24, 2020, https://itsgoingdown.org/welcome-to-the-party-the-george-floyd-uprising-in-nyc; "The World Is Ours: The Minneapolis Uprising in Five Acts," *It's Going Down*, June 12, 2020, https://itsgoingdown.org/the-world-is-ours-the-minneapolis-uprising-in-five-acts; Puget Sound Anarchists, "The World Opens Up: Recalling the First Week of the Uprising in Seattle," *It's Going Down*, October 22, 2020, https://itsgoingdown.org/the-world-opens-up-recalling-the-first-week-of-the-uprising-in-seattle.

62   Haslett, "Magic Actions."

63   "Welcome to the Frontlines: Beyond Violence and Nonviolence," *Chuǎng*, June 8, 2020, https://chuangcn.org/2020/06/frontlines; "Tools and Tactics in the Portland Protests," *CrimethInc.*, August 3, 2020, https://crimethinc.com/2020/08/03/tools-and-tactics-in-the-portland-protests-from-leaf-blowers-and-umbrellas-to-lasers-bubbles-and-balloons. For an excellent discussion of this division of labor see *CrimethInc.*, "Siege of the Third Precinct."

64   #IndianWinter, "Standing Rock: The Story of a Heroic Resistance," *ROAR Magazine*, November 19, 2016, https://roarmag.org/essays/standing-rock-no-dapl-protests.

65   *CrimethInc.*, "Accounts from the Battle of Grant Park: How Chicago Demonstrators Pushed Back the Police and Nearly Toppled a Statue," July 21, 2020, https://crimethinc.com/2020/07/21/accounts-from-the-battle-of-grant-park-how-chicago-demonstrators-pushed-back-the-police-and-nearly-toppled-a-statue; James Stephens and J.J. McAfee, "In the Streets of Philadelphia," *Hard Crackers*, June 14, 2020, https://hardcrackers.com/in-the-streets-of-philadelphia.

66   Phil A. Neel, "The Spiral: Epilogue to the French edition of *Hinterland: America's New Landscape of Class and Conflict*," Field Notes, *Brooklyn Rail*, September 2020, https://brooklynrail.org/2020/09/field-notes/The-Spiral-Epilogue-to-the-French-Edition-of-Hinterland-Americas-New-Landscape-of-Class-and-Conflict.

67   Wohlleben, "Memes Without End."

68   "At the Wendy's: Armed Struggle at the End of the World," *Ill Will*, November 9, 2020, https://illwill.com/at-the-wendys.

69   *CrimethInc.*, "Siege of the Third Precinct."

70   With the exception of Shemon Salam, who predicted the rebellion. See "Black Mutations," 2020.

71   Johnathan M. Metzl, *Dying of Whiteness: How the Politics of Racial Resentment Is Killing America's Heartland* (Basic Books, 2019).

72   Shemon Salam and Arturo Castillon, "The Return of John Brown: White Race-Traitors in the 2020 Uprising," *Ill Will*, September 4, 2020, https://illwill.com/print/the-return-of-john-brown-white-race-traitors-in-the020-uprising. Additional essays by this prolific duo appear in the collection *The Revolutionary Meaning of the George Floyd Uprising* (Darjala Press, 2021).

73   "Twin Cities Protest Death of George Floyd: Day 3," *Unicorn Riot*, May 28, 2020, https://unicornriot.ninja/2020/twin-cities-protest-death-of-george-floyd-day-3.

74   Yannick Giovanni Marshall, "Black Liberal, Your Time is Up," *Al Jazeera*, June 1, 2020, https://www.aljazeera.com/opinions/2020/6/1/black-liberal-your-time-is-up; We Still Outside Collective, "Black Leadership and Other White Myths," *Ill Will*, June 4, 2020, https://illwill.com/print/on-the-black-leadership-and-other-white-myths; Haslett, "Magic Actions."

75   Belew's remarks were stunning in their recklessness and scholarly malpractice. "When I hear reports of the U-Haul trucks, the pellets [pallets] of bricks left at opportune places, passing out bombs and incendiary devices to people who are already angry during the peaceful protests," she told credulous local reporters, who had sought out her expertise as a self-identified scholar of the far right, "those actions across multiple cities indicate some central planning." This sweeping conspiracy to engineer Black-led resistance, she argued, was likely done by white supremacists, manipulating hapless dupes coast to coast. In addition to denying the agency of Black militants, this conjecture also made yet another national news event germane to Belew's own expertise. But unless Belew has evidence none of us have seen, the "reports" she refers to with such scholarly gravitas amounted to specious social media rumors that any serious observer viewed with credulity. The "bait bricks" canard that Belew repeated had already been challenged by *Rolling Stone*, which did not need expertise in the far right to smell a rat. See Katie Kim and Lisa Capitanini, "Extremist Groups May be Infiltrating Protests," *NBC Chicago*, June 5, 2020, https://www.nbcchicago.com/news/local/extremist-groups-may-be-infiltrating-protests/2285094; E.J. Dickson, "People Claim Authorities Are Intentionally Planting Bricks to Bait Protesters," *Rolling Stone*, June 3, 2020.

76   Tim Bruno, "The Fireworks: On Rumor and Counter-Revolution (After Jean Genet)," *Hard Crackers*, October 24, 2001, https://hardcrackers.com/the-fireworks.

77   Liaisons, "Warning," *New Inquiry*, September 9, 2020, https://thenewinquiry.com/blog/warning.

78   Bruno, "Fireworks."

79   Shemon Salam, "The Rise of Black Counter-Insurgency," *Ill Will*, July 30, 2020, https://illwill.com/the-rise-of-black-counter-insurgency; *The Only Way Out Is Always Through the Police* (Research & Destroy NYC, 2020), https://researchdestroy.com/the-only-way-out-is-always-through-the-police-the-2020-new-york-george-floyd-riots.pdf.

80   Laura Rodríguez Presa, "'This is a Step Back.' Latino Activists Speak Out About Racial Tension with Black Chicagoans on Southwest Side amid George Floyd Fallout," *Chicago Tribune*, June 3, 2021.

81   Idris Robinson, "How it Might Should Be Done," *Ill Will*, August 16, 2020, https://illwill.com/how-it-might-should-be-done.

82   W.E.B. Du Bois, *The Souls of Black Folk* (Oxford University Press, 2007), 3.

83   David Roediger and Elizabeth Esch, *The Production of Difference: Race and the Management of Labor in US History* (Oxford University Press, 2012).

84   In a class I took some years ago, Charlie Post called this latter theory "the garbage can theory of ideology." By contrast, Thomas J. Sugrue's sketch of the proletariat in

NOTES

postwar Detroit in *The Origins of the Urban Crisis: Race and Inequality in Postwar Detroit* (Princeton University Press, 1998) is a classic study of racial chauvinism emanating, at least in part, from below.

85 George Rawick makes this point compellingly in the 1964 essay "The American Negro Movement," reprinted in George Rawick, *Listening to Revolt: Selected Writings* (Charles H. Kerr, 2010) 1–29.

86 "Abolish the White Race by Any Means Necessary," *Race Traitor* 1, (Winter 1993): 2, archived at https://theanarchistlibrary.org/library/race-traitor-abolish-the-white-race-by-any-means-necessary.

87 See Salam and Castillon, "Return of John Brown"; Wohlleben, "Memes Without End," *Ill Will*, May 16, 2021, https://illwill.com/memes-without-end; Nevada, "In the Wake of an Erosion," *The New Inquiry/Liaisons*, July 16, 2021, https://thenewinquiry.com/blog/in-the-wake-of-an-erosion. *Ill Will* also began a series on race treason called "Desertions," see https://illwill.com/series/desertions.

88 "Black Armed Joy: Some Notes Towards a Black Theory of Insurrectionary Anarchy," *Haters Cafe*, January 18, 2022, https://haters.noblogs.org/post/2022/01/18/black-armed-joy-some-notes-towards-a-black-theory-of-insurrectionary-anarchy.

89 Jarrod Shanahan, "The Big Takeover," in this volume.

90 ACLED, "Demonstrations and Political Violence in America: New Data for Summer 2020," September, 2020, https://acleddata.com/2020/09/03/demonstrations-political-violence-in-america-new-data-for-summer-2020; Adrian Wohlleben, "Weapons and Ethics," *Ill Will*, September 18, 2020, https://illwill.com/weapons-and-ethics.

91 Research and Destroy, *Only Way Out Is Always Through the Police*.

92 For additional perspective see the anonymous report back: "'Breewayy or the Freeway': The Rise of America's Frontliners and Why Louisville Didn't Burn," *It's Going Down*, October 15, 2020, https://itsgoingdown.org/breewayy-freeway-american-frontliners.

93 In the wake of Kenosha, Adrian Wohlleben penned a brilliant and beautiful reflection on this question. See "Weapons and Ethics," *Ill Will*, September 18, 2020, https://illwill.com/weapons-and-ethics.

94 Leonard Zeskind and Devin Burghart, "Is America's Militia Movement on the Rise?" Type Investigations, *The Nation*, September 9, 2013, https://www.typeinvestigations.org/investigation/2013/09/09/americas-militia-movement-rise.

95 See Matthew N. Lyons, "Caution Doesn't Make Us Safe: A Review of PRA's Report on the MAGA Movement," *Three-Way Fight*, February 17, 2022, https://threewayfight.org/caution-doesnt-make-us-safe-a-review-of-pras-report-on-the-maga-movement.

96 Zhandarka Kurti and I discuss the history of the US abolitionist tradition in detail in *States of Incarceration*, chapter 5, alongside a critical assessment of its current terrain. We have previously written about the crossroads facing US abolitionism in "Prelude to a Hot American Summer," and "The Dangerous Seduction of Reform," *Brooklyn Rail*, September 2020.

97 Alex Vitale, *The End of Policing* (Verso, 2017); Joy James, "Airbrushing Revolution for the Sake of Abolition," *Black Perspectives*, July 20, 2020, https://www.aaihs.org/airbrushing-revolution-for-the-sake-of-abolition; Revolutionary Abolitionist Movement, *Burn Down the American Plantation: Call for a Revolutionary Abolitionist Movement* (2017).

98 Garrett Felber, "The Struggle to Abolish the Police Is Nothing New," *Boston Review*, June 8, 2020. For the original articulation of nonreformist reforms, a concept popularized in recent time by abolitionist Ruth Wilson Gilmore, see André Gorz, *Strategy for Labor: A Radical Proposal* (Beacon Press, 1967).

99 Dan Berger, Mariame Kaba, and David Stein, "What Abolitionists Do," *Jacobin*, August 24, 2017, https://jacobin.com/2017/08/prison-abolition-reform-mass-incarceration.

100 See Beth Richie, *Arrested Justice: Black Women, Violence, and America's Prison Nation* (NYU Press, 2012).

101 Char Adams, "Cities Vowed in 2020 to Cut Police Funding—But Budgets Expanded in 2021," *NBC News*, December 28, 2021, https://www.nbcnews.com/news/nbcblk/cities-vowed-2020-cut-police-funding-budgets-expanded-2021-rcna9864.
102 Kay Gabriel, "Defund Is a Strategy," *Verso* (blog), June 7, 2021, https://www.versobooks.com/blogs/news/5096-defund-is-a-strategy.
103 Du Bois, *Black Reconstruction*, 3–16, 55–83, 391.
104 Angela Davis, *Abolition Democracy: Beyond Empires, Prisons, and Torture* (AK Press, 2005), 69, 91–93.
105 See, for instance, Allegra M. Mccleod, "Envisioning Abolitionist Democracy," *Harvard Law Review* 132 (2019): 1613–49.
106 Eric Foner, *Reconstruction: America's Unfinished Revolution 1863–1877* (Harper, 1988).
107 Noel Ignatiev, "The American Blindspot: Reconstruction According to Eric Foner and W.E.B. Du Bois," *Labour/Le Travail* 31 (Spring 1993): 245.
108 Gus Breslauer, "Mutual Aid: A Factor of Liberalism," *Regeneration Magazine*, November 27, 2020, archived at https://autonomynews.org/mutual-aid-a-factor-of-liberalism.
109 Noel Ignatiev, "Alternative Institutions or Dual Power?" in *Treason To Whiteness Is Loyalty to Humanity*, ed. Geert Dhondt, Zhandarka Kurti and Jarrod Shanahan (Verso, 2022), 359–63.
110 Wohlleben, "Memes Without End."
111 No New Jails NYC, *Close Rikers Now: We Keep Us Safe*, (No New Jails NYC, 2019), https://drive.google.com/file/d/1NPW9cNv6AsbKYF_se4d8lIHQ5cyHOvOx/view.
112 Zhandarka Kurti, "Police Power in the Aftermath of Black Lives Matter," *Social Justice* 47, no. 3/4 (2020): 139.

Afterword: Toward Something Else

1 International Workingmen's Association, "General Rules," October 1864, https://www.marxists.org/history/international/iwma/documents/1864/rules.htm.
2 A good start for following these traditions back to their common grounding is Kristin Ross's *Communal Luxury: The Political Imaginary of the Paris Commune* (Verso, 2015).
3 This is a central theme throughout my work, and has benefited immensely from the work of Ruth Wilson Gilmore, namely *Golden Gulag: Prisons, Surplus, Crisis, and Opposition in Globalizing California*, (University of California Press, 2007).
4 C.L.R. James, Grace C. Lee, and Cornelius Castoriadis, *Facing Reality* (Berwick Editions, 1974) 131; Henry Miller, *Henry Miller on Writing* (New Directions, 1964).
5 Lester Bangs, "Do the Godz Speak Esperanto?" *Cream* 3, no. 7 (December 1971): 40.
6 Mary Barnard, *Sappho: A New Translation* (University of California Press: 2019).
7 This fantastic essay, originally circulated privately, has subsequently appeared in print: Don Hamerquist, "Ferguson," in *A Brilliant Red Thread*, ed. Luis Brennan (Kersplebedeb and PM Press, 2023), 291.
8 With regards to Hamerquist's point that I was *fetishizing militancy and spontaneism*, if I am honest, I'm still doing the work to move beyond that one.
9 Tobi Haslett, "States of Incarceration: Tobi Haslett with Zhandarka Kurti and Jarrod Shanahan," *Brooklyn Rail*, October 2022, https://brooklynrail.org/2022/10/field-notes/States-of-Incarceration-Zhandarka-Kurti-and-Jarrod-Shanahan-with-Tobi-Haslett.
10 As ever, Phil Neel is on the case. See *Hinterland America's New Landscape of Class and Conflict* (Reaktion / Field Notes, 2018). See also S.W., "Semi-Automatic Subjects," Lake Effect Collective (blog), April 10, 2025, https://lakeeffect.noblogs.org/post/2025/04/10/semi-automatic-subjects.
11 Jarrod Shanahan, "The Show Must Go On," *Hard Crackers*, September 30, 2020, https://hardcrackers.com/show-must-go.
12 Patrick Wolfe, *Traces of History: Elementary Structures of Race* (Verso, 2016); J. Sakai, *Settlers: The Mythology of the White Proletariat* (Kersplebedeb and PM Press, 2014). Noel was wrong to dismiss *Settlers* as cavalierly as he did. This is a book every American

NOTES

leftist must contend with. Its polemical style and macho, maximalist politics make it a poor substitute for a political foundation. But that's not the point. It is a provocation, and any disagreements with it should be hard-won by reading it closely and clarifying one's own position. As of this writing, the United Auto Workers have once more risen from the grave long enough to pull the movement back down into it, this time it's the righteous struggle for a free Palestine, and I only wish more comrades would, as the young people say: #READSETTLERS. Wolfe, by contrast, is far more careful, nuanced, and rigorous. Which also means its way less fun to read and debate.

13   Check out the Lake Effect Collective: https://lakeeffect.noblogs.org.

14   Shanahan and Kurti, *States of Incarceration.*

15   Elizabeth Henson, "Aux Armes: May Day at Olive Grove," *Elizabeth's Substack*, May 7, 2024, https://elizabethhenson.substack.com/p/aux-armes-may-day-in-the-olive-grove.

16   Xtn Alexander and Matthew Lyons, eds., *Three-Way Fight: Revolutionary Politics and Antifascism* (PM Press and Kersplebedeb, 2024).

17   Zhana Kurti and I have raised and further substantiated this challenge in our books *States of Incarceration: Rebellion, Reform, and America's Punishment System* (Field Notes/Reaktion, 2022) and *Skyscraper Jails: The Abolitionist Fight Against Jail Expansion in New York City* (Haymarket, 2025).

18   Vortex Group, *The George Floyd Uprising* (PM Press, 2023); E.P. Thompson, *The Making of the English Working Class* (Vintage, 1993), 832.

19   Friedrich Nietzsche, *Beyond Good and Evil*, trans. Judith Norman (Cambridge University Press, 2002), 32.

About the Authors

Jarrod Shanahan is the author of *Captives* (Verso, 2022); coauthor of *States of Incarceration* (Field Notes, 2022), *City Time* (NYU Press, 2025), and *Skyscraper Jails* (Haymarket, 2025); coeditor of *Treason to Whiteness Is Loyalty to Humanity* (Verso, 2022); and founding editor of *Hard Crackers: Chronicles of Everyday Life*. He works as an associate professor of criminal justice at Governors State University.

A.M. Gittlitz is the author of *I Want to Believe: Posadism, UFOs, and Apocalypse Communism* (Pluto Press, 2020), the forthcoming *Metropolitans*—a materialist history of the New York Mets, and the cohost of the *Antifada* podcast.

ABOUT PM PRESS

PM Press is an independent, radical publisher of critically necessary books for our tumultuous times. Our aim is to deliver bold political ideas and vital stories to all walks of life and arm the dreamers to demand the impossible. Founded in 2007 by a small group of people with decades of publishing, media, and organizing experience, we have sold millions of copies of our books, most often one at a time, face to face. We're old enough to know what we're doing and young enough to know what's at stake. Join us to create a better world.

PM Press
PO Box 23912
Oakland, CA 94623
www.pmpress.org

PM Press in Europe
europe@pmpress.org
www.pmpress.org.uk

FRIENDS OF PM PRESS

These are indisputably momentous times—the financial system is melting down globally and the Empire is stumbling. Now more than ever there is a vital need for radical ideas.

In the many years since its founding—and on a mere shoestring—PM Press has risen to the formidable challenge of publishing and distributing knowledge and entertainment for the struggles ahead. With hundreds of releases to date, we have published an impressive and stimulating array of literature, art, music, politics, and culture. Using every available medium, we've succeeded in connecting those hungry for ideas and information to those putting them into practice.

Friends of PM allows you to directly help impact, amplify, and revitalize the discourse and actions of radical writers, filmmakers, and artists. It provides us with a stable foundation from which we can build upon our early successes and provides a much-needed subsidy for the materials that can't necessarily pay their own way. You can help make that happen—and receive every new title automatically delivered to your door once a month—by joining as a Friend of PM Press. And, we'll throw in a free T-shirt when you sign up.

Here are your options:

- **$30 a month** Get all books and pamphlets plus a 50% discount on all webstore purchases

- **$40 a month** Get all PM Press releases (including CDs and DVDs) plus a 50% discount on all webstore purchases

- **$100 a month** Superstar—Everything plus PM merchandise, free downloads, and a 50% discount on all webstore purchases

For those who can't afford $30 or more a month, we have **Sustainer Rates** at $15, $10, and $5. Sustainers get a free PM Press T-shirt and a 50% discount on all purchases from our website.

Your Visa or Mastercard will be billed once a month, until you tell us to stop. Or until our efforts succeed in bringing the revolution around. Or the financial meltdown of Capital makes plastic redundant. Whichever comes first.

The George Floyd Uprising

Edited by Vortex Group

ISBN: 978-1-62963-966-6
$22.95   288 pages

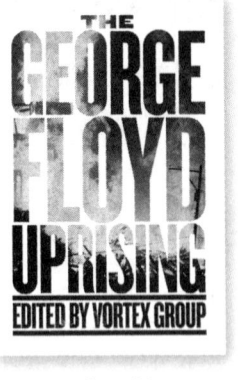

In the summer of 2020, America experienced one
of the biggest uprisings in half a century. Waves of
enraged citizens took to the streets in Minneapolis
to decry the murder of George Floyd at the hands of
the police. Battles broke out night after night, with
a pandemic-weary populace fighting the police and
eventually burning down the Third Precinct. The revolt soon spread to cities
large and small across the country, where protesters set police cars on fire,
looted luxury shopping districts, and forced the president into hiding in a bunker
beneath the White House. As the initial crest receded, localized rebellions
continued to erupt throughout the summer and into the fall in Atlanta, Chicago,
Kenosha, Louisville, Philadelphia, and elsewhere.

Written during the riots, *The George Floyd Uprising* is a compendium of the
most radical writing to come out of that long, hot summer. These incendiary
dispatches—from those on the front lines of the struggle—examine the revolt
and the obstacles it confronted. It paints a picture of abolition in practice,
discusses how the presence of weapons in the uprising and the threat of armed
struggle play out in an American context, and shows how the state responds to
and pacifies rebellions. *The George Floyd Uprising* poses new social, tactical, and
strategic plans for those actively seeking to expand and intensify revolts of the
future. This practical, inspiring collection is essential reading for all those hard at
work toppling the state and creating a new revolutionary tradition.

*"Exemplary reflections from today's frontline warriors that will disconcert liberals but
inspire young people who want to live the struggle in the revolutionary tradition of
Robert F. Williams, the Watts 65 rebels, and Deacons for Defense and Justice."*
—Mike Davis, author of *Planet of Slums* and *Old Gods, New Enigmas*

*"This anthology resists police and vigilante murders. It is not an easy read. We will
not all agree on its analyses or advocacy. Yet, its integrity, clarity, vulnerability, love
and rage are clear. As a librarian who archives liberators and liberation movements, I
recognize essential reading as a reflection of ourselves and our fears. With resolution,
this text resonates with narratives of mini-Atticas. The 1971 prison rebellion and
murderous repression by government and officialdom reveal the crises that spark
radical movements and increasing calls for self-defense. This volume offers our
cracked mirrors as an opportunity to scrutinize missteps and possibilities, and
hopefully choose wisely even in our sacrifices."*
—Joy James, author of *Resisting State Violence: Radicalism, Gender, and Race in
U.S. Culture*

It Did Happen Here: An Antifascist People's History

Edited by Moe Bowstern, Mic Crenshaw, Alec Dunn, Celina Flores, Julie Perini, and Erin Yanke

ISBN: 978-1-62963-351-0
$21.95   304 pages

Portland, Oregon, 1988: the brutal murder of Ethiopian immigrant Mulugeta Seraw by racist skinheads shocked the city. In response disparate groups quickly came together to organize against white nationalist violence and right-wing organizing throughout the Rose City and the Pacific Northwest.

It Did Happen Here compiles interviews with dozens of people who worked together during the waning decades of the twentieth century to reveal an inspiring collaboration between groups of immigrants, civil rights activists, militant youth, and queer organizers. This oral history focuses on participants in three core groups: the Portland chapters of Anti-Racist Action, Skinheads Against Racial Prejudice, and the Coalition for Human Dignity.

Using a diversity of tactics—from out-and-out brawls on the streets and at punk shows, to behind-the-scenes intelligence gathering—brave antiracists unified on their home ground over and over, directly attacking right-wing fascists and exposing white nationalist organizations and neo-nazi skinheads. Embattled by police and unsupported by the city, these citizen activists eventually drove the boneheads out of the music scene and off the streets of Portland. This book shares their stories about what worked, what didn't, and ideas on how to continue the fight.

"By the time I moved my queer little family to Portland at the turn of the millennium, the city had a reputation as a homo-friendly bastion of progressive politics, so we were somewhat taken aback when my daughter's racially diverse sports team was met with a burning cross at a suburban game. So much progress had been made yet, at times, it felt like the past hadn't gone anywhere. If only we'd had It Did Happen Here. *This documentary project tells the forgotten history of Portland's roots as a haven for white supremacists and recounts the ways antiracists formed coalitions across subcultures to protect the vulnerable and fight the good fight against nazi boneheads and the bigoted right. Through the voices of lived experience,* It Did Happen Here *illuminates community dynamics and lays out ideas and inspiration for long-term and nonpolice solutions to poverty and hatred."*
—Ariel Gore, author of *We Were Witches*

We Go Where They Go: The Story of Anti-Racist Action

Shannon Clay, Lady, Kristin Schwartz, and Michael Staudenmaier with a Foreword by Gord Hill

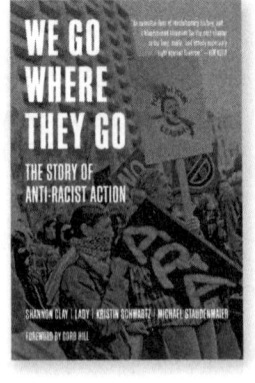

ISBN: 978-1-62963-972-7 (paperback)
978-1-62963-977-2 (hardcover)
$24.95/$59.95   320 pages

What does it mean to risk all for your beliefs? How do you fight an enemy in your midst? *We Go Where They Go* recounts the thrilling story of a massive forgotten youth movement that set the stage for today's antifascist organizing in North America. When skinheads and punks in the late 1980s found their communities invaded by white supremacists and neo-nazis, they fought back. Influenced by anarchism, feminism, Black liberation, and Indigenous sovereignty, they created Anti-Racist Action. At ARA's height in the 1990s, thousands of dedicated activists in hundreds of chapters joined the fights—political and sometimes physical—against nazis, the Ku Klux Klan, antiabortion fundamentalists, and racist police. Before media pundits, cynical politicians, and your uncle discovered "antifa," Anti-Racist Action was bringing it to the streets.

Based on extensive interviews with dozens of ARA participants, *We Go Where They Go* tells ARA's story from within, giving voice to those who risked their safety in their own defense and in solidarity with others. In reproducing the posters, zines, propaganda, and photos of the movement itself, this essential work of radical history illustrates how cultural scenes can become powerful forces for change. Here at last is the story of an organic yet highly organized movement, exploring both its triumphs and failures, and offering valuable lessons for today's generation of activists and rabble-rousers. *We Go Where They Go* is a page-turning history of grassroots antiracism. More than just inspiration, it's a roadmap.

"I was a big supporter and it was an honor to work with the Anti-Racist Action movement. Their unapologetic and uncompromising opposition to racism and fascism in the streets, in the government, and in the mosh pit continues to be inspiring to this day."
—Tom Morello

"Antifa became a household word with Trump attempting and failing to designate it a domestic terrorist group, but Antifa's roots date back to the late 1980s when little attention was being paid to violent fascist groups that were flourishing under Reaganism, and Anti-Racist Action (ARA) was singular and effective in its brilliant offensive. This book tells the story of ARA in breathtaking prose accompanied by stunning photographs and images."
—Roxanne Dunbar-Ortiz, author of *Loaded: A Disarming History of the Second Amendment*

Another War Is Possible:
Militant Anarchist Experiences in the Antiglobalization Era

Tomas Rothaus
with a Foreword by CrimethInc.

ISBN: 979-8-88744-105-4
$28.95   416 pages

This is history come to life.

At the turn of the century, the movement against capitalist globalization exploded onto the world stage with mass mobilizations in Quebec City, Washington, Genoa, and other cities. Anarchists faced off against heads of state, captains of industry, and riot police by the thousands. While the authorities sought to bend all living things to the profit imperative, anarchists set out to demonstrate a way of fighting that could open the road to a future beyond capitalism. The twenty-first century was up for grabs. And every time, Tomas Rothaus was there, fighting on the front line.

In *Another War Is Possible*, we follow Tomas from his days as a young militant to his tenure editing the publication *Barricada*. In vivid prose, he recounts the lessons he learned from veterans of the Spanish CNT—his first experience trading blows with police in the streets of Paris—and his adventures slipping across borders to participate in epoch-making riots. With Tomas, we breathe tear gas, we tear down fences, we tour the squats and battlefields of three continents.

Along the way, Tomas shows that the tragedies of the twenty-first century were not inevitable—that another war was possible. His testimony is proof that another world remains possible today.

"*Another War Is Possible is a compelling invitation to revolutionaries of the past, present, and future to think critically and historically about their years of struggle. Rothaus's captivating memoir of global justice militancy beyond puppets and platitudes is painfully honest, admirably humble, and at times simply hilarious.*"
—Mark Bray, author of *Antifa: The Anti-Fascist Handbook*

"*In an age where anarchist ideas are being both embraced by a new generation of activists and demonized by the rich and powerful, Rothaus shines a light onto those who were punching Nazis and fighting the police before the rise of Trumpism. Part riot diary and part personal reflection,* Another War Is Possible *is a must-read for anyone looking for both an exciting page-turner and an inside look at militant anticapitalist and antifascist resistance.*"
—*It's Going Down*

Revolution in 35mm: Political Violence and Resistance in Cinema from the Arthouse to the Grindhouse, 1960-1990

Edited by Andrew Nette and
Samm Deighan

ISBN: 979-8-88744-060-6
$29.95   384 pages

Revolution in 35mm: Political Violence and Resistance in Cinema from the Arthouse to the Grindhouse, 1960-1990 examines how political violence and resistance was represented in arthouse and cult films from 1960 to 1990.

This historical period spans the Algerian war of independence and the early wave of postcolonial struggles that reshaped the Global South, through the collapse of Soviet Communism in the late 1980s. It focuses on films related to the rise of protest movements by students, workers, and leftist groups, as well as broader countercultural movements, Black Power, the rise of feminism, and so on. The book also includes films that explore the splinter groups that engaged in violent, urban guerrilla struggles throughout the 1970s and 1980s, as the promise of widespread radical social transformation failed to materialize: the Weathermen and the Black Liberation Army in the United States, the Red Army Faction in West Germany and Japan, and Italy's Red Brigades. Many of these movements were deeply connected to culture, including cinema, and they expressed their values through it.

Twelve authors, including film critics and academics, deliver a diverse examination of how filmmakers around the world reacted to the political violence and resistance movements of the period and how this was expressed on screen. This includes looking at the production, distribution, and screening of these films, audience and critical reaction, the attempted censorship or suppression of much of this work, and how directors and producers eluded these restrictions.

Including over two hundred illustrations, the book examines filmmaking movements like the French, Japanese, German, and Yugoslavian New Waves; subgenres like spaghetti westerns, Italian *poliziotteschi*, Blaxploitation, and mondo movies; and films that reflect the values of specific movements, including feminists, Vietnam War protesters, and Black militants. The work of influential and well-known political filmmakers such as Costa-Gavras, Gillo Pontecorvo, and Glauber Rocha is examined alongside grindhouse cinema and lesser-known titles by a host of all-but-forgotten filmmakers, including many from the Global South that deserve to be rediscovered.

Sticking It to the Man: Revolution and Counterculture in Pulp and Popular Fiction, 1950 to 1980

Edited by Andrew Nette and Iain McIntyre

ISBN: 978-1-62963-524-8
$29.95   336 pages

From Civil Rights and Black Power to the New Left and Gay Liberation, the 1960s and 1970s saw a host of movements shake the status quo. The impact of feminism, anticolonial struggles, wildcat industrial strikes, and antiwar agitation was felt globally. With social strictures and political structures challenged at every level, pulp and popular fiction could hardly remain unaffected. While an influx of New Wave nonconformists transformed science fiction, feminist, gay, and Black authors broke into areas of crime, porn, and other paperback genres previously dominated by conservative, straight, white males. For their part, pulp hacks struck back with bizarre takes on the revolutionary times, creating vigilante-driven fiction that echoed the Nixonian backlash and the coming conservatism of Thatcherism and Reaganism.

Sticking It to the Man tracks the changing politics and culture of the period and how it was reflected in pulp and popular fiction in the US, UK, and Australia from the 1950s onward. Featuring more than 300 full-color covers, the book includes in-depth author interviews, illustrated biographies, articles, and reviews from more than 30 popular culture critics and scholars. Works by science-fiction icons such as J.G. Ballard, Ursula Le Guin, Michael Moorcock, and Octavia Butler, street-level hustlers turned bestselling Black writers Iceberg Slim and Donald Goines, crime heavyweights Chester Himes and Brian Garfield, and a myriad of lesser-known novelists ripe for rediscovery are explored, celebrated, and analyzed.

Contributors include Gary Phillips, Woody Haut, Emory Holmes, David Whish-Wilson, Susie Thomas, Bill Osgerby, Kinohi Nishikawa, Devin McKinney, Scott Adlerberg, Andrew Nette, Victor J. Banis, Cameron Ashley, Mike Dalke, Danae Bosler, Rjurik Davidson, Rob Latham, Michael Gonzales, Iain McIntyre, Donna Glee Williams, Nicolas Tredell, Brian Coffey, James Doig, Molly Grattan, Brian Green, Eric Beaumont, Bill Mohr, J. Kingston Smith, Steve Aldous, David Foster, Joe Weixlmann, and Cheryl Morgan.

Lucasville: The Untold Story of a Prison Uprising, 2nd ed.

Staughton Lynd
with a Preface by Mumia Abu-Jamal

ISBN: 978-1-60486-224-9
$20.00   256 pages

Lucasville tells the story of one of the longest prison uprisings in United States history. At the maximum security Southern Ohio Correctional Facility in Lucasville, Ohio, prisoners seized a major area of the prison on Easter Sunday, 1993. More than 400 prisoners held L block for eleven days. Nine prisoners alleged to have been informants, or "snitches," and one hostage correctional officer, were murdered. There was a negotiated surrender. Thereafter, almost wholly on the basis of testimony by prisoner informants who received deals in exchange, five spokespersons or leaders were tried and sentenced to death, and more than a dozen others received long sentences.

Lucasville examines both the causes of the disturbance, what happened during the eleven days, and the fairness of the trials. Particular emphasis is placed on the interracial character of the action, as evidenced in the slogans that were found painted on walls after the surrender: "Black and White Together," "Convict Unity," and "Convict Race." An eloquent Foreword by Mumia Abu-Jamal underlines these themes. He states, as does the book, that the men later sentenced to death "sought to minimize violence, and indeed, according to substantial evidence, saved the lives of several men, prisoner and guard alike." Of the five men, three black and two white, who were sentenced to death, Mumia declares: "They rose above their status as prisoners, and became, for a few days in April 1993, what rebels in Attica had demanded a generation before them: men. As such, they did not betray each other; they did not dishonor each other; they reached beyond their prison "tribes" to reach commonality."

"Mr. Lynd is a masterful storyteller and he has a hell of a story to tell. [He] has written a definitive history of one of the longest prison riots in US history and its aftermath. That alone is worth the price of admission.... What makes the book unique in the historical sense is the remarkable range of primary and secondary sources; Lynd writes with a lawyer's pen but a poet's ear.... This book is a reminder that prisoners—even death row prisoners—are human beings, too. Lucasville is a resounding affirmation of our common humanity."
—Michael Mello, author of The Wrong Man: A True Story of Innocence on Death Row

Facebooking the Anthropocene in Raja Ampat: Technics and Civilization in the 21st Century

Bob Ostertag

ISBN: 978-1-62963-830-0
$17.00   192 pages

The three essays of *Facebooking the Anthropocene in Raja Ampat* paint a deeply intimate portrait of the cataclysmic shifts between humans, technology, and the so-called natural world. Amid the breakneck pace of both technological advance and environmental collapse, Bob Ostertag explores how we are changing as fast as the world around us—from how we make music, to how we have sex, to what we do to survive, and who we imagine ourselves to be. And though the environmental crisis terrifies and technology overwhelms, Ostertag finds enough creativity, compassion, and humor in our evolving behavior to keep us laughing and inspired as the world we are building overtakes the world we found.

A true polymath who covered the wars in Central America during the 1980s, recorded dozens of music projects, and published books on startlingly eclectic subjects, Ostertag fuses his travels as a touring musician with his journalist's eye for detail and the long view of a historian. Wander both the physical and the intellectual world with him. Watch Buddhist monks take selfies while meditating and DJs who make millions of dollars pretend to turn knobs in front of crowds of thousands. Shiver with families huddling through the stinging Detroit winter without heat or electricity. Meet Spice Islanders who have never seen flushing toilets yet have gay hookup apps on their phones.

Our best writers have struggled with how to address the catastrophes of our time without looking away. Ostertag succeeds where others have failed, with the moral acuity of Susan Sontag, the technological savvy of Lewis Mumford, and the biting humor of Jonathan Swift.

"With deep intelligence and an acute and off-center sensibility, Robert Ostertag gives us a riveting and highly personalized view of globalization, from the soaring skyscapes of Shanghai to the darkened alleys of Yogyakarta."
—Frances Fox Piven, coauthor of *Regulating the Poor* and *Poor People's Movements*

"If you want an insightful, witty panorama of this brave new world we are making, follow Osterlag around it for a year—or read this book."
—Jeremy Brecher, author of *Strike!* and *Common Preservation*

The Hands That Crafted the Bomb: The Making of a Lifelong Antifascist

Josh Fernandez

ISBN: 979-8-88744-023-1
$22.95   256 pages

Josh Fernandez is a community college professor in Northern California who finds himself under investigation for "soliciting students for potentially dangerous activities" after starting an antifascist club on campus.

As Fernandez spends the year defending his job, he reflects on a life lived in protest of the status quo, swept up in chaos and rage, from his childhood in Boston dealing with a mentally ill father and a new family to a move to Davis, California, where, in the basement shows of the early '90s, Nazi boneheads proliferated the music scene, looking for heads to crack. His crew's first attempts at an antifascist group fall short when a member dies in a knife fight.

A born antiauthoritarian, filled with an untamable rage, Fernandez rails against the system and aggressively chooses the path of most resistance. This leads to long spates of living in his car, strung out on drugs, and robbing the whiteboys coming home from the clubs at night. He eventually realizes that his rage needs an outlet and finds relief for his existential dread in the form of running. And fighting Nazis. Fernandez cobbles together a life for himself as a writing professor, a facilitator of a self-defense collective, a boots-on-the-ground participant in Antifa work, and a proud father of two children he unapologetically raises to question authority.

"Fernandez is scathing on the corporate-minded liberals who talk about equity and diversity, antiracism, and gay rights but can't deal with people actually defending themselves or challenging authority. What he offers instead isn't heroics or militant slogans or even measured analysis—it's the messy story of a 'fucked-up person' trying to 'channel rage into something less destructive,' a guy who tends to run face-first into danger but also has the good sense to run away screaming when confronted with a knife-wielding racist. Fernandez's account of violence, trauma, and loneliness is hard to read in places, but there's an underlying sweetness here, a hopefulness about flawed people helping each other out, a sense that if we can get past the lies, we can remake this world together."
—Matthew N. Lyons, author of *Insurgent Supremacists: The U.S. Far Right's Challenge to State and Empire*